The Making of International Human Rights

The 1960s, Decolonization and the Reconstruction of Global Values

This book fundamentally reinterprets the history of international human rights in the post-1945 era by documenting how pivotal the Global South was for their breakthrough. In stark contrast to other contemporary human rights historians who have focused almost exclusively on the 1940s and the 1970s – heavily privileging Western agency – Steven L. B. Jensen convincingly argues that it was in the 1960s that universal human rights had their breakthrough.

This is a groundbreaking work that places race and religion at the center of these developments and focuses on a core group of states that led the human rights breakthrough, namely Jamaica, Liberia, Ghana and the Philippines. They transformed the norms upon which the international community today is built. Their efforts in the 1960s postcolonial moment laid the foundation – in profound and surprising ways – for the so-called human rights revolution in the 1970s when Western activists and states began to embrace human rights.

Steven L. B. Jensen is a researcher at the Danish Institute for Human Rights. His current research, funded by the Danish Research Council (2015–2017), focuses on the history of economic and social rights after 1945. He has previously published on genocide, HIV/AIDS, global health and development, and 1960s politics and has held positions with the Danish Ministry of Foreign Affairs and the United Nations. He is the winner of the 2015 Ester Boserup Thesis Prize and the 2015 Rene Cassin Thesis Prize (Special Mention).

Human Rights in History

Edited by

Stefan-Ludwig Hoffmann, *University of California, Berkeley*
Samuel Moyn, *Harvard University*

This series showcases new scholarship exploring the backgrounds of human rights today. With an open-ended chronology and international perspective, the series seeks works attentive to the surprises and contingencies in the historical origins and legacies of human rights ideals and interventions. Books in the series will focus not only on the intellectual antecedents and foundations of human rights, but also on the incorporation of the concept by movements, nation-states, international governance and transnational law.

Also in the series:

Eleanor Davey, *Idealism beyond Borders*
Fisch, trans. Mage, *The Right of Self-Determination of Peoples: The Domestication of an Illusion*
Hong, *Cold War Germany, the Third World, and the Global Humanitarian Regime*
Fehrenbach and Rodogno, *Humanitarian Photography: A History*
Hoffmann, *Human Rights in the Twentieth Century*
Snyder, *Human Rights Activism and the End of the Cold War: A Transnational History of the Helsinki Network*
Winter and Prost, *René Cassin and Human Rights: From the Great War to the Universal Declaration*

The Making of International Human Rights

The 1960s, Decolonization and the Reconstruction of Global Values

STEVEN L. B. JENSEN

The Danish Institute for Human Rights

CAMBRIDGE
UNIVERSITY PRESS

CAMBRIDGE
UNIVERSITY PRESS

University Printing House, Cambridge CB2 8BS, United Kingdom

One Liberty Plaza, 20th Floor, New York, NY 10006, USA

477 Williamstown Road, Port Melbourne, VIC 3207, Australia

4843/24, 2nd Floor, Ansari Road, Daryaganj, Delhi - 110002, India

79 Anson Road, #06-04/06, Singapore 079906

Cambridge University Press is part of the University of Cambridge.

It furthers the University's mission by disseminating knowledge in the pursuit of
education, learning and research at the highest international levels of excellence.

www.cambridge.org
Information on this title: www.cambridge.org/9781107531079

© Steven L. B. Jensen 2016

First published 2016
Reprinted 2016
First paperback edition 2017

A catalogue record for this publication is available from the British Library

Library of Congress Cataloging in Publication data
Jensen, Steven L. B., 1973– author.
The making of international human rights : the 1960s, decolonization,
and the reconstruction of global values / Steven Jensen,
the Danish Institute for Human Rights.
New York, NY : Cambridge University Press, 2016.
Series: Human rights in history
Includes bibliographical references.
LCCN 2015039219   ISBN 9781107112162 (hardback)
LCSH: Human rights – History – 20th century.   Decolonization –
History – 20th century.   United Nations. Commission on Human Rights.
LCC JC571.J468   2016
DDC 341.4/8 – dc23
LC record available at http://lccn.loc.gov/2015039219

ISBN 978-1-107-11216-2 Hardback
ISBN 978-1-107-53107-9 Paperback

Contents

Acknowledgments

I would like to thank The Danish Institute for Human Rights, the Saxo-Institute at the University of Copenhagen and the Centre for Advanced Security Theory for funding my research that led to this book. Helle Porsdam was a great support – always positive and encouraging and assisting me in bridging the disciplines of history and law in both practical and academic ways. I would also like to thank Ole Wæver and Eva Maria Lassen for letting me pursue my own path.

I am grateful to Professor Paul Kahn and Yale Law School for hosting me as Visiting Researcher for six months in 2011. As an academic community, it is a truly rewarding place to reside. Yale Law School librarian Margaret Chisholm has become a friend and her dedication to the legacy of civil rights activist Bayard Rustin is inspirational. I am grateful to Augustinus-Fonden, Oticon-Fonden and Knud Højgaards Fond for making my research visit viable.

Some people say "it takes a village" – well for me it actually took several cities. A number of people I gratefully count as friends invited me into their homes making my archive visits economically feasible and socially a lot more joyful. Special thanks goes to Nancy and Richard Turnbull, Clare Turnbull and Nicholas Tims and Ismay and Elodie (London), Tatjana Lichtenstein and Chris Ernst (Austin), Lesley and Kevin Scott-Morrison (Boston), Frances and Danny McCaul, Sinead Ryan and Peter Andersen, Tanya Siraa and Joe Wandall, Susan Timberlake and Gerald Walzer (all Geneva). Michelle Neita in Jamaica opened many more doors for me than just those of her fabulous B&B Neita's Nest by introducing me to people who helped me pursue the Jamaica story. A heartfelt thanks to her, Charmaine, Graham and Duncan and Karen Hutchison for many insights into Jamaican society.

At the libraries and archives I visited I have been blessed with great assistance from dedicated archivists. Alice Nemcova at the OSCE Archive in Prague and Allen Fisher at the LBJ Library were brilliant. Adriano Goncalves, Carla Bellota and their colleagues at the UN Library in Geneva have over several years and numerous visits been truly remarkable in their support. This project would not have been possible without their advice, expertise and their constant willingness to help me pursue sources through a wide array of UN processes to piece together the larger story presented here.

I owe a particular word of thanks to Samuel Moyn, Ryan Irwin, Sarah Snyder, Mark Bradley, Barbara Keys, Robert Brier, Chris Dietrich, Roland Burke, Nathan Kurz, Patrick William Kelly, Andrew Preston, Simon Stevens, Stefan-Ludwig Hoffmann and Jan Eckel for their valuable time, exchanges or encouragement on several occasions. Rasmus Mariager has been a great friend and a constant discussion partner that made a straying historian feel at home at the Saxo-Institute. Hanne Hagtvedt Vik and her management of the Oslo Contemporary International History Network have been wonderful and enabled me to do archival work and interviews in Jamaica and elsewhere. I would also like to thank OCIHN participants Paul Gordon Lauren, Susan Pedersen, Daniel Maul and Marc Frey for valuable comments on a key part of my work.

Hugh Small enabled me to be a fly on the wall at Jamaican Cabinet meetings in the early 1960s and challenged me on my knowledge of Jamaican history. I am grateful to Sir Alister McIntyre, Elaine Melbourne and Ann and Michael Richardson for their valuable insights that gave me a better understanding of the truly remarkable person and diplomat that Egerton Richardson was. Professor Rupert Lewis and Ambassador Patricia Durrant were instrumental in enabling me to bring the findings of my research back to Jamaica and present the forgotten story of Jamaica's pivotal role to a Jamaican audience at the University of the West Indies and at the Jamaican Ministry of Foreign Affairs.

The Society for Historians of American Foreign Relations (SHAFR) gave me an opportunity to present my findings to an important audience at a critical stage of my research. It was an honor and privilege to do so. I am grateful for the work of my Ph.D. Review Committee consisting of Jay Winter, Jarna Petman and Poul Villaume. A special word of gratitude goes to the two anonymous peer reviewers of the book manuscript. Both provided a thoughtful and engaging assessment with numerous great suggestions that have strengthened the final version of the manuscript.

I would like to thank my colleagues at the Danish Institute for Human Rights for listening to me telling stories from the archives and seeing the potential in my research findings and prodding me along. The Saxo-Institute was a good academic home and allowed me the space and time to concentrate on the actual writing. A special word of thanks should go to Marie Juul Petersen, Charlotte Flindt Petersen, Charlotte Kristof-fersen, Kim Bidstrup, Louise Holck, Thomas Gammeltoft-Hansen, Tomas Martin, Annali Kristiansen, Sita Michael Bormann, Niels Nymann Erik-sen, Klaus Petersen, Kristine Kjaersgaard, Niklas Olsen and Alexandre Bernier. The participants at the 2012 Venice Academy on Human Rights were a particular joyful bunch to become acquainted with.

My family and friends have kept me grounded. I apologize for the long absences. The Betts family provided me with a wonderful workspace during an important last stretch. There is one who deserves special praise and appreciation for so many more reasons than I can capture here. Heidi Nadine Betts has motivated, challenged, helped and inspired me throughout and been ever so patient. She has joined me on many of the journeys undertaken for my research and in the process become a recording artist of amazing quality. She has also been an editor and critic extraordinaire – my own personal Grammar Queen so to speak – and has made this manuscript so much better than I would ever have thought possible. Her presence was felt every step of the journey and her presence is there on every single page – always for the better.

I dedicate this book to my maternal grandparents David and Enyd Llewellyn. To you grandma and grandpa – in loving memory!

Negotiating universality – an introduction

On June 14, 1993, the Secretary-General of the United Nations Boutros Boutros-Ghali delivered the opening address to the World Conference on Human Rights held in Vienna. The world had undergone massive political transformations in the preceding four years and the Vienna conference's purpose was to lay new foundations for international human rights protection in the post–Cold War era. Since 1945, the evolution of international human rights had been closely linked to the United Nations. The Cold War and North–South debates had for almost fifty years determined the uneasy existence of human rights at the United Nations.

Boutros-Ghali's speech was a subtle reflection on these historical realities and on the nature of human rights as he explained that:

> Human rights should be viewed not only as the absolute yardstick which they are, but also as a synthesis resulting from a long historical process. As an absolute yardstick, human rights constitute the common language of humanity. Adopting this language allows all peoples to understand others and to be the authors of their own history. Human rights, by definition, are the ultimate norm of all politics.
>
> As an historical synthesis, human rights are in their essence, in constant movement. By that I mean that human rights have a dual nature. They should express absolute, timeless injunctions, yet simultaneously reflect a moment in the development of history. Human rights are both absolute and historically defined.[1]

This was a paradoxical but honest assessment of a complex phenomenon in international politics, diplomacy and law – a phenomenon that with

---

[1] A/CONF.157/22: Address by the Secretary-General of the United Nations at the Opening of the World Conference on Human Rights, June 14, 1993, p. 3.

the 1945 UN Charter had become a purpose and a vision to guide the work of the United Nations. Boutros-Ghali gave an open invitation to the historian to become engaged in understanding the role of human rights in twentieth-century international politics. Human rights were after all both absolute and timeless as well as historically defined and in constant movement.

In recent years, human rights have become a rapidly expanding field of historical research. Exciting new studies and interpretations have been put forward. While I gratefully acknowledge the inspiration drawn from these works, my research has guided me in a very different direction than recent historiography. Jamaica and Liberia will therefore emerge in this work as influential normative powers in twentieth-century politics, and I present the duality of race and religion as the driving forces in the breakthrough of international human rights law and politics. The 1960s will, crucially and again diverging from the increasingly accepted narrative, feature as the central period in this longer Cold War story combined with a new emphasis on the significance of decolonization. What follows is the story of these until-now, little-acknowledged players in a forgotten decade who played such a decisive role in shaping our contemporary world. This calls for elaboration.

Decolonization made a crack in the world running from South to North and East to West. From this tectonic shift, the issue of human rights emerged and over time achieved global prominence. This transformation was not just a result of structural changes in the international system of states: It was also a story of agency where the lead proponents were, in fact, a group of states from the Global South that explored and used this global transformation to reform the norms of international society and create a platform for human rights in international politics. It took time before this change became visible. The consequence of the time lag was that the source of this tectonic shift remained hidden and clouded our understanding of the emergence of human rights. The breakthrough and trajectory of international human rights has been misdated and misunderstood.

The decolonization process, described as the largest transfer of sovereign power in the history of humankind,[2] deserves greater attention

---

[2] Jeffrey Herbst (2004), "Let Them Fail: State Failure in Theory and Practice," *When States Fail: Causes and Consequences*. Edited by Robert Rotberg. Princeton, NJ, p. 312; See also James Sheehan (2008), *Where Have All the Soldiers Gone? The Transformation of Modern Europe*. New York, p. 167.

not just as an essential part of the twentieth-century historical experience but also for the emergence of human rights. It represented the transformation from a world of empires to the world of quasi-functional sovereign states we live in today.[3] Decolonization transformed the normative backdrop upon which human rights were projected on the world stage from the 1940s and the decades that followed. In the hierarchical world of empire, human rights had only a limited opportunity to shape global politics. The notion of the universality of human rights was anathema to this world system. After decolonization, human rights were negotiated in a more horizontal system of states, at least in formal terms, and the notion of universality now operated in a world where some of its most powerful barriers had subsided. "Decolonization was a precondition that 'Europe' might again be associated with and worthy of an egalitarian universalism" as Jan Werner-Müller rightfully observes in his study of twentieth-century European political thought.[4]

Sovereignty still dominated; it actually expanded with decolonization and remained a major barrier, but a structural change of the world system had taken place and the transformation process was in itself significant for human rights. The European imperial powers, among the most powerful opponents of universality in the first two decades after the Second World War, went through a political process that reformed their views on human rights as they were increasingly liberated from their own empire in the middle decades of the twentieth century. It transformed their approaches to foreign policy and international human rights diplomacy. This was not merely a journey of self-discovery. They were guided toward these new positions. At the same time, and in a not unrelated process, the United States confronted its own long-lasting and foundational tradition of racism by disbanding the Jim Crow system of formalized racial

---

[3] See Susan Pedersen's work on the League of Nations: Susan Pedersen (2006), "The Meaning of the Mandates System: An Argument," *Geschichte und Gesellschaft*, vol. 32, pp. 560–582; Susan Pedersen (2015), *The Guardians. The League of Nations and the Crisis of Empire.* Oxford, p. 13. See also Frederick Cooper (2005), *Colonialism in Question: Theory, Knowledge, History.* Berkeley, CA, p. 231; Frederick Cooper (2014), *Citizenship between Empire and Nation. Remaking France and French Africa, 1945-1960.* Princeton, NJ; A. G. Hopkins (2008), "Rethinking Decolonization," *Past and Present*, vol. 200, no. 1, pp. 241–247; Matthew Connelly (2000), "Taking off the Cold War Lens: Visions of North-South Conflict during the Algerian War for Independence," *American Historical Review*, vol. 105, no. 3, pp. 739–769; Christian Reus-Smit (2013), *Individual Rights and the Making of the International System*, Cambridge, p. 161.

[4] Jan-Werner Müller (2010), *Contesting Democracy. Political Ideas in Twentieth-Century Europe.* New Haven, CT, p. 157.

segregation in the South – a century after slavery had been abolished with the Civil War. The Communist regimes led by the Soviet Union believed that the end of colonialism would deliver ideological gains, which it initially did. They would, however, find themselves unable to reform their societies as the norms of international society evolved over time. None of the abovementioned states were at the vanguard of the rise of human rights in the 1960s.

"The geography of international law" had changed, one diplomatic observer noted in a significant 1962 UN debate on the future of law and international relations.[5] The 1960s were a decade where the colonial, the anticolonial and the postcolonial met and overlapped. A large number of new subjects of international law had emerged with the creation of so many new states. Cold War ideological battles were extended to the sphere of international law. A new approach to international relations was one expression of the tectonic shift. Among the matter that emerged from this shift was universality.

The new focus on the universality of human rights was supported by two elements: an increased emphasis on universality as a principle of international law and universality as a founding principle for the type of international organization that the United Nations embodied. In these processes, universality was promoted and contested, codified and rejected – but above all it was negotiated. This is worthy of our attention. Actually, it may be said that with the normative breakthrough for human rights in the 1960s, the total of the United Nations as an international organization during this decade proved to be more than the sum of its parts. The lived experience of human rights in the member states with the widespread violations during this era – and after – would support this claim.

The hypothesis about this important connection between decolonization and human rights provides a challenge to some of the existing literature. From within postcolonial studies, human rights have been strongly criticized, frequently linking human rights with Western essentialism and neocolonialist agendas, but it may be that this critique has only been able to sustain itself through its amnesia about the postcolonial moment, that is, its own historical foundations. If a number of key countries from the Global South were the driving force behind the breakthrough of universal human rights, how Western, then, is the concept of human rights? There

---

[5] Mr. Lannung (Denmark), UN General Assembly, 17th session, 756th meeting, November 9, 1962, p. 111.

remain important questions to be asked about how international human rights emerged.

The emphasis on the link between human rights and decolonization also calls for a word of caution. Decolonization was a multifaceted and complex process, where its aspirations soon encountered harsh political realities on a national, regional and global scale. What came to pass was that "amidst one of the great political openings of the twentieth century, the closures of a particular decolonization were becoming visible."[6] The exercise of power soon manifested itself forcefully and repressively. My intention has not been to overstate the nexus between human rights and decolonization but that the nexus exists in a more refined way than previously understood, and that it is important.

This becomes evident when recognizing that several developments in late 1962 represented a crucial turning point that led to the breakthrough for human rights law and politics. At this juncture, and in the aftermath of the Cuban Missile Crisis in October, three major developments took place at the United Nations that set human rights on a new political trajectory.

The first development was that the UN human rights project that had been faltering for a decade and a half was essentially reborn in late 1962 around the issues of race and religion. This brought a whole new dynamic to the field as it reflected global political developments central to this period and challenged and transformed East–West positions on international human rights. This dynamic secured the breakthrough for human rights to become international law.

The second development was that newly independent Jamaica joined the United Nations at the 1962 UN General Assembly Session and imme-diately initiated a process that provided a new and longer-term framework for human rights to evolve and expand. In the process, Jamaica became the major broker of progress on human rights in the 1960s, facilitating important innovations in human rights politics – at the United Nations and beyond – leaving a long-lasting and profound legacy.

The third development was that human rights became an integrated component of broader international norm-making efforts. In 1962, the UN initiated a process to elaborate "the principles of international law concerning friendly relations and co-operation among states based on the UN Charter." It was part of a push from Communist states to promote Nikita Khrushchev's campaign for peaceful coexistence and have this

---

[6] Frederick Cooper (2002), *Africa Since 1940. The Past of the Present*. Cambridge, p. 71.

notion reflected in international law. The outcome of this UN process, which lasted from 1962 to 1970, was the foundational document for the Helsinki Final Act. In subtle but important ways, it reflected human rights principles that would facilitate the inclusion of human rights in the 1975 Helsinki Final Act. If the Helsinki Final Act was instrumental during the late 1970s in elevating human rights in international relations and in inspiring activism, the backdrop for this development lies in the 1960s in a context rather different than the Conference on Security and Cooperation in Europe (CSCE) and European détente.

Yet despite this, the 1960s has remained almost a forgotten decade in human rights historiography.[7] The primary focus has been on the 1940s and the early rise of human rights. More recently, the 1970s has emerged as the other period at the center of attention for human rights history.[8] In two recent major international anthologies on postwar human rights, there is only one out of thirty articles that focuses on the 1960s.[9]

There are obvious reasons for the focus on the 1940s and the 1970s. The 1940s saw the development of the milestone document that shaped the field, namely the 1948 Universal Declaration of Human Rights.[10] The 1970s saw the global embrace of human rights by numerous international and national NGOs, forging a number of social movements. In response to the alleged human rights breakthrough in the 1970s, it is

---

[7] One notable exception is Roland Burke (2010), *Decolonization and the Evolution of International Human Rights*. Philadelphia, PA.

[8] See Samuel Moyn (2010), *The Last Utopia. Human Rights in History*. Cambridge, MA; Michael Cotey Morgan (2010), "The Seventies and the Rebirth of Human Rights," *The Shock of the Global. The 1970s in Perspective*. Edited by Niall Ferguson *et al.* Cambridge, MA, pp. 237–250; Akira Iriye, Petra Goedde and William I. Hitchcock (eds.) (2012), *The Human Rights Revolution: An International History*. Oxford; Jan Eckel and Samuel Moyn (eds.) (2012), *Moral für die Welt? Menschenrechtspolitik in den 1970er Jahren*. Freiburg; Barbara Keys (2014), *Reclaiming American Virtue. The Human Rights Revolution of the 1970s*. Cambridge, MA.

[9] See Stefan-Ludwig Hoffmann (ed.) (2011), *Human Rights in the 20th Century*. Cambridge; and Iriye, Goedde and Hitchcock, *The Human Rights Revolution*. The article is by Barbara Keys on Greece and antitorture politics in the late 1960s and early 1970s (Barbara Keys (2012), "Anti-Torture Politics: Amnesty International, the Greek Junta, and the Origin of the Human Rights 'Boom' in the United States,"). The claim is made in a couple of other instances that an article covers the 1960s but the actual text and footnotes reveal a different story. The editors of *The Human Rights Revolution* write that human rights "became a major concern in international politics in the 1960s and 1970s," but they have done little to address this conclusion about the 1960s in the edited volume. See "Introduction," p. 5.

[10] For a recent take on this history, see Christopher N. J. Roberts (2015), *The Contentious History of the International Bill of Human Rights*. Cambridge.

important to emphasize that while it was significant that international NGOs advocated for and media disseminated news features on human rights worldwide, it was equally significant when states negotiated – in this case, several binding human rights treaties – and concluded them. On the latter point, there was a definite breakthrough in the 1960s.

Until the early 1960s, the Universal Declaration of Human Rights carried limited weight in international politics. There was, however, one area in which the Universal Declaration played a concrete role. It had become an important source of inspiration in the drafting of constitutions in newly emerging states. By the early 1960s, the Declaration, for example, had been applied in the drafting of constitutions in more than twenty African countries.[11] By 1962, as the UN human rights project still floundered, there was a lesson to be learned from this development: Human rights were coming in from the South.

The breakthrough occurred rapidly. In July 1963, a legal advisor in the U.S. State Department wrote about the Commission on Human Rights and its "prolonged effort expended on human rights covenants which may never be completed and which, if completed, may never be widely ratified as treaties."[12] Three years later, at the end of 1966, three major human rights treaties had been completed, with ratifications already having occurred for the International Convention on Elimination of All Forms of Racial Discrimination adopted in December 1965. It was this Convention and the race issue itself that enabled the completion in 1966 of the two Covenants on civil and political rights and on economic, social and cultural rights that by then had been underway for eighteen years.

"Treaties reflect politics," writes Beth Simmons in her influential book *Mobilizing for Human Rights*.[13] It is therefore relevant to try and understand the nature of these political developments. The story seen from the perspective of 1962's influence begets quite a different historical context, with a different set of actors and a different trajectory and causalities regarding the human rights breakthrough than those stories focusing on

---

[11] Egon Schwelb (1963), *Human Rights and the International Community*. Chicago, IL, p. 51; See also Charles O. H. Parkinson (2008), *Bills of Rights and Decolonization. The Emergence of Domestic Human Rights Instruments in Britain's Overseas Territories.* Oxford.

[12] Document 258, "Memorandum From the Deputy Legal Advisor of the Department of State (Meeker) to the Assistant Secretary of State for International Organization Affairs (Cleveland)," July 16, 1963, *Foreign Relations of the United States, 1961–1963*, Vol. 25, p. 573.

[13] Beth Simmons (2009), *Mobilizing for Human Rights: International Law in Domestic Politics.* Cambridge, p. 12.

the 1940s and the 1970s. It also connects these three periods in a way that is unseen in existing human rights research. The book thereby addresses significant gaps in the research literature and in our knowledge of how human rights evolved in the post-1945 era.

The existing human rights literature is extremely comprehensive and covers a wide range of disciplines. It is impossible here to do justice to the research field. Since 2010, the discipline of history has been one of the most vibrant contributors to human rights scholarship, with an outburst of new research. This comes on the back of previous work by scholars such as Paul Gordon Lauren, Johannes Morsink and others published during the 1980s and 1990s.[14] During the 2000s, but before the recent boom, important contributions were made by scholars including A. W. Brian Simpson, Mary Ann Glendon, Lynn Hunt and Jay Winter.[15] Susan Waltz placed particular emphasis on the role of small states, especially in the drafting of the 1948 Universal Declaration of Human Rights.[16] Their contributions stand out as important independent works and offer different perspectives to the strong focus on the 1970s in the recent historiography since 2010.[17] One of the limitations of this literature is a

---

[14] See, for example, Paul Gordon Lauren (1983), "First Principles of Racial Equality: History and the Politics and Diplomacy of Human Rights Provisions in the UN Charter," *Human Rights Quarterly*, vol. 5, no. 1, pp. 1–26; Paul Gordon Lauren (1998), *The Evolution of International Human Rights: Visions Seen*. Philadelphia, PA; Johannes Morsink (1999), *The Universal Declaration of Human Rights: Origins, Drafting and Intent*. Philadelphia, PA; Gudmundur Alfredsson and Asbjørn Eide (1999), *The Universal Declaration of Human Rights: A Common Standard of Achievement*. The Hague.

[15] A. W. Brian Simpson (2001), *Human Rights and the End of Empire. Britain and the Genesis of the European Convention*. Oxford; Mary Ann Glendon (2001), *A World Made New. Eleanor Roosevelt and the Universal Declaration of Human Rights*. New York; Lynn Hunt (2008), *Inventing Human Rights. A History*. New York; Jay Winter (2008), *Dreams of Peace and Freedom: Utopian Moments in the 20th Century*. New Haven, CT. See also Micheline Ishay (2004), *The History of Human Rights. From Ancient Times to the Globalization Era*. Berkeley, CA.

[16] See Susan Waltz (2001), "Universalizing Human Rights: The Role of Small States in the Construction of the Universal Declaration of Human Rights," *Human Rights Quarterly*, vol. 23, no. 1, pp. 44–72; Susan Waltz (2002), "Reclaiming and Rebuilding the History of the Universal Declaration of Human Rights," *Third World Quarterly*, vol. 23, no. 3, pp. 437–448; Susan Waltz (2004), "Universal Human Rights: The Contribution of Muslim States," *Human Rights Quarterly*, vol. 26, no. 4, pp. 799–844. I believe there is better evidence for Waltz's goal of placing due emphasis on the contributions of non-Western states to the evolution of human rights in the diplomatic processes studied in the present book.

[17] There are several excellent historiographical essays about human rights history. See, for example, Reza Afshari (2007), "On Historiography of Human Rights Reflections on Paul Gordon Lauren's *The Evolution of International Human Rights: Visions Seen*," *Human Rights Quarterly*, vol. 29, no. 1, pp. 1–67; Stefan-Ludwig Hoffman (2011),

limited awareness of the 1960s' human rights foundations on which the 1970s' developments rest.

Roland Burke's excellent 2010 book *Decolonization and the Evolution of International Human Rights* is one of very few books that address the 1960s in some detail. It provides a comprehensive and insightful overview of Third World diplomacy from the 1955 Bandung Conference to the 1968 World Conference for Human Rights held in Tehran. The book is particularly strong in addressing the nuances of the debates at the United Nations as well as the later "rise of cultural relativism" as a challenge to human rights.[18] It does not, however, capture important catalytic factors such as the strategic impact of the race–religion equation and the nuances of the five-year Jamaica-led preparation process for the 1968 human rights year and what this also says about the role of the Global South. Daniel Whelan's book *Indivisible Human Rights*, also from 2010, captures similar themes, providing a rich account of the drafting of the Human Rights Covenants at the United Nations and offering a long-term perspective from 1945 to 2009 on the development of a key conceptual and political dimension of international human rights thinking. However, its thematic focus also carries a limitation: The 1960s receive limited treatment despite the fact that 1968 is presented as a turning point in how the understanding of the indivisibility of human rights evolved.[19]

The UN Intellectual History Project produced ten volumes from 2004 to 2009 on a whole range of topics that have been key in the UN's work since 1945, including a book on the history of *Human Rights at the UN*. It is a rich, comprehensive and informative work that unfortunately manages to largely ignore the 1960s – apart from twelve pages on the Convention on Elimination of All Forms of Racial Discrimination[20] – thereby

---

"Introduction: Genealogies of Human Rights," *Human Rights in the 20th Century*. Edited by Stefan-Ludwig Hoffman. Cambridge, pp. 1–26; Philip Alston (2013), "Does the Past Matter: On the Origins of Human Rights," *Harvard Law Review*, vol. 126, no. 7, pp. 2043–2081. See also Abigail Green (2014), "Humanitarianism in Nineteenth-Century Context: Religious, Gendered, National," *The Historical Journal*, vol. 57, no. 4, pp. 1157–1175. For an excellent piece on historiography focusing on the United Nations see Sunil Amrith and Glenda Sluga (2008), "New Histories of the United Nations," *Journal of World History*, vol. 19, no. 3, pp. 251–274.

[18] Burke (2010), *Decolonization and the Evolution of International Human Rights*, p. 113.
[19] Daniel J. Whelan (2010), *Indivisible Human Rights. A History*. Philadelphia, PA.
[20] Roger Normand and Sarah Zaidi (2008), *Human Rights at the UN: The Political History of Universal Justice*. Bloomington, IN, pp. 260–272. For a separate work that constitutes a broad UN history, see Mark Mazower (2012), *Governing the World: The History of an Idea, 1815 to the Present*. New York.

providing a rather limited view of a critical and transformative period for the UN and for the subject matter of the book. More recently, Jan Eckel's *Die Ambivalenz des Guten*, from 2014, which focuses on human rights in international politics since the 1940s, has provided a wide-ranging and detailed study. In a 900-page book on this topic, the 1960s can hardly be avoided. The book does cover issues such as decolonization, the case against the Greek military Junta in the European regional human rights system from 1967, the evolution of Amnesty International and importantly the debates about the creation of an inter-American human rights system during the 1960s; but despite giving attention to several relevant developments during the decade, Eckel still argues that the UN human rights agenda focused almost exclusively on condemning colonialism and on racial discrimination.[21] I hope to show in this book why this perception deserves to be nuanced.

In his 2013 book *Individual Rights and the Making of the International System*, Christian Reus-Smit argued that there was a discrepancy between studies of decolonization and human rights. Decolonization studies seldom mentions the politics of human rights and "histories of the international human rights regime ignore, to all intents and purposes, the politics of decolonization."[22] Reus-Smit's provides an accurate analysis of the reasons for this, namely a deeply ingrained but problematic assumption "that if decolonization was about rights, it was about collective rights not individual rights; and that the international codification of human rights was a Western project."[23] The limited historiography that has grappled with the nexus between human rights and decolonization has tended to focus on the right to self-determination, rejecting the idea that human rights were central to the anticolonial movements.[24] Self-determination

---

[21] The quote in German reads: "so stand die Menschenrechtsagenda der Vereinten Nationen in den sechziger Jahren praktisch ausschliesslich im Zeichen der Verurteilung von Kolonialismus und Rassendiskriminierung," see Jan Eckel (2014), *Die Ambivalenz des Guten. Menschenrechte in der internationalen Politik seit den 1940ern*. Göttingen, p. 263.

[22] Reus-Smit (2013), *Individual Rights and the Making of the International System*, p. 152.

[23] Ibid., p. 152. It is a little paradoxical that Reus-Smit builds his analysis mainly through the traditional focus on the right to self-determination – which in his view universalized sovereignty – since the scope of Global South human rights engagement went well beyond this issue and that the broader focus more significantly substantiates the point about the nexus between decolonization and human rights that Reus-Smit argues.

[24] See Moyn (2010), *The Last Utopia*, pp. 84–119; Samuel Moyn (2012), "Imperialism, Self-Determination, and the Rise of Human Rights," *The Human Rights Revolution*. Edited by Akira Iriye, Petra Goedde and William I. Hitchcock, Oxford, pp. 158–178;

was certainly an important issue but has led to the Global South agency on human rights being viewed from a too narrow perspective. The Global South engagement with human rights was broader in scope. The literature rarely differentiates between the 1950s when decolonization had yielded few results and the 1960s when the postcolonial era had begun. Fabian Klose has provided a useful account of human rights and the anticolonial struggles in the 1950s.[25]

It is fair to say that Samuel Moyn's 2010 book *The Last Utopia: Human Rights in History* rebooted the international human rights historiography and challenged the notions on which much of the historical understanding of human rights was based. Moyn firmly places the 1970s as the period where human rights had their breakthrough. To a large extent, he discards the importance of earlier periods, including the 1940s. It is a compelling work, but overwhelming archival evidence would suggest a more nuanced narrative. Moyn's emphasis on the 1970s almost presents itself as a kind of Big Bang historiography, with human rights emerging – in his own words – "in the 1970s seemingly from nowhere."[26] *The Last Utopia* highlights 1977 as a particularly important breakthrough moment. However, I would suggest rather forcefully that a more gradual process was at play – albeit a process with important breaks and discontinuities – which make the 1960s a vital decade and also allows the 1940s some relevance. Samuel Moyn has forced us to take a new critical look at this early UN period where the Universal Declaration of Human Rights was drafted and which has achieved such iconic status. It is relevant to reassess the role of the 1940s in light of his critique, while also giving due attention to the contributions this era made to later developments.

This book's focus is on the politics and diplomatic processes that established human rights as a field of international politics and international law. It does not – as so many other books do – focus on the interpretative practices and institutional expressions that emerged afterward such as the

Jan Eckel (2010), "Human Rights and Decolonization: New Perspectives and Open Questions," *Humanity: International Journal of Human Rights, Humanitarianism and Development*, vol. 1, Fall, pp. 111–135.

[25] Fabian Klose (2013), *Human Rights in the Shadow of Colonial Violence. The Wars of Independence in Kenya and Algeria*. Philadelphia, PA. There is scope for a more complex engagement with the issue of self-determination, see, for example, Bradley Simpson (2013), "Self-Determination, Human Rights and the End of Empire in the 1970s," *Humanity: International Journal of Human Rights, Humanitarianism and Development*, vol. 4, no. 2, pp. 239–260.

[26] Moyn (2010), *The Last Utopia*, p. 3.

UN treaty body system or through human rights jurisprudence. It does, however, owe a debt to scholars who have related law to the study of meaning and social imaginaries.

In his book *The Cultural Study of Law*, the American legal scholar Paul Kahn has argued that to understand the power of law, we must start by looking at the legal imagination instead of paying too much attention to legal institutions, since by the emergence of the latter, law's power has already established itself, for example, with courts. The legal imagination has "the power to represent the world one way rather than another, to create expectations among one set of possible answers, and to limit our capacity even to imagine alternatives."[27] The power of law is first constituted in a belief of law's rule represented in ideas and practices and only later does institutional decision-making appear. The notion of meaning in the context of law is a central concept for both Paul Kahn and Robert Cover. For the study of law, Kahn has argued that "if we approach law's rule as the imaginative construction of a complete worldview, we need to bring to its study those techniques that take as their object the experience of meaning."[28] Robert Cover emphasizes the narratives or normative universes that shape the legal prescriptions that are elaborated. This is law as more than rules – these narratives constitute a "world in which we live."[29]

These understandings have been developed in the context of studying American law but they are applicable to the study of international human rights law. The completion of the human rights Covenants in the 1960s is not just an irrelevant stepping stone somehow linking the 1940s and the 1970s. The Covenants are an expression of the fact that there was a much wider "legal imagination" at play in the international diplomacy. There are worlds of meaning in the decision-making processes that shaped the evolution of international human rights during the Cold War and they are an important part of the history of human rights.

The Cold War was traditionally defined by a focus on global conflict, military escalation and strategies of containment, national security and

[27] Paul Kahn (1999), *The Cultural Study of Law. Reconstructing Legal Scholarship*. Chicago, IL, pp. 135–136.

[28] Ibid., p. 2. See also Charles Taylor (2002), "Modern Social Imaginaries," *Public Culture*, vol. 14, no. 1, pp. 91–124; Charles Taylor (2007), *Modern Social Imaginaries*. Durham, NC.

[29] Robert Cover (1995), "Nomos and Narrative," *Narrative, Violence and the Law. The Essays of Robert Cover*. Edited by Martha Minow, Michael Ryan and Austin Sarat. Ann Arbor, MI, p. 96.

the nuclear threat – all linked to international power politics. It is therefore difficult to argue for the centrality of human rights and international law during the Cold War without addressing the issue of power. Both Cover and Kahn address the relationship between law and power in ways that may enlighten our understanding of the dynamics of UN diplomacy in the early 1960s. Robert Cover argued that "there is a radical dichotomy between the social organization of law as power and the organization of law as meaning."[30] In Cover's understanding, law operates on both levels – distinct and intersecting. Power was never far removed from the Cold War dynamics but its preponderance had limitations.

The normative universe behind decolonization was one of the instances where in Cover's words "The uncontrolled character of meaning exercises a destabilizing influence upon power."[31] This provides ample space to study agency and political change because "it is in the nature of our self-consciousness that power always reveals itself as failing to fill the entire possibility of human freedom."[32] The exercise of power was not stagnant. It was shaped by and responded to international developments. This created a space for human rights to shape international politics and diplomacy. Meaning and power interacted and this interchange was important.

A central tenet of this book is to study a process that I have labeled "negotiating universality." Human rights evolved through various stages of diplomatic negotiations, political contestations and larger historical processes, and throughout the whole period, the various actors were engaged in negotiating universality. The meaning of universality was a dynamic concept around which a larger political, diplomatic and legal history unfolded. Furthermore, the actors who advocated for and against it changed significantly throughout the period. Universality is the central claim underpinning contemporary human rights. It is the source of the most significant debate in the human rights field from the 1940s and onward, namely universalism versus relativism. It is also the key concept around which many of the contestations surrounding human rights revolve.

The rhetorical uses and the contexts in which universality was applied shaped the human rights story in fundamental ways. Human rights first needed to become a recognized international language, then to become

---

[30] Ibid., p. 112
[31] Ibid., p. 112.
[32] Kahn (1999), *The Cultural Study of Law*, p. 139.

legally binding standards in international law, in order to finally be disseminated through advocacy and activism and through institutional infrastructure and political processes. In the process, it also became part of a wider social imaginary from which these actions were nurtured and drew legitimacy. Human rights gained legitimacy through these protracted processes but we have failed to understand how broad based these processes actually were.

By emphasizing the "negotiating" part, I have wanted to instill chronology and precedent as the main guiding principles in the history of this evolution and as important factors in how human rights historiography is conducted. The historiography has until recently been too influenced by an intent narrative emerging from the United Nations based around the idea for an International Bill of Human Rights. This narrative focuses on the stated intent from the 1940s that the Universal Declaration was to be followed by a Human Rights Covenant as its logical next step. The latter took eighteen years to finalize and then it took another ten years before the two Covenants entered into force, by which the story has jumped from the 1940s to the 1970s without acknowledging that a fundamental reshaping of the human rights work took place in the 1960s. A different dynamic intervened in the process. It was a dynamic that challenges the widely perceived understanding that the Cold War human rights history was one where civil and political rights throughout were pitched against economic and social rights as a natural part of the ideological struggles.[33]

As this is a story of the development of international norms and international law, it should be recognized that legal standards developed in conditions we would label historically contingent can become an authoritative source of law for a later period. Set and established norms can have a fascinating and nuanced creation process. In regard to human rights,

---

[33] Daniel J. Whelan and Jack Donnelly (2007), "The West, Economic and Social Rights, and the Global Human Rights Regime: Setting the Record Straight," *Human Rights Quarterly*, vol. 29, no. 4, pp. 908–949. For the subsequent journal debate, see: Alex Kirkup and Tony Evans (2009), "The Myth of Western Opposition to Economic, Social and Cultural Rights?: A Reply to Whelan and Donnelly," *Human Rights Quarterly*, vol. 31, no. 1, pp. 221–238; Daniel J. Whelan and Jack Donnelly (2009), "Yes, a Myth: A Reply to Kirkup and Evans," *Human Rights Quarterly*, vol. 31, no. 1, pp. 239–255; Susan L. Kang (2009), "The Unsettled Relationship of Economic and Social Rights and the West: A Response to Whelan and Donnelly," *Human Rights Quarterly*, vol. 31, no. 4, pp. 1006–1029; Daniel J. Whelan and Jack Donnelly (2009), "The Reality of Western Support for Economic and Social Rights: A Reply to Susan L. Kang," *Human Rights Quarterly*, vol. 31, no. 4, pp. 1030–1054.

there are important links and connections in time and space, which have not been adequately understood. This does not make the creation processes arbitrary; indeed, there was often a very high bar set for what could be adopted as human rights law as the lengthy processes indicate. The point is rather that the enhanced focus on chronology, precedent and, by extension, political impact leads us toward a greater sense of historicity in the human rights narratives. This is important because there have been major gaps and omissions in the historical narratives and this has left its mark on both the cross-disciplinary human rights research and human rights practice.

The title of the book *The Making of International Human Rights* draws its inspiration from the British social historian E. P. Thompson's influential book *The Making of the English Working Class* from 1963. Thompson emphasized agency as a driving factor in the emergence of the working class in eighteenth- and nineteenth-century England. The English working class was "present at its own making." The working class was not merely a byproduct of industrialization or structural forces – just like human rights were not a waste product of international organization or of détente policies. Thompson explained his choice of title in the following manner, "*Making*, because it is a study in an active process, which owes as much to agency as to conditioning."[34] I recognize this sentiment and want to emphasize an agency perspective that not just complements or enriches a focus on structural changes in the international state system in the twentieth century but without which we cannot adequately understand the specific processes by which human rights obtained political and legal traction internationally.

This approach has taking me in surprising directions and has enabled me to uncover new histories and new causalities. I have been inspired by the new international history, which emphasizes multinational and multiarchival approaches.[35] The book is based on archival research in ten different countries (Jamaica, Denmark, the United States, Czech Republic,

---

[34] E. P. Thompson (1963), *The Making of the English Working Class*. London, p. 9.

[35] See, for example, Erez Manela (2007), *The Wilsonian Moment: Self-determination and the International Origins of Anticolonial Nationalism*. Oxford; Burke (2010), *Decolonization and the Evolution of International Human Rights*; Sarah Snyder (2011), *Human Rights Activism and the End of the Cold War. A Transnational History of the Helsinki Network*. Cambridge; Ryan Irwin (2012), *The Gordian Knot. Apartheid and the Unmaking of the Liberal World Order*. Oxford; Nico Slate (2012), *Colored Cosmopolitanism. The Shared Struggle for Freedom in the United States and India*. Cambridge, MA.

Switzerland, France, Italy, the Netherlands, the United Kingdom and Trinidad and Tobago). This has helped rethink the existing, and at times limiting, narratives surrounding both human rights history and other scholarly disciplines. I believe my findings will bring new perspectives not just on the history of human rights but also on wider aspects of twentieth-century history. This is where both the multinational and the multiarchival approaches have provided the greatest dividends.

The book's structure is in itself a historical argument. With half of the eight historical chapters focusing on a six-year timeframe in the 1960s, the book's claim about the centrality of the political transformations that took place during this period is there on display.[36] The story, however, begins with the Second World War, where human rights began to receive considerable political attention internationally, culminating with their inclusion in the UN Charter. It ends with the 1993 Vienna World Conference on Human Rights, where UN Secretary-General Boutros-Ghali speaks so eloquently. In between lies the Cold War period and decolonization, adding a critical North–South dimension to this history. The main objective has been to write a new international history of human rights during the Cold War – the period when human rights emerged from at best a peripheral notion to become a central part of the global political, legal and moral discourse. A second objective has been to integrate the developments of the 1960s into the human rights historiography.

---

[36] The fact that the book rarely covers gender or women's rights should, however, not be seen as an argument concerning their significance. Their absence is mainly part to the fact that the issues were covered in a parallel UN structure, namely the Commission on the Status of Women and would have required an equally detailed study of this Commission's debates and how the issues debated there moved through other UN bodies. This is a worthy research project in itself but is outside the scope of this work. Furthermore, women's rights became a lot more central on the political agenda during the 1970s, which receives less attention here compared with the previous decade. On gender and women's rights, see Jean Quataert (2009), *Advocating Dignity. Human Rights Mobilizations in Global Politics*. Philadelphia, PA, pp. 149–182; Allida Black (2012), "Are Women 'Human'? The UN and the Struggle to Recognize Women's Rights as Human Rights," *The Human Rights Revolution: An International History*. Edited by Akira Iriye, Petra Goedde and William I. Hitchcock. Oxford, pp. 133–155; Celia Donert (2014), "Whose Utopia? Gender, Ideology, and Human Rights at the 1975 World Congress of Women in East Berlin," *The Breakthrough. Human Rights in the 1970s*. Edited by Jan Eckel and Samuel Moyn. Philadelphia, PA, pp. 68–87; Roland Burke (2015), "Competing for the Last Utopia? The NIEO, Human Rights, and the World Conference for the International Women's Year, Mexico City, June 2015," *Humanity: International Journal of Human Rights, Humanitarianism and Development*, vol. 6, no. 1, pp. 47–62.

In order to achieve this, the overarching questions shaping this book have been: How did universal human rights emerge during the Cold War era to become a defining set of political, legal and moral norms and values for the international community? What were the historical processes by which human rights overcame strong international and domestic opposition to become the representative notion for universality in international law, politics and ethics? What global political transformations shaped this emergence from 1945 to 1993?

"Power carries its own conviction"

The early rise and fall of human rights, 1945–1960

"The chief novelty of the Declaration was its universality"
Rene Cassin, UN General Assembly, December 9, 1948[1]

"Its moral force cannot rest on the fact of its universality – or practical universality – as soon as it is realized that it has proved acceptable to all for the reason that it imposes obligations upon none."
Hersch Lauterpacht (1949), "The Universal Declaration of Human Rights"[2]

It is December 7, 1948. The "International Bill of Human Rights" is one of many agenda items. It has been two years in the making. The delegates are now reaching decision time on the future of human rights in the work of this international organization. We are in Guadeloupe – the French island territory in the Caribbean. The occasion is the third West Indian Conference of the Caribbean Commission.

Half a world away the UN General Assembly is in session in Paris. The Commission on Human Rights has presented the "Draft International Declaration on Human Rights" to the Assembly. After more than two months of debate stretching over eighty-five meetings the Third Committee of the UN General Assembly votes to adopt the document that one week earlier, upon the initiative of French delegate Rene Cassin, was renamed the "Universal Declaration of Human Rights." The debate in the Third Committee ends on December 7, 1948.

Meanwhile back in Guadeloupe, the delegates prepare themselves for the human rights debate. The item was placed on the agenda in 1946

---

[1] Mr. Cassin (France), UN General Assembly, 3rd session, 180th meeting, December 9, 1948, p. 866.
[2] Hersch Lauterpacht (1949), "The Universal Declaration of Human Rights", *The British Yearbook of International Law 1948*. London, p. 372.

when it was decided that the Caribbean Commission should consider developing a regional "Bill of Human Rights and Obligations."[3] In a 1945 debate in the State Department, the distinguished African American diplomat Ralph Bunche, who served on the Caribbean Commission, recognized that the Caribbean was a testing ground for the Atlantic Powers' "treatment of colonial peoples."[4] The 1948 human rights debate proved a case in point. The colonial powers in the Caribbean, the United Kingdom, France and the Netherlands, view the agenda item with great concern. They have tried to end the debate before it began because they viewed it as being against their interests. They have lobbied their American ally for support to stultify the debate and the United States obliged. While the United States did not want to "muzzle" the delegates it would "stand firmly against any attempt to take positive action which might involve serious controversy with the other three national sections."[5] Using the unfinished UN debate on the Universal Declaration of Human Rights as an alibi and as a claim to their goodwill, the aim of France, the United Kingdom, the Netherlands and the United States was to block the debate.

Back in Paris, the debate has moved to the Plenary after the Third Committee adopted the Universal Declaration. It is in this forum that formal endorsement by the United Nations has to take place. On December 10, 1948, The Universal Declaration of Human Rights is adopted with forty-eight states in favor and eight states abstaining. Eleanor Roosevelt predicts that the Declaration will be "the Magna Carta of all mankind."[6]

In Guadeloupe, the rhetoric is less magnanimous. In what must be one of the first statements on the relationship between human rights and international development aid, the Trinidadian delegate opened by stating "the Bill of Rights required for the West Indies was a 'Dollar Bill', as such idealistic objectives must necessarily depend upon the improvement

---

[3] See Recommendation 8 from "Report by Secretary-General on the Action taken by the metropolitan and territorial Governments on the Recommendations of the previous session of the West Indies Conference and on the work of the Commission since the previous session." U.S. National Archives, RG/59/150/70/28/6 – Box 40, File: Report by Secretary-General on Progress of West Indies Conference. The Commission was established in 1942 in response to the region's increased strategic importance during the Second World War.

[4] Jason Parker (2008), *Brother's Keeper: The United States, Race, and Empire in the British Caribbean, 1937–1962*. Oxford, p. 70, see also pp. 52–55; Rafael Cox Alomar (2009), *Revisiting the Transatlantic Triangle: The Constitutional Decolonization of the Eastern Caribbean*. Kingston, pp. 18–24.

[5] U.S. National Archives, RG/59/150/70/28/6 – Box 40: U.S. Department of State, "Draft Declaration of Human Rights (Item 5); Background Information for use of the United States Commissioners on the Caribbean Commission," November 22, 1948, p. 12.

[6] Mrs. Roosevelt (USA), UN General Assembly, 3rd session, 180th meeting, December 9, 1948, p. 362.

of economic circumstances."[7] The Trinidad delegate moves to close the debate on a regional adaptation of the UN Bill of Human Rights. The colonial masters could not have asked for more.

Other delegates express greater interest in the draft UN Declaration. The delegates from Guadeloupe and British Guyana are particularly impressed with the Article on the right to an adequate standard of living.[8] The delegate from Puerto Rico calls for establishing a Committee that would "submit concrete proposals for practical implementation of the Declaration in the life of the Caribbean people." The Caribbean Commission should not wait for further action from "the United Nations or the Metropolitan Governments."[9] The Puerto Rican delegate submits a resolution calling for concrete implementation as soon as the Declaration is approved by the UN. This is three days before the UN vote on December 10, adopting the Universal Declaration. The Puerto Rican resolution is adopted and is transferred to the conference Drafting Committee. Here the colonial powers manage to neutralize its recommendation on human rights.[10] They were successful in ensuring that the debate had no real effect against the wishes of several of the Caribbean delegations. At the same time, they celebrate in Paris the adoption of the Universal Declaration as a great achievement.

Historians strongly disagree on how to understand the human rights legacy from the 1940s. The Universal Declaration has been described both as "a monumental achievement"[11] and as a "funeral wreath laid on the grave of wartime hopes."[12] The human rights developments of the 1940s have been captured under headings such as "A New Deal for the World" and "A World Made New"[13] as well as "Death by Birth" and as

---

[7] U.S. National Archives, RG 59/150/70/UD 07D 68 – Box 39 (Caribbean Commission series): Mr. Gomes (Trinidad), 3rd West Indian Conference, Daily Journal no. 6, December 7, 1948.

[8] This was Article 22 in the Draft Bill – see E/800, "Report of the Third Session of the Commission of Human Rights, May–June 1948," p. 13 (in the UDHR, it appears as Article 25). Available at: www.un.org/en/ga/search/view_doc.asp?symbol=E/800 (accessed on September 16, 2015).

[9] U.S. National Archives, RG 59/150/70/UD 07D 68 – Box 39 (Caribbean Commission series): Mr. Ramos Antonini (Puerto Rico), 3rd West Indian Conference, Daily Journal no. 6, December 7, 1948.

[10] U.S. National Archives, RG 59/150/70/UD 07D 68 – Box 39: 3rd West Indian Conference, "Recommendations of the Conference," January 28, 1949.

[11] Daniel J. Whelan (2010), *Indivisible Human Rights. A History.* Philadelphia, PA, p. 60.

[12] Samuel Moyn (2010), *The Last Utopia. Human Rights in History.* Cambridge, MA, p. 2.

[13] Elizabeth Borgwardt (2005), *A New Deal for the World: America's Vision for Human Rights.* Cambridge, MA; Mary Ann Glendon (2001), *A World Made New. Eleanor Roosevelt and the Universal Declaration of Human Rights.* New York.

a "stillborn" project.[14] These directly opposed interpretations call for a balanced assessment of this period.

The story of the real-time events occurring in December 1948 in Guadeloupe and Paris, between colonial territory and metropole, illustrates an important point about the history of human rights. It is often a history of the simultaneous coexistence of proclamation and denial. As human rights started to emerge, new techniques of curtailment also developed. Part of the historian's challenge is to uncover the existence of this proclamation–denial nexus and how it has been part of the dynamics that have driven change in international human rights politics. Sovereignty and domestic jurisdiction versus human rights constitutes one version of this nexus. Universality versus relativism is another. The combined process of proclamation and denial in the decade after 1945 merits the label an "early rise and fall of human rights." It is not a traditional temporal narrative of "rise and fall" but rather a dual dynamic happening simultaneously as part of wider political battles. The 1940s remains a starting point for the contemporary human rights story. The question is: In what way?

"Searching for a new universalism": the UN Charter and human rights

The outbreak of the Second World War spelled the end of interwar international organization. "The Wilsonian Moment" did not last long after the First World War. The United States abandoned the League of Nations from the outset and non-European actors rapidly became disillusioned when realizing that the principle of self-determination – a core principle of President Wilson's plan – did not extend beyond the European continent.[15] It was undone by the return of traditional European power politics. Despite important efforts in specific areas of its mandate the League suffered a protracted collapse after 1933 when the Nazis took power in Germany.[16] By the outbreak of the war the League of Nations was a symbol of failure in most quarters.

In October 1940, a group of former League of Nations officials presenting themselves as the *International Consultative Group of Geneva* issued a report on the "Causes of the Peace Failure 1919–1939." It was

---

[14] See, respectively, Moyn (2010), *The Last Utopia*, pp. 44–83 and Samuel Moyn (2010), "Human Rights in History," *The Nation*, August 11, 2010.

[15] Erez Manela (2007), *The Wilsonian Moment: Self-Determination and the International Origins of Anticolonial Nationalism*. Oxford.

[16] Patricia Clavin (2013), *Securing the World Economy. The Reinvention of the League of Nations 1920–1946*. Oxford.

an assessment of the political, economic and spiritual causes of why international organization had failed. The group identified among the political causes that the post–First World War settlement had required "a new political morality, the substitution of responsibility for power" that never materialized. The failure of collective security in Europe and the flawed relationship between the doctrine of sovereignty and international state obligations was highlighted. The most revealing part of the report was a discussion of the spiritual factors causing the crisis of democracy:

> men everywhere are searching for a new universalism. It is rightly believed that international society has become so interdependent that it will only be able to live in a harmonious and orderly fashion if some fundamental common convictions concerning man and society are held by all nations, however different they may remain in all other respects.[17]

The Group identified what they believed were the three existing conceptions of universalism: the communist, the humanistic and the Christian. Human rights were mentioned nowhere under these categories. Communist universalism was described as "impressive and real, but it arrives at universality through a process of destruction of all values (and those who hold them)." It was not a tempting proposition. Humanistic universalism was seen as based on a "faith in human reason" believing that by universalizing education in its values conflicts could be averted and a better world would develop. The Group believed that "the weakness of this type of universalism has been its facile optimism concerning the nature of men and the power of human reason."[18] It was naïve when facing the nature of power.

The Group found the third option the most appealing. It reflected the worldview of the group. Christian universalism was based on an understanding that only by this common faith could humans live together and overcome the conflicts that emerged. It was an understanding that saw "the growth of Christianity as the only world-wide religion and in the emergence of a new ecumenical consciousness the ground for hope that the Christian faith may once more become the integrating force in Western civilization."[19] It was a notion that installed a hierarchy elevating Western civilization and projecting Christian universalism upon the whole world. It bore the imprint of the colonial world order. It was a universalism of

---

[17] International Consultative Group of Geneva (1940), "Causes of the Peace Failure 1919–1939," *International Conciliation*, October, no. 363, p. 367.
[18] Ibid., p. 368.
[19] Ibid., p. 368.

the particular that was unable to imagine a world outside its own system of values and beliefs.

The report was published a few months after the Fall of France. If the Consultative Group's analysis reflected mainstream political thinking about international organization in 1940, it is safe to say that human rights were not part hereof – not even when the focus was on developing "a new universalism." By 1945, human rights had become a central element in the founding document for the new postwar international organization. What happened in between?

The Atlantic Charter, launched by President Roosevelt and the British Prime Minister Winston Churchill in August 1941, is often viewed as a starting point for the new thinking on human rights in international affairs despite the fact that it did not contain the actual words. The historian Elizabeth Borgwardt has argued that its statement about establishing a peace after the war where "all the men in all the lands may live out their lives in freedom from fear and want," with its emphasis on individuals and not state interests was "positively revolutionary" and "marked a defining, inaugural moment for what we now know as the modern doctrine of human rights."[20] The Charter did help define war aims and stimulated international interest beyond the allied nations who signed onto the Charter. It aroused interest in the colonies as it included a provision on self-determination. Its timing, coming after Roosevelt's Four Freedoms speech to Congress earlier in 1941, may support Borgwardt's view that it was a starting point for U.S. projection of a New Deal international order upon the world.

Churchill, however, had a very different ambition. He retreated from the universalistic interpretations of the Atlantic Charter. In his understanding it did not apply to colonial settings but merely to the occupied European countries. Politically, it was a tenuous position that revealed major tensions between a colonial order and the tendency toward universalistic war aims for this global conflict. Churchill's alliance was tenuous because it consisted of European governments that had been forced into exile. By autumn 1940 European exile governments and exiled representatives from many other countries had settled in London making it the center of the war effort. Britain was leading this alliance that served as a symbol of European opposition to Nazi expansion on the continent.

A government-in-exile is an oxymoron because the term government normally implies a political entity that has control over its given

[20] Borgwardt (2005), *A New Deal for the World*, p. 4.

territory – the state. Exile undermines this meaning. France, Belgium and the Netherlands had showed considerable military and political weaknesses when they were occupied by Germany. The fact that the European governments in exile in London had lost control over their territory and the ability to protect their citizens but still managed their colonial possessions – some of them providing invaluable natural and human resources to the war effort – was bound to challenge perceptions about the legitimacy of the existing colonial world order. It was little surprise if people outside Europe – for example in colonial settings – were inspired to think differently about the organization of international affairs. Exile was an experience of displacement that stimulated new political thinking and ideas about international organization, European integration and human rights. Rene Cassin, who was legal advisor to Charles de Gaulle's Free French movement, was one of several exiles who would come to play an influential role in shaping the UN's future human rights work.[21]

In the months after the Atlantic Charter human rights made a more direct imprint on the notion of international organization. With the Soviet Union joining the Allied war effort after the German invasion in the summer of 1941 and the United States joining in December 1941 after Pearl Harbor, Roosevelt and Churchill met again shortly after the attack. During the Christmas period they prepared what became the United Nations Declaration, which was issued for wider signatory support on January 1, 1942. It was based on the principles of the Atlantic Charter and contained a commitment "to preserve human rights and justice in their own lands as well as in other lands." The Declaration was short, less than 200 words, but human rights were mentioned in this, the first document of the United Nations. The wording "as well as in other lands" recognized that human rights were an issue of international concern.

By January 1942, the Alliance against the Axis powers had been reconfigured. The war effort was now led by the United States, Great Britain and the Soviet Union replacing the more tentative alliance of Great Britain and its exiled partners. The latter were subsequently sidelined from much of the wartime decision-making much to their frustration and dismay. As Stalin, Churchill and Roosevelt were agreeing on how to divide up

---

[21] Two others were the Czechoslovakian Egon Schwelb, UN Deputy Director for Human Rights 1947–1962, and the Belgian Marc Schreiber, UN Director for Human Rights 1966–1977. Schwelb also became a leading international human rights scholar after the Second World War. See Rene Cassin's introduction to Schwelb alongside Schwelb's biographical profile and bibliography in the *Human Rights Journal: International and Comparative Law* (1971), vol. 4, no. 2–3, pp. 194–205.

Europe, they also set out to detail the principles and structures of the future United Nations. In August 1944, diplomats from the three major powers gathered at Dumbarton Oaks in the United States. By October they had come up with a proposal for the organization of the United Nations. Both the Soviet Union and Great Britain had little interest in making human rights a central part of the United Nations and with only one reference to human rights the Dumbarton Oaks proposals reflected their views. The Chinese Government had been invited to join at the last stages but their request for a stronger role for human rights was ignored. The omission was widely criticized and the insertion of human rights into the UN Charter would be among the most significant changes made during the United Nations Conference in San Francisco that opened in April 1945.[22]

The criticism that was aired reflected a number of developments that had taken place between 1940 and 1945. During the war legal experts and some non-governmental organizations had started defining a set of international human rights standards.[23] These efforts helped to ensure that human rights became part of the work of the United Nations. A first requirement for their consideration was that a more specific language for human rights was developed. One significant effort was the "model international bill of human rights" prepared by the transnational American Law Institute between 1941 and 1944. Their draft was promoted at San Francisco and would later be used by the UN Commission on Human Rights.

Norwegian historian Hanne Hagtvedt Vik has concluded that during the Second World War there existed "an ongoing transnational conversation on the rights of individuals."[24] It was this conversation that converged at the San Francisco conference and challenged the convictions held by the major powers. Another factor was the role of public opinion, which was particularly important in the United States. A large number of NGO representatives who represented many walks of American life was

---

[22] Borgwardt (2005), *A New Deal for the World*, pp. 142–143; Mark Mazower (2004), "The Strange Triumph of Human Rights," *The Historical Journal*, vol. 47, no. 2, p. 392.

[23] Jan Herman Burgers (1992), "The Road to San Francisco: The Revival of the Human Rights Idea in the Twentieth Century," *Human Rights Quarterly*, vol. 14, no. 4, pp. 468–474.

[24] Hanne Hagtvedt Vik (2012), "Taming the States: The American Law Institute and the 'Statement of Essential Human Rights'," *Journal of Global History*, vol. 7, no. 3, p. 481.

part of the U.S. delegation to the San Francisco conference.[25] It served as an effective publicity exercise for the Americans who also had the recently deceased President Franklin D. Roosevelt's legacy to consider. The NGOs lobbied to strengthen the human rights provisions. The British looked on with some alarm.[26]

The Latin American countries were also effective advocates. The 1940s were a relatively liberal period in Latin America with emphasis on constitutional developments and with a twenty-nation contingent to the San Francisco conference they were able to influence the outcome.[27] Other smaller states, for example, New Zealand, also supported a stronger role for human rights in the Charter. Their efforts and the fact that the United States became to a certain degree supportive of the positions held by the above-mentioned actors meant that the Charter differed from the Dumbarton Oaks draft and included human rights references throughout the document.

It is rare in international diplomacy to give prominence to a notion in which there is neither an actual definition nor even an agreed meaning. The human rights provisions in the UN Charter operated somewhere between an imaginary for a just international order and as rhetorical devices that provided idealistic gloss on the *realpolitik* of the era. Despite the very different motivations, the inclusion in the UN Charter was significant because it defined human rights as being part of the field of multilateral diplomacy. Without this inclusion the human rights story may have had a very different dynamic and historical trajectory in the postwar era.

At first reading, human rights feature prominently in the UN Charter with a total of seven references. They appear in the second paragraph of the preamble where "faith in fundamental human rights, in the dignity and worth of the human person, in the equal rights of men and women" is reaffirmed. They appear in Article 1 on the "Purposes of the United Nations" as a non-discrimination provision that focuses on respecting human rights "without distinction as to race, sex, language or religion." Article 55 contains the first reference to the universality of human rights

[25] Glenn Tatsuya Mitoma (2008), "Civil Society and International Human Rights: The Commission to Study the Organization of Peace and the Origins of the UN Human Rights Regime," *Human Rights Quarterly*, vol. 30, no. 3, pp. 607–630.

[26] Borgwardt (2005), *A New Deal for the World*, p. 189.

[27] Mary Ann Glendon (2003), "The Forgotten Crucible: The Latin American Influence on the Universal Human Rights Idea," *Harvard Human Rights Journal*, vol. 16, pp. 27–30; Burgers (1992), "The Road to San Francisco," pp. 474–475.

by the United Nations.[28] Article 68 determines that a UN human rights commission will be established so that the organization can perform its functions. Human rights thereby appear in the UN Charter as a vision, a purpose, a goal for international cooperation with a specific institutional mechanism and with defined roles for the UN General Assembly (Article 13) and the Economic and Social Council (Article 62).

It is, however, equally appropriate to view the 1945 UN Charter as a barrier to an international legal order based on respect for human rights because it was designed also with this purpose. Article 2 gives privileged status to the principle of sovereignty and to domestic jurisdiction as it determines that "Nothing contained in the present Charter shall authorize the United Nations to intervene in matters which are essentially within the domestic jurisdiction of any state or shall require the Members to submit such matters to settlement under the present Charter." The domestic jurisdiction provision protected state sovereignty. It became a central part of UN diplomacy and was a formidable barrier to overcome. It clashed with both the promotion of the human rights provisions and with Article 55 on the nature of international cooperation. In this light, it was no coincidence that the human rights language was couched in weak terms such as encouragement and respect instead of enforceability. It was proclamation and denial all in one.

The Charter also had colonial hypocrisy written into its human rights provisions. Human rights were not made part of Chapter 11 which contained a "Declaration regarding Non-Self-Governing Territories" dealing with the colonial territories of European Allied powers. The next Chapter, however, established an International Trusteeship System for the colonial possessions from the League of Nations Mandate system and any territory removed from "enemy states as a result of the Second World War" (Article 77). This mainly covered the German colonies taken after the First World War. In Chapter 12 human rights were deemed relevant as a basic objective of the Trusteeship System that included "to encourage respect for human rights and for fundamental freedoms for all without distinction as to race, sex, language or religion, and to encourage recognition of the interdependence of the peoples of the world" (Article 76 c).

It was a victor's settlement mainly protecting British and French colonial interests. This arbitrary application of human rights meant a double

---

[28] The UN "shall promote … universal respect for, and observance of, human rights and for fundamental freedoms without distinction as to race, sex, language or religion."

standard for colonial territories. Respect for human rights was to be encouraged in Tanganyika but not in neighboring Kenya, which was under British rule, and not in Angola, controlled by Portugal, but in neighboring South West Africa (today Namibia) because these territories had a different status at the United Nations. The latter, held as a League of Nations mandate by South Africa, who from 1948 were eager to extend apartheid rule in the territory, would be an especially tragic example of how the double standard was applied. This post–First World War invention of the League of Nations[29] was held suspended in legal limbo throughout the Cold War with bloody consequences and with a lasting, negative effect on the international human rights system in operation today. The situation across Southern Africa would play a significant role in shaping human rights politics at the United Nations during the Cold War.

Mark Mazower has asked "What to make of the fact that Jan Smuts, the South African statesman, helped draft the UN's stirring Preamble?"[30] Mazower implies that because the Preamble of the Charter was primarily drafted by the South African leader Jan Smuts, it was tainted with the "moral mission of empire."[31] This agenda remained prevalent in the mid-1940s and in the decade that followed but it did not stand alone. A reason for this is that while one may influence language one cannot necessarily control meaning. Meanings are contested and change and meanings transcend state borders. The UN Charter, the Universal Declaration of Human Rights and the wider UN diplomacy carry these complexities and contradictions within their own historical trajectories. The UN Charter had a dual nature. This would be part of its legacy because to such a large extent it defined the legal and political field on which multilateral diplomacy unfolded and shaped the evolution of human rights.

The new vernacular: from Charter to Universal Declaration, 1945–1948

Where the UN Charter helped define the field of multilateral diplomacy, the Universal Declaration provided human rights with a language and specific content. It defined specific provisions and standards from which

---

[29] Susan Pedersen (2006), "The Meaning of the Mandates System: An Argument," *Geschichte und Gesellschaft*, vol. 32, no. 4, pp. 560–582.

[30] Mark Mazower (2010), *No Enchanted Palace: The End of Empire and the Ideological Origins of the United Nations*. Princeton, NJ, pp. 19, 61.

[31] Ibid. See also Saul Dubow (2008), "Smuts, the United Nations and the Rhetoric of Race and Rights," *Journal of Contemporary History*, vol. 43, no. 1, pp. 45–74.

human rights debates could emerge. It was also a statement from which a number of concepts had been filtered away. Some of these were deemed inappropriate, some deemed more relevant for a convention due to their level of specificity while others were omitted since they could not obtain a majority during the UN negotiations. The latter could have added an interesting dimension to human rights thinking. One example was "the right to social justice" that was promoted by France, Lebanon and Belgium. Its meaning was both open-ended and politically significant and its inclusion could have had its own juridical–political dynamics in international diplomacy and jurisprudence. It did not obtain the necessary backing and instead the Third Committee settled for a "right to social security." The example illustrates a larger point, namely that there was not a clear East–West divide on civil and political rights versus economic, social and cultural rights.[32] There was general support for the inclusion of the whole range of rights.

Despite the absence of any implementation or accountability measures, the Universal Declaration offered greater specificity to the UN Charter provisions. The Declaration provided a specific vernacular for human rights that until then had been only loosely defined in various draft proposals developed during the 1940s and in some historical documents. Universality became the central notion around which many subsequent human rights debates evolved. The title of the document supported this but it was only ten days before its adoption, on November 30, 1948, that the title was changed from "International Declaration" to "Universal Declaration." The change of this one word carried, quite literally, a world of meaning.

The Commission on Human Rights was established in 1946. The UN Economic and Social Council (ECOSOC) decided in June 1946 that the

---

[32] Daniel J. Whelan and Jack Donnelly (2007), "The West, Economic and Social Rights, and the Global Human Rights Regime: Setting the Record Straight," *Human Rights Quarterly*, vol. 29, no. 4, pp. 908–949. See also Daniel J. Whelan (2010), *Indivisible Human Rights*. In an analysis of U.S. proposals during the drafting of the 1948 Universal Declaration of Human Rights, Sally-Anne Way has pointed to the proactive approach that the United States took regarding economic, social and cultural rights during 1947 submitting proposals for the Universal Declaration on these areas. These proposals would later influence the drafting of the Convention on Economic, Social and Cultural Rights. Sally-Anne Way argues for greater nuance: "The standard narratives of the history of human rights and the history of economic, social and cultural rights need to be revised to recognize the distinctly different picture of the US position that emerges here." See Sally-Anne Way (2014), "The 'Myth' and Mystery of US History on Economic, Social and Cultural Rights: The 1947 'United States Suggestions for Articles to Be Incorporated in an International Bill of Rights'," *Human Rights Quarterly*, vol. 36, no. 4, p. 897.

first main task for the Commission was to prepare an international bill of human rights. ECOSOC also asked for a compilation of all existing human rights treaties and other relevant documentation to support the work. This task was assigned to the Canadian John Humphrey and led to a preliminary draft based on cross-examination of this information.[33] The drafting of standards was not the only development in this field during this time. Human rights featured elsewhere in the emerging United Nations system. They became part of the mandate of new UN agencies such as the World Health Organization. The 1946 WHO Constitution described health as one of the fundamental rights and included a nondiscrimination provision focusing on "race, religion, political belief, economic or social condition." Beginning in 1944, the International Labour Organization (ILO) also developed a strong human rights focus. It was important for the longer-term developments that human rights were inscribed in the mandates of the various UN agencies during the 1940s.[34]

The task for the Commission on Human Rights was defined around three elements, namely drafting an international declaration, an international convention and implementation measures. The full Commission met for the first time in February 1947 and from here the drafting process took off. The Commission on Human Rights established a Drafting Committee for the international bill of human rights and work continued during several sessions in 1947 and 1948. This process saw particularly constructive contributions from the philosopher–diplomat Charles Malik from Lebanon, the Confucian Renaissance man Peng-Chun Chang from China, Law professor and social movement veteran René Cassin from France, the judge and educator Hernán Santa Cruz from Chile and Eleanor Roosevelt as a skillful chairwoman. In August 1948, ECOSOC transmitted the Commission's draft Declaration to the General Assembly. The draft convention and draft measures of implementation were sidelined for the time being. The focus was on adopting a Declaration and the 1948 UN General Assembly witnessed the broadest and most comprehensive debate thus far.[35]

---

[33] Glendon (1999), *A World Made New*, pp. 32, 48.

[34] On ILO, see Daniel Maul (2012), *Human Rights, Development and Decolonization: The International Labour Organization, 1940–1970*. Basingstoke, p. 77. See Benjamin Mason Meier (2010), "Global Health Governance and the Contentious Politics of Human Rights," *Stanford Journal of International Law*, vol. 46, no. 1. Available at: www.unc.edu/~meierb/Meier%202010.pdf (accessed on September 16, 2015).

[35] For a comprehensive drafting history of the Universal Declaration, see Johannes Morsink (1999), *The Universal Declaration of Human Rights: Origins, Drafting and Intent.*

Critical voices had appeared during the process of preparing the Declaration. The American Bar Association passed a resolution in 1948 condemning the Universal Declaration partly on racial grounds.[36] An intriguing and controversial statement came from the American Anthropological Association (AAA) in 1947. Always interpreted as a strongly cultural relativist statement[37] defending the varied expressions of cultures, its more realist analysis of power and critical commentary has been overlooked. Its stated ambition was to explore whether the UN Declaration could "be applicable to all human beings, and not be a statement of rights conceived only in terms of the values prevalent in the countries of Western Europe and America."[38] This was similar to the task that the Commission on Human Rights was grappling with – a point that the AAA statement did not recognize.

The Statement rejected a biological frame of perceiving cultures and Man, thereby arguing an anti-racist position opposed to the American Bar Association. It criticized the impact of colonialism on non-Western cultures and essentially called for a more reflexive understanding of the legacy of colonialism on contemporary developments around the world. The promoters of an international human rights declaration could not ignore this dynamic between past and present. The AAA statement argued that the ideology of empire had legitimized its practice of power in such a way that "The hard core of *similarities* between cultures has consistently been overlooked."[39] The nature of these similarities was not explained, an obvious failure by the AAA given the nature of the topic, but this idea potentially had a universalistic bent. The analysis of power contained another interesting element as the Statement explained that:

Religious beliefs that for untold ages have carried conviction, and permitted adjustment to the Universe have been attacked as superstitious, immoral, untrue. And, *since power carries its own conviction*, this has furthered the process

---

Philadelphia. See also Glendon (1999), *A World Made New*. New York; Jay Winter and Antoine Prost (2013), *René Cassin and Human Rights. From the Great War to the Universal Declaration*. Cambridge; and for a useful overview of Peng-Chun Chang's contribution see Frédéric Krumbein (2015), "P. C. Chang – The Chinese Father of Human Rights," *Journal of Human Rights*, vol. 14, no. 3, pp. 332–352.

[36] Borgwardt (2005), *A New Deal for the World*, p. 267.

[37] See Karen Engle (2001), "From Skepticism to Embrace: Human Rights and the American Anthropological Association from 1947–1999," *Human Rights Quarterly*, vol. 23, no. 3, pp. 536–559.

[38] American Anthropological Association (1947), "Statement on Human Rights," *American Anthropologist*, vol. 49, no. 4, p. 539.

[39] Ibid., p. 540.

of demoralization begun by economic exploitation and the loss of political autonomy.[40]

The belief that "power carries its own conviction" is a realist understanding of the practice of power with much broader applicability. Power was not just domination but brought its own system of values. The American Anthropological Association was basically arguing that if the Declaration project was to have any meaning then power had to civilize itself and its convictions. It was a shift from realist understanding to idealist prescription. The two world wars that had originated in Europe had led people in the colonies to question "the superior ways of their rulers" and the legitimacy of colonial rule:

> The religious dogmas of those who profess equality and practice discrimination, who stress the virtue of humility and are themselves arrogant in insistence on their beliefs have little meaning for peoples whose devotion to other faiths makes these inconsistencies as clear as the desert landscape. Small wonder that these people, denied the right to live in terms of their own cultures, are discovering new values in old beliefs they had been led to question.[41]

The AAA statement has continued to vex the relativist versus universality debate. Its cultural relativism is certainly there on display but merely emphasizing this reduces its complexity since it was also outspoken on the relationship between human rights and self-determination. This played into what became an important United Nations debate over the next three decades. It was a debate that would come to reveal the problems of cultural relativism because it became closely connected to authoritarian rule.[42] At the same time, the American Anthropological Association with its restrictive emphasis on culture was blind to the appeal that human rights actually had for anticolonial politics. This appeal led to a complex anticolonial grappling with human rights that gave them renewed international attention during the 1950s.

By the time the draft Declaration was placed before the UN General Assembly in 1948, there had been several human rights controversies at the UN. These issues loomed over the 1948 General Assembly negotiations. In 1946, India challenged South Africa over its discriminatory treatment of Indians. South Africa claimed this was an issue protected by domestic jurisdiction and not an issue for the United Nations; however,

---

[40] Ibid., p. 541.
[41] Ibid., p. 541.
[42] Roland Burke (2010), *Decolonization and the Evolution of International Human Rights.* Philadelphia, PA, p. 113.

India secured backing to keep it on the UN agenda. It was the first conflict over human rights to be brought before the United Nations but despite being on the agenda for three sessions, it did not lead to any action. It mainly proved how weak the authority of the UN could be.[43]

In February 1947, the Soviet Union passed legislation banning their citizens from marrying foreign nationals. It soon became an international issue. In August 1948 ECOSOC passed a resolution referencing Charter provisions on human rights and fundamental freedoms that deplored "legislative or administrative provisions which deny women the right to leave her country of origin and reside with her husband in any other."[44] This significant step demonstrated that before the Universal Declaration was proclaimed the Council had taken the position that the right to leave any country, including one's own, and the right to marry without limitation due to nationality were part of the rights and freedoms that the Charter aimed to protect.[45] It was a substantial recognition but with limited consequence. The debate over the Soviet wives followed what would become a familiar cold war pattern of tit-for-tat exchanges between East and West in the human rights debates. Freedom of information was also subject to special attention during the late 1940s and to a large extent it followed the same Cold War pattern. The normative work on freedom of information lingered for decades because of this.[46]

A third significant controversy during this period also started in 1947. It concerned the former Axis states – Hungary, Bulgaria and Romania. Since they were on the losing side in the Second World War, they became party to peace treaties instructing them to uphold human rights and fundamental freedoms, including freedom of expression and association, freedom of the press and freedom of worship. Throughout 1948, the United States and British governments protested over the increasing "sovietization" of the three countries, which was incompatible with their human rights obligations. The process culminated in 1949 when Hungary and Bulgaria imposed long prison sentences on a Cardinal and a number of pastors for espionage and high treason.[47] The controversy was an

---

[43] Saul Dubow (2008), "Smuts, the United Nations and the Rhetoric of Race and Rights," pp. 67–71.

[44] Andrew Martin (1953), "Human Rights and World Politics," *The Yearbook of World Affairs 1951*. New York, p. 69.

[45] Ibid., pp. 69–70.

[46] Jan Eckel (2014), *Die Ambivalenz des Guten. Menschenrechte in der Internationalen Politik seit den 1940ern.* Göttingen, pp. 123–135.

[47] Andrew Martin (1953), "Human Rights and World Politics," *The Yearbook of World Affairs 1951*. New York, pp. 72–74.

indication of how freedom of religion would become central to human rights developments during the Cold War.

It was also a central theme in the 1948 UN debate in the Third Committee. The relevant draft article focused on "freedom of thought, conscience and religion." The Soviet Union felt that the article discriminated in favor of religious freedom and wanted this article to be reduced to "freedom of thought and freedom to perform religious services" with both made dependent on provisions of national law. The Soviet proposal, which omitted freedom of conscience and freedom of religion, was met with strong opposition. The Philippines called it "clearly reactionary in character."[48] There was wide support for the Commission's draft article.[49] A similar pattern followed in the next debate on freedom of opinion and freedom of expression which the Communist states sought to curtail. This also continued in the debate on freedom of movement, which the Soviets were accused, no doubt with the case of the Soviet wives in mind, of seeking to nullify.[50]

There was also another attack on freedom of thought, conscience and religion, namely, from Saudi Arabia who opposed including the freedom to change religion or belief in the Universal Declaration. They wanted this to be deleted. The Saudi position was, however, opposed by a clear majority with Pakistan playing an important role by endorsing the freedom to change religion or belief.[51] Cuba was a strong supporter of freedom of religion to the extent that they argued for a separation of the article into two parts: one on freedom of thought and conscience and one on freedom of religion to elevate the significance of the latter. The majority of states supported the unity of the freedoms expressed and wanted to maintain it. It was an important decision because this General Assembly debate created the precedents for the future international human rights language and here "freedom of thought, conscience and religion" were a unified

---

[48] Mr. Aquino (the Philippines), UN General Assembly, 3rd session, Third Committee, 127th meeting, November 9, 1948, p. 396.

[49] The Commission's draft Declaration is available at: www.un.org/en/ga/search/view_doc .asp?symbol=E/800 (accessed on September 16, 2015).

[50] Mr. Santa Cruz (Chile), UN General Assembly, 3rd session, Third Committee, 120th meeting, November 2, 1948, p. 317.

[51] Mr. Zafrulla Khan (Pakistan), UN General Assembly, 3rd session, 182nd Meeting, December 10, 1948, p. 890. For an interesting profile of Muhammad Zafrulla Khan, who was Pakistan's first Minister for Foreign Affairs and Commonwealth Relations, see Victor Kattan (2015), "Decolonizing the International Court of Justice: The Experience of Judge Sir Muhammad Zafrulla Khan in the South West Africa Cases," *Asian Journal of International Law*, vol. 5, no. 2, pp. 310–355.

principle.[52] This decision would have great significance especially after it had been confirmed as an international legal standard in the 1960s.

Cuba was part of the Latin American contingent that promoted a broad human rights agenda. They were among the most vocal supporters of the unity of civil, political, economic and social rights believing that with this unity "the twentieth century had witnessed the development of a new concept of liberty which it was important to clarify in the declaration."[53] The Third Committee debate revealed that there was a broad consensus on this approach. There was debate on the specific wording of most articles but the overall concept that the Declaration should combine the broad range of rights was not questioned anymore. The British delegate even called the social rights at the end of the document "a climax."[54]

Where the Soviet Union had been challenged by the debate on freedom of religion, the Communist states went on the offensive in the matter of racial discrimination. They highlighted the United States "custom of lynching," which President Harry S. Truman's Commission on Civil Rights had acknowledged in their report from 1947, and the petition to the UN by the National Association for the Advancement of Colored People (NAACP) protesting the discrimination against African Americans in the United States. This pattern of attacks over race and religion were only at an early stage. The attacks were also directed at South Africa who in 1948 was in the process of introducing apartheid rule. The position of the South African government had hardened on the issues debated at the UN General Assembly. They defended not just a racial hierarchy but also a wider civilizational hierarchy that was now being challenged. They were "pained" by the human rights debate that "was very different from that to which the League of Nations had happily been accustomed."[55] The League of Nations had done more to support a South African view of "European civilization." It was a view that extended its hierarchies beyond race to the inferiority of women as the South African delegate explained, "Men and women had and always would have

[52] For an in-depth and insightful study of the drafting of the article on "freedom of thought, conscience and religion" in the Universal Declaration, see Linde Lindkvist (2014), *Shrines and Souls. The Reinvention of Religious Liberty and the Genesis of the Universal Declaration of Human Rights.* PhD Dissertation, Lund University.

[53] Mr. Perez Cisneros (Cuba), UN General Assembly, 3rd session, Third Committee, 104th meeting, October 16, 1948, p. 164.

[54] Mr. Corbet (UK), UN General Assembly, 3rd session, Third Committee, 179th meeting, December 7, 1948, p. 885.

[55] Mr. Te Water (South Africa), UN General Assembly, 3rd session, Third Committee, 112th meeting, October 25, 1948, p. 240.

different rights."[56] This distanced them further from the principles of the United Nations since the UN Charter had explicitly recognized the equality of the sexes that had been, according to another delegate, "a triumph for the women of the world."[57] It was two irreconcilable worldviews that were clashing since the work on the Declaration was attempting to establish universal standards while the South Africans made no effort to hide their fundamentally opposite position that "there could be no universality in the concept of equality."[58] It was a very blunt and revealing statement that represented a worldview that would occupy the attention of the UN for decades to come.

The adoption of the Universal Declaration of Human Rights on December 10, 1948, did leave a question mark about its claim to universality. This influenced the reception outside the United Nations. Contemporary observers were divided on how to interpret the political significance of the Universal Declaration. While Eleanor Roosevelt evoked the Magna Carta and the delegate from Pakistan saw it as an "epoch-making event,"[59] a leading legal expert, Hersch Lauterpacht, described the Universal Declaration in a distinctly less appreciative mode. Lauterpacht, who was professor of law at Cambridge, denounced the "fictitious authority" with which the Declaration's proponents surrounded it. Lauterpacht delivered a damning critique because of the Declaration's lack of legally binding force. It was a direct critique of Roosevelt herself who had argued the U.S. viewpoint that the document should have no legal force whatsoever.[60] Lauterpacht was particularly harsh in his critique of the self-perceived universality:

Its moral force cannot rest on the fact of its universality – or practical universality – as soon as it is realized that it has proved acceptable to all for the reason that it imposes obligations upon none...

---

56 Mr. Te Water (South Africa), UN General Assembly, 3rd session, Third Committee, 95th meeting, October 6, 1948, p. 92.
57 Miss Bernardino (Dominican Republic), UN General Assembly, 3rd session, Third Committee, 98th meeting, October 9, 1948, p. 108.
58 Mr. Te Water (South Africa), UN General Assembly, 3rd session, Third Committee, 95th meeting, October 6, 1948, p. 92.
59 Mr. Zafrulla Khan (Pakistan), UN General Assembly, 3rd session, Third Committee, 182nd meeting, December 10, 1948, p. 890.
60 Lauterpacht quoted Eleanor Roosevelt for stating, "It is not a treaty; it is not an international agreement. It is not and does not purport to be a statement of law or of legal obligation." Hersch Lauterpacht (1949), "The Universal Declaration of Human Rights," *The British Yearbook of International Law 1948*. London, p. 358.

Lauterpacht continued:

There are no rights unless accompanied by remedies. That correlation is not only an inescapable principle of juridical logic. Its absence connotes a fundamental and decisive ethical flaw in the structure and conception of the Declaration.[61]

It was a critique that the Director of the UN Human Rights Division, John Humphrey, described as "brilliant and devastating" as it came from a leading authority within the international legal community.[62] Humphrey and others had faced the prospect of achieving no international document at all and they opted for the compromise that was possible. Decades later, Humphreys felt that time had vindicated this approach. From the perspective of the late 1940s it was a strategy with a great amount of uncertainty. Lauterpacht's critique was certainly legitimate.

"The warring conceptions of human rights," 1949–1954

The Universal Declaration was, as argued by Jay Winter and Antoine Prost, the last major political and moral act on which the Great Powers of the wartime alliance agreed.[63] The Cold War quickly affected the United Nations and the international human rights work that had to operate under this evolving political conflict. In 1949, Roger Baldwin, the founder of the American Civil Liberties Union, pointed out that "in the tortured development of an international morality through the United Nations, the years 1948 and 1949 mark the laying of cornerstones of universality in human rights." During the 1950s Roger Baldwin would, through the International League for the Rights of Man, do more than almost anyone else to test the limits of the new international human rights diplomacy. The League was the leading international human rights NGO in the 1950s and had a strong focus on colonial rule with South West Africa featuring particularly prominently. The League assisted local African leaders in petitioning their case for protection and independence

---

[61] Ibid., pp. 372–373.

[62] John P. Humphrey (1994), *On the Edge of Greatness: the Diaries of John Humphrey, First Director of the United Nations Division of Human Rights.* Edited by A. J. Hobbins. Montreal, vol. 1, p. 36.

[63] The Soviet Union actually abstained from the vote but Winter and Prost write "They were part of the alliance, however repugnant the regime. A United Nations without them, a Universal Declaration without at least their tacit approval, would make no sense at all." Winter and Prost (2013), *René Cassin and Human Rights*, p. 239.

before the UN Committees in New York.[64] The League's efforts were strongly opposed by the colonial powers.

In his 1949 article, Baldwin admitted he was guessing about the emergence of an international morality because with the world becoming torn between East and West, it was uncertain how progress would occur since "the warring conceptions of human rights are central to the aspirations of both sides."[65] This was an overly idealistic interpretation of the Cold War power struggle as the arms race, the competition for hegemonic control over states and outbreaks of violent conflict, for example, in Korea, rarely had human rights as a central consideration. Human rights would be instrumentalized for ideological purposes but power operated on its own terms. As a global conflict this instrumentalization was a proclamation that also exposed denial. The gaps between ideals and reality grew ever more apparent on issues like racial discrimination and the very different understandings of what democracy and freedom entailed.

The developments in Europe are a case in point. Winston Churchill had been wary of human rights language and its universalistic aims in a global setting but he was an active proponent of human rights regionally. In Europe, human rights could play directly into the East–West confrontation and could help consolidate democracy and the rule of law in Western Europe. Churchill was a driving force behind the creation of the Council of Europe and supported the drafting of the European Convention on Human Rights.

The European Convention offered a strong legal and political statement against Soviet hegemony in Eastern Europe. It contained implementation measures that – although optional – potentially gave the Convention a binding status. The Convention, with an accompanying Court, is today regarded as the strongest regional human rights system and as an expression of European values. This is the result of much later developments. Its foundation was weak in the early phases. The European

---

[64] Roger S. Clark (1981), "The International League for Human Rights and South West Africa 1947–1957: The Human Rights NGO as Catalyst in the International Legal Process," *Human Rights Quarterly*, vol. 3, no. 4, pp. 101–136; Meredith Terretta (2012), "We Had Been Fooled into Thinking that the UN Watches over the Entire World": Human Rights, UN Trust Territories, and Africa's Decolonization," *Human Rights Quarterly*, vol. 34, no. 2, pp. 329–360; Jan Eckel (2013), "The International League for the Rights of Man, Amnesty International and the Changing Fate of Human Rights Activism from the 1940s through the 1970s," *Humanity*, vol. 4, no. 2, pp. 183–214.

[65] Roger N. Baldwin (1949), "The International Bill of Rights," *Great Expressions of Human Rights*. Edited by R. M. MacIver. New York, p. 210.

system developed very little jurisprudence in the first two decades. An institutional legal culture was nurtured inside the organization itself but it only started playing a wider legal–political role in Europe after 1968. The European standards were also an iterative process with, for example, freedom of movement, important to the Helsinki Process in the 1970s, only becoming a human right in the European system through a 1963 Protocol to the Convention. This was after the UN had negotiated language on such a provision. In addition, Great Britain and France, in part worried by the applicability in colonial territories, only signed onto the implementation measures in 1966 and 1974, respectively, after the human rights breakthrough inside the United Nations. Similar to the United Nations, the smaller states were quicker at endorsing the human rights framework as part of their political agenda.

Furthermore, the European Convention was almost abandoned before it was developed. The Committee of Ministers under the new Council of Europe was at its first meeting in August 1949 deciding on the agenda for the Parliamentary Assembly. The French foreign minister Schumann and his British counterpart Ernest Bevin wanted the European Convention struck off the agenda, which would have blocked its actual development. The Danish Foreign Minister Gustav Rasmussen and his Irish counterpart Sean MacBride opposed this citing the great public interest that human rights had aroused among their respective publics. They wanted to keep it on the agenda of the Assembly. It ended with a vote and a minority of four secured that the majority of seven did not have the two-thirds majority to remove it from the agenda.[66] It was a close call but it allowed the Parliamentary Assembly to act and they moved quickly. The European Convention was approved in 1950. It is possible that the Convention project could have survived a lost vote but it would have followed an unknown political trajectory as the main priorities of early European integration lay elsewhere. It illustrates the less than solid foundations that the project was built on.[67]

After the UN had adopted the Universal Declaration in December 1948, the Commission on Human Rights worked in the following years on defining the standards for a broad range of legally binding rights as well as implementation measures. The Commission argued over whether

---

[66] See *Council of Europe: Papers of the First Session of the Committee of Ministers, August 8–13, 1949*. Council of Europe Archives.

[67] See Marco Duranti (2012), "The Holocaust, the Legacy of 1789 and the Birth of International Human Rights Law: Revisiting the Foundation Myth," *Journal of Genocide Research*, vol. 14, no. 2, pp. 159–186.

there should be one or two Covenants. In 1950, the General Assembly decided that one Covenant should be the way forward. The argument in favor of one Covenant was based on the indivisibility of civil, political, economic, social and cultural rights, on avoiding a hierarchy between the rights and to avoid delays in ratification and implementation of economic and social rights.[68] The argument against a single Covenant was that the implementation processes of the various rights were different in nature and that one single Covenant would be a convoluted and confused document. The latter point was illustrated by a draft of the Covenant from April 1951. It contained seventy-three articles and it was unclear whether the implementation measures applied to all of the substantive articles on civil and political rights and on economic, social and cultural rights. The issues moved back and forth between the Commission and the General Assembly in the early 1950s. It was decided in 1952 to have two separate Covenants and progress could now be made in finalizing the provisions although the Soviet Union tried to have this decision reversed in 1953 and again in 1954. In 1954, the Commission on Human Rights finalized the Covenants and transferred them to the General Assembly. It was not a straightforward process as a major political change had occurred that once again seriously questioned the validity of the whole human rights project.

In 1953, immediately after Dwight D. Eisenhower became President of the United States, the Americans told the Commission on Human Rights that given the international political climate, the United States could not support the Covenants, did not believe that they would be widely ratified and were themselves unlikely to ever ratify them. It reflected increasing domestic opposition to American engagement in human rights issues and a struggle for control of U.S. foreign policy. The Eisenhower administration was reacting to a move from the U.S. Congress where the so-called Bricker Amendment, aiming to limit the President's ability to negotiate international agreements, was gaining wide support.[69] It was a political move attacking both the United Nations and intended to counter the possible impact that international human rights developments might have on racial segregation in the American South. The Presidential administration obliged in order to block the Amendment from being passed by

---

[68] Whelan (2010), *Indivisible Human Rights*, p. 117.
[69] For an interesting analysis of the "Bricker Amendment Battle," see Elizabeth Borgwardt (2012), "'Constitutionalizing' Human Rights: The Rise and Rise of the Nuremberg Principles," *The Human Rights Revolution. An International History*. Edited by Akira Iriye, Petra Goedde and William I. Hitchcock. Oxford, pp. 78–82.

Congress, thus preventing the Executive Branch's ability to act independently on foreign affairs from being severely restricted. The statement to the UN, however, cited the current international political climate, for example, reflected in the Korean War, as the reason behind the American withdrawal.

The announcement met with great disappointment among many member states as it questioned the Commission's future. The Philippines was particularly vocal believing that progress had previously been made in bleak times. It was "true that totalitarian states would probably find it impossible to ratify instruments which set out to protect fundamental human rights, since their whole system was based on a denial of these rights," but the Philippines delegate continued "the adoption of the covenants would serve as a beacon to the oppressed peoples of totalitarian states."[70] René Cassin noted that U.S. pessimism was disquieting as it was not without its supporters but he urged that an effort to push ahead with the Covenants should be made as the "political circumstances, which were unfavourable at the moment, might change."[71] The drafting process continued but was effectively blocked from making real progress given the political and ideological conditions under which it was being developed. The Covenants would have a long and arduous journey before them after their transfer in 1954 from the Commission to the General Assembly. The hopes of the mid-1940s appeared a distant memory.

Stalemate and new explorations, 1955–1960

By the mid-1950s the human rights project appeared stymied. The UN Secretary-General Dag Hammarskjold allegedly gave the Director of the UN Human Rights Division, John Humphrey, the following instruction on how to manage the UN human rights work: "There is a flying speed below which an airplane will not remain in the air. I want you to keep the program at that speed and no greater."[72] This appears to have been the level of ambition for human rights at the United Nations in 1955. It

---

[70] Mr. Ingles (the Philippines), Commission on Human Rights, 9th session, 340th meeting, April 8, 1953.

[71] Mr. Cassin (France), Commission on Human Rights, 9th session, 341st meeting, April 9, 1953.

[72] John P. Humphrey (1984), *Human Rights & the United Nations: A Great Adventure.* New York, p. 205; See also Jeff King and A. J. Hobbins (2003), "Hammarskjöld and Human Rights: the Deflation of the UN Human Rights Programme 1953–1961," *Journal of the History of International Law*, vol. 5, no. 2, pp. 337–386.

would not stay that way but whether and when progress would happen lay in an unknown future.

In hindsight 1955 was by no means an uninteresting year for what came to pass with human rights. While there appeared to have been a stalemate – and powerful actors certainly preferred this situation – there were new signs of the times where the meaning and relevance of human rights was the subject of exploration. In October 1955 a young British lawyer representing the "English Human Rights movement" meet with a member of the Strasbourg-based Council of Europe secretariat. The lawyer explained that representatives from the group, including several members of Parliament had met with the British Government to promote their cause. In a June 1955 meeting the Lord Chancellor had explained the government's position and informed them that regarding the group's human rights work there would be "no official support as their pro-gramme depended on full application in all British dependent territories." This meant that the self-proclaimed movement was "comparatively dor-mant" but as the young lawyer explained "they were still watching for any legal case where a question of human rights arises and where the movement could consequently take a stand with proper publicity."[73] In 1960, the young British lawyer, also known as Peter Benenson, would finally find a cause that offered the necessary political traction to establish a human rights movement. According to legend, Benenson read a story in the newspaper one morning in autumn 1960 about two Portuguese students who in a bar had given a toast for freedom and subsequently been arrested by the dictatorship for this act. In reading this article, Peter Benenson was allegedly moved to make the plight of political prisoners his cause. It became a founding moment for Amnesty International that Benenson went on to establish in 1961.[74]

The story of the October 1955 meeting is telling as it sheds light on the prehistory of Amnesty International. It illustrates that the creation of Amnesty was not merely a spur of the moment thing as legend has it. It was a result of a six-year strategic exploration by Benenson for a cause that would give human rights traction by capturing the imagination of

---

[73] Council of Europe Archive, Strasbourg, Central Archives, Box 1847, file 12128: "The Human Rights Movement in the United Kingdom," Confidential meeting note, October 6, 1955 (Mr. A McNulty and Mr. P. Benenson).

[74] Tom Buchanan (2002), "'The Truth Will Set You Free': The Making of Amnesty Interna-tional," *Journal of Contemporary History*, vol. 37, no. 4, pp. 575–597. Peter Benenson was for a while in the intervening period involved with the organization *Justice*, which became the British section of the International Commission of Jurists.

a critical mass of people that would spur action. The story of the moral revulsion that Benenson had felt in late 1960 should be balanced with the story of a political process where a key element was the gradual realization that a human rights movement was built not by seeking government permission but instead by distancing itself and basing it on its own terms in civil society. Timing was also a factor. From its early beginning in 1961, Amnesty International's evolution happened in a decade where human rights were gaining more traction than they had in the 1950s.

Another reason that 1955 was an interesting year was due to the Bandung Conference that took place in April, hosted by the Indonesian government, with representatives from twenty-nine Afro-Asian states, including many representatives from territories that were not yet independent. This high-profiled event was notable for the significant attention that human rights received. It is widely regarded as a landmark event in the emergence of the Third World and the Non-Aligned Movement but as Roland Burke has argued it also "marked out many of the basic contours that came to define key human rights battles, such as that on self-determination."[75] It is striking to notice how clearly a Third World commitment to human rights was expressed at Bandung, including specific endorsements of the Universal Declaration of Human Rights and the Draft Covenants on Human Rights. It acknowledged a broad range of human rights issues, including questions of individual freedom, religious liberty and democratic governance and these debates consumed more of the conference "than the often mythologized question of non-alignment."[76] There was little doubt that the question of self-determination consumed the attention of the participating states. The echoes from Bandung were loud and clear at the 1955 session of the UN Commission on Human Rights, which was meeting in Geneva in parallel with the Bandung Conference and had the right to self-determination as one of its major agenda items.

Both draft Covenants had as Article 1 the right to self-determination – a right that did not feature in the Universal Declaration. Despite having passed on the draft Covenants in 1954 for completion by the General Assembly the debate still lingered on in the Commission on Human Rights. The right to self-determination was introduced into the Covenant

---

[75] Burke (2010), *Decolonization and the Evolution of International Human Rights*, p. 13; See also Roland Burke (2006), "'The Compelling Dialogue of Freedom,' Human Rights at the Bandung Conference," *Human Rights Quarterly*, vol. 28, no. 4, pp. 947–965.

[76] Burke (2010), *Decolonization and the Evolution of International Human Rights*, p. 33.

negotiations in 1950. It was a controversial anticolonial move but also connected with the wider set of international norms established by the UN Charter in which self-determination had been included. Western states criticized the Article for being either a territorial or a group right or for being a principle and not a right and therefore not appropriate for legal documents on individual human rights. Nevertheless, the right to self-determination became part of the 1950s UN human rights diplomacy and added further controversy and complexity to its East–West and North–South intersections. It initiated a complex Western engagement with this issue that would move from criticism of the notion of self-determination as a human right throughout the 1950s and 1960s, where in 1966 it was adopted as the opening article in both Covenants, to an embrace in the 1970s when Western countries applied the principle as part of the Helsinki negotiations directed at Soviet control in Eastern Europe. This points, however, to longer-term developments.

The 1955 Commission on Human Rights revealed many of the tensions at stake. The Western states did not have a unified position and the British were concerned with what positions the United States would take. The United States was cautious but had to acknowledge that self-determination had been an important factor in its own founding. The Soviet Union was very supportive due to its anticolonialist relevance but was at the same time exposed to criticisms about the lack of self-determination in Eastern Europe. Afro-Asian states were, however, the ones driving the debate forward. Their delegates had the added bonus of being able to refer to the speeches, which their heads of state were delivering at Bandung almost simultaneously. It was India, the Philippines, Pakistan and Egypt who were infusing the debate with the political realities that the world was facing. In contrast, the United States was suggesting that the question could be referred to a Committee for study of what self-determination meant and how it should be defined. This did not sit well with the "Bandung Countries." The Indian delegate asked, referring to states that had recently achieved independence, "Did the Commission think that the peoples of India, Pakistan, Burma and Ceylon would have awaited with resignation the deliberations of professors and jurists?" He then went on to outline the glaring contradictions of the global situation that served as a backdrop to the Commission debate:

There was a curious phenomenon in the field of the right to self-determination to which he must draw attention. It was a fact that the territories of the vanquished Powers of the second world were already free or were in the process of liberation – for instance, Libya and Somaliland. The dependent territories of those Powers that had been vanquished in the first world war were the responsibility of the United Nations under the Trusteeship System; but what was the position of these dependent territories that were under the control of those Powers that had emerged victorious from both world wars? Was the lesson which the peoples of those territories had to draw that their best hope for freedom lay in their being on the defeated side in a world war?[77]

This patchwork approach to either independence or continued colonial rule was one of the historical ironies and inconsistencies that was becoming a pressing issue for the international community to address. The European imperial powers, however, were trying to hold off on this and carefully guarded the debates at the United Nations – especially in the context of human rights. It was a pattern that would continue for the rest of the decade. Despite a more organized Afro-Asian grouping who were elaborating their human rights stance, for example, at several conferences for African states in the late 1950s, human rights at the UN remained in a stalemate. By the end of 1960, the General Assembly's Third Committee had adopted less than a third of the articles of the Covenants.[78] It was a slow process that like Peter Benenson's human rights project was searching for political traction to take it forward.

In the latter half of the 1950s, France, Britain and the other colonial rulers were increasingly being challenged on both power and principles. Decolonization was starting to take off but policies changed slowly. The conservatism of the British Colonial Office was felt on its foreign policy and this would continue for several years despite the existence of some alternative voices. In one instance, a Foreign Office official argued for a very different approach to self-determination. In opening an internal Foreign Office debate the official pointed out:

Self-determination would appear to be an ideal subject for a resolution which would show up Soviet policy for what it is. Unfortunately, the legalistic attitude we have adopted on this question has limited our freedom of action for we have taken the line in the discussions on the Human Rights Covenants that self-determination is not a right but a principle and abstained on Article 1 of the Draft Covenants . . . As a result of this unforthcoming attitude we have in fact

---

[77] Mr. Dayal (India), Commission on Human Rights, 11th session, 505th meeting, April 25, 1955, p. 18.

[78] By the end of 1960, the Third Committee had adopted the Preambles and twenty-six articles of the draft Covenants. At this point, there were fifty-seven articles still to be considered, as well as a number of new articles that had been proposed. British National Archives (Kew), FO 371/161043, U.K. Initiatives at the UN, folder "P.Q. Parliamentary Question, Mr. Lipton, January 30, 1961."

put ourselves in the position of appearing to be opponents of a concept which has always been a cardinal feature of the evolution of the Commonwealth and which is consistently denied by the Soviet Government to the peoples under their domination.[79]

This dissenting viewpoint was articulated three days after the building of the Berlin Wall which marked a new stage in the Cold War and high-lighted the realities of Soviet domination in Eastern Europe. This had always been part of the context of the UN debates on self-determination but the cost of exploiting this had been viewed as too high by the European imperial powers. The Berlin Wall could have been a valid reason to bring human rights issues to the forefront of global politics but the debate that followed inside the British Foreign Office showed that even in 1961 such a move was not to Western liking.

The human rights project of the 1940s was not stillborn but it arrived on the international scene without any privileged birthright. It had to make its own way through the world. One must therefore be careful when presenting the 1940s as a natural starting point for the emergence of human rights because an historical account must better reflect the lack of continuity in their evolution. The 1940s was not the breakthrough era for human rights but the fact that human rights featured so prominently in the Charter, however, is important because it invariably brings us back to the earliest phases of UN history when trying to explain the genesis of international human rights. At a minimum, the UN Charter defined human rights as part of the field of multilateral diplomacy. The drafting of the 1948 Universal Declaration remains an impressive piece of intellectual and normative work by any standard but the wider context in which the document emerged calls for a more moderate and less triumphant narrative to describe the human rights developments in this period.

It is also necessary to give due attention to the UN Charter as an enabler of these developments. The UN Charter was sufficiently rich in meaning to become the source for reinterpreting the nature and purpose of the United Nations. These various interpretations reflected the tides of international politics and changed the norms guiding the international state system. It is in these processes that one can capture the making of human rights and better understand its 1940s' beginnings. Human rights were interacting with the global forces of change. Against the backdrop

[79] British National Archives (Kew), FO 371/161043, "Possibility of an initiative in the United Nations in the field of human rights," Foreign Office Circular/memo from August 16, 1961 (Entry by E. E. Key).

of a colonial order, human rights had little hope of becoming a global phenomenon. It was only with the decline of colonialism that human rights could more fully emerge. This fact places human rights closer to the center of 1960s' international politics, more precisely as part of the world that decolonization made.

2

"The problem of freedom"

The United Nations and decolonization, 1960–1961

"Africa is engaged in a complete juridical revolution."
    Abdoulaye Wade (Senegal), African Conference on the Rule of Law,
            January 1961[1]

"We fear to be led astray by a dialogue in which the colonizers speak just like those who seek their own freedom."
        Ahmed Benhima (Morocco), UN General Assembly, 1961[2]

On August 16, 1961, Willy Brandt, the mayor of West Berlin, sent a letter to President John F. Kennedy in response to the worst crisis facing his city since the Soviet blockade in 1948. Three days earlier, the Berlin Wall had been erected by the Soviet and East German authorities, dividing the city, families and friends, and raising questions about the international status of Berlin and the relationship between the two Germanys – questions that were at the epicenter of the Cold War conflict.[3]

Willy Brandt asked for American support to bring the situation before the United Nations as a major human rights violation. He believed that a Western political initiative that emphasized the Soviet Union's flagrant abuse of the Universal Declaration of Human Rights inside the East German zone was necessary and beneficial to the West. The United States

---

[1] Statement by Abdoulaye Wade in: International Commission of Jurists (1961), African Conference on the Rule of Law, Lagos Nigeria, pp. 58–59.
[2] Mr. Ahmed Benhima (Morocco), UN General Assembly, 16th session, 1064th meeting, November 24, 1961, p. 816.
[3] A useful account of the political responses to the Berlin Wall by Willy Brandt and the Kennedy administration is found in Arne Hoffman (2007), *The Emergence of Détente in Europe: Brandt, Kennedy and the Formation of Ostpolitik*. Berlin, pp. 27–42.

opposed the idea. This was made clear to Brandt in a meeting on August 20 with Vice President Lyndon B. Johnson and General Lucius Clay. They had been asked by President Kennedy to travel to West Berlin to show American support to the people of Berlin and their political leaders.[4]

A few days later the UN General Assembly was facing a heated debate over events in Bizerte, Tunisia, in July 1961 and the United States had little appetite for a human rights debate over Berlin.[5] In Bizerte, French forces had killed several hundred Tunisians when they had tried to claim sovereignty over a French military base on Tunisian soil, which was supporting the French war effort in neighboring Algeria. The Bizerte incident had angered the Afro-Asian group of countries. The United States had to respond to this political crisis and they did not see any value in making the Berlin Wall a human rights issue at the United Nations. The German Federal Government decided in favor of the U.S. position and Willy Brandt's request was sidelined.

Willy Brandt's idea did create interest in the British Foreign Office, which considered a human rights initiative on "freedom of movement" at the 1961 United Nations General Assembly session. The discussion had started in May 1961 when the new British Ambassador to the United States David Ormsby-Gore proposed an initiative on "Freedom of information." There was interest in a British initiative but "Freedom of information" was deemed problematic due to highly restrictive regulations enforced in a number of colonial territories. In early August 1961, the focus had changed to a resolution on "democratic freedom" focusing on "free elections, free speech and freedom of political party life."[6]

Immediately after the Berlin Wall was erected, the British focus shifted toward a human rights initiative on "freedom of movement." This proposal was seen as having several advantages and meant that Britain "could meet the wishes which Herr Brandt has expressed, to see the Russian violations of human rights there raised in the United Nations."[7] As the internal

---

[4] See "Report by Vice President Lyndon B. Johnson on his visit to Germany, 19–20 August 1961" and "Memorandum of Conversation" (Mayor Brandt and Amrehn with Ambassador Dowling and Bohlen), August 20, 1961, LBJ Library (Austin, TX), Vice Presidential Security File, Box 2.

[5] Ibid.

[6] British National Archives (Kew), FO 371/161043, "Possibility of an initiative in the United Nations in the field of human rights," Foreign Office circular/memo, August 16, 1961.

[7] British National Archives (Kew), FO 371/161043, "Possibility of an initiative in the United Nations in the field of human rights," Foreign Office circular/memo, August 17, 1961.

Foreign Office debate unfolded, problems arose. One official mentioned that when the article on "freedom of movement" in the Covenant on Civil and Political Rights had been negotiated in 1959, it had actually caused considerable problems for the United Kingdom. The Colonial Office believed that the U.K. would be rather vulnerable on this issue due to situations in the colonies. Furthermore, it was stated that the United Kingdom had "not accepted the doctrine . . . that human rights are the subject of international obligation and therefore that specific breaches are not covered by the domestic jurisdiction provisions of Article 2(7)" of the UN Charter.[8] It meant that official British policy was that human rights were not an issue of legitimate international concern. By early September, it was acknowledged that the British human rights initiative at the 1961 UN General Assembly was dead on arrival due to limitations in U.K. policies. The wider initiative was too risky for the British. Human rights were therefore not directly linked to the handling of the Berlin question at the UN.

Hence, crisis management won over the principled concern voiced by Brandt of a clear Western interest in raising the human rights dimensions of the Berlin situation. In 1962, Brandt explained this political vision, arguing that on "the topic of human rights . . . we have to think in terms of changing conditions within the bounds of a balance of power that cannot be changed at first."[9] The International Commission of Jurists shared Brandt's view in their 1962 report *The Berlin Wall – A Defiance of Human Rights* but this NGO effort had limited impact on wider opinion.[10]

Freedom of movement between East and West and related human rights had not yet in any significant way become issues to be used strategically with the aim of transforming Cold War relations. The Council of Europe could not serve this purpose. It had to be a matter for a wider international forum, namely the United Nations. Brandt believed human rights could constitute the beginning of a transformative approach, but in August 1961, the East–West conflict over human rights was still seen as a zero-sum game. The Western powers had little appetite for leveraging the Berlin Wall issue in the United Nations, given the racial situation in the United States and the colonial issues that several European states were

---

[8] Ibid. See statements in "File August 17–September 6."

[9] Quoted in Hoffman (2007), *The Emergence of Détente in Europe*, p. 75. See also Willy Brandt (2003), *Erinnerungen*. Munich, pp. 60–65.

[10] International Commission of Jurists (1962), *The Berlin Wall – A Defiance of Human Rights*. Geneva, p. 5.

facing. There was also no coherent Western strategy to use human rights in this world forum. Any change in the international political significance of human rights at this point in time would have to come from another source. It did.

This chapter examines the debates on decolonization at the United Nations General Assembly in 1960 and 1961. The debates were about the nature of colonialism and how to bring colonialism to an end. The debates demonstrated that every member state had to adjust to a new global reality and to a new world in the making. For many member states, it was comparable to debating a new UN Charter outlining the future purpose of the organization. These UN debates signified a new trajectory for human rights norms in international relations, which would lead to their legal breakthrough during the 1960s. Decolonization was a structural change in the international state system. This change initially inspired a turn toward international law-making but also brought forward other profound questions. As the historian Matthew Connelly has argued concerning decolonization: the organization of "the transfer of power first appeared as a pressing, practical matter. But that was merely a premonition of a larger problem that continues to trouble the postcolonial world: What was the real nature and extent of decolonization?"[11] It is a question worth asking.

1960: "colonialism of souls"

"Every age has its own imperatives," the Guinean president Sékou Toure explained to the 1960 General Assembly. President Toure spoke about colonialism the morning after the General Assembly had witnessed chaotic scenes during its plenary debate. The Soviet leader Nikita Khrushchev allegedly slammed his shoe on his desk in protest and the plenary meeting was abandoned amid the controversies that ensued.

Toure tried to bring the debate back on track. He wanted to impress on the General Assembly the great importance decolonization had for the African and Asian states. He explained that "There can be no doubt that the problem of freedom is the greatest problem in the world. No people and no thinking person can think that freedom is divisible or that

---

[11] Matthew Connelly (2002), *A Diplomatic Revolution. Algeria's Fight for Independence and the Origins of the Post-Cold War Era.* Oxford, p. 249; See also John Darwin (1984), "British Decolonization since 1945: A Pattern or a Puzzle?," *Journal of Imperial and Commonwealth History*, vol. 12, no. 2, p. 187.

it belongs to a single people, race or religion."[12] The topic of ending colonialism became the defining debate of the 1960 General Assembly – a session that would be a watershed moment between two versions of the United Nations.

The momentum behind decolonization was evident as seventeen newly independent states joined the United Nations in 1960. Sixteen of these were African countries and included large swathes of West and Central Africa. Colonialism was an ideological, political and military battleground of great significance to the major Cold War powers and the newly independent states. The differences between the colonial powers and the new African states was made clear in a statement by Liberia that drew attention to the ironic claim by a "certain European Head of State that in discussing Africa the United Nations is meddling in the domestic affairs of his country."[13] The meaning of sovereignty was a central aspect of the debate, which was also about defining the imperatives of a new age.

Sékou Toure's statement about "the problem of freedom" was echoed by other states. A Latin American delegate quoted Toure's statement at length, complimented the new states for the emphasis they were placing on human rights at the United Nations and took advantage of the topic to criticize the Soviet Union for its colonialist regime of terror and silence that suppressed man's conscience and his freedom to create, to speak, to write and to worship. The Soviet system practiced a "colonialism of souls."[14]

---

[12] Mr. Sékou Toure (Guinea), UN General Assembly, 15th session, 903rd Meeting, October 13, 1960, p. 691. Sékou Toure offers a good illustration of the chasm that existed among a number of Third World leaders between their progressive messages at the United Nations and the brutal reality of their domestic rule. Guinea became independent in October 1958 after a rapid French withdrawal, which the scholar Ebere Nwaubani has called a "scorched-earth retreat." It was bound to leave the country of 2.6 million people – with only fifteen secondary schools, no tertiary institutions, an illiteracy rate of 95 percent and an economy wholly dependent on France – in a chaotic and devastating situation. Ebere Nwaubani (2001), *The United States and Decolonization in West Africa, 1950–1960*. Rochester, NY, p. 210. One of Toure's early decisions in October 1958 with both real and symbolic significance was to abolish the profession of lawyer because that profession according to him expressed a "legal formalism which is not only useless but incompatible with the social realities of a young African nation." This was a starting point for a brutal and arbitrary dictatorial rule where foes and allies alike would suffer at best mock trials before long-term imprisonment or execution based on the whims of the President. International Commission of Jurists (1971), "Justice in Guinea," *The Review*, December, no. 7, p. 4.

[13] Mr. Dosumu-Johnson (Liberia), UN General Assembly, 15th session, 931st meeting, December 1, 1960, p. 1070.

[14] Mr. Alvarez Restrepo (Colombia), UN General Assembly, 15th session, 929th meeting, November 30, 1960, pp. 1040–1041.

Nikita Khrushchev had not wanted the discussion to take this direction. Khrushchev himself had proposed that priority should be given to the debate on ending colonialism. The Soviet Union wanted to gain political advantage from the unfinished decolonization process by presenting itself as its leading proponent at the United Nations. Khrushchev had submitted a draft Declaration on decolonization that the Soviet Union wanted the General Assembly to endorse. After lengthy deliberation, the Declaration that was endorsed distinguished itself from the Soviet proposal – most notably by emphasizing the importance of human rights to the process of ending colonialism.

The Soviets hailed themselves as champions of anticolonialism. This agenda formed part of a larger political campaign for "peaceful coexistence" that Khrushchev had been promoting for some time. A formal settlement of the post–Second World War European political order, including a peace treaty between the two Germany's, was the "question of questions" for Khrushchev, but his campaign for peaceful coexistence was not limited to the European theater of the Cold War.[15] He saw the 1955 Bandung Conference where twenty-nine Asian and African countries had met as reflecting his principles of peaceful coexistence.[16] This exemplified how the legacy of Bandung, and related conferences in Africa in the intervening period, was evoked to shape the outcome of the 1960 General Assembly debate on colonialism.[17]

This frame of reference provided an opportunity for the Afro-Asian countries to assert their agenda. This received some sympathy as reflected on by a Latin American delegate who vividly compared their plight in the process of achieving independence with the Odyssey and drew the following lesson, "We cannot allow despair to lead them, by logical

---

[15] Nikita Khrushchev (1959), "On Peaceful Coexistence," *Foreign Affairs*, vol. 38, October, no. 1, p. 10.

[16] Ibid., p. 9.

[17] There were twenty-four different countries that made references to Bandung during the debate. These references came in two versions. There were references specific to Bandung (11 countries – Cambodia, Iran, Ceylon, Burma, Mali, Laos, Nepal, Iceland, the United States, Congo-Brazzaville and Cyprus) or references jointly to Bandung and the African follow-up conferences (1958 in Accra, 1959 Monrovia and 1960 Addis Ababa) that addressed similar concerns and included human rights in the Declarations from these meetings. These broader references were made by thirteen countries (Czechoslovakia, Ghana, Ethiopia, Poland, Libya, Egypt, Ukraine, Sudan, Nepal, Indonesia, Togo, the USSR and Morocco). The statements could contain multiple references to the abovementioned conferences. Some states repeated references in different interventions.

reaction, to accept the totalitarian Charybdis after having escaped from the Colonialist Scylla."[18]

The Afro-Asian countries arrived well prepared. It was not just that the political developments since Bandung had started to change the relationship between race and the Cold War.[19] The Bandung Conference, the 1958 and 1960 Conferences of African Independent States held in Accra and Addis Ababa, respectively, at the level of Head of States and the 1959 Monrovia meeting for Foreign Ministers had helped define common positions on issues that were now before the United Nations. They countered the Soviet move by tabling a separate draft Declaration that had been negotiated over several weeks by approximately forty Afro-Asian member states. Its language drew to a large extent on the Bandung Declaration and the other conferences that had given prominence to human rights and the UN Charter. They took the issue out of the hands of the Soviet Union and turned the debate in a different direction. The United Kingdom, despite Prime Minister Macmillan's "Wind of Change" speech earlier that year, contributed little to the discussion. They did, however, acknowledge that the Afro-Asian group had "succeeded in emancipating the subject of granting of independence to all colonial countries and peoples from the tendentious and unconstructive language of the Soviet draft declaration."[20] The Soviet Union tried to reinstate language from their original proposal but faced strong opposition and had to agree to the Afro-Asian draft that famously became known as General Assembly Resolution 1514: *Declaration on the Granting of Independence to Colonial Countries and Peoples.*

The Declaration is viewed as an expression of the Third World's insistence on close linkages between human rights and self-determination. This is not without reason, but this understanding has overshadowed the subtleties in the human rights language in the Declaration. The affirmation of faith in the UN Charter and the Universal Declaration of Human Rights carries a meaning that is broader than self-determination. The emphasis on "human rights and fundamental freedoms for all without distinction as to race, sex, language or religion" shows that this went beyond the

---

[18] Mr. Benites Vinueza (Ecuador), UN General Assembly, 15th session, 933rd meeting, December 2, 1960, p. 1102.

[19] Jason C. Parker (2006), "Cold War II: The Eisenhower Administration, the Bandung Conference, and the Reperiodization of the Postwar Era," *Diplomatic History*, vol. 30, no. 5, p. 890.

[20] Mr. Ormsby-Gore (UK), UN General Assembly, 15th session, 947th meeting, December 14, 1960, p. 1276.

notions of race. Religion was also central. This was reaffirmed in the call for decolonization "without distinction as to race, creed and colour" of the remaining territories that had not attained independence. Religion was an important feature of the human rights debates at the 1960 General Assembly.[21]

Furthermore, the scope of the text was universal in nature, whereas the Soviet draft was intended as an attack on European colonialism. Universality was regularly evoked in the debate, referring either specifically to human rights or to the ethos of the United Nations.[22] The combination of the two was a reason why the United Nations became such an important forum for the emergence of human rights in the 1960s. The Afro-Asian states were commended for emphasizing "the essential principle of universality."[23] The Pakistani delegate stated, "The basis of the United Nations is universality. From this principle it derives its greatest strength," but he also reminded the Assembly about "the history of man which teaches us that freedom has never been won with words."[24]

This highlighted the dilemmas of the Afro-Asian achievement in shaping the Declaration on decolonization and independence. Ending colonialism had for the first time been high on the United Nations agenda. The Afro-Asian group had developed a rather coherent strategy based on the UN Charter and human rights. They had performed well in the diplomatic dealings at the UN General Assembly, where a substantial number of these countries were operating for the first time. However, this was not enough to achieve support from the United States. President Eisenhower personally intervened, instructing that the United States would not back the Declaration, much to the dismay of the Secretary of State Christian Herter and the U.S. Ambassador James Wadsworth, who was "shocked and disheartened" by the decision to reject what he considered a constructive draft that partly focused on Soviet imperialism.[25] The United States

[21] See the chapter "The Hymn of Hate."

[22] See in particular statements delivered during the 1960 UN General Assembly Plenary Debate by the following countries: Argentina (p. 1008), Pakistan (p. 1058), Peru (p. 1060), Mali (p. 1066), Guinea (p. 1083), Japan (p. 1094). Guatemala (p. 1098), Ireland (p. 1138), Lebanon (p. 1162) and Venezuela (p. 1200). Page numbers refer to the Summary Records from the UN General Assembly, Plenary, 15th session.

[23] Mr. Aiken (Ireland), UN General Assembly, 15th session, 935th meeting, December 5, 1960, p. 1138.

[24] Mr. Hasan (Pakistan), UN General Assembly, 15th session, 930th meeting, December 1, 1960, p. 1058.

[25] Roland Burke (2010), *Decolonization and the Evolution of International Human Rights.* Philadelphia, PA, pp. 55–56.

abstained alongside the major colonial powers of Portugal, Belgium, Spain, South Africa, the United Kingdom and France. It appears that the Odyssey from colonialism to independence did not just have to navigate a course between Scylla and Charybdis. It was also navigating a world of one-eyed Cyclops.

The vote by the colonial powers was less surprising. There were multiple agendas and interests shaping policy decisions in the metropoles as the developments in Algeria and Southern Africa showed. It gave the Eastern Bloc the possibility to mobilize their appeal. The Soviet Union therefore voted in favor of the Declaration despite being sidelined on the actual content. The Soviet Union presented the Declaration as a significant achievement and went on to promote the agenda in the coming years based on the Declaration – even though human rights provisions were embedded in the text. The Soviets saw a larger ideological opportunity to pursue an anticolonialist agenda and ignored the fact that the Declaration contained the seed of what Robert Cover called a new *jurisgenesis* – the creation of a new legal meaning – around human rights. The anticolonialist critique was a politically tempting and powerful means to attack Western "neocolonialist" designs for the world or, as the Romanian delegate explained, "the tiger does not turn vegetarian just because his prey becomes scarce and elusive."[26]

1961: "we have no desire to be faced with a multiplication of Congos"

By autumn 1961, when the General Assembly reconvened, little had changed. The sole new member was Sierra Leone, as opposed to sixteen new members the previous year, who fully endorsed the strong human rights provisions secured by the Afro-Asian group of nations in the *Declaration on the Granting of Independence to Colonial Countries and Peoples*.[27]

If little had changed regarding implementation of the Declaration, the situation on the ground had become worse. It seemed as if atrocities abounded, with ongoing or brewing crises in Algeria, Angola, Bizerte (Tunisia), Congo, South Africa, South West Africa and Southern Rhodesia dominating the debate. Finding responses to these multiple crises in

---

[26] Mr. Mezincescu (Romania), UN General Assembly, 15th session, 932nd meeting, December 2, 1960, p. 1077.
[27] Mr. Collier (Sierra Leone), UN General Assembly, 16th session, 1057th meeting, November 17, 1961, p. 700.

Africa was a prominent feature of the 1961 debate on ending colonialism. In addition, there had been the failed U.S. Bay of Pigs invasion in Cuba and the Soviet–East German building of the Berlin Wall in August 1961. It was a year of international crisis.

It was the Soviet Union who pushed the agenda but was again rebuffed by the Afro-Asian group. A key group of Afro-Asian states made significant efforts at consulting a broad array of member states to reach a consensus. From the outset, these states shaped the debate placing emphasis on the rule of law and human rights. Nigeria was among the leading actors pursuing this moderating role. Their Foreign Minister Jaja Wachuku led this approach and spoke about finding solutions to the situations in South Africa, Rhodesia and South West Africa. Wachuku believed that these countries could no longer resist the impact of independence on the continent and described his country's problem with apartheid as one of South Africa not respecting the "rule of law."[28] Coming a year after the Sharpeville massacre that killed sixty-nine protesters and led to further entrenchment of white apartheid rule, it was a surprisingly modest critique. The emphasis on the rule of law, however, had its reasons.

Earlier in 1961, Nigeria had hosted the largest gathering ever of African jurists on African soil to debate the principle of the rule of law and its importance for the new political developments on the continent and a hopefully democratic future. It was organized by the International Commission of Jurists (ICJ) and Liberty, the Nigerian section of the ICJ. The conference brought together several Ministers of Justice, Chief Justices and other prominent legal experts from twenty-three African countries with a total of 194 participants. Most states were newly independent, had recently undergone a constitution-making process and were facing the early challenges of statehood with enthusiasm, hope and great concern since the African states "had broken into a universe composed of powerful and organised states" and had to find their position in this world. Other nations were on the brink of such political change but still faced great uncertainty and instability in the transition.

T. O. Elias, the Nigerian Minister of Justice and the leading African legal scholar during this era, opened the debate. He spoke of apartheid in South Africa as "an unparalleled example of the prostitution of the judicial process in recent times" but admired the "courageous stand"

---

[28] "Our quarrel with South Africa is only that the power is in the hands of a microscopic minority that does not want to respect the rule of law," Mr. Wachuku (Nigeria), UN General Assembly, 16th Session, 1050th meeting, November 9, 1961, p. 610.

taken by the U.S. Supreme Court on discriminatory racial laws in "the last few years" under the Warren court.[29] This drew Elias toward a larger conclusion on the role of law – a point that may help explain the moderate Nigerian position in the United Nations in the 1961 debate. Elias struck a hopeful theme, which was widespread during the first half of the 1960s, when he emphasized that "law is a civilizing as well as a stabilizing influence in human society, and the true jurists are some of the most unyielding defenders of its prerogatives."[30] Few in the conference room were likely to challenge this view.

The debates at the African Conference on the Rule of Law showed great insight as to legal developments around the world, and it was also here that the idea of an African Human Rights Convention and an African Court of Human Rights was first put forward.[31] This debate resonated well beyond the conference and caught the interest of the Council of Europe and was highlighted at the United Nations.[32] The proposal was the result of a larger political dynamic, which was equally as much about manifesting continent-wide independence as it was about the role of law in modernizing African sociocultural and political structures. "Africa is engaging in a complete juridical revolution," the Senegalese legal scholar Abdoulaye Wade argued, and he continued by elaborating a liberal vision for Africa's future development where equality was the central component:

In any listing of human rights, one right is frequently treated separately, or even neglected altogether: the right to equality. Although often proclaimed, it is in fact the most violated. Without equality there cannot be democracy. Is it the blood link, the survival of the mentality of tribalism, that frequently results in nepotism? The essential condition for equality is undeniably to pass from the tribal form and mentality to the modern form of co-existence of individuals, safeguarded by

[29] Statement by T. O. Elias in: International Commission of Jurists (1961), *African Conference on the Rule of Law, Lagos Nigeria, 3–7 January 1961 – A Report on the Proceedings of the Conference*. Geneva, p. 45.

[30] Ibid., p. 55.

[31] Francois Amorin from Togo made the suggestion. He made reference to similar regional developments in Europe and plans in Latin America. It subsequently became part of the conference recommendations, known as "The Law of Lagos." It would be another two decades before an African Convention came into existence in 1981.

[32] See, for example, Hermod Lannungs statement to the Third Committee, 1397th meeting, October 18, 1966 – five years after the Lagos Conference – and compare with the full draft of statement in Rigsarkivet (Danish National Archives), Danish UN Mission, 119.L.22a/1.1 – Box 257. From Council of Europe, see Letter from A. B. McNulty to G. K. J. Amachree, Attorney-General's Office Nigeria, March 3, 1961, Council of Europe Archives, Strasbourg, Box 1815, File 12113: Human Rights in Nigeria.

institutions which to some degree guarantee standards of reciprocal behaviour among citizens. We therefore feel that the future of democracy in Black Africa is strongly bound up with institutionalization . . . one of the essential lines of development of our societies.[33]

The notion of equality was without doubt a major reason for the emphasis on human rights by countries from the Global South. Wade elaborated on his analysis by emphasizing that the West had given Africa various ideas and institutions – including the rule of law – that were no longer in dispute and were considered "common property." The emphasis on the importance of institutions in the African context also reflected a wider belief in the United Nations as an international institution that could meet the aspirations of the newly independent countries. Wade acknowledged the inspiration of the Universal Declaration of Human Rights on constitution making in Africa where the inviolability of freedom of religion, freedom of assembly, freedom of opinion and freedom of association were proclaimed as principles to be upheld in the new states and were also universal requirements.

The challenge for Africa, Wade argued, would be to address two issues that the continent was facing as it emerged as an independent actor in the international system. The two issues were underdevelopment and Africa's place in the international system of states. It was between these two challenges that the African state now found itself. The development process needed to bring the complex element of judicial institutions into social and political life in order to establish a democratic system based on the rule of law.[34] It was a system that could not merely abstain from the violation of freedoms. The State had to provide positive benefits to its people.

Law had a special role in realizing this vision and the Nigerian delegates were particularly active in this debate. The country had achieved independence only three months earlier in October 1960, with a constitution that included a bill of rights that set a trend for many other British colonies achieving independence.[35] Both the Nigerian Prime Minister and the Chief Justice spoke at the conference, highlighting human rights as "fundamental in a civilized society." The chairman of the Nigerian

---

[33] Statement by Abdoulaye Wade in: International Commission of Jurists (1961), *African Conference on the Rule of Law, Lagos Nigeria*, pp. 58–59.
[34] Ibid., s. 67.
[35] Charles O. H. Parkinson (2008), *Bills of Rights and Decolonization. The Emergence of Domestic Human Rights Instruments in Britain's Overseas Territories*. Oxford, p. 17.

section of the ICJ provided a strong international outlook on these matters that showed that the participating jurists' engagement on rule of law
and human rights issues had both a strong African and an international
dimension. He asked:

When nations reach the stage where the right of freedom of movement is determined by the colour of your skin; where the right of freedom of expression is
determined by one's political allegiance; where the right of freedom of worship
is determined by the State in which one lives, where is the sanctity of the Rule of
Law?[36]

These were the questions raised by African diplomats and others from
the Global South that were demanding answers from the international
community. They were changing the whole dynamic of how human rights
were perceived at the United Nations.

The 1961 debate in the UN General Assembly on ending colonialism
was, according to the Dutch Foreign Minister Joseph Luns, essentially
about "the closing of an era."[37] Decolonization meant that a new international system was in the making. In 1961, however, the process appeared
mainly to bring to the world's attention more examples of how violent
this transformation could become. The Bizerte incident in Tunisia was an
expression of the brutality of the Algerian war. The war had lasted seven
years and had cost the lives of several hundred thousand people. The
debate contained numerous references to the July incident at Bizerte. As a
critique of French behavior, these statements received renewed relevance
during the debate after French authorities in October killed around hundred peaceful Algerian demonstrators in what was called a "race hunt"
in the streets of Paris.[38]

The Congo also featured prominently in discussions. The crisis there
had consumed considerable diplomatic effort by the United Nations and
led in September 1961 to the death of UN Secretary-General Dag Hammarskjöld, who had been en route to cease-fire negotiations. The Indian
delegate Krishna Menon did not mince words in his articulate assessment
of the legacy of Belgian colonialism:

There is no greater condemnation of colonialism than what is taking place in the
Congo ... The very fact that a metropolitan country, after years of rule, leaves

---

[36] Statement by Chief Arthur Prest in: International Commission of Jurists (1961), *African Conference on the Rule of Law, Lagos Nigeria*, p. 89.
[37] Mr. Luns (the Netherlands), UN General Assembly, 16th Session, 1049th Meeting, November 8, 1961, p. 587.
[38] Mr. Bourguiba (Tunisia), UN General Assembly, 16th Session, 1057th Meeting, November 17, 1961, p. 694.

a territory in such a state of anarchy that, after its withdrawal, civil war and outside intervention follow, provides the worst picture of colonial rule that has come before this Assembly.[39]

The immediate ramifications of this legacy for the international community's handling of the decolonization process was most poignantly expressed when Pakistan stated: "We have no desire to be faced with a multiplication of Congos."[40] The sad reality was that this was already on the horizon.

Belgium's rapid departure from the Congo in 1960 had an almost immediate impact in Angola. The city of Leopoldville in Congo had been a center of Angolan exile politics and the departure triggered events in Angola, where local insurrections started in 1961.[41] These insurrections hardened the position of the Portuguese regime and led to a rapid and costly escalation of military forces on the ground. By the time the UN General Assembly convened in September 1961, the death toll had reached more than 50,000 Africans and 2,000 Europeans and had caused large-scale population displacement.[42] Further violent conflict would spill over into the other Portuguese territories of Mozambique and Guinea.

Portugal became the target of continual criticism at the United Nations comparable to the criticism raised against South Africa.[43] It was not lost on other member states that the colonial power was a "small and backward European nation" and that it took advantage of support from its powerful Western allies as it "engaged in the deliberate massacre of the African population."[44] Portugal's defense was that their colonial possessions were an integrated part of the country's constitutional order and that it was a matter of internal jurisdiction and not of colonialism.

---

[39] Mr. Menon (India), UN General Assembly, 16th Session, 1058th Meeting, November 20, 1961, p. 713.

[40] Mr. Iqbal (Pakistan), UN General Assembly, 16th Session, 1061st Meeting, November 22, 1961, p. 763.

[41] Malyn Newitt (2007), "Angola in Historical Context," *Angola – The Weight of History*. Edited by Patrick Chabal and Nuno Vidal. London, pp. 72–82. On Mozambique, see Joao M. Cabrita (2000), *Mozambique – The Tortuous Road to Democracy*. London, pp. 24–31.

[42] In the 1961 debate on ending colonialism, these figures for the number of deaths were quoted citing the international press. They are listed as official figures in Gerald J. Bender (1978), *Angola under the Portuguese. The Myth and the Reality*. London, p. 158.

[43] For an insightful analysis of the security dependency between Portugal's colonial rule and South African national security, see Jamie Miller (2012), "Things Fall Apart: South Africa and the Collapse of the Portuguese Empire 1973–74," *Cold War History*, vol. 12, no. 2, pp. 183–204.

[44] Mr. Ba (Mali), UN General Assembly, 16th Session, 1064th Meeting, November 24, 1961, p. 822.

It was an argument that convinced very few, and Portugal was criticized for its "legalistic fiction adopted for the purposes of evading the provisions of the Charter."[45] This point made by Cyprus – a newly independent European country – was presented in the context of a larger strategic lesson and prediction in favor of decolonization that Cyprus drew for the West, namely that:

The final liquidation of colonialism will be a source of strength to the United Nations in many ways by rendering the Western Powers freer in their policies, thus fortifying and broadening the common front for freedom and human rights as the basis of peace.[46]

The Western powers were managing so many different political agendas in this transformative process that such clarity of vision did not emanate from these powers themselves. They could speak the language, express support in principle, but their actions were too often questionable. Morocco stated a widely felt sentiment, namely that "We fear to be led astray by a dialogue in which the colonizers speak just like those who seek their own freedom."[47]

The Communist Bloc tried to exploit the situation but there was a noticeable change. The 1960 Declaration had established a platform for human rights in the debates on ending colonialism and the Soviet Union could not ignore this. In the context of race and colonialism, they would, over the coming years, opt for political overreach by becoming promoters of civil and political rights.[48] It was an indication of a new flank for international human rights diplomacy that would be used strategically in the human rights breakthrough over the next years.

The Western states did in direct rhetorical clashes criticize the Soviet Union and the other Communist countries on human rights grounds, for example, the denial of freedom of movement, but otherwise Western positions were generally passive or defensive on the human rights dimensions of this debate. This debate also extended to the situation in South West Africa, Rhodesia and South Africa – countries where, according to one

---

[45] Mr. Rossides (Cyprus), UN General Assembly, 16th Session, 1064th Meeting, November 24, 1961, p. 812.

[46] Ibid., p. 812.

[47] Mr. Benhima (Morocco), UN General Assembly, 16th session, 1064th meeting, November 24, 1961, p. 816.

[48] The following quote illustrates the Soviet approach; "We advocate granting the dependent peoples the widest democratic rights and freedoms, including freedom of speech, the Press, freedom of association and the right to elect their organs of power on the basis of universal suffrage," Mr. Lapin (the USSR), UN General Assembly, 16th session, 1048th meeting, November 7, 1961, p. 580.

African delegate, "the despicable system of racial discrimination is exalted to the level of State dogma."[49] The unsatisfactory Western responses to the problems faced in Africa would receive lengthy treatment by two of the diplomats who were active in the 1961 debate on ending colonialism. Although representing two different constituencies – being Ghanaian and British, respectively – they presented similar analyses of the problems.

The British diplomat, Hugh Foot, had long been a colonial adminis-trator before representing the United Kingdom at the United Nations. He had been particularly successful as Governor General of Jamaica during the 1950s and played an important role in preparing the country for independence. He had also helped broker the Cypriot independence pro-cess under very difficult circumstances. His statement at the 1961 debate was a rather traditional British statement criticizing the "neoslavery of the Soviet system" while denying that the situation in Southern Rhodesia was in any way comparable to that of South Africa.

Within a year, Hugh Foot had resigned from his post as Ambassador to the United Nations after more than thirty years in British government ser-vice, his tipping point being Britain's policy toward Southern Rhodesia. In June 1962, the General Assembly had called for a constitutional con-ference in Southern Rhodesia, with only Great Britain, South Africa and Portugal voting against this proposal. Hugh Foot had worked for a U.K. policy change away from being "champions of the status quo." He saw this as an untenable position for Britain. Foot explained this in a highly critical memorandum from August 1962, which he subsequently went to London to defend. It stated that "we speak of peaceful change, but we can point to no effective action to bring it about in the southern part of Africa."[50]

With no change of government policy in sight after his discussions with the British Foreign Minister Alec Douglas-Home and the prospect of having to defend this position at the UN General Assembly, Hugh Foot resigned. The "Wind of Change" that British Prime Minister Harold Macmillan announced in his 1960 speech delivered in South Africa was still a phenomenon that was subject to border controls and could get stuck in customs.[51] Tragically, as in Angola and Mozambique, the story of Southern Rhodesia would be one of enduring violence.

---

[49] Mr. Maka (Guinea), UN General Assembly, 16th session, 1058th meeting, November 20, 1961, p. 710.

[50] Hugh Foot (1964), *A Start in Freedom*. London, p. 220.

[51] For an interesting perspective on the political significance of Macmillan's speech in the Southern African context, see Saul Dubow (2011), "Macmillan, Verwoerd and the 1960 'Wind of Change' Speech," *The Historical Journal*, vol. 54, no. 4, pp. 1087–1114.

In his 1964 memoir, *A Start in Freedom*, Hugh Foot provided his own vivid image of the situation in Africa – a situation that had so dominated the 1960 and 1961 debates on ending colonialism. He explained to the reader that:

When I have been speaking in America and trying to describe modern Africa as I see it, I have spoken about Africa as a great house of many separate rooms. We look into one room and see encouraging constructive work going forward. We look into another room and we are uneasy and disturbed by what we see. In another room what we see going on seems dangerous, misguided, wrong. But in all the separate rooms the effort goes forward. Meanwhile down in the cellars – in the southern states of Africa – the fuses are already lit. They are likely to cause explosions which will blow not only the cellars but the whole house sky high.[52]

It was powerful imagery that captured the risks facing the African continent and the international community. It went to the core of the decolonization process and the global struggles for power and control affecting Africa as it vividly described the problem of freedom, where political power was the prerogative of an unrepresentative and oppressive minority. Hugh Foot evoked a scenario of race war that would affect the development of the whole continent for years to come. Foot also highlighted that the outcomes of decolonization and independence were not predetermined. They were shaped by a variety of political processes at different levels.[53] This makes it an imperative to understand with greater detail and nuance how human rights and the global transformations of this era evolved.

Many of the interventions by the African countries in the 1960–1961 debates on ending colonialism appear restrained in comparison with the risks posed by the real-life scenarios being played out on the African continent. Their emphasis on the rule of law and human rights contained self-interest, but the belief in international institutions and international law was a moderate strategy to achieve their goals. The focus on an orderly transition was exemplified by the Nigerian proposal of making December 1, 1970, a deadline for ending colonialism. This was a modest compromise compared with the Soviet proposal of bringing an end to colonialism by 1962 – a one-year deadline in a world with a large number of colonial territories remaining. Nigeria made the proposal to counter the Soviet propaganda attempt. It would have enabled a planned transition

---

[52] Foot (1964), *A Start in Freedom*, p. 228.
[53] Frederick Cooper (2002), *Africa Since 1940. The Past of the Present*. Cambridge, p. 66, 71.

from colonialism to independence contrary to the Soviet proposal. It was not a radical call for self-determination.

Hugh Foot also took a critical position on the Western approach to the problems of freedom brought before the United Nations:

> We show no indignation when we see political slavery or economic exploitation or social injustice. When subject people talk about freedom we call them "emotional." When they urge some positive policy of liberation we call them "reckless." When resolutions are passed in the United Nations with the overwhelming support of the world we call them "utterly lacking in responsibility." In a world full of explosive danger we seem to have no higher ideal than the maintenance of the status quo.[54]

There can be little doubt that the Ghanaian Ambassador Alex Quaison-Sackey would endorse this description. The *Declaration on Granting Independence and Ending Colonialism* was always conceived as a transformative document against the status quo. The Ghanaian Ambassador, also active in the 1960–1961 debates, emphasized the Afro-Asian authorship of the document and believed that the Declaration shared the same prominence as the UN Charter and the Universal Declaration of Human Rights. Quaison-Sackey explained that "If indeed Africa was a forgotten continent at the time of the promulgation of the Charter of the United Nations in 1946, the Declaration calling for an immediate end to colonial rule in all territories that are not independent has redressed the balance."[55]

Like Nigeria's, the Ghanaian approach at the UN General Assembly was one of moderation in the negotiations. Both tried to play a constructive role in diffusing tensions between the Netherlands and Indonesia over the future status of the island of West Irian. This controversy reflected a tense relationship since Indonesia's bloody path to independence in the 1940s. In the debate, the Netherlands offered UN involvement and self-determination to the people of West Irian, while Indonesia demanded sovereign control of the island and threatened war. A number of countries from the Global South supported a process that allowed self-determination for the people of West Irian in deciding the territory's future status. These countries supported the colonial power's proposal

---

[54] Ibid., pp. 231–232.
[55] Mr. Quaison-Sackey (Ghana), UN General Assembly, 16th session, 1057th meeting, November 17, 1961, p. 692. It was a viewpoint echoed by other delegates, for example, Guinea, who saw the 1960 Declaration as "a just atonement for the serious omissions of San Francisco," see Mr. Maka (Guinea), UN General Assembly, 16th session, 1058th meeting, November 20, 1961, p. 710.

rather than showing allegiance to a nonaligned partner that had even been the host of the Bandung Conference. Alliances were not always clear-cut.

The human rights language was also not just limited to race but emphasized "race, creed or colour."[56] It thereby gave emphasis to religion as a human rights concern and positioned the topic of human rights with a greater sense of nuance and critical edge in relation to the Cold War superpowers – a point that is too often overlooked in the human rights literature. In his 1963 book, *Africa Unbound: Reflections of an African Statesman*, Quaison-Sackey elaborated on this point. He believed that the Cold War divisions might be "Africa's opportunity to serve." The human rights diplomacy of a country like Ghana was presented in a self-image of neutrality, nonalignment and a self-proclaimed objective idealism:

> as long as the Soviet Union and the United States assume antipodal positions on world problems and attempt to entice into their orbit any number of other countries, so long will there be a need for a group of countries to remain outside the two camps – a group of countries that will approach international issues as objectively as possible and speak out for justice, morality and human rights.[57]

Just like Hugh Foot, the Ghanaian Ambassador found himself arguing with the British Foreign Minister Alec Douglas-Home. In December 1961, the British Foreign Minister had asserted that the "United Nations was in danger of collapse because it was changing its purpose from an organization committed to keeping the peace to one concerned with liquidating colonialism."[58] To the contrary, Quaison-Sackey believed that ending colonialism would contribute greatly to the maintenance of peace in

---

[56] See Mr. Quaison-Sackey (Ghana), UN General Assembly, 16th session, 1057th meeting, November 17, 1961, p. 687; see also Mr. Dosumu-Johnson (Liberia), UN General Assembly, 16th session, 1054th meeting, November 14, 1961, p. 639.

[57] Alex Quaison-Sackey (1963), *Africa Unbound. Reflections of an African Statesman.* New York, p. 118. It is important to understand that Ghana's UN diplomacy was conducted from New York by a skilled and independently minded small group of diplomats who were not necessarily relying on instructions from Accra or some of Kwame Nkrumah's ill-conceived ideas. This gave them freedom to maneuver on a range of international issues and define a policy position on the merits of diplomatic dealings taking place in New York. One insightful study argues that Ghana's UN delegation "became a virtually independent subsystem of Ghana's foreign policy," and from the late 1950s, "set a high standard for other newly independent states to follow," W. Scott Thompson (1969), *Ghana's Foreign Policy 1957–1966: Diplomacy, Ideology, and the New State.* Princeton, NJ, pp. 52–53.

[58] Alex Quaison-Sackey (1963), *Africa Unbound*, p. 165.

the world. The two positions expressed different worldviews and strategic priorities and, according to the Ghanaian Ambassador, differences between tradition and a new world in the making – between Europe and the Afro-Asian countries. The established nation-states could cling to their beliefs but it was unfair, Quaison-Sackey stated, to conclude that "any departure from what they have come to accept and cherish in faith is necessarily suspect or will lead to the end of the world."[59] He was echoing Hugh Foot's critique of the British emphasis on the status quo.

Quaison-Sackey, who in 1964 became the first African President of the UN General Assembly, ended his argument by laying down a gauntlet that would be echoed in human rights diplomacy in the next five years. It was a testimony to the pivotal role played by the African and Asian countries in the breakthrough for international human rights law during this era and proved to be prophetic:

Universal standards there must be, and the very existence of the United Nations is a testimony to that conviction; but those universal standards must be evolved by all nations, and they can be evolved only by the agreement arrived at in the conflict of debate, in the acceptance of new ideas and in the willingness to grant others the rights one expects for himself.[60]

In this process, Ghana and the Philippines together would secure the foundations for the international human rights system we know today. Hugh Foot would return as British UN Ambassador in 1964 when the Labour government of Harold Wilson came to power. In this capacity, he would become a valuable supporter – a "foot in the door" of the great powers so to speak – when one of the colonies in which he had served as Governor set about transforming the whole approach to human rights by the international community only two months after its independence.

The 1961 debate on ending colonialism finished on an uncertain note. Nigeria and Liberia prepared and widely consulted on a moderate resolution that supported decolonization, most notably by establishing a Special Committee with seventeen members that would become a new United Nations forum for monitoring the implementation of the Declaration. There was no deadline set for ending colonialism and no position on how Indonesia and the Netherlands should resolve their issues over West Irian.

---

59 Ibid., p. 165.
60 Ibid., p. 166.

There were worrying signs with violent conflicts and protracted political crisis visible on the international horizon. There was, however, a development at the 1961 General Assembly session that pointed toward new "universal standards." The direct cause was a planned agenda item on "Manifestations of Racial Prejudice and National and Religious Intolerance" that the 1961 General Assembly ended up ignoring. At the last moment, Ghana, Guinea and Ethiopia pushed for a resolution that saved this item by placing it on the agenda for the 1962 General Assembly.[61] It was from this agenda item that the whole UN human rights project would be put on track after many years in the doldrums. From there, it would reach a whole new level of significance in international law, change international norms and help shape a new moral imagination with global outreach. The 1960s would prove to be a transformative decade for human rights.

---

[61] See Resolution 1684, UN General Assembly, 16th session, 1081st meeting, December 18, 1961.

3

From Jamaica with law

The rekindling of international human rights, 1962–1967

"How can the history of this West Indian futility be written? What tone shall the historian adopt? . . . The history of the islands can never be satisfactorily told. Brutality is not the only difficulty. History is built around achievement and creation and nothing was created in the West Indies."

V. S. Naipaul (1962), *The Middle Passage. The Caribbean Revisited*[1]

On August 7, 1962, a former Texan school teacher and a young Jamaican trade union leader spoke in Innswood – a center for sugarcane farming in Jamaica – in front of a crowd of 4,000 sugarcane workers and their families. The Texan's speech touched on the bonds of sympathy that existed between Jamaica and the United States and on the race issue by emphasizing "the equality of man regardless of race or color and the need to maintain individual freedom against all encroachments." According to one report, the speech "evoked a wild, enthusiastic response, completely overshadowing the skillful talks of the Jamaican . . . trade union leader Hugh Shearer."

It was no doubt a memorable occasion. Not only because it was part of Jamaica's Independence celebrations, but also because the Texan schoolteacher would, fifteen months later, become the 36th President of the United States when John F. Kennedy was assassinated in Dallas on November 22, 1963.[2] As President, Johnson would remain true to his

---

[1] V. S. Naipaul (1962), *The Middle Passage. The Caribbean Revisited*. London, p. 20.

[2] The above quotes are from: "Report on Vice President Johnson's Visit to Jamaica for Independence Celebrations (August 5–8, 1962)," JFK Library (Boston, MA), NSF Box 123. For the manuscript of Lyndon B. Johnson's (LBJ) Innswood speech, see "Statement by Vice President Lyndon B. Johnson to Sugar Cane Workers, Innswood, Jamaica, August 7, 1962," LBJ Library (Austin, TX), Box 68, Statements of LBJ, Vice President,

call for racial equality as he battled for and secured the collapse of the Jim Crow legal system in the American South through the Civil Rights Act (1964) and the Voting Rights Act (1965), which were milestones in a remarkable legislative record.

Vice President Lyndon B. Johnson had traveled to Jamaica for a three-day official visit as the personal representative of President Kennedy to join the Independence celebrations. During his visit, Johnson traveled extensively around the island, visiting slum dwellers in Kingston where new housing was under construction, speaking at two Peace Corps youth camps and for the sugarcane workers in between meetings with Prime Minister Alexander Bustamente and leading government ministers. The formal ceremony took place in Kingston and Johnson witnessed the raising of the Jamaican flag at the moment of independence, which took place at midnight between August 5 and August 6, 1962.

As part of his outreach, Johnson also traveled to Montego Bay, the island's second largest city, where he spoke to an estimated crowd of 6,000 people. He brought a message of cooperation within the hemisphere to secure freedom and independence – clearly alluding to Cuba only ninety miles away from Jamaica. He also challenged Jamaica to think beyond its domestic concerns and to consider the role the country should "play on the world stage, in the Caribbean region, in the Organization of American States, in the Western Hemisphere and through the United Nations in the world at large."[3] Little did Lyndon B. Johnson know how seriously and to what effect the Jamaican Government would address this challenge.[4]

Far from being overshadowed, Hugh Shearer – the Jamaican trade union leader and newly appointed Cabinet Minister speaking with

July 7–August 20, 1962. Johnson had trained as a teacher and worked as such – an experience he would refer to in his Voting Rights Address on March 15, 1965 to a Joint Session of Congress.

[3] "Report on Vice President Johnson's Visit to Jamaica for Independence Celebrations (August 5–8, 1962)," JFK Library (Boston, MA), NSF Box 123. The transcript of Lyndon B. Johnson's Montego Bay speech is available but he appears to have improvised extensively from the prepared text, "Remarks by Vice President at Charles Square, Montego Bay, Jamaica, August 8, 1962," LBJ Library (Austin, TX), Box 68, Statements of Lyndon B. Johnson, Vice President, July 7–August 20, 1962.

[4] In an otherwise interesting article that significantly revises and elevates the importance of Lyndon B. Johnson's (LBJ's) contribution as a Vice-President to the foreign policy agenda of the Kennedy administration by focusing on LBJ's foreign travels, Mitchell Lerner dismisses LBJ's trip to Jamaica as a "mundane expedition" that "saw Johnson attend a flag-raising ceremony, lunch with Princess Margaret, and deliver a collection of small gifts that included a signed first edition of *Profiles in Courage* to the new government." There clearly was something much more significant at stake as this chapter will show. See Mitchell Lerner (2010), "A Big Tree of Peace and Justice: The Vice-Presidential Travels of Lyndon Johnson," *Diplomatic History*, vol. 34, no. 2, p. 359.

Johnson at Innswood – would go on to deliver his country's first speech to the UN General Assembly two months later. The speech would initiate a transformation of international human rights work. Jamaica became the main broker of progress in UN human rights diplomacy from 1962 to 1968 – a period that witnessed its breakthrough as human rights were transformed into international law with binding obligations on states.

It was through a remarkable vision for a different international order and through skilful diplomatic efforts that Jamaica came to play this prominent role. The country has had a profound and long-lasting effect on international human rights work. It is a legacy worth understanding in greater detail. The Jamaica story is of interest for several reasons, not the least being that they obtained their independence at the same time decolonization was sweeping across Africa and Asia, changing the composition of the United Nations dramatically.

It is of little surprise that a small state favored a system of states based on international rules and norms. What is striking is the scope and persistence of Jamaica's human rights diplomacy in the 1960s. They gave new strategic direction to the faltering UN human rights diplomacy. Through this process, they had managed by the end of the decade to tie together the nascent or disparate human rights efforts of various international actors into a more coherent whole. Jamaica helped shape international NGO work on human rights, energized the regional human rights work under the Council of Europe, provided a political platform that Soviet dissidents from 1968 would explicitly rely on and brokered political change and significant innovation in international law in several other ways. Human rights were never the same after this.

Jamaica's international human rights diplomacy was nurtured by the country's often conflicted historical past and the protracted constitutional moment that saw Jamaica move from colonial rule via adult suffrage and self-government into independence during the period between 1938 and 1962. It was also based on a refined reading of international current affairs at the moment of independence. Jamaica entered multilateral diplomacy at the United Nations in the shadow of the 1962 Cuban Missile Crisis and in the midst of the Cold War political order that had effectively locked down the human rights project since the late 1940s. A novel approach was required.

The protracted constitutional moment – Jamaica, 1938–1962

In 1962, a Jamaica-based lawyer wrote about a new constitutional trend happening in the territories that were being transformed from colonial status to independent statehood. Entitled "Fundamental Rights – the Need for a New Jurisprudence," the author S. S. Ramphal explained: "Constitutions often contain within themselves the seeds of growth and change, and of no other provisions of the new Constitutions is this more likely than those which seek to guarantee respect for fundamental human rights."[5]

The move toward independence removed external political restraints and the constitution-making process introduced new concepts, guarantees and constitutional forms relating to human rights that went well beyond the British constitutional tradition and common law. The exact nature of the guarantees would be determined by "the degree to which they enjoy the status of a superior law against which normal legislative authority cannot prevail." The article argued that the political parties were willingly imposing legal restraints on the executive and legislative powers by including these guarantees in the new independence constitutions, ensuring various safeguards against discrimination and developing a system where "judicial authority is in each case paramount."

Ramphal outlined the ramifications of this rise of human rights. It might have been a "parting gift" during decolonization but it was a gift chosen by the "fledging state itself."[6] He wrote, "The need for a new jurisprudence in this border country between law and policy is real and inescapable. A new and exciting field of judicial authority is opening up, but for the most part the country is rugged and the way is uncharted."[7] Decolonization was bringing constitutional and political innovations on a wider international scale.

Jamaica was a construction of empire. The legacies of slavery and colonialism rested heavily on the economic and social conditions in the 1930s even if emancipation of the slaves had occurred a century before. The legacy of colonialism and the plantation economy meant that poverty was still widespread. Jamaican society was sharply divided on two closely

---

[5] S. S. Ramphal (1962), "Fundamental Rights – The Need for a New Jurisprudence," *Caribbean Quarterly*, vol. 8, no. 3, p. 140. Ramphal later became Attorney General and Foreign Minister for British Guyana and Secretary-General of the Commonwealth from 1975 to 1990. As a law student in London during the 1950s Ramphal became greatly inspired by Norman Manley's vision for the West Indies. He first encountered this vision during a talk given by Manley at the London School of Economics. For more on Ramphal's background and international career, see "Transcript of Interview of Shridath Ramphal by Richard Jolly, London, 14–15 January 2002," UN International History Project (available at UN Library in Geneva).

[6] Ramphal (1962), "Fundamental Rights – The Need for a New Jurisprudence," p. 142.

[7] Ibid., p. 140.

related issues – race and class.[8] About 90 percent of the population was of African descent.

The political transformations that led to independence played a significant role in shaping Jamaica's vision of international relations. Jamaica went through a protracted constitutional moment as the country moved through a long process of political reform starting after widespread labor riots in 1938 and culminating with independence in August 1962. The labor riots in 1938, where fourteen people were killed and many more injured from gunshot wounds, was in many ways the birth moment of modern Jamaica. It led directly to the creation of two political parties, which helped spark a process of political reform.

The two parties – the Jamaica Labour Party and the People's National Party (PNP) – became the dominant parties in Jamaican politics. Both were affiliated with trade union movements that were part of their political base.[9] The political rivalry between the respective founders Alexander Bustamente and Norman Manley, who both remained as party leaders until the late 1960s, defined the direction the country took in the immediate aftermath of the 1938 riots. Half cousins and of mixed race, they were rivals for the role of "father of the nation."

The PNP party program from 1940 had three basic goals: self-government, political democracy based on universal suffrage and economic and social reforms.[10] PNP was a socialist party affiliated with the Labour Party in Britain. The Jamaica Labour Party (JLP) operated much more on the basis of Bustamente's charisma and political improvisation with a program that had a more narrow focus on trade union objectives than the PNP program. Bustamente's party had a strong following among the working masses and the poorest part of the population.[11]

The outbreak of the Second World War changed the global strategic importance of the Caribbean from which local politics could benefit. In November 1944, universal adult suffrage was introduced through

---

[8] Anita Waters (1999), "Half the Story: The Uses of History in Jamaican Political Discourse," *Caribbean Quarterly*, vol. 45, no. 1, p. 62. See also Colin A. Palmer (2014), *Freedom's Children. The 1938 Labor Rebellion and the Birth of Modern Jamaica*. Chapel Hill, NC.

[9] A useful account of the turbulent trade union politics in the years that followed is provided in: Gerald Horne (2007), *Cold War in Hot Zone. The United States Confronts Labor and Independence Struggles in the British West Indies*. Philadelphia, PA.

[10] Wendell Bell (1964), *Jamaican Leaders. Political Attitudes in a New Nation*. Berkeley, CA, p. 18.

[11] Jason C. Parker (2008), *Brother's Keeper: The United States, Race, and Empire in the British Caribbean, 1937–1962*, Oxford, p. 29.

a new constitution that secured political democracy with limited self-government under continued British rule. An election was called, which Bustamente and the JLP won. Importantly, this election introduced formally a two-party system where government and opposition roles would move back and forth between the two parties. During the years that followed – and especially in the 1950s – wider self-government was introduced through several constitutional changes.

In 1955 Norman Manley and the PNP came to power under the system of self-government. The party was to the left of the JLP with a socialist program, but both parties were clearly Western oriented in their political outlook. They were also very aware of global race issues. In early July 1959, the Manley government announced that Jamaica would introduce a policy of trade sanctions toward South Africa because of its apartheid system.[12] It was an independently minded and assertive position, and a strong signal inside the Commonwealth, that outraged the South Africans. It was also a creative way of applying the constitutional political changes that had developed over the past two decades. The South Africans demanded that the United Kingdom as the colonial power should step in and block the initiative.[13] The South Africans were no doubt worried about the trend this could establish first in the British Caribbean and thereafter beyond this region. The Jamaican sanctions policy was at this point an unseen move and a possible new precedent – only comparable with India's actions against South Africa at the United Nations in 1946.

The sanctions policy had been debated within the governing PNP since 1957. The PNP had also consulted the British on this matter, who had requested the Jamaican government not to pursue it further.[14] After further consideration, this was not acceptable to the Jamaicans, who subsequently went ahead. The question was what type of policy the introduction of trade sanctions against South Africa actually was. The South Africans believed it was a matter of foreign policy and therefore the

---

[12] "Jamaica Bans S. African Goods," *The Jamaica Gleaner*, July 2, 1959, p. 1 (front page), Newspaper Collection, National Library of Jamaica, Kingston.

[13] "The Ban: S. Africa Complains," *The Jamaica Gleaner*, July 3, 1959, p. 1 (front page); "Jamaican Cabinet Was Put Under Pressure," *The Jamaica Gleaner*, July 5, 1959, p. 1 (front page).

[14] "SA Ban Decided on Last Year," *The Jamaica Gleaner*, July 7, 1959, pp. 1, 11. This whole process pre-dates the establishment of an international boycott movement which took form in 1959 and 1960 in response to developments inside South Africa, see Christabel Gurney (2000), "'A Great Cause': The Origins of the Anti-Apartheid Movement, June 1959-March 1960," *Journal of Southern African Studies*, vol. 26, no. 1, pp. 123–144.

prerogative of the colonial power. The Jamaicans argued that it was a matter of trade policy, and since the responsibility for this had been devolved to Jamaica through the agreements on self-government, it was their own decision to make. It was a refined use of legal and constitutional provisions to pursue a policy objective of great importance to the Jamaican government. It was both a practical and a visionary view of using law that the Jamaicans would take with them to United Nations three years later. As Manley explained the political rationale behind Jamaica's introduction of sanctions:

The ban on trade with South Africa is a logical and proper act done in respect of a country which denies to its own people all the basic human rights and denies to coloured people all over the world every right of human rights intercourse ... Since we cannot send a coloured athlete to South Africa, nor even a cricket team, with any pretence of dignity, why should we send our goods?[15]

From 1954 Manley had been connected with the International League for the Rights of Man. He was at the same time a national political leader and linked to the leading international human rights NGO of the era.[16] Norman Manley had a more structured approach to government and to planning than Bustamente, and he introduced a policy of private sector–led growth in close collaboration with the Governor of Jamaica, Hugh Foot, to secure economic and social development in Jamaica.[17] This secured good growth rates in the late 1950s, and as the prospect of independence grew nearer, there was some basis for optimism about the future.

At the time of independence, Jamaica had a well-functioning two-party system, a relatively well-functioning system of government and civil service in which Jamaican-born persons played an increasingly important role. It was a vastly different situation to many of the other colonial territories achieving independence during these years. The country also had a well-established legal tradition and system – at least partly inherited

---

[15] "SA Ban decided on last year," *The Daily Gleaner* (Jamaica), July 7, 1959, pp. 1 and 11.
[16] See Norman Manley Papers, National Archives of Jamaica (Spanish Town), "Letter from Roger Baldwin (The League for the Rights of Man) to Norman Manley," March 17, 1954, Folder A/4/60/2B/16. See also "Letter from Norman Manley to Roger Baldwin, September 24, 1954," Box 9: Internal Correspondence and Papers/Advisory Committee and Board of Directors, Papers of the International League for the Rights of Man, New York Public Library.
[17] See, for example, Norman Manley Papers, National Archives of Jamaica (Spanish Town), "Letter From Hugh Foot to Norman Manley, August 24, 1953," Folder 4/60/2B/16.

from the British – and had also gained experience in international politics and in dealing with national, regional and global interests between the British and the Americans.

In terms of human rights, the Jamaicans were well positioned to engage on the broad spectrum of civil, political, economic or social rights or specifically on issues related to race and religion. The combination of being a creation of empire and having experienced a relatively well-prepared and progressive path to independence may have put Jamaica in a unique place to be a human rights broker on the international scene.[18]

This is supported by interesting data about the values and attitudes held by leaders in Jamaica in the late 1950s and 1960s. During this period American sociologist Wendell Bell made detailed surveys and interviewed Jamaican politicians, leading civil servants and other elite groups. In his study Bell asked, "What should Jamaica's global alignments be?" Bell also asked which of the two Cold War superpowers "has been morally right more often in recent years." Out of 188 respondents, 83 percent said the United States, 1 percent answered the Soviet Union and 16 percent about the same. The reasons given were based on commitment to the principles of democracy and fear and suspicion of Soviet methods and motives.[19] It was a clear preference in favor of the United States and the Western camp, but there were qualifications in some responses that criticized U.S. racial policies and McCarthyism. Cases of discrimination and racial attacks in the United States were widely reported in the Jamaican media.

Bell also surveyed views on the effectiveness of the superpowers in the Cold War competition. He asked which of the two superpowers was "more effective in winning over to its point of view the people living in the so-called underdeveloped countries of the world?" Here, 56 percent believed the Soviet Union was most effective, 24 percent believed that the United States was more effective and 20 percent about the same.[20]

---

[18] I have left out the domestic developments in Jamaica after independence where frustrations soon grew over poverty and lack of economic opportunity. International trade, aid, Jamaica's Western allegiance and its stance over Cuba did not provide the dividends for economic development that had been hoped for when independence was achieved. The economic growth and social development did not continue in the 1960s and the 1970s and political violence grew. In the 1980 election, 750 people were killed in election-related violence. See Waters (1999), "Half the Story," p. 71. See also the chapter on Jamaica in Vijay Prashad (2007), *The Darker Nations. A People's History of the Third World*. New York, pp. 224–244. Jamaica's own human rights record has also been frequently criticized over the last decades. This context is important not to lose sight of but is not part of this study.

[19] Bell (1964), *Jamaican Leaders*, p. 152.

[20] Ibid., p. 161.

Competition between the superpowers was a central part of shaping the dynamics of decolonization.

The Jamaican respondents were concerned with achieving both political freedom and economic advancement at the same time. They focused on the Soviet's ability to capitalize on people's despair in underdeveloped countries and the forceful Soviet propaganda on poverty-stricken peoples. The responses did not reflect an endorsement of the Soviet Union. There were few illusions among the respondents that the Soviet agendas represented "false promises of utopia."[21] It was therefore not surprising that Hugh Shearer in February 1963 announced that the official government policy was opposed to Communism and firmly aligned with the West. This alignment had become apparent during the Cuban Missile Crisis only a few months earlier.

Wendell Bell concluded by attempting some predictions on "Jamaica's precarious future." He saw both great potential and problems on the horizon. The latter focused on disillusionment with the pace of social reform and with cynicism about political democracy itself. Bell, however, emphasized the great potential and saw in Jamaica's political attitudes and their approach in the postcolonial world a source of Western renewal. Bell believed that Jamaica may actually take:

> the lead among the new nations in seeking the welfare of humanity as a whole . . . It is possible that Jamaica can become a symbol to the world, to the developed and underdeveloped, to the committed and uncommitted nations alike . . . Jamaica could prove to the world . . . that a nation can be concerned not just with its own welfare, but with the welfare of all people everywhere; and that a nation can put humanity even above its own newly won national sovereignty. In sum, Jamaica could prove that some key ideas underlying Western thought still have vigor and meaning, that a belief in progress, reason, and the perfectibility of man carries with it a force that can help make the vision of a 'better world' come true.[22]

It was a hugely idealistic but thought-provoking observation and a huge task to perform for a small island state with a population of less than 2 million. Nevertheless, this is what Jamaica set out to achieve.

Setting a new agenda, 1962–1964

Jamaica had only been a member of the United Nations for three weeks when it delivered its first speech to the General Assembly on October 8, 1962. Hugh Shearer started by extending his country's greetings to

---

[21] Ibid., p. 163.
[22] Ibid., pp. 172–173.

another newly independent country and UN member state, Algeria, and acknowledged their long struggle to secure freedom. The simultaneous independence and UN membership of Algeria and Jamaica in 1962 captures well the political extremes of the decolonization era. Jamaica's and Algeria's stories were a tale of two colonies that almost resembled the best and the worst of times in the decolonization process. Their path to independence had followed parallel timelines but brutally dissimilar trends.

Algeria, like Jamaica, had also experienced labor riots and calls for political reform in the late 1930s that had mobilized a new political movement which would have a strong influence on what unfolded. While Jamaica achieved universal suffrage in 1944 in the context of the Second World War, a massacre of several thousand people took place in May 1945 in the Algerian town of Setif as a response by French officials to protests against colonial rule during celebrations marking the end of the World War. The massacre escalated an increasingly brutal struggle over political control in Algeria. In the 1950s, while Jamaica embarked on further constitutional reform and self-government combined with economic growth, Algeria succumbed to a long bloody war marked by atrocities, leaving several hundred thousand people dead. Jamaica's and Algeria's arrival into the world of multilateral diplomacy was very different and these experiences shaped the trajectories of their diplomatic efforts.[23]

The Jamaican government believed that it was tantamount for the UN to intensify its efforts on human rights. The goal was to find peaceful solutions to the problems facing the international community. In his 1962 speech to the General Assembly, Hugh Shearer projected an idealistic image of Jamaica as an example to the rest of the world on both race and religion. As an immediate step, Jamaica called for the creation of an international human rights year with a worldwide collaborative effort to revitalize interest and "seek co-operative methods of curing the denial of human rights whenever and wherever such a condition persists."[24] Jamaica presented their proposal with a focus on the

---

[23] See, for example, Jeffrey James Byrne (2009), "Our Own Special Brand of Socialism: Algeria and the Contest of Modernities in the 1960s," *Diplomatic History*, vol. 33, no. 3, pp. 427–447; Nils Gilman (2015), "The NIEO: A Reintroduction," *Humanity*, vol. 6, no. 1, p. 6.

[24] Ibid., p. 378. This proposal immediately caught the interest of the International League for the Rights of Man. See letter from Roger Baldwin to Mr. J. M. Lloyd (Jamaica's representative to the Third Committee in 1962), October 23, 1962, and letter from J. M. Lloyd, Ministry of External Affairs, Jamaica, to Roger Baldwin, November 5,

relationship between human rights and development. This was the angle that the leading and well-informed national newspaper *The Jamaica Gleaner* took in their coverage of Shearer's speech. The international collaboration for advancing human rights was linked to the question of world trade and giving the "under-developed countries... a fair chance of achieving economic independence."[25] It entailed a statement of strong support for international institutions and multilateral diplomacy.

At the 1963 General Assembly session, Jamaica was determined to pursue the idea of a human rights year. In his 1963 speech to the General Assembly, Hugh Shearer took the opportunity to advocate his government's proposal. The Cuban Missile Crisis had loomed large over Jamaica's entry as an independent nation into international affairs and over the 17th General Assembly in 1962, which had taken place in the shadow of the crisis. Shearer addressed the wider strategic implications of this crisis and the nuclear threat on the values of the international state system:

Often in the history of nations and civilizations a whole generation lives out its little life by the rules and standards of a bygone age, oblivious of the fact that the current of history and the march of ideas have passed it by. Let it not be said that in this generation one nation continued to dispute with the other about areas of national sovereignty, about means of protecting national security, ignorant of the fact that the hydrogen bomb has eliminated the resort to force as a means of settling international disagreements.[26]

An epochal shift had occurred with the threat of the nuclear arms race. From the perspective of the Jamaican government, the current of history pointed toward overcoming national sovereignty and the march of ideas involved human rights as ideals and as legally binding agreements between states. Human rights started to look like a possible means to advance both détente and social justice.

The designation of 1968 as "International Human Rights Year" was a simple idea and not necessarily very noteworthy. Jamaica had two things in mind. The first was that the International Human Rights Year should be an event promoting human rights. The second was that 1968 should be a target for progress in the field of human rights guiding UN efforts

---

1962, Box 22: General Correspondence, Jamaica, Papers of the International League for the Rights of Man, New York Public Library.
[25] "Editorial: Human Rights," *The Jamaica Gleaner*, October 10, 1962, p. 10, Newspaper Collection, National Library of Jamaica, Kingston.
[26] Mr. Hugh Shearer (Jamaica), UN General Assembly, 18th session, 1228th meeting, October 4, 1963, p. 1.

over the next five years.[27] This proposal paved the way for a new and more structured approach. A five-year preparation period could provide a comprehensive program of work and a much more strategic elaboration of human rights. The frequent ceremonial and denialist rhetoric of many of the UN human rights debates could be challenged in new ways if a target, with relative broad appeal, was looming in the near distance.

Jamaica's speech to the 1963 General Assembly added a new concrete proposal to the idea of an International Human Rights Year, proposing that an international conference on human rights should be organized in 1968 for all member states to attend. It would be the first world conference on human rights. Recognizing the momentum behind the race issue, and speaking only five weeks after the march on Washington where Martin Luther King Jr. had expressed his dream of racial reconciliation, Hugh Shearer provided concrete examples of what the international conference should address:

[The] delegations to that conference would report on the advances made in their own countries in eliminating particular denials of human rights in whatever form and by whatever name – apartheid, segregation, Jim Crow, or colour prejudice.[28]

It was the responsibility of the Jamaican Ambassador to the United Nations, Egerton Richardson, to ensure backing for their resolution. If passed, it would secure the formal endorsement of 1968 as international human rights year. By December 1963, with the item before the Third Committee, Ambassador Richardson had secured endorsement for the resolution from eighteen cosponsoring countries.[29]

No opposition was voiced by any member state. The Soviet Union was among the supporters who, as they stated, placed the Universal Declaration as an instrument of highest importance alongside the 1960 *Declaration on the Granting of Independence to Colonial Countries and Peoples*

---

[27] Ibid., p. 3.
[28] Ibid., p. 3. Other issues proposed were slavery, condition of refugees and right of asylum. The Explanatory Memorandum also mentioned freedom of information. See A/5493/Add.1: Jamaica: Request for the Inclusion of an Additional Item in the Agenda of the Eighteenth Session – "Designation of 1968 as International Year for Human Rights," Explanatory Memorandum, September 18, 1963.
[29] The countries cosponsoring with Jamaica were Afghanistan, Argentina, Brazil, Costa Rica, El Salvador, Ecuador, Ghana, Guatemala, India, Iraq, Italy, Ivory Coast, Liberia, Nigeria, Saudi Arabia, Trinidad and Tobago, Uganda and Uruguay. This covered seven Latin American countries, five African countries, two Arab countries, two Caribbean countries, two Asian countries and one European country. A/5660, UN General Assembly 18th Session, Report of the Third Committee, December 11, 1963, p. 1.

and the *UN Declaration on the Elimination of All Forms of Racial Discrimination* approved only two weeks earlier on November 20, 1963.[30] The United Kingdom noted with surprise that the Soviet Union, which had not voted in favor of the Universal Declaration in 1948, was now showing such concern about human rights progress by 1968.[31]

The Commission on Human Rights debated this in February–March 1964 and decided that a separate Committee for the International Human Rights Year should be established. The Commission endorsed the idea of an international conference on human rights in 1968 and stated that the new Committee should give special attention to this issue. The International Conference was now elevated to the major event of 1968 with a three-fold purpose: (1) to review progress, (2) to evaluate the effectiveness of the UN human rights methods and (3) to formulate a program of further measures to be pursued after the 1968 human rights year.[32] The third point was a new development that gave longevity beyond the target year.

The proposal was on track and Jamaica was being recognized as a leader in the human rights field. This development would continue as the program of work was elaborated. Jamaica was fast-tracked into membership of the Commission on Human Rights. Egerton Richardson was appointed Chairman of the new Committee in June 1964, and in this capacity, the Jamaican Ambassador immediately took the lead in defining the whole process.[33] His role would come to be one balancing the vision behind the Jamaican proposal, the mandate provided for the work

---

[30] Mr. Ostrovsky (the USSR), UN General Assembly, Third Committee, 1283rd Meeting, December 6, 1963, p. 383. Soviet leader Nikita Khrushchev offered in April 1963 a possible explanation for the Soviet engagement on human rights. After the Cuban Missile Crisis was resolved, there were hopes for a change in international relations. As Khrushchev explained to an Italian journalist, "Genuine détente . . . can be created by the joint efforts of all peoples . . . Peoples should get to know each other better . . . [but] we communists have never agreed, and never will agree, to the idea of peaceful coexistence in ideologies. In this there can be no compromise." From this perspective, human rights can maybe be regarded as a continuation of the Cold War by other means. Quote from Melvyn Leffler (2007), *For the Soul of Mankind. The United States, The Soviet Union and the Cold War.* New York, p. 169.

[31] Mr. Attlee (UK), UN General Assembly, Third Committee, 1283rd Meeting, December 6, 1963, p. 384. See also report from the Netherlands representative highlighting the Jamaican leadership behind the proposal, Ministerie van Buitenlandse Zaken (1964), *Verslag over de Achttiende Algemene Vergadering van de Verenigde Naties, New York, September 17–December 17, 1963*, 77 edn. The Hague.

[32] Commission on Human Rights, Report on the 20th Session, February 17–March 18, 1964, ECOSOC, 37th Session, E/3873.

[33] See ST/SG/AC.5/3: Programme of Measures and Activities, June 25, 1964.

and the different agendas of the member states involved in the evolution of the human rights system. While progress in getting to this point had been rapid, now Cold War agendas came knocking more forcefully at the door. Jamaica, in its role as broker for the future of the UN human rights program, would find itself at the center of these diplomatic struggles. The Jamaican UN Ambassador used his unique set of skills to meet the challenges ahead.

The Jamaican broker, 1962–1965

At the end of June 1962, a Jamaican delegation visited Washington as part of the preparations for independence a few weeks later. Led by Prime Minister Bustamente, Egerton Richardson was part of the delegation, which also included several government ministers. Richardson had been promoted to the position of Financial Secretary in 1956 during Norman Manley's term in office. He was an example of how Jamaicans of African descent were able to reach the highest levels of government and civil service during the period of self-government leading up to independence. Richardson had worked his way up through the system, achieving positions normally earmarked for white colonial officials. Described as immensely capable with a refined intellect, he helped break the glass ceiling for civil servants of African descent.[34] He was one of the main advisors during the independence negotiations where the Jamaican constitution was prepared. The U.S. Embassy in Kingston clearly respected him, and in providing background on the delegates from Jamaica, they wrote:

Described by some as the most powerful man in the Jamaican Government, Financial Secretary Richardson may emerge as the most impressive member of the delegation. He has a reputation as an excellent negotiator, and a ruthless

---

[34] Richardson received a grant to study at Oxford when he was in his early forties. Here, he received a year-long one-person tutorial with the political economist Thomas Balogh (later Lord Balogh). Balogh had come to England in 1930 from Hungary with John Maynard Keynes as his mentor. In the 1950s, Balogh focused on the economics of poverty – a relevant topic for a Jamaican civil servant – and he and Richardson developed a good relationship. Balogh was controversial in his critique of other economists, but Richardson would have been exposed to the most advanced debates on international economic issues. Richardson brought Balogh to Jamaica around 1960 to work on Jamaica's first economic development plan. Balogh was advisor to several Labour governments and a Minister of Energy in the 1970s.

administrator. Serious-minded, sometimes stern . . . there is wide agreement that he is highly color conscious.[35]

This was a unique set of competences for someone at the center of UN human rights diplomacy in the 1960s. Ambassador Richardson would veer between being a neutral, combative and a continually constructive broker in his efforts to find solutions to the many issues that were to arise while breaking new ground in the human rights field.

Egerton Richardson became UN Ambassador immediately upon independence. He only had a matter of weeks to prepare Jamaica's positions on a whole range of international issues before the General Assembly started. Before arriving in New York, he gave an indication of the approach Jamaica might take during a meeting with the British High Commissioner to Jamaica. Richardson explained that Jamaica was under some pressure from African Americans to play a positive role at the United Nations.[36] The latter had, dissatisfied with a number of African representatives at the UN, expressed the need for a moderate and responsible "black" voice that could hold its own with other states. The statement revealed the at times uneasy relationship between African Americans and diplomats from African countries. Jamaica was being called on to bridge this gap, echoing the appeal Lyndon Johnson made during his visit. The source of this pressure is not mentioned, but it is almost certain that it came from the U.S. civil rights leader Roy Wilkins from the National Association for the Advancement of Colored People (NAACP).[37] This is one reason for the Jamaican human rights initiative that Richardson developed.

---

[35] American Consular-General to U.S. Department of State, Washington, "Biographic Information on Bustamente Visit to Washington and London," Foreign Service Dispatch, June 14, 1962, JFK Library (Boston), National Security File, Box 123 (Jamaica).

[36] British National Archives (Kew), DO 181/33, Letter from British High Commissioner C. N. Diggines to British UN Mission, New York, August 20, 1962.

[37] This conclusion is based on an analysis of the list of attendees for the independence celebrations in early August. Ralph Bunche participated as representative for the UN Secretary-General but he would hardly qualify as "American Negro Opinion." Harry Belafonte was invited but was unable to attend. Adam Clayton Powell, member of the U.S. House of Representatives, did participate but Roy Wilkins stands out as the most likely source. Wilkins was Director of the National Association for the Advancement of Colored People (NAACP) and joined Lyndon Johnson on some of the Vice-President's site visits during their trip to Jamaica. See British National Archives (Kew), FO 371/161994. The former Governor Hugh Foot also attended. On Roy Wilkins and the NAACP, see Yvonne Ryan (2014), *Roy Wilkins: The Quiet Revolutionary and the NAACP*. Lexington, KY.

Another reason was the international position in which Jamaica found itself when becoming a member of the United Nations and determining its own foreign policy in more specific terms. On issues of race, decolonization and apartheid, there was an affinity with Africa. The Jamaicans, however, also felt concerned about how the Afro-Asian Bloc was acting at the United Nations. Richardson was a diplomat who represented Jamaica's moderate outlook and considered each issue on its merit after careful preparatory study. There is also little doubt that Jamaica saw itself as a nation that was politically more developed and sophisticated compared with most of the African nations.

Geographically, Jamaica belonged to the Latin America and Caribbean region and the country did seek membership in the Organization of American States (OAS), but this was not a straightforward process. While they had strong backing from Costa Rica, other countries in the region saw Jamaica as too closely associated with the United Kingdom. There was opposition to Jamaica mainly because of the unsettled status of British Honduras (Belize) – a territory to which Guatemala laid claim. These opposing states, including Guatemala, did not want a British ally in the OAS and rejected Jamaican membership. It made for an uneasy relationship with the group that would have been the natural affiliation.

Jamaica did have amicable relations with its former colonial master. It had a Western outlook and its political institutions and traditions had close ties to Britain. The British High Commissioner in Kingston even suggested that Jamaica could be considered worthy of membership of the North Atlantic Treaty Organization (NATO). The idea did not have much traction in London. Decolonization meant something. From one side, it meant independence; from the other, it meant withdrawal. This was reflected in a British policy paper on Jamaica from 1963 that stated:

It is the fact that in the 1960s the United Kingdom is unable to devote to the Commonwealth as a whole the assistance – financial, economic, military, cultural or technical – which we should be glad to do; and it becomes unrealistic to divert too much of those scarce resources to a territory, no matter how friendly, which strategically is of no importance to this country; which is not embarrassingly poor . . . which is unlikely to have views of any issues of general importance which would seriously affect Ministers in London formulating British policy.[38]

Those closer to the Jamaicans, for example, British UN diplomats, were less condescending in their tone and consistently praised their Jamaican

---

[38] British National Archives (Kew), DO 200/53, "A Policy for Jamaica" – Memo by the Commonwealth Relations Office, November 5, 1963.

counterparts for the excellent quality of their interventions, but the overall message was clear: Jamaica had to manage on its own. In these early stages in 1962 and 1963, it appeared that Jamaica did not naturally fit within the specific groups of alliances. In response, they charted their own way through the world with a political initiative that strongly affirmed the values upon which Jamaica wanted the international system to be based.

The human rights initiative had a broader foundation as Jamaican diplomacy operated within a larger framework that included a strong focus on reforming international trade in the direction of a system that was fairer for the new states and with an emphasis on the United Nations as a peacekeeping organization. When the United Nations in 1964 faced a major political and financial crisis over its peacekeeping mandate, it was Egerton Richardson who mobilized the Commonwealth states into clarifying their contribution to UN peacekeeping in order to tackle this serious problem. The United Kingdom acknowledged Richardson's achievement as "excellent and timely."[39]

Human rights, reforming international trade and peacekeeping were the triad of issues on which Jamaica initially built its multilateral diplomacy. The approach meant a strong investment in the United Nations. Jamaica wanted "to see greater use made of the machinery of negotiation, enquiry, mediation, conciliation, arbitration, judicial or other peaceful means of settling disputes."[40] The human rights initiative was based on a very ambitious vision of civilizing international relations. It was a hopeful vision but not one merely based on naïve idealism. Richardson knew well the severity of the international situation and the deeply concerning economic and political situation that many of the newly independent states were in. The approach he outlined was a survival strategy for the postcolonial world. It was a very particular reading of the state of international affairs and an illustration of the fact that sometimes a situation or political scenario can appear so critical and so dire that realism can only express itself meaningfully through an idealistic and transformative worldview.

These efforts were from 1964 backed by the official Jamaican Foreign Policy. In June 1964, Prime Minister Bustamente issued this policy and

---

[39] British National Archives (Kew), DO 200/182, "United Nations Peacekeeping," Letter from UN Department, British Foreign Office, November 1, 1965.

[40] British National Archives (Kew), DO 200/182, Ministry Paper 40: Activities of the Ministry of External Affairs during the year 1965 with a forecast for 1966–1967.

strategy, which contained a strong commitment to human rights.[41] The 1964 Jamaican Foreign Policy is possibly the first human rights–focused foreign policy strategy developed by any country. It came thirteen years before the much better-known efforts in the late 1970s by the Carter administration to integrate human rights in U.S. foreign policy.

The policy had not been developed based on a lengthy strategy process, although the process had, importantly, involved all heads of Jamaica's overseas missions. It was prepared in response to criticisms from the opposition party in the Jamaican parliament over the lack of an officially declared policy. The two main parties competed in representing a progressive, independent and Western-oriented foreign policy, and despite various statements by the Government on its foreign policy, the opposition led by Norman Manley pushed for more.[42] The policy was launched in the House of Representatives by the government on June 24, 1964 and was a synthesis of what Jamaica had been focusing on since independence.[43] It was a strategy focusing on multilateralism, with a strong commitment to the United Nations and the Commonwealth. It was based on the obvious recognition of Jamaica "as a small nation in a world of power-blocs."[44] It supported "Western hemisphere solidarity," close collaboration with African countries in their efforts against colonialism and apartheid and argued for "a new pattern of world trade" that would allow fuller participation of developing countries in the international trade system. First and foremost, it was a policy dedicated to human rights.

The policy argued for the removal of all forms of discrimination based on race, sex, color and religion and committed Jamaica to speaking out against discrimination wherever it was practiced, which signified a clear internationalist stand on human rights. It called for universal adult suffrage and the rule of law to uphold the principle "of freely elected democratic Government and parliamentary practices" as a measure against totalitarian rule – a position that had relevance in Southern Africa, behind the Iron Curtain and in neighboring Cuba. It also declared as a goal "the achievement for all peoples everywhere of the fullest measure of

---

[41] British National Archives (Kew), DO 200/182, "The Foreign Policy of Jamaica," June 1964, British National Archives.

[42] See statement on March 31, 1964 by Norman Manley to the House of Representatives. National Library of Jamaica (Kingston), *Jamaica Hansard: Proceedings of the House of Representatives Session, 1964–1965*, vol. 1, March 31–June 25, 1964, p. 4.

[43] Ibid. See statement by Donald Sangster on June 24, 1964.

[44] British National Archives (Kew), DO 200/182, "The Foreign Policy of Jamaica," June 1964, British National Archives.

Human Rights."[45] The policy highlighted the recent appointment of the Jamaican UN Ambassador as Chairman of the Special Committee on Human Rights, seeing it as an illustration of how Jamaica would focus its resources at the United Nations "in areas of particular interest to Jamaica." Egerton Richardson had the Government's formal backing, but then again, he had also played an influential role in developing and applying the principles reflected in the Jamaican foreign policy strategy.

From the outset of his chairmanship, Ambassador Richardson gave a forceful vision for the human rights year. His working paper explained that the:

ceremonies and celebrations should be such as to dramatize the deeper meaning of individual liberty, and to illustrate how narrow is the dividing line between a scrupulous observance of the obligation to respect human rights and fundamental freedoms in our political, economic and social relationships and an effective denial of these rights.[46]

Richardson was keenly aware that underlying the often embracing and elevated rhetoric aired in UN human rights debates there was in fact a continuing denial of these rights by the same UN member states. He was determined to challenge this status quo and look for new solutions. The Working Paper included two distinct proposals. One was an elaboration of the idea for an international conference on human rights to be held in 1968. The Soviet Union, the United States and the United Kingdom expressed clear reservations about this idea, but it appeared likely that it would generate widespread support from the Afro-Asian nations. The Costa Rican delegate, an important ally of Jamaica, strongly supported the idea and placed it in a larger context. For him, the Working Paper:

reflected a general desire to do something new and effective to promote the cause of human rights and the feeling that action could no longer be deferred. The idea of an international conference in 1968 had been born of that feeling of urgency.[47]

The second proposal tackled a major stumbling block in the preparation of the human rights conventions, namely the measures of implementation. The main outstanding questions for finalizing the draft Covenants on civil and political rights and on economic, social and cultural rights

---

[45] Ibid., p. 2.
[46] ST/SG/AC.5/3: Programme of Measures and Activities, June 25, 1964, p. 6.
[47] ST/SG/AC.5/SR.5: Mr. Volio (Costa Rica), Committee on the International Year for Human Rights, July 10, 1964, p. 5.

were "whether one form of international machinery or another, or any international machinery at all, aimed at ensuring implementation of these agreements should be provided for."[48] This was a critical component if the human rights conventions were to have any real significance. These measures would involve international monitoring and some degree of accountability, without which the legally binding nature of a convention would have little meaning and no dynamic process to support the elaboration of its standards over time. Richardson set as an aim that by the beginning of the 1968 Human Rights Year the two draft Covenants and other human rights conventions, including those on racial discrimination and religious intolerance, should be completed with effective measures of implementation included.

Richardson had requested that "reminiscences of the Cold War" be kept out of the Committee negotiations, but with similarly worded interventions by the three Communist states (Poland, the Soviet Union and Ukraine) emphasizing that the most important tasks for the Committee had to be the eradication of "apartheid, colonialism, neo-colonialism, fascism, neo-fascism and militarism," this appeared unlikely from the outset. The Soviet delegate even called for the Committee to have as one of its goals the eradication of colonialism by 1965. It was similar to the Soviet demands during the 1960 and 1961 debates on ending colonialism. The Danish representative on the Committee noted that the Soviet policy of promising more than could be achieved did not necessarily appeal to the African delegations.[49]

In his 1964 speech to the General Assembly, Hugh Shearer elaborated further on the aims. Jamaica was hoping that the international conference could provide an "opportunity of taking a fresh look at the whole human rights programme," which should include a critical assessment of the work of the Commission on Human Rights. Jamaica saw human rights in a larger strategic context for the international community, explaining that:

The existence of the United Nations as an institution of collective security and international cooperation presupposes the corresponding existence of an international legal order.[50]

---

[48] Ibid., p. 7.

[49] Memo from the Danish UN Mission to Foreign Ministry (Copenhagen), "Udvalget vedrørende det internationale menneskerettighedsår 1968," Danish National Archives (Rigsarkivet), Danish UN Mission in New York, 119.L.22a/3, Box 259, p. 7.

[50] Hugh Shearer (Jamaica), UN General Assembly, 19th session, 1293rd meeting, December 7, 1964, p. 12.

FIGURE 1. Soon after its independence in 1962, Jamaica became recognized as a leader in UN human rights diplomacy. In June 1964, the Jamaica's UN Ambassador Egerton Richardson was appointed Chairman of the newly established Committee for the International Year for Human Rights. *Source*: United Nations Photos

It was a legal order in which human rights were to be a central component. Shearer therefore called for "encouraging the progressive development of international law and its codification" and for the General Assembly to elaborate the principles of international law at the 1964 session in order to contribute "to the rule of law throughout the world."[51]

The United States strongly opposed a separate international human rights conference. They would only accept a special session of the General Assembly in New York. According to a report from UN Ambassador Adlai Stevenson, the United States convinced Costa Rica and Turkey to keep the conference within the confines of the General Assembly and at minimal cost. This was included in the resolution for the November meeting of the Committee on the International Human Rights Year.

Ambassador Richardson lashed out in what the U.S. Ambassador called "a vicious campaign to persuade the weak delegates that the resolution was designed to kill the idea of a conference." According to

[51] Ibid., p. 12.

FIGURE 2. Jamaican UN Ambassador Egerton Richardson with colleagues from Poland, the Philippines and Italy during a July 1964 working session of the Committee for the International Year for Human Rights. *Source*: United Nations Photos

Stevenson, the Jamaican Ambassador gave a strongly worded assessment of the UN human rights work as he called:

[the] Human Rights Commission incompetent, ineffective, and said it was killing United Nations initiatives in Human Rights, that it was unrepresentative of the United Nations, and that the best way to make sure that any conference on human rights was ruined was to let the Human Rights Commission participate in its organization. Furthermore, he stated that the present members on the Human Rights Commission had no interest in human rights.[52]

Richardson also "as on previous occasions,... insulted the USSR." Why this should have been a major concern to a U.S. diplomat remains unclear, but Richardson did not fold to the pressure of U.S. demands. Instead, he convinced the other delegates from developing nations to keep the idea of an international conference, outside the UN's formal structures, alive.

[52] Document 318, "Airgram from the Mission to the United Nations to the Department of State," November 24, 1964, *Foreign Relations of the United States, 1964–68*, Vol. 34, p. 562.

Richardson had told a U.S. diplomat that he needed some "Big Power" to support the idea. He had hoped that the United States would do this, but since this was not forthcoming, he instead secured the necessary support from the United Kingdom. Adlai Stevenson noted, "this determination is now evident and Richardson seemingly will settle for nothing less."[53]

For Richardson, the 1968 conference was not just an event. It was a target that offered the opportunity to drive change at the international level. By early December, he had secured backing from the United Kingdom and would not let the proposal falter. The British diplomats informed their American counterparts that the U.K. delegation "was under firm instructions not to alienate Amb. Richardson."[54] At a meeting on December 14, 1964, the U.K. Ambassador to the UN Lord Caradon made it clear to the Americans that he was an enthusiastic supporter of the Jamaican Ambassador's proposal as he believed it was important that the United Nations was seen to be doing more in the human rights field. Lord Caradon (also known as Hugh Foot) was reappointed British UN Ambassador after the new Labour government took office in October 1964. Having served as Governor to Jamaica from 1951 to 1957, he was well acquainted with Richardson. There is no doubt about the great mutual trust and respect that existed between Lord Caradon and the Jamaicans.[55] This partly explains his support but there was also another reason. A change was emerging in British thinking during these months – one that would lead to a major shift in U.K. policy on human rights.

Defining the new UN human rights diplomacy, 1964–1967

On October 19, 1964, Egon Schwelb, who had been Deputy Director of the UN Human Rights Division from 1947 until 1962, wrote to the British Foreign Secretary, urging the Foreign Office to initiate "a thorough study and analysis . . . of the policy pursued by United Kingdom representatives on Human Rights questions in various United Nations organs over the last twelve years or so."[56] Schwelb, who had been legal

---

[53] Ibid., p. 563.

[54] Ibid., p. 563, footnote 4.

[55] See, for example, British National Archives (Kew), DO 181/33, Jamaica and the United Nations, Letter from British High Commission, January 24, 1963, to Commonwealth Relations Office, London.

[56] British National Archives (Kew) LAB 13/2409, Letter from Egon Schwelb to Foreign Secretary Gordon Walker, October 19, 1964. At this point, Schwelb was based at Yale Law School.

advisor to the Czechoslovak Exile Government in London during the Second World War, sent the letter four days after Labour's election victory, pleading for a more constructive British approach. He commented that after a promising engagement in the late 1940s, the United Kingdom had become "one of the most restrictive and conservative forces and allowed governments whose dedication to Human Rights was, to say the least, open to considerable doubt, to appear as champions of freedom and democracy." Schwelb pointed to the U.K. position that domestic jurisdiction trumped a legitimate focus on human rights, the U.K. viewpoint that the UN Charter had given states no obligation regarding human rights and their undermining of universality by going against provisions that extended human rights to individuals in colonial territories all amounted to what Schwelb described as "bad politics, bad public relations and out of line with British tradition."[57]

The letter struck a nerve with the new Labour government. In January 1965, a cross-ministerial Working Group on Human Rights was established to review the United Kingdom's international human rights policy. It was in direct response to Egon Schwelb's letter.[58] At its first meeting on February 23, 1965, the Working Group dealt with the interpretation of UN Charter obligations and the colonial policies, which were the two main issues that had determined the U.K. human rights policy.

The UN Charter issue implied a shift from emphasizing Article 2(7) on domestic jurisdiction to emphasizing Articles 55 and 56 on principles of international cooperation, including promoting "universal respect for, and observance of, human rights and fundamental freedoms for all without distinction as to race, sex, language, or religion." It would be a significant shift from a Charter interpretation essentially negating the existence of international human rights to a view that regarded human rights as a positive obligation. The Foreign Office favored this change, arguing that "our aim was to get into line with other States; it was unfortunate that because of our colonial preoccupations, we had slipped behind in this respect. Colonial difficulties would continue but we should be better placed to promote human rights and to defend our record."[59] The U.K. government was gradually moving to a position that declared human rights a legitimate matter of international concern. It would take

---

[57] Ibid.

[58] British National Archives (Kew), LAB 13/2409, "Note by the Foreign Office: United Kingdom Policy towards Human Rights in the United Nations," January 29, 1965.

[59] British National Archives (Kew), LAB 13/2409, Statement by K.R.C. Pridham (Foreign Office), "Review of U.K. Human Rights Policy: Record of Meeting," February 23, 1965.

until April 1966 before this policy announcement was made, but the new British thinking emerging from late 1964 did enable Lord Caradon to support Jamaica's efforts.[60]

The U.S. State Department was concerned that the Human Rights Conference would be used as a platform for "race and other propaganda issues."[61] The race issue featured prominently within the Administration at a meeting held on January 21, 1965 regarding the creation of a UN High Commissioner on Human Rights.[62] Concern was expressed that domestic groups would use the Commissioner to seek further publicity on race relations in the United States.[63] Ambassador Franklin H. Williams from the U.S. Mission to the United Nations mentioned that these groups were "already appealing directly to foreign delegations in New York," so a UN Commissioner on Human Rights "would not create a new situation." The contrary was actually the case, since:

a balanced and objective human rights reporting system would be helpful and was urgently needed to offset the ignorance and disbelief in New York with respect to US progress in eliminating race discrimination – the US was already exposed and the situation could not be worse.[64]

This shows the differing views on human rights that existed inside U.S. diplomatic circles. The example also illustrates that by 1965 all member states had to if not constructively engage, then at least scramble to find their own preferred solutions to human rights progress within the United Nations. In November 1965, the OAS declared its full support for the 1968 Human Rights Year and would soon after turn their

---

[60] Steven L. B. Jensen (2014), "'Universality Should Govern Our Small World of Today': The Cold War and UN Human Rights Diplomacy 1960–1968," *Human Rights in Europe during the Cold War*. Edited by Rasmus Mariager, Karl Molin and Kersti Brathagen. London, pp. 56–72.

[61] Document 318, "Airgram from the Mission to the United Nations to the Department of State," November 24, 1964, *Foreign Relations of the United States, 1964–68,* Vol. XXXIV, p. 563.

[62] President Kennedy had suggested the creation of UN High Commissioner on Human Rights in his 1963 General Assembly speech. Roger S. Clark (1972), *A United Nations High Commissioner for Human Rights.* The Hague.

[63] U.S. civil rights groups had made earlier attempts using UN machinery to address racial segregation in the United States. See Carol Anderson (2003), *Eyes off the Prize. The United Nations and the African American Struggle for Human Rights 1944–1955.* Cambridge. See also Mary Dudziak (1988), "Desegregation as a Cold War Imperative," *Stanford Law Review*, vol. 41, pp. 61–120.

[64] Document 323, Memorandum of Conversation. Subject: Proposals for a UN Commissioner on Human Rights. Washington, January 21, 1965. *Foreign Relations of the United States, 1964–68, Vol. 34,* p. 569.

attention toward completing an Inter-American Convention on Human Rights.[65] The momentum was clear and new strategies had to be found. The Jamaican initiative was shifting the boundaries of the international debate.

By the spring of 1965, direct opposition to the international human rights conference had disappeared. The debate revealed divisions between the West and the East, but the process had sufficient momentum not to be undermined by these. Rene Cassin was concerned that "nothing was said about international machinery for implementing human rights," whereas the Soviet delegate was able to argue that "an excessive preoccupation with that aspect might divert attention from the more important task of promoting human rights."[66] It was one of a number of incoherent Soviet positions put forward as the debate on human rights shifted and became more concrete concerning the steps forward.

Western delegates (Canada, the United States) highlighted the importance of focusing on the rights of the individual, while delegates from Communist states focused on ending colonialism and on neo-Nazism (Poland and the USSR). The idea of engaging regional human rights mechanisms was proposed by European and Latin American countries – the regions where such mechanisms existed. Poland argued that "the drafting of the Covenants in final form should constitute the most important objective for the United Nations in the human rights field."[67] The motives behind this position were questionable. However, it was starting to look as if the push from developing countries and the momentum from the preparations for the human rights year were providing dividends for the codification of both civil and political rights and economic, social and cultural rights.

Richardson and his closest allies, including the Philippines, which held the post of Chairman of the Commission on Human Rights, had achieved what they wanted. The recent prominence of the race issue in the codification of human rights and the centrality of apartheid and colonialism in UN debates had made the Communist states engage more than ever before in the human rights work across a broader spectrum of rights,

---

[65] See A/CONF.32/PC/SR.7 – Mr. Martins (Uruguay), Preparatory Committee for the International Conference on Human Rights, May 18, 1966.

[66] Mr. Cassin (France) and Mr. Yakovlev (the USSR), Commission of Human Rights, 21st Session, 846th meeting, April 12, 1965, p. 7, 10.

[67] Mr. Dabrowa (Poland), Commission of Human Rights, 21st session, 846th meeting, April 12, 1965, p. 6.

FIGURE 3. The Committee on the International Year for Human Rights in session in New York in February 1965, debating "the deeper meaning of individual liberty" as a theme for the celebrations in 1968. *Source*: United Nations Photos

including civil and political. This created new possibilities but it did not mean that the battle for the future of the human rights program was over. It would increasingly be over what at first glance were procedural issues but, in reality, were of significant substantive value to international human rights work. The most significant debates were about the involvement of external stakeholders in the 1968 conference, namely the regional human rights mechanisms and civil society, and the setting of the conference agenda.

In March 1966, Costa Rica, the Philippines, Sweden, the United Kingdom and the United States proposed that an invitation be sent to the regional intergovernmental bodies involved with human rights allowing them to participate in the UN human rights work. The Soviet Union would not accept this idea. The Soviets would later explain that they had no issue with inviting the Organization of African Unity and the League of Arab States but could not accept the "Council of Europe, because that organization had nothing to do with the preparation of the conference and was dedicated to the struggle against the socialist States, thus a thorny political issue might arise."[68] When the five states withdrew their joint proposal over a procedural matter, it was Jamaica that secured the backing for a resolution which ensured the "cooperation of competent regional inter-governmental organizations in observing 1968 as International Human Rights Year."[69] It was a crucial intervention because the Council of Europe used the Tehran Conference and the human rights year to energize the regional human rights work in Europe. This new European development was initiated in 1969–1970 and drew direct inspiration from the Jamaica-initiated human rights year.[70]

The Soviet Union and other Communist states were performing a peculiar balancing act. They were all in favor of pushing the human rights agenda forward when it focused on race, apartheid and colonialism but blocked any practical step, no matter how minor, that would expand human rights work since it could widen the human rights issues addressed. Their blocking of efforts could even be on such apparently minor issues as criticizing the request for a temporary expansion of staff in the UN Division of Human Rights to support the International Conference. The Soviets presented a line of reasoning that was very compatible with Richardson's earlier assertion of the narrow dividing line between human rights promotion and denial. The Soviet representative stated that:

The Division of Human Rights had sufficient staff to prepare the documentation. The United Nations human rights programme included many activities which were clearly of secondary importance such as the study of everyone to be free from arbitrary arrest, detention and exile, the question of an international code of police ethics and the study of the right of an arrested person to communicate with those whom it was necessary to consult in order to ensure his defence or to protect his interests. If the Division of Human Rights postponed these studies, it

---

[68] A/CONF.32/PC/SR.2, Mr. Nasinovsky (the USSR), Preparatory Committee for the International Conference on Human Rights, May 10, 1966.

[69] E/CN.4/L.845/Add.5: Draft report of the Commission on Human Rights on the Work of the Twenty-Second Session on International Year for Human Rights, April 2, 1966.

[70] Council of Europe Archive (Strasbourg), Box 1847, Dossier 12130: International Human Rights Year 1968, "Recommendation 548 (1969) on the Programme of Action Relating to Human Rights after the International Human Rights Year 1968" (adopted by Consultative Assembly on January 30, 1969) and "Appendix V – CN/Del/Concl. (70) 186." See also Ed Bates (2010), *The Evolution of the European Convention on Human Rights: From Its Inception to the Creation of a Permanent Court of Human Rights*. Oxford, pp. 257–263.

would have sufficient staff and resources to make adequate preparations for the Conference.[71]

Richardson called for support to go against these blocking maneuvers. He was concerned with what he regarded as foot-dragging by the Western countries and their lack of commitment. He wanted them to mobilize their "renowned legal and human rights experts." Richardson believed that Western fears that the conference would degenerate into political debate should be countered by the West taking initiative by presenting new ideas for international human rights work.[72] He also highlighted the importance of the work of NGOs and its value to the Conference.

The Soviet Union was focused on limiting the role of the NGOs. At a 1967 Preparatory Committee meeting, they used the recent revelations of financial support from the U.S. Central Intelligence Agency (CIA) to a number of international NGOs as evidence that inviting the NGO sector to the Conference "would be to poison its atmosphere. They should be rigidly excluded."[73] This was an issue where there was vocal opposition from several other states and a procedure was eventually found that allowed NGOs to participate in the 1968 Conference but only after extensive foot-dragging from within the Preparatory Committee.[74] Ambassador Richardson had been a strong advocate of NGO involvement and actively promoted this at the United Nations. He reached out to these organizations to mobilize them for human rights work, although he did not hesitate to criticize NGOs for not having sufficiently intensified their efforts.[75]

The agenda for the 1968 Conference was another contentious issue. Racial discrimination and apartheid were soon established as major

---

[71] A/CONF.32/PC/SR.8: Statement by Mr. Nasinovsky (the USSR), Preparatory Committee for the International Conference on Human Rights, Summary Record of the 8th Meeting, May 19, 1966, p. 11.

[72] See U.S. National Archives, RG 59/250/7/20, Soc 14, Box 3205: "1968 Human Rights Conference," Telegram 4802 from U.S. United Nations Mission to Secretary of State, May 6, 1966.

[73] A/CONF.32/PC/SR.35: Statement by Mr. Nasinovsky (the USSR), Preparatory Committee for the International Conference on Human Rights, July 20, 1967, p. 3.

[74] See A/CONF.32/PC/SR.43–45: Mr. Schreiber (UN Division of Human Rights), Preparatory Committee, March 18–19, 1968.

[75] See speech by Egerton Richardson delivered to the "OPI Annual Conference for the Non-Governmental Organisations," September 13, 1967, Box 43: International Year for Human Rights (1968), Papers of the International League for the Rights of Man, New York Public Library.

agenda items alongside the badly worded item on "the universal realization of the right of peoples to self-determination and of the speedy
granting of independence to colonial countries and their influence on the
promotion of human rights and fundamental freedoms." The third major
item was the development of a long-term program for the advancement
of women.[76] Other agenda items such as "to strengthen the defence of
human rights and freedoms of individuals" and "international machinery
for effective implementation of international instruments" were becoming minor items.[77] What was becoming uncertain was the extent to which
there would be a real debate on human rights norms, standards, promotion and protection and not just acrimonious naming and blaming.

It was on this point that Jamaica suffered its most significant defeat.
Throughout the preparation period for the human rights year, Jamaica
had been advocating various models for furthering human rights protection, including national commissions on human rights, the creation of a
UN High Commissioner for Human Rights, stronger mandated measures
for the Commission on Human Rights in dealing with concrete human
rights violations,[78] creation of a Human Rights Council to replace the
Commission on Human Rights[79] and ensuring a substantive evaluation of
the international human rights efforts to be reviewed in Tehran. Jamaica
was committed to fighting racial discrimination and apartheid. There is
no doubt that finding effective measures to tackle apartheid in South
Africa was high on Ambassador Richardson's diplomatic agenda. It was
a stated objective of Jamaican foreign policy. The problem was that too
many member states did not live up to the principled agenda of a broader
human rights program but instead were increasingly more interested in
compartmentalizing human rights based on narrow self-interest and a
renewed emphasis on sovereignty.

The Jamaican Ambassador gave the best analysis of the Conference's
possible demise. He delivered it two years before the delegates gathered
in Tehran. Speaking at a meeting of the Preparatory Committee in May
1966, Richardson said about the agenda of the Conference:

---

[76] A/6354: "First Progress Report of the Preparatory Committee for the International
Conference on Human Rights," UN General Assembly, 21st Session, June 22, 1966.

[77] Ibid., p. 5.

[78] This proposal was presented in collaboration with Italy and Morocco. See E/CN.4/
L.923/Rev.1: CHR, 23rd session, March 15, 1967.

[79] U.S. National Archives, RG 59/250/7/20, Soc 14, Box 3205: "1968 Human Rights
Conference," Telegram 4908 from U.S. United Nations Mission to Secretary of State,
May 16, 1966.

There was no risk that racial discrimination and apartheid would not be amply discussed; the danger was that they might become the central focus of the Conference. The Committee should take every precaution to prevent the Conference from degenerating into a political debate which could more appropriately be held in other forums of the United Nations. If, for instance, colonialism was included in the agenda, the Conference might become involved in a discussion of the unresolved question of whether self-determination applied to peoples as well as nations, thus setting off a process of recrimination which was likely to extend to other items of the agenda.[80]

Richardson then went on to outline what a constructive approach at the conference would be:

The objective should be a discussion of <u>apartheid</u>, for example, solely from the point of view of the possible application of human rights techniques as a means of dissuading States from aiding and abetting the South African Government's policy.[81]

It was this combined focus on concrete normative development with remedies or specific measures for action in the human rights field that was at the heart of the Jamaican approach and would be behind one of the few lasting legacies from the Tehran Conference. This approach was applied during 1968 as a direct response to the escalating conflicts in a number of countries around the world, and it was a legacy that involved real innovation in international law.

The Jamaican vision easily embraced the interrelatedness and indivisibility of human rights. It is noteworthy that when a series of international seminars were to be organized in the run up to the 1968 Conference, Jamaica decided to host a seminar on civil and political rights that elaborated the principles for the effective realization and protection of civil and political rights at the national level. This does not fit the typical view of what human rights priorities developing nations had. The UN seminar, held in April 1967, showcased Jamaica but also proved a larger point, namely that there was another way forward for the new nations than the "trend toward single-party hegemony in the new Commonwealth."[82] The significant challenges of ensuring economic and social development

---

[80] A/CONF.32/PC/SR.7: by Mr. Richardson (Jamaica), "Agenda of the Conference," Preparatory Committee for the International Conference on Human Rights, May 18, 1966, pp. 6–7.

[81] Ibid., p. 7.

[82] SO 216/3 (13) AME 1967 – WP 8: UN Human Rights Seminar on the Effective Realization of Civil and Political Rights at the National Level, Kingston, Jamaica, April 25–May 2, 1967. Working Paper 8 by Victor B. Grant, Attorney-General, Jamaica, p. 29.

were taking their toll on Jamaican politics but there were still lessons to be learned.

An ageing Norman Manley spoke to the international delegates, and Ambassador Richardson consolidated his new partnership with a leading NGO actor, Sean MacBride, from the International Commission of Jurists, who also represented Amnesty International. The Kingston Seminar itself defined six essential features for the effective realization and protection of civil and political rights at the national level, highlighting, for example, the need for Ombudsmen or national human rights commissions, thereby pushing the limits of UN human rights debate from general standards to specific measures required in country-level implementation.[83]

Jamaica was the location for some of the richest human rights debates in this era. In December 1967, as a precursor to the human rights year, the Jamaican Council for Human Rights was established. It was a national NGO founded by a large group of concerned citizens, many with legal knowledge aiming to "challenge at every level the infringement of human rights in every constitutional way known to us as citizens."[84] Within six months, they were in public and, with great detail, exposing the brutal practices of the Jamaican police force against civilians – practices that were endorsed by leading politicians.[85] The idealistic self-image from the earliest days of Jamaican independence was starting to crack. The 1968 International Human Rights Year would be the culmination of Jamaica's remarkable international leadership in the human rights field. Much had changed in the human rights field since 1962. As 1967 ended, the world was entering what would prove to be a dramatic and eventful year.

Jamaica was not the only member of the United Nations that worked to strengthen and expand the role of human rights. They would not have achieved much without supporters and other states that took the lead on specific issues. The timing also worked to their benefit. As Jamaica joined the United Nations in 1962, they could build on the momentum created by a significant number of states pushing for International Conventions on Elimination of Racial Discrimination and Elimination of Religious

[83] S. S. Ramphal (1968), "Toward a Just Multi-Racial Society," *Toward an NGO Strategy for the Advancement of Human Rights* [Conference Report], The International NGO Conference on Human Rights, Paris, September 1968, p. 74.

[84] "Jamaica Human Rights Council Inaugurated," *The Jamaica Gleaner*, December 12, 1967, p. 27, National Library of Jamaica (Kingston).

[85] Jamaican Council for Human Rights (1968), *Government, The Police and Personal Freedom*. Kingston.

Intolerance. The new emphasis on making human rights into international law and the preparations for the human rights year were parallel processes that mutually reinforced each other from 1962 and onward. The latter gave the process a longer-term strategy and structure that the UN human rights project had never had before.

What is clear is that during this period no other UN member state worked so systematically or with the same clarity of vision as Jamaica did to promote human rights as universal principles to guide international relations. When necessary, Jamaican diplomats took a combative approach to protect the integrity of their vision, but they also provided the most innovative proposals for expansion of the international human rights system with a greater degree of state accountability. This was in itself an important role in a decade where United Nations human rights diplomacy was a decisive factor in determining the future of international human rights work.

In 1962, the Trinidad-born author V. S. Naipaul published the book *The Middle Passage. The Caribbean Revisited* based on a year-long journey he took in 1960 and 1961 through the region, visiting several nations on the brink of independence. He journeyed through Trinidad, British Guyana, Suriname, Martinique and Jamaica. His was a somber account that dealt with the legacies of slavery and colonialism and the current state of race relations. Naipaul offered a challenge to the historian. He asked, how could the history of "this West Indian futility" be told when history was "built around achievement and creation and nothing was created in the West Indies."[86] Naipaul's critique deserves a response because at the exact moment he was publishing his account, newly independent Jamaica was rising up well beyond claims of Caribbean futility and lack of achievement to set a new direction for the United Nations and for an international legal order where human rights was an important aspect of international affairs. It played directly into the East–West and North–South dynamics of the Cold War and decolonization. It was a profound vision and it came from Jamaica with law.

[86] V. S. Naipaul (1962), *The Middle Passage. The Caribbean Revisited*. London, p. 20.

4

The making of a precedent

Racial discrimination and international human rights law, 1962–1966

"A community without law is but a shell."

John F. Kennedy, United States, UN General Assembly,
September 25, 1961[1]

"If I rise to this rostrum, it is essentially to salute this historic event. The twentieth of November 1963 will be, to our mind, as historic as 10 December 1948."

Mr. Ghorbal, United Arab Republic/Egypt, UN General Assembly,
November 20, 1963[2]

International human rights law has been built on a foundation of race. The Convention on Elimination of All Forms of Racial Discrimination from 1965 established the major precedent that made human rights into international law accompanied by some measures of implementation. The 1965 Convention paved the way for the universal legal recognition of civil, political, economic, social and cultural rights elaborated in the Human Rights Covenants from 1966.[3] This claim is well

---

[1] Speech by John F. Kennedy (USA), UN General Assembly, 16th Session, September 25, 1961. Available at: www.jfklibrary.org/Asset-Viewer/DOPIN64xJUGRKgdHJ9NfgQ .aspx (quote appears at 2:45 minutes) (accessed on September 16, 2015).

[2] Mr. Ghorbal (United Arab Republic/Egypt), UN General Assembly, 18th session, 1261st meeting, November 20, 1963, p. 15.

[3] This is not how the standard account of the story is presented. In the influential 1500-page textbook *International Human Rights in Context: Law, Politics and Morals* (3rd edn., 2007, Oxford) edited by Henry J. Steiner, Philip Alston and Ryan Goodman, the Convention on Elimination of All Forms of Racial Discrimination is hardly mentioned at all and the normative foundations are clearly defined as civil, political, economic, social and cultural rights (see Table of Contents). The UN Intellectual History

supported by both chronology and precedent. There are four decisive UN General Assembly debates in the period 1962–1966 that together represent the breakthrough for international human rights law. These debates show how race transcended the sacred notions of sovereignty so closely guarded by many UN member states and secured that a wider range of human rights standards became international law.

The chapter aims to reinterpret the standard version of how the human rights Covenants came into existence by focusing on the making of legal and diplomatic precedents in the 1960s. In this context, the 1965 Convention on Elimination of All Forms of Racial Discrimination and the buildup to this is pivotal. The Convention was prepared and finalized during one General Assembly Session and was based on the 1963 Declaration on Elimination of All Forms of Racial Discrimination.[4] At the time the Convention was completed, the two Covenants had been under way for seventeen years and were still not finalized. They were only finalized and adopted in 1966. Race was the issue that forced the hand of UN member states and came to the rescue of the international human rights project.

To understand these developments, it is necessary to also look at the legal and political imagination that shaped the breakthrough. The breakthrough derived from deeper political meanings about law, universality, equality and justice linked to the emerging international political and social order in the first half of the 1960s.[5] Negotiating universality

Project dedicated a full volume to the history of human rights at the United Nations. The authors see it as a separate process to the human rights Covenants and ignore the obvious links and what it says about the evolution of international human rights. They do, however, make the important observation that the convention was "the first of the international instruments to bridge the artificial divide between civil and political rights and economic, social and cultural rights that had been created as a result of the polarization over the international bill of rights." Roger Normand and Sarah Zaidi (2008), *Human Rights at the UN: The Political History of Universal Justice*, Bloomington, IN, p. 272. Paul Gordon Lauren is the scholar who has probably given the most attention to the nexus between race and UN human rights diplomacy. In a brief passage on the Convention, he notices that it broke the "political deadlock" that had existed. Paul Gordon Lauren (1998), *The Evolution of International Human Rights: Visions Seen.* Philadelphia, PA, p. 254.

4 Due to the political controversies over a major funding crisis for the United Nations, the 1964 General Assembly session was largely abandoned and the various Committees did not perform substantive work. On human rights, it is fair to say that the 1965 General Assembly followed the 1963 session. On the background for the 1964 crisis, see Ilya V. Gaiduk (2012), *Divided Together. The United States and the Soviet Union in the United Nations, 1945–1965.* Washington, DC.

5 Paul Kahn (1999), *The Cultural Study of Law. Reconstructing Legal Scholarship.* Chicago, IL, pp. 135–136.

entailed much more than drafting legal standards. The process offers an insight into the dynamics of international organization in the shift from the colonial world order to the postcolonial world.

Between 1959 and 1960, a number of states – mainly European – witnessed a series of anti-Semitic attacks. The attacks received widespread attention as fears about anti-Semitism resurfaced and became an issue for the United Nations. In December 1960, the General Assembly passed a resolution condemning all manifestations and practices of racial, religious and national hatred in all spheres of society as violations of the UN Charter and the Universal Declaration of Human Rights. All governments were asked to take the necessary measures to prevent these attacks from happening. The item almost fell off the agenda after the 1961 UN General Assembly but was saved at the last moment by three African states. The issue was therefore on the agenda for the 1962 General Assembly.

The debate that opened in the Third Committee on October 29 would prove a turning point. October 1962 had been an eventful month, with the world appearing to be on the brink of a nuclear war during the Cuban Missile Crisis. In the United States, the domestic news agenda – visible for all delegates to the UN General Assembly – had been dominated by the court-ordered admission to the University of Mississippi of the African American student James Meredith. The Kennedy administration had sent in federal armed forces to uphold and secure Meredith's admission. Massive violence had ensued due to protests against his admission. Two people died and dozens were injured. The question of racial discrimination and segregation in the United States was a great problem for the conduct of American foreign policy. It received worldwide attention and raised doubts about the ideals that the country claimed to represent. It also allowed for easy propaganda for America's opponents. A considerable problem was that it was a reality that diplomats from African, Asian and Caribbean were experiencing themselves on a regular basis when they looked for housing or visited a restaurant in Washington DC or when they traveled around the country, including the journey to their own missions in New York and the United Nations. There were many incidents of this kind and they were something the Kennedy and later the Johnson administration could not ignore.[6] The UN debates on racial

---

[6] Renee Romano (2000), "No Diplomatic Immunity: African Diplomats, the State Department, and Civil Rights, 1961–1964," *Journal of American History*, vol. 87, no. 2, pp. 546–579; Mary Dudziak (2002), *Cold War Civil Rights. Race and the Image of American Democracy*. Princeton, NJ.

discrimination were viewed through the lens of the political risks that the issue incurred for the Americans. It was not yet seen as a risk that could also involve an opportunity – although that is how the process turned out in the years between 1962 and 1966.

The two main topics in the influential UN General Assembly debate in 1962 were racial discrimination and religious intolerance. At the start of the debate, a group of nine Francophone African states presented a resolution calling for the drafting of a Convention on Elimination of All Forms of Racial Discrimination.[7] The resolution ensured that the primary focus of the debate would be about race and racial discrimination.

The Israeli delegate described the 'swastika epidemic' that had inspired the debate. This included bombs thrown at Jewish schools, synagogues set on fire, swastikas painted on buildings and desecration of Jewish cemeteries. He warned against dismissing the incidents as the work of lunatics. In describing the anti-Semitic attacks, the Israeli delegate concluded that:

It was ironical that the more law-abiding and liberal countries were the most reluctant to take action against those who would trample their laws and liberties underfoot ... Freedom of expression could not properly be exploited to propagate concepts branded as inherently criminal.[8]

The Israeli delegate then criticized the Soviet Union for the treatment of its Jewish population, labeling it as cultural discrimination. This stimulated a series of verbal attacks by Arab states, who aired criticisms against Israel over Palestine and the treatment of Arabs. The Mauritanian delegate, who had cosponsored the draft resolution, intervened to request that:

While the United Nations tended to be basically political, an effort should be made to view certain problems from a social and humanitarian, rather than an ideological and partisan, point of view and in any case to divorce those problems from the cold war.[9]

The idea that the human rights project could be separated from the Cold War was voiced frequently. The goal was that the human rights debate would be more principled and be separated from the political pressures

---

[7] UN Document A/C.3/L.1006, October 25, 1962, Resolution proposed by Central African Republic, Chad, Dahomey (Benin), Guinea, Ivory Coast, Mali, Mauritania, Niger and Upper Volta.

[8] Mr. Comay (Israel), UN General Assembly, Third Committee, 17th Session, 1165th meeting, October 29, 1962, p. 156.

[9] Mr. Kochman (Mauritania), UN General Assembly, Third Committee, 17th Session, 1165th meeting, October 29, 1962, p. 157.

of the Cold War logic on international relations. The reason for this was obvious as the shadow of the Cuban Missile Crisis was hanging over the debate. However, the ambition behind the separation also came from an understanding that decolonization was a different logic and historical phenomenon with its own set of issues needing political attention outside the Cold War dynamics. There was a longer historical tradition of racial discrimination and the legacies of colonialism that many states wanted to confront. They wanted to place these issues at the center of United Nations diplomacy. As stated by Senegal, "Racial discrimination was still the rule in the African colonial territories and in South Africa, and was not unknown in other parts of the world," and while Senegal regarded itself as being at the frontline in attacking discrimination wherever it occurred, "The time had come to bring all States into that struggle, and in that regard a convention on the elimination of racial discrimination would be of the greatest usefulness."[10] There was a great belief that international law could be an important instrument to achieve justice and greater equality.

Egypt believed that the moral weight of a declaration on racial discrimination "would pave the way for the elaboration of binding instruments applicable to all States and people."[11] From the perspective of Mali, "the argument of racial supremacy must be demolished once and for all," and for this purpose, a Convention on racial discrimination "was absolutely essential."[12] Liberia had taken concrete action by testing the relevance of international law in the fight against racial discrimination. Liberia and Ethiopia had brought South Africa before the International Court of Justice to test the legality of South Africa's claim to South West Africa based on a League of Nations mandate. Liberia believed that this claim had no standing in international law. They tried therefore to put apartheid on trial.[13] The outcome of this case would prove to have a direct effect on the Human Rights Covenants in 1966.

---

[10] Mr. Kane (Senegal), UN General Assembly, Third Committee, 17th session, 1167th meeting, October 30, 1962, p. 168.

[11] Mr. Ghorbal (United Arab Republic), UN General Assembly Third Committee, 17th Session, 1168th meeting, October 31, 1962, p. 172. Please note that the statement refers to "instruments" in the plural.

[12] Mrs. Rousseau (Mali), UN General Assembly, Third Committee, 17th Session, 1169th meeting, October 31, 1962, p. 179.

[13] Ryan Irwin (2010), "Apartheid on Trial: South West Africa and the International Court of Justice, 1960–66," *International History Review*, vol. 32, no. 4, pp. 619–642.

It was not just African states who looked toward applying international law to the issue of race. It was a step strongly supported by the Latin American countries, the Communist countries and others. There was no real opposition voiced in the debate. The Philippines – one of the most active promoters of the human rights project since the creation of the UN – was a voice of caution. The Philippines was in favor of drafting the Convention but correctly warned that "While there was no lack of lip-service to the charter and the Universal Declaration, there was insufficient cooperation in the form of faithful compliance with their provisions."[14] The Philippines was concerned with the lengthy process of formulating a convention and therefore placed responsibility on Governments to immediately take practical action. The Polish delegate stated that since racism violated the rights and freedoms of millions of individuals, it had to be "fought at both the national and the international level." The measures that Poland suggested were strong and superseded the concerns as regards sovereignty normally expressed from that political camp. The Convention:

> should include provisions making it obligatory for contracting States to revoke all discriminatory laws directed against any one group of the population, prohibit racial discrimination by law, eliminate administrative discrimination and take long-term educational action among both youths and adults.[15]

Poland was willing to shift the existing parameters of the human rights debate because the topic was racial discrimination. It was a preview of the diplomatic struggle that was to come.

There was a general tone of consensus regarding the proposal for a declaration and a convention but there was also well-known controversy. The Soviet delegate ignited a sharp ideological exchange when requesting an explanation from the U.S. delegate on why racism prevailed in the country to the extent that "armed forces had had to be called in to safeguard the rights of negroes during the recent incidents in Mississippi."[16] The United States delegate, who had earlier asked about the situation concerning the Jews in the Soviet Union, replied by claiming that:

---

[14] Mr. Reyes (the Philippines), UN General Assembly, Third Committee, 17th Session, 1167th meeting, October 30, 1962, p. 166.

[15] Mrs. Dembinska (Poland), UN General Assembly, Third Committee, 17th Session, 1167th meeting, October 30, 1962, p. 166.

[16] Mr. Ostrovsky (the USSR), UN General Assembly, Third Committee, 17th Session, 1170th meeting, November 1, 1962, p. 187.

What was really significant was the fact that the United States Government had placed its full strength and prestige behind the efforts to protect the rights and liberties of one individual. The State existed to serve the citizen, not the citizen to serve the State.[17]

The Soviet delegate responded by denying discrimination against Jews and then attacked the United States on voting rights, on discrimination in housing, work and education. The racism in the United States was compared with South Africa and then turned to what was a difficult issue, namely that racism "was so prevalent in the United States that it affected even the diplomatic representatives of the African and Asian countries in New York and Washington." This hit a sore spot. The diplomats from the Third World were not unaccustomed to suffering racial discrimination and even violence in the United States.[18] These problems were not limited to the diplomatic corps in New York. There were big problems with finding decent housing for diplomatic staff from many of the newly independent states because of the widespread discrimination against people of color in racially segregated Washington DC. They faced a bitter reality and the Soviet Union was offered a useful diplomatic tool for their Cold War propaganda.

It may appear that Mauritania's ambition to divorce the problems of racial discrimination from the Cold War failed. One should, however, be careful to separate this high-profiled controversy from the actual outcome when assessing this – and other – diplomatic debates. In reality, Mauritania and the thirty-three states that cosponsored the resolution achieved what they wanted from the debate. The resolution calling for a Declaration on Elimination of All Forms of Racial Discrimination followed by a Convention on the same was adopted unanimously in the Third Committee and later by the General Assembly on December 7, 1962. For now, the project was on track and it appeared that the UN human rights work had received a new lease of life after a long period in the shadows. Decolonization was its source of energy.

"A declaration of universal and unrestricted intent"

The Declaration on Elimination of All Forms of Racial Discrimination was a top priority for the 1963 General Assembly session. It was decided

---

[17] Mrs. Tree (USA), UN General Assembly, Third Committee, 17th Session, 1170th meeting, November 1, 1962, p. 188.
[18] Dudziak (2002), *Cold War Civil Rights*, pp. 228–231.

that it would be the first item to be addressed. The determination to see it completed was evident. The Declaration in itself was awarded great significance, but at the same time, it was made clear that it was a stepping stone to completing a legally binding human rights Convention. The world had changed dramatically in only a few years and the United Nations had to take a strong position against racial discrimination since "contemporary politics could not be separated from the question of racial discrimination."[19]

The change was reflected in the language used to describe racism and racial discrimination by the member states. Descriptions of racism like "the shame of the Century" and "the social cancer of the modern times" were among many examples where the meaning of race in a United Nations human rights context undermined the legitimacy of racial segregation.[20] The statements, however, went beyond this and outlined the wider strategic implications of the issue of racial discrimination. Tunisia called attention to the "explosive situation which racial discrimination might create in certain parts of the world...it was clear that South Africa represented a potential hotbed of armed conflict."[21] The Soviet delegate compared the debate on race with the signing of the Partial Nuclear Test Ban Treaty in August 1963. The "happy outcome" of the latter after "lengthy negotiations would be a good omen for the Committee's work."[22] Racial discrimination was being viewed in the context of détente. This helped inspire the turn toward international law-making in the human rights field.

Law was in the air in the Third Committee. The different delegations invested the meaning they applied to it – their legal imagination so to speak – in the negotiations on the Declaration on Elimination of All Forms of Racial Discrimination. This can be witnessed both from the many areas where there was consensus and from the areas where disagreement and tension arose. The strong quest for universality that was often evoked – and that helped mediate solutions to some of the contentious issues – was also an expression of this legal imagination. The delegate from the Central

[19] Miss Wachuku (Nigeria), UN General Assembly, Third Committee, 18th session, 1220th meeting, October 3, 1963, p. 43. Nigeria was paraphrasing a Ghanaian statement.
[20] Quoted from statements by Mauritania (1215th meeting) and Czechoslovakia (1218th meeting).
[21] Mr. Razgallah (Tunisia), UN General Assembly, Third Committee, 18th session, 1216th meeting, October 1, 1963, p. 23.
[22] Mr. Ivanov (the USSR), UN General Assembly, Third Committee, 18th session, 1215th meeting, September 30, 1963, p. 19.

African Republic expressed it in more elaborate terms by returning to the failings of the Universal Declaration of Human Rights from 1948 in an interestingly argued critique:

Through clever manoeuvres the Declaration [UDHR] had been deprived of binding force, and it stood merely as a body of principles whose abstract and inert nature seemed to embolden those who would raise discriminatory practices to the level of State norms. How different a picture was presented by South Africa and by the United States, for instance, which was doing all it could to eliminate racial discrimination within its boundaries.

His delegation considered the draft Declaration [on racial discrimination] to be no more than a step towards the conclusion of an international convention ensuring the unconditional application of the principles of the Universal Declaration of Human Rights on the subject of non-discrimination.[23]

The implications here are important. They highlight the significance of the 1960s UN human rights diplomacy. Africa was present at the moment when human rights acquired real meaning – namely as legally binding universal standards, and they were a driving force in the process. It is therefore too simplistic to claim that human rights are Western values imposed on the international community. The binding nature of human rights was carried forward by an Afro-Asian push or as one African delegation explained it, "To those who sought to stem a revolutionary tide with routine and static texts, Africa would reply with the logic of an oppressed continent."[24]

The way the statement from the Central African Republic had referred to South Africa and the United States in the debate on racial discrimination was symbolic for the whole debate. The events in these two countries were formative in shaping the debate. The references to apartheid and the South African situation were numerous. They highlighted racial discrimination as a threat to peace and international security. The South African attempt to explain the country's policy and deny the existence of any human rights violations impressed no one.[25]

---

[23] Mr. Kombet (Central African Republic), UN General Assembly, Third Committee, 18th session, 1217th meeting, October 1, 1963, p. 32.

[24] Mrs. Aribot (Guinea), UN General Assembly, Third Committee, 18th Session, 1218th meeting, October 2, 1963, p. 36. See also statement by Gabon, "The United Nations was gradually changing from a centre for deliberations to a practical tool for the establishment and maintenance of the international rule of law and justice, and the Committee should not lag behind in that process," Mr. Nyoundou (Gabon), UN General Assembly, Third Committee, 18th session, 1220th meeting, October 3, 1963, p. 44.

[25] Mr. Schalkwyk (South Africa), UN General Assembly, Third Committee, 18th session, 1218th meeting, October 2, 1963, p. 37.

The meaning of racial discrimination in America was far more interesting. Reflected clearly in the debate, the UN diplomats were well-informed about the situation both from residing in the United States and from following political developments and the news coverage. There were thirteen member states that commented on race relations in the United States during the 1963 debate. Of these, seven were positive, four were negative and two countries gave neutral commentary.[26] The positive assessments had a political rationale and an element of self-interest. It was beneficial for member states greatly concerned with racial discrimination to highlight the transformative process that race relations were undergoing in America and the role of active government in securing this. It provided international encouragement to the U.S. Government and showed a path toward improving international relations. The positive assessments were directed toward the U.S. Government's "remarkable efforts" and were frequently addressed directly to President Kennedy.

The negative assessments were either ideological or expressed shock over individual atrocities. This highlighted the uncertainty over the direction and the likelihood of success for the civil rights struggle in the United States. The Albanian delegate stated that if the United States government had really wanted to end racial discrimination, "the shameful practice would have been eliminated long ago."[27] The Costa Rican delegate addressed the Birmingham atrocity of September 15, 1963, where four young girls died in a church bombing for which the Ku Klux Klan was responsible, as he:

regretted profoundly that the efforts of the United Nations had not succeeded in abolishing the degrading discriminatory practices of which non-whites were the victims, particularly in Africa, and *that even today bombs were exploding in churches and killing Negro children.*[28]

The United States could not avoid giving an interpretation of the deeper meaning of ending racial discrimination when delivering their statement to the Third Committee. It was the U.S. Ambassador Adlai Stevenson who was assigned this responsibility. His speech was part U.S. history lesson,

[26] The countries were Mauritania, India, Ceylon, Morocco, Senegal, Cameroon and Central African Republic (all positive); Albania, Cuba, Costa Rica and Guinea (negative); and Uruguay and United Kingdom (neutral). The U.S. situation was addressed in fourteen statements as Albania addressed it negatively in two separate interventions.

[27] Mr. Lamani (Albania), UN General Assembly, Third Committee, 18th session, 1217th meeting, October 1, 1963, p. 30.

[28] Mr. Redondo (Costa Rica), UN General Assembly, Third Committee, 18th session, 1216th meeting, October 1, 1963, p. 26. My italics.

part accolade to those who had been or were fighting to end segregation, part a defense of his government's record and part a reflection on the nexus between human rights and social transformation.

Stevenson spoke of the three American revolutions: the war for national independence, the Emancipation Proclamation to free slaves in the 1860s and the third revolution through which the country was passing "to ensure greater freedom and full human rights for all citizens."[29] The statement described the numerous forms of discrimination that African Americans had suffered in the century between the second and third revolutions and the government's various legislative, regulatory and enforcement strategies, including the University of Mississippi case with federal enforcement of the Supreme Court decision on desegregation of education. The wider international meaning of the social transformation that the United States was undergoing was not lost on the Americans, and Stevenson tried to portray it positively:

> The reaction of world opinion showed that people throughout the world recognized the difference between a country which was having racial trouble because it was unwilling to make progress and a country which was having trouble precisely because it was making progress.[30]

Distancing themselves from South Africa was the least that could be expected from the United States when giving meaning to the brutality faced by civil rights activists in the American South. The message that legislative and administrative measures could be used to destroy a system of racial discrimination was not lost on the audience. To deliver the full meaning of the U.S. statement, Stevenson would, however, borrow credibility from an event at the Lincoln Memorial a month earlier, "As one of the speakers participating in the recent march on Washington had said, the fight for human rights was not for the sake of the Negro, but for the sake of the image, the idea, and the aspiration of America itself."[31] It shows how these negotiations of universal standards were highly aware of contemporary developments happening almost in real time outside the confines of the UN meeting rooms.

The American statement stood out for another reason. It was the only one that included a self-critical assessment of the situation in their

---

[29] Mr. Stevenson (USA), UN General Assembly, Third Committee, 18th session, 1217th meeting, October 1, 1963, p. 30.
[30] Ibid., p. 30.
[31] Ibid., p. 30. The speaker referred to was the German-American Rabbi Joachim Prinz from the American Jewish Congress.

country. The United States used this as a platform to turn the focus to global realities that were certainly worth challenging:

How many Members of the United Nations would validly claim that their societies were free of discrimination based on race, religion, tribe or caste? The ferment and revolution of the current era must go deeper than nationalism. They must be used to extend the frontiers of the human intellect and to embody the principles of freedom in existing institutions.[32]

The Declaration contained a lengthy preamble and eleven articles. The preamble affirmed the principles of dignity and equality of all human beings, including equality before the law based on the UN Charter and the Universal Declaration of Human Rights. It also condemned colonialism and all segregation based on the 1960 *Declaration on the Granting of Independence to Colonial Countries and Peoples*. The Declaration proclaimed that racial discrimination was "scientifically false, morally condemnable and socially unjust" and had no justification "in theory or in practice." Furthermore, it proclaimed that government policies based on racial superiority or hatred was not just a violation of human rights but a risk to international peace and security. The articles specified the principles calling for governments to rescind discriminatory legislation, for equal access to all public facilities and to public services and for the right of effective remedy against discrimination based on race, color or ethnic origin. The Declaration specifically condemned apartheid.

The main controversy was over the measures to be taken to curtail any promotion of racist ideas or statements. Israel, the Communist Bloc and many Third World states wanted strict measures against any expression of racism while the Western states argued against it to protect freedom of expression and freedom of association. The latter argued that the stricter provisions of prosecuting and outlawing racist expressions and organizations were against the agreed standards in the Universal Declaration as long as the individuals in question were not inciting or using violence. The disagreement was the subject of many attempts at consensus with countries in the African group playing a moderating role but eventually these attempts failed. The Declaration was approved in the Third Committee on October 28 but with seventeen abstentions.[33] Falling short of universal endorsement was seen as a failure that would curtail the significance of the Declaration.

---

[32] Ibid., p. 30.
[33] See record from the Third Committee's 1245th meeting, October 28, 1963.

At the General Assembly, the Declaration sparked off a debate over this issue captured in Article 9. In a last gasp effort by Argentina, a new amendment that aimed to balance promotion and incitement in the provision on prosecution was proposed just before the vote in the General Assembly on November 20, 1963. The amendment did not fully meet the aspirations of the Western group, but the significance of the vote was clear to everyone. The amendment was approved and the *Declaration on the Elimination of All Forms of Racial Discrimination*, as it was entitled, was adopted unanimously. The unanimous vote in the General Assembly was cause for celebration for the large majority of the delegations. They celebrated the historical achievement of what Australia called "a declaration of universal and unrestricted intent."[34] Egypt probably expressed best the feeling of achievement, stating: "If I rise to this rostrum, it is essentially to salute this historic event. The twentieth of November 1963 will be, to our mind, as historic as 10 December 1948."[35] This, if anything was, was a ringing endorsement of the universal human rights project at the United Nations from a country from the Global South.

Two days later, John F. Kennedy was assassinated in Dallas, Texas, and Lyndon B. Johnson was inaugurated as President. From the outset of his presidency, Johnson made civil rights a priority for his administration, persisting to end racial segregation and achieve formal racial equality.[36] With Johnson at the helm, major legal and policy reform on racial discrimination was carried forward, something that was unsurpassed in any other period in the nation's history. In the two-year period between the United Nations adopting the Declaration and the Convention on Elimination of All Forms of Racial Discrimination, significant change happened in racial politics in the United States. Both processes reflected global political transformations and they intersected in several ways.

The passing of the 1964 Civil Rights Bill, which included economic and social rights, was a major achievement but it had one serious omission: the African Americans' right to vote. In March 1965, Johnson placed a Voting

---

[34] Mr. Hay (Australia), UN General Assembly, 18th session, 1261st meeting, November 20, 1963, p. 11.

[35] Mr. Ghorbal (United Arab Republic/Egypt), UN General Assembly, 18th session, 1261st meeting, November 20, 1963, p. 15.

[36] Memorandum for the President, "Civil Rights Activities During the First 100 Days," April 15, 1964 by Lee C. White, LBJ Library (Austin, TX), Papers of LBJ – President 1963–1969, Box 2, Ex & Gen Hu. See also Robert Caro (2012), *The Passage of Power. The Years of Lyndon Johnson*. New York.

Rights Act before Congress. This was fully in line with Johnson's political views, but his actions were also forced by violent events in the South
that shocked many Americans. On March 7, ABC interrupted a television broadcast of "Judgement in Nuremberg" to bring a news item from
Selma, Alabama. The news item showed state troopers and local police
viciously assaulting peaceful and unarmed protesters, including killing a
white clergyman who was among the civil rights protesters. While the
Selma protests caught the national imagination, the tense standoff continued. The Johnson administration tried to convince Alabama Governor
George Wallace to take responsibility and resolve the crisis. He would
not and this became the impetus for sending in federal troops and for the
most remarkable speech of Johnson's presidency.

On March 15, 1965, Johnson delivered a carefully crafted and tele-
vised speech before a Joint Session of Congress where he came out in
full force on the issue of voting rights.[37] It was a profoundly American
speech in tone, content and meaning, but it is hard to ignore its international dimension. It was 45 minutes and 20 seconds of a master class
in human rights diplomacy.[38] Johnson opened by saying that he was
speaking "for the dignity of man and the destiny of democracy" and then
linked the American revolution, the Civil War and the recent events in
Selma, Alabama, together as an evocation of the challenges posed "to
the values and the purposes and the meaning" of the American nation.
He called on all the legislators to live up to their sacred oath to uphold
the Constitution and approve the Voting Rights Act with urgency because
"we have already waited a 100 years and more and the time for waiting
is gone." In a move that would have angered the intransigent Southern politicians, Johnson declared that "The real hero of this struggle
is the American Negro. His actions and protests, his courage to risk
safety, and even to risk his life, have awakened the conscience of this
nation."

A high point was when Johnson stated that "There is no issue of
state's rights or national rights. There is only the struggle for human
rights." With that, Lyndon B. Johnson ripped through the foundations

---

[37] See Garth Pauley (2007), *LBJs American Promise. The 1965 Voting Rights Address*.
College Station, TX.
[38] The speech lasted for 36 minutes and 40 seconds and was interrupted by 8 minutes
and 40 seconds of applause. See the website of the LBJ Library: www.lbjlibrary
.org/lyndon-baines-johnson/speeches-films/president-johnsons-special-message-to-the-
congress-the-american-promise/ (accessed on September 16, 2015).

of a century of failed post–Civil War reconstruction that had nurtured Jim Crow and brought the debate on race in America up to date with the global normative developments and standards of international law-making in 1965.[39] Johnson knew that he had a very wide audience that stretched well beyond the borders of America. He acknowledged this international constituency: "I recognize that from outside this chamber is the outraged conscience of a nation, the grave concern of many nations and the harsh judgment of history on our acts."

The speech had a profound, almost physical effect on many of the lis-teners present in Congress and around the country. The Associate Justice of the U.S. Supreme Court Tom C. Clark wrote to Johnson the following day, "Dear Lyndon. The Address last night was the greatest. I was so proud that if I had been close enough I'd have kissed you for it."[40] A similar experience was reported from among the international media rep-resentatives as an exalted female Japanese journalist said about Lyndon B. Johnson, "He can cause affection."[41]

The vast majority of letters received by the White House on the Voting Rights Speech praised Johnson's statement in glowing terms. Among the small minority of angry letters, there was one from Mr. and Mrs. Cronin from Clinton, Maryland. They wrote to the President a few days later with these words, "Why was the United Nations flag flown in Selma March 16 demonstration. I too am an American citizen. I demand an investigation."[42] The letter by the Cronin family referred to the blue United Nations flag that had been flown at Selma. Local African American high school students had carried the UN flag alongside the American Stars and Stripes in opposition to the Confederate flag on display en route.[43] The carrying of the UN flag was a symbolic indication of the importance given to this organization by the civil rights protesters. It required no

---

[39] For a good account, including that of the U.S. Supreme Court's role in paving the way for Jim Crow legislation, see Lawrence Goldstone (2011), *Inherently Unequal: The Betrayal of Equal Rights by the Supreme Court, 1865–1903*. New York.

[40] Letter from Tom C. Clark, Associate Justice, Supreme Court of United States, LBJ Library (Austin, TX), Papers of LBJ – President 1963–1969, Box 68, EX SP 2–3/ 1965/HU 2–7/PRO/C.

[41] "Note from Katie Louchheim, Deputy Assistance Secretary for Community Advisory Services, March 24, 1965." LBJ Library (Austin, TX), Papers of LBJ – President 1963–1969, EX SP 2–3/1965/HE – Box 67.

[42] Telegram from Mr. and Mrs. John E. Cronin, Clinton, MD, March 18, 1965, LBJ Library (Austin, TX), Papers of LBJ – President 1963–1969, Box 69, EX SP 2–3/1965/HU 2–7/ CON/C.

[43] See Thomas Borstelmann (2001), *The Cold War and the Color Line*. Cambridge, MA, p. 189.

investigation but the letter illustrated how support for continued racial segregation was linked to opposition to the United Nations.

The aftermath of Johnson's Voting Rights speech made it clear that it was intended for the widest possible circulation. A special booklet version was sent to every African Ambassador to the United States. On May 8, 1965, a finely printed version of the speech was sent to every African Head of State with a letter from President Johnson explaining that this was the "definitive position of this administration."[44]

Johnson's determination and his masterly legislative skills ensured that the Voting Rights Act passed with remarkable speed despite a Southern attempt at filibuster. Lyndon B. Johnson signed the Act on August 6, 1965. It had immediate effect as U.S. law. The timing was good, given the focus of the upcoming session of the General Assembly due to start in New York the following month. The drafting of a Convention on Elimination of All Forms of Racial Discrimination was on the agenda. It was an agenda item that carried real political weight and came with political momentum behind it.

"The ideals of any civilized society"

The United States opened the 1965 UN General Assembly debate on the Draft International Convention on Elimination of all Forms of Racial Discrimination. They had a point to prove and therefore outlined a catalog of actions taken by the United States Government in the last two years to end racial discrimination, with particular emphasis on the Civil Rights Act, the Voting Rights Act and the 1964 Economic Opportunities Act.[45] The impact of these changes was clear at the United Nations. In 1963, there had been thirteen member states that highlighted the U.S. domestic situation on race. In the 1965 debate on the Convention, which was substantially longer than the 1963 debate, only two states referred to race relations in the United States.[46] The perception of the United States had changed – at least for the time being. Furthermore, the eyes of most delegations were on a bigger prize – an international legal instrument

---

[44] Letter from May 8, 1965; see, for example, box on Mauritania, LBJ Library (Austin, TX).

[45] Miss Willis (USA), UN General Assembly, Third Committee, 20th session, 1299th meeting, October 11, 1965, pp. 57–58.

[46] The UN official records of the 1965 debate are about double in length (number of pages) compared with those of the 1963 debate.

on racial discrimination that would firmly establish universal norms and would be binding on states that ratified the Convention.

The determination to complete the Convention was widespread and it was therefore agreed not to have a general debate. Instead, the Third Committee proceeded directly to negotiate the preamble and substantive articles based on the draft prepared by the Commission on Human Rights. This approach did not mean that issues of a more principled nature were not raised. The Third Committee remained "an arena for battles of words" over the meaning of human rights in the modern world.[47] When the Canadian delegate claimed ownership of human rights by talking about "the traditional Western concept of human rights,"[48] other member states immediately took issue with this self-perception. The Venezuelan delegate, from the outspoken Latin American contingent, responded that "the Western countries had no reason to pride themselves on their advanced moral concepts, since it was in those countries that racial discrimination had originated and still existed."[49] It was in 1965 clearly difficult to make the claim that human rights were a Western invention or Western imposed, without standing corrected by countries from the Global South. From Africa, the Tanzanian delegate responded equally firmly:

With respect to the Canadian representative's statement, the Western world clearly had nothing to teach the developing countries in the matter of human rights; indeed, it was the Western world that had given birth to colonialism and slavery, while the developing countries had suffered as a result.[50]

[47] Mr. Cochaux (Belgium), UN General Assembly, Third Committee, 20th session, 1368th meeting, December 8, 1965, p. 458.
[48] Mr. Macdonald (Canada), UN General Assembly, Third Committee, 20th session, 1345th meeting, November 17, 1965, p. 324.
[49] Mr. Zuloaga (Venezuela), UN General Assembly, Third Committee, 20th session, 1345th meeting, November 17, 1965, p. 326.
[50] Mr. Waldron-Ramsey (Tanzania), UN General Assembly, Third Committee, 20th session, 1345th meeting, November 17, 1965, p. 327. This statement illustrates the ongoing negotiations over the meanings of human rights that took place during this significant period in the 1960s. The statement by Waldo Waldron-Ramsey should also be seen in the context of the domestic developments in Tanzania. Tanganyika (from 1964, Tanzania) became a one-party state under Julius Nyerere's leadership shortly after its independence. As Meredith Terretta has argued, "the Nyerere regime, continuing in the revolutionary spirit of Africa's liberation from foreign rule, became deft at presenting itself, on a Pan-African and global stage, as pro-human rights while making clear that the state of Tanzania would be the sole entity to define and to implement rights and thus would reject any critiques coming from the global North." Meredith Terretta (2013), "From Below and to the Left? Human Rights and Liberation Politics in Africa's Postcolonial Age," *Journal of World of History*, vol. 24, no. 2, p. 401. It should be mentioned that

If the elephant in the room in these UN debates had always been about having a realistic debate on human rights violations in the respective countries, instead of the peculiar blend of proclamation and denial, it was also the Tanzanian delegate who most directly attacked the legal formalism that was so prevalent when member states explained their domestic situation. He expressed his:

> surprise that almost all delegations thought it necessary to say that discrimination did not exist in their countries. There were no doubt very few countries in the world whose legislation contained provisions favouring discrimination. But it was surely hardly possible to make the same blanket affirmation when it was no longer the sphere of law and principles that was concerned but that of custom and practice.[51]

This reality check spoke to larger issues related to the human rights project. Even if the debate focused on elaborating specific legal standards article by article, these allowed plenty of room for debate about their wider meaning. One of these debates was about the meaning of "civilized society." Senegal and Colombia had jointly submitted a proposed paragraph for inclusion in the preamble, which read "Convinced that the existence of racial barriers is repugnant to the ideals of any civilized society." A number of states asked the sponsors what the meaning of "civilized society" was. It did not have a standard meaning in terms of law and there was, according to one delegation, "probably no universally applicable definition of the term."[52] Senegal provided a remarkable explanation outlining the relationship between power and principle and, by extension, what constituted political legitimacy in international affairs:

> 'civilized society' meant any normative society guided by an ethical outlook whose fundamental general principles were laid down in the Universal Declaration of Human Rights; its opposite was savage society, which was dominated by the idea of might is right.[53]

Tanzania were rather active in UN human rights debates in the formative period leading up to 1968 but that their proposals to expand, for example, fact-finding mechanisms in Southern Africa did not go unopposed by other Global South actors, who worked toward allowing a broader application of such human rights monitoring procedures. This can be seen, for example, in the 1967 debates in the Commission on Human Rights and in ECOSOC.

[51] Mr. Waldron-Ramsey (Tanzania), UN General Assembly, Third Committee, 20th session, 1301st meeting, October 12, 1965, p. 71.

[52] Mrs. Mantzoulinos (Greece), UN General Assembly, Third Committee, 20th session, 1300th meeting, October 12, 1965, p. 63.

[53] Mr. Sy (Senegal), UN General Assembly, Third Committee, 20th session, 1301st meeting, October 12, 1965, p. 71.

Its meaning was still regarded as uncertain, and therefore, the sponsors, now joined by Brazil, decided to neutralize the issue and insert the word 'human' instead so the negotiations could proceed. This was the easy solution.[54] The interchangeable use of the words "civilized" and "human" raises an interesting question, namely whether the evolution of human rights with its notion of universality is the twentieth-century expression of the civilizing process?[55] The issue did not disappear with the amended text for the preamble. It arose in the final statements after the Third Committee adopted the Convention. Here it was presented as one "of the great pioneering instruments by means of which the United Nations was laying the groundwork for civilized life on an ever-increasing scale."[56] International law was awarded a unique role and purpose. If the civilizing and pioneering nature of the Convention was recognized, what was implied?

The quest for universality is one important element. The debate was not merely negotiating a legal instrument with universal standards. The process of reaching that point meant that the aspired universality of endorsement created a strategy aimed at disciplining the proceedings to avoid a politicized outcome that the Afro-Asian Bloc and others believed would undermine the whole effort to prepare a Convention on racial discrimination. The international law-making ambition was another element. This made the negotiations over sovereignty a central piece of the puzzle. Sovereignty was both guarded and transcended. The 1965 debate on racial discrimination was mainly weighted in favor of the latter. The defense of sovereignty, which traditionally was a dominant feature of UN debates, appeared weakened. There was both a formal aspect and a dynamic point involved. The formal point was linked to international law. States would, on becoming party to the Convention, accept obligations where they were not only accountable to their own people but also would "assume a legal responsibility to the international community."[57] Jordan expressed this more dynamic interpretation most eloquently when arguing that:

---

[54] This was adopted. The preamble read, "Convinced that the existence of racial barriers is repugnant to the ideals of any human society."

[55] Norbert Elias (2000) (original in 1939), *The Civilizing Process.* London.

[56] Mr. Macdonald (Canada), UN General Assembly, Third Committee, 20th session, 1374th meeting, December 15, 1965, p. 504.

[57] Miss Hart (New Zealand), UN General Assembly, Third Committee, 20th session, 1347th meeting, November 18, 1965, p. 340.

The meaning of sovereignty had changed. It had lost its absolute character. By joining the United Nations, States lost their competence to give an a priori interpretation of sovereignty. Jordan did not consider that its sovereignty would be in any way diminished if it acceded to a convention on racial discrimination which had implementation clauses of reasonable magnitude, designed to safeguard human dignity.[58]

It was perhaps not all member states that would go this far in their understanding of sovereignty. It illustrated, however, the extent to which the efforts to eliminate racial discrimination during the 1960s had taken a crack at the hard nut of international law-making – the problem of sovereignty.

Another pioneering element came from what one delegate called "accelerating history,"[59] namely the process of decolonization that had so rapidly transformed the United Nations. It was a historical process that was highlighted by a number of states. "It had spurred the United Nations," stated the Belgian delegate, adding:

the movement for the liberation of the formerly dependent countries had had a determining influence on the progress achieved in the field of human rights, although during that historic phase, the struggle to protect individuals against arbitrary action by Governments might have suffered a momentary eclipse.[60]

Then the Belgian delegate gave special mention to Ghana and the Philippines for "having envisaged practical means of guaranteeing the rights of the individual against arbitrary governmental action."[61] They were among the leading actors in this debate and their joint and coordinated efforts actually laid the foundation for the UN human rights treaty body monitoring system in existence today.

Ghana's and the Philippines' major concern regarding the outcome of the negotiations was whether the Convention would become a "Dead Letter" law. This concern shaped the negotiation strategy, and the many compromises made, both regarding the substantive articles and the

---

[58] Mr. Sharaf (Jordan), UN General Assembly, Third Committee, 20th session, 1347th meeting, November 18, 1965, p. 337.

[59] Mr. Beltramino (Argentina), UN General Assembly, Third Committee, 20th session, 1355th meeting, November 26, 1965, p. 385.

[60] Mr. Cochaux (Belgium), UN General Assembly, Third Committee, 20th session, 1349th meeting, November 19, 1965, p. 345.

[61] Ibid., p. 345.

measures of implementation. It was linked to the need for universality of support for the provisions in the Convention. This blended firm principles with a sense of moderation that sought consensus. Ghana and the Philippines were the lead proponents of this approach with numerical backing from the Afro-Asian group on occasions where Cold War controversies could lead "ultimately to a convention which was more of a political propaganda sheet than an attack on racial discrimination."[62]

An example of this played out after the United States and Brazil sponsored an amendment that would secure the inclusion of anti-Semitism in the Convention. This was countered by a proposal by the Soviet Union to include a mention of Nazism and neo-Nazism, which would provide a degree of legitimacy to their often-repeated attacks on West Germany. It led to a heated exchange involving the United States, the Soviet Union, Israel, Sudan and others that risked derailing the debate. As the controversy flared more widely, the Middle East politics became part of the discussion. The Sudanese delegate made the following association: "For the Arabs, Israel was what South Africa was to the African nationalists and Zionism was the equivalent of apartheid."[63] This pattern of accusations would continue in the following years with a detrimental impact, but at this juncture, it was defused. The Afro-Asian group used their numerical weight to announce that they would vote against all proposals and amendments to the preamble and new articles in an effort to stop the controversy.[64] It meant a return to the draft from the Commission on Human Rights. Whatever the historical significance was behind the claim to include anti-Semitism, it risked blocking progress on the Convention. It could also lead to an article with a flawed definition of the existing forms of racial discrimination. The diplomacy of negotiating universality was also an exercise in diffusion or neutralization when political controversy was instrumentalized for certain purposes. As the Ghanaian delegate explained:

The references proposed in the amendments were simply out of place in the Convention, and, since it was claimed that the formula 'all forms of racial discrimination' would cover any new manifestations which might arise in the future, there

---

[62] Miss Aguta (Nigeria), UN General Assembly, Third Committee, 20th session, 1313th meeting, October 21, 1965, p. 123.

[63] Mr. Abdel-Rahim (Sudan), UN General Assembly, Third Committee, 20th session, 1312th meeting, October 20, 1965, p. 116.

[64] Mrs. Warzazi (Morocco), UN General Assembly, Third Committee, 20th session, 1310th meeting, October 19, 1965, p. 109.

was no reason why it should not be considered adequate to cover anti-Semitism, Nazism, and so forth.[65]

Another contentious issue regarding the substantive articles was the provision in Article 4 incurring an obligation to prosecute racist expressions and organizations. This debate echoed the debate in 1963, in which concerns regarding the freedom of expression and upholding the principles of the Universal Declaration of Human Rights were raised. The outcome in 1965 did not differ, and a number of Western and Latin American member states would again state their critique and reservations over this alleged infringement.

The substantive articles were finalized relatively fast. It was instead the implementation measures that dominated the debate and would be a pioneering element of the Convention. Ghana and the Philippines prepared the drafts that guided the negotiations. The significance came from the recognition that these measures "would no doubt constitute a precedent for future conventions relating to human rights."[66] The motives behind the widespread backing for implementation measures differed among states. The Soviet Union saw the implementation measures of the Convention as what would ensure respect for the 1960 *Declaration on the Granting of Independence to Colonial Countries and Peoples* and the 1963 *Declaration on Elimination of All Forms of Racial Discrimination* – both documents that the Soviet Union gave particular emphasis. The Ivory Coast argued that without these measures, "the Convention would be like a body without a head or a worker without tools."[67] The implementation measures were important because they moved human rights into the areas of monitoring and accountability, without which a convention would hardly be different from a declaration.

The proposal evolved around the creation of an eighteen-person Committee for the Convention. It would serve as an impartial body with independent experts and as a means to ascertain that states were applying the provisions of the Convention. The Committee would receive state reports and would report relevant information to other bodies in the UN system. It was also proposed that there should be a body

[65] Mr. Lamptey (Ghana), UN General Assembly, Third Committee, 20th session, 1313th meeting, October 21, 1965, p. 122.

[66] Mrs. Ramaholimihaso (Madagascar), UN General Assembly, Third Committee, 20th session, 1345th meeting, November 17, 1965, p. 326.

[67] Mrs. Berrah (Ivory Coast), UN General Assembly, Third Committee, 20th session, 1345th meeting, November 17, 1965, p. 323.

responsible for conciliation between state parties to the Convention in case of disputes. Finally, an individual right to petition was outlined. The monitoring Committee was adopted but the conciliation idea was eventually downplayed, although a referral to the International Court of Justice for deciding on state disputes was maintained in the final version.

The right to petition sparked the most controversy. It was controversial because it directly challenged state sovereignty. The Western states, Latin American and many of the African states wanted a strong provision. Others – including Communist countries and France – were pushing for a separate protocol. As France explained, "the new idea of the right of petition would thus enter into international law without impairing the mandatory nature of the Convention as a whole. Since the protocol would be separate from the Convention, its ratification could be made optional."[68] It was hardly a new idea. France had actually promoted the idea themselves during the 1948 negotiations on the Universal Declaration. The French proposal was not acceptable to the sponsors. As Ghana explained, a separate protocol would mean a separate ratification process, which would invite States to ignore this element. An optional clause inside the Convention would involve a separate position on the issue of petition but ensure ratification of the whole Convention and facilitate an easier way of changing a position on the matter. As compromises were sought, the proposal was watered down regarding the functions of the monitoring Committee that would receive petitions. Lebanon most firmly argued against the weak compromise. The draft presented would:

introduce a system of very limited scope which would not meet the desired objective of imposing on States a moral obligation to eliminate all forms of racial discrimination in their territory. The committee envisaged would in fact be little more than a post office.[69]

The "post office" Committee would only receive petitions, inform states and summarize them in an annual report. The proposal by Lebanon called for the establishment of a system in which the Committee would deal with the complaints received and make its own set of recommendations. It would allow a more dynamic treaty practice for this human rights convention and this was seen as a bare minimum by many states. It was a solution far from what was preferred by two Latin American delegations

---

[68] Mr. Combal (France), UN General Assembly, Third Committee, 20th session, 1357th meeting, November 25, 1965, p. 393.

[69] Miss Tabbara (Lebanon), UN General Assembly, Third Committee, 20th session, 1362nd meeting, December 2, 1965, p. 427.

that wanted a world court of human rights. Highlighting the challenges in its international human rights policy, the United Kingdom, which had not signed up to the right of petition in the European Convention on Human Rights, found itself in the contradictory position of being unable to vote in favor while hoping that the article "would command a large majority."[70] On December 2, 1965, the Third Committee approved the Lebanese amendments. For the first time, a right to petition was introduced in the United Nations human rights system. It had been a contentious issue since the 1940s. Race created the new precedent.

The final controversy was over the "colonialist clause" and also linked to the right to petition. Some African states wanted to secure the right to petition for people living in colonial territories and found support from the Communist Bloc. The states with colonial possessions were unwilling to grant a direct right of petition to individuals in these territories as this bypassed the state remedial procedures in the process of petitioning the Committee on Elimination of Racial Discrimination. It was a well-designed ideological setup for linking racial discrimination to colonialism and promoting it as such under the banner of universalism. There was a strong pushback led by the United Kingdom, who claimed it was directed against them, since a country like South Africa would never sign on to the Convention. The proposal was not successful for a variety of reasons and this drew a sharp response from Egypt, linking it to the Western arguments against Article 4 on prosecution of racist expressions:

The Committee had also been told of the existence of certain liberties in the Western world; yet when article 15 of the draft Convention had come up for discussion, the colonialist Powers had decided that freedom of expression was not for export.[71]

At the end of the negotiations, the member states could reflect on the meaning of completing the first major international human rights convention. The significance was not lost on anyone. It was a major achievement for the leading facilitators. The final statement by Ghana reflected the transnational experience of the color line symbolized in their President Kwame Nkrumah. He had gone to the United States as a young student in the 1930s and had come "face to face with racial discrimination." He had also experienced "the subtlety of racial discrimination"

---

[70] Lady Gaitskell (UK), UN General Assembly, Third Committee, 20th session, 1363rd meeting, December 2, 1965, p. 431.
[71] Mr. Abdul-Hamid (Egypt), UN General Assembly, Third Committee, 20th session, 1374th meeting, December 15, 1965, p. 507.

when he went to the United Kingdom in 1945 to study and ended up as an organizer of the 5th Pan-African Congress in Manchester. Nkrumah hosted the 1958 Accra Conference for independent African states, where human rights were made central to their political agenda.[72] Against this backdrop, it is little surprise that Ghana felt that the adoption of the Convention on Elimination of All Forms of Racial Discrimination by the General Assembly was "its finest hour."[73]

The race issue had engaged the Soviet Union in the human rights project in a substantial way, and in the view of the Soviet Union, the "Third Committee had scored a brilliant victory," but they saw the actual negotiation process in a very different light. The drafting had been "obstructed by many obstacles raised by the imperialist and colonialist powers," but this would not have a lasting effect according to the Soviet delegate because "The future . . . would unmask the hypocrites."[74] It certainly would, but not in the way the Soviet delegate expected. The International Convention on the Elimination of All Forms of Racial Discrimination was adopted unanimously by the General Assembly on December 21, 1965. Its immediate significance would become evident the following year when the International Covenants on Civil and Political Rights and on Economic, Social and Cultural Rights were completed and adopted.

The 1966 Covenants on human rights

During the 1966 Covenants debate, the International Convention on Elimination of all Forms of Racial Discrimination was referred to a total of 120 times by forty-nine different member states. It was a constant point of reference throughout the debate.[75] The Convention on racial

---

72 See Alex Quaison-Sackey (1963), *Africa Unbound. Reflections of an African Statesman.* New York, pp. 70–73. Quaison-Sackey was the Ghanaian Ambassador to the United Nations. In 1964, he was the first African to become President of the General Assembly.

73 Mr. Lamptey (Ghana), UN General Assembly, 20th session, 1406th meeting, December 21, 1965, pp. 10–11. Two months later, in February 1966, Nkrumah was ousted in a military coup.

74 Mr. Chkhikvadze (the USSR), UN General Assembly, Third Committee, 20th session, 1373rd meeting, December 14, 1965, p. 501.

75 It was only a very small minority of these cases where the Convention was not referred to as a positive precedent to be applied in the drafting of the Covenants. It was mainly France and India that argued against the use of the Convention on racial discrimination as a precedent. The Communist Bloc tended to use sovereignty arguments and the denial of the individual having a status in international law in their attempts to counter the proposals they opposed.

discrimination was the precedent that inspired the completion of the Covenants.

By the start of the Covenants debate, Bulgaria, Ghana, Pakistan and Ecuador had ratified the Convention. The Convention had opened for signature on March 7, 1966, with nine states signing the Convention on that day – the majority being the Communist states of Eastern Europe.[76] Declaring a position on the Convention on racial discrimination had become a measure of credibility going into the Covenants debate in 1966. The American UN Ambassador Arthur Goldberg lobbied intensely with the Johnson administration to approve U.S. signature of the Convention. After a meeting with the President in September 1966 where the Convention on racial discrimination was discussed, Goldberg succeeded. The United States signed the Convention on Elimination of All Forms of Racial Discrimination on September 28, 1966, the same week that the Third Committee started its 1966 session.

The Soviets declared a position beyond signing the Convention on the first day. In the period that followed, the Soviet press ran a number of stories about the Convention.[77] In May 1966, the Soviet foreign policy journal *International Affairs* published its first article ever on human rights. The article "The Nations Repudiate Racism" was written by the Soviet delegate to the Third Committee. It gave an account of the negotiation process at the UN and targeted the United States and South Africa for its racial policies – for the latter aptly calling apartheid "from the womb to the tomb" racism – linking as many times before the issue to colonialism, Nazism and Western hypocrisy. The journal article was a propaganda piece that downplayed the Afro-Asian countries significant contribution and celebrated the efforts by the USSR and other Communist states. The publication of articles on international human rights debates in the journal and in the Soviet press was still a noteworthy new trend.[78]

The debate in the Third Committee opened with the Draft Covenant on Economic, Social and Cultural Rights and the focus was the implementation mechanisms. The debate went back to 1950, when it had been

---

[76] The nine states were Belarus, Brazil, Central African Republic, Greece, Israel, the Philippines, Poland, the Soviet Union and Ukraine.

[77] Airgram from American Embassy, Moscow, April 12, 1966, "UN Convention on Racial Discrimination as a Device for Future Soviet Propaganda," U.S. National Archives (College Park, MD), Soc 14, Central Foreign Policy Files, 1964–1966, Box 3203.

[78] See V. Chkhikvadze (1966), "The Nations Repudiate Racism," *International Affairs*, May, no. 5, pp. 49–54. The journal was started in 1954 and was published in English and French language editions from 1955.

FIGURE 4. Arthur Goldberg, The U.S. Ambassador to the United Nations, signing the Convention on Elimination of All Forms of Racial Discrimination on
September 28, 1966, in the office of UN Secretary-General U Thant (seated right).
Goldberg lobbied President Lyndon B. Johnson to approve a U.S. signature before
the vital 1966 UN General Assembly began as a sign of commitment to strengthen
the U.S. standing in the final debates on the two human rights Covenants.
Source: United Nations Photos

decided to split the drafting of the Human Rights Covenant into two separate documents – a Covenant on civil and political rights and a Covenant
on economic, social and cultural rights. The decision was criticized by
the Communist states in the early stages of the 1966 debate. The historic
reference was an attempt to legitimize a current concern by these states,
namely avoiding strong implementation measures.

It was here that the Convention on Racial Discrimination was first
used as a precedent. Both Italy and the United States submitted a proposal on the establishment of a monitoring Committee for the Covenant
on Economic, Social and Cultural Rights. They were both modeled on
the Committee established in the Convention on racial discrimination,
though the United States applied the most elaborate measures for the
functioning of the Committee. It made the United States the strongest
proponent of the most advanced implementation measures on economic,

social and cultural rights. It was a position that had been maturing inside the Johnson Administration in the weeks and months leading up to the UN Covenants debate.[79] The Communist states were strongly resisting this proposal. Hungary and Czechoslovakia used sovereignty and noninterference as arguments against establishing a Committee for the Covenant. The Soviet Union argued that it had always contended that creation of special bodies should be avoided – even though this had not been its position in the 1960 debate on colonialism or in the 1965 debate on the Convention on racial discrimination. They wanted the state reports on economic, social and cultural rights to be a matter for the UN Economic and Social Council (ECOSOC) instead. This would limit the attention to the implementation of human rights due to the broad focus and heavy agenda of the ECOSOC. It was also a body consisting of and controlled by member states and not one with, at least in principle, independent experts such as the committees established under the Convention – known as treaty bodies.

The developing countries were divided on the issue of a Committee – some were in favor of a Committee because it was a practical method to secure a dynamic implementation, others expressed great concerns about the financial burdens on their countries in funding participation in such a system. The Communist opposition and this division meant that the support to the proposal for a Committee did not appear sufficiently strong and therefore the United States and Italy decided to withdraw their respective proposals before they were put to the vote. It was one of the few occasions where the model of the Convention on racial discrimination was not applied but it had been used strategically to push toward a Committee model and had placed the Communist Bloc on the defensive in areas that allegedly were close to their interests. It is beyond doubt that in this decisive debate on a system to strengthen state accountability for the implementation of economic, social and cultural rights, the United States was by far the most progressive member state, while the Soviet Union and the other Communist states undermined the efforts to promote these rights. This had a long-term impact on the international human rights system. It raises interesting questions about the Cold War human rights

---

[79] During these preparations, the U.S. position had been discussed and approved at a high level – possibly as high as Secretary of State Dean Rusk. The U.S. position is evident from the UN debate and from archive material in the U.S., British and Danish Foreign Ministry archives. The best documentation exists in the British National Archives (Kew), FO 371/189938, including the draft U.S. proposal. See also U.S. National Archives (College Park, MD), RG 59/250/7/20/4, Box 3207, Folder SOC14-4.

story, namely who supported what and what was the nature of this support. To argue that there was a clear divide where the West supported civil and political rights and the Communist East supported economic and social rights is too simplistic, bordering on misleading.[80]

There is little doubt that the adoption of the Convention on racial discrimination created a precedent for adoption of international legal instruments in the field of human rights and provided an incentive to complete the Covenants. In addition, there were five areas where the impact of the International Convention on Elimination of All Forms of Racial Discrimination as a precedent was noticeable, with the eighteen-person human rights Committee and the right to petition being the most significant.[81]

The proposal for an eighteen-person Committee to oversee implementation of the Covenant on Civil and Political Rights was put forward and this time it prevailed. The arguments varied from those stating that without the Committee, the Covenant would be a mere reiteration of the Universal Declaration and "the Third Committee would have wasted fifteen years"[82] to a more dynamic understanding of the Committee's role in international relations. On the latter, Iraq argued that "States were being drawn irresistibly towards interdependence and the United Nations had the task of reconciling the search for an international order with the principle of State sovereignty." This inspired Iraq to support the proposed human rights Committee as it could undertake "an effort to facilitate an exchange between the United Nations and its member states," the Iraqi statement continued, "The world was at present developing so rapidly and changes taking place were so far-reaching that action must be taken immediately."[83] Other delegates also supported this view, seeing human rights in a strategic light, with Jamaica arguing, "there was no better starting point for the sacrifice of a portion of sovereignty than in the field of human rights."[84]

---

[80] For more on this point, see Daniel J. Whelan and Jack Donnelly (2007), "The West, Economic and Social Rights, and the Global Human Rights Regime: Setting the Record Straight," *Human Rights Quarterly*, vol. 29, no. 4, pp. 908–949.

[81] The other three were: (a) the states eligible to become parties to the covenant, (b) amendment procedures and (c) involvement of NGOs.

[82] Mrs. Barish (Costa Rica), UN General Assembly, Third Committee, 21st session, 1416th meeting, November 8, 1966, p. 227.

[83] Mrs. Afnan (Iraq), UN General Assembly, Third Committee, 21st session, 1417th meeting, November 8, 1966, p. 237.

[84] Mrs. Robinson (Jamaica), UN General Assembly, Third Committee, 21st session, 1417th meeting, November 8, 1966, p. 238.

There was greater momentum behind the creation of a Human Rights Committee for the Covenant on Civil and Political Rights and that meant that the idea could not be discarded. The challenge was over the scope of its functions and here the right to petition was a decisive battleground as it was "both the central theme of the Covenant and the main obstacle to its adoption."[85] Those critical of the idea again evoked sovereignty and denied that individuals were subjects of international law. This met with criticism from many sides. The Ghanaian delegate elaborated on this in a way that was a reminder of the crucial role the country had played the previous year in negotiating the implementation measures for the Convention on racial discrimination. Reflecting on the nature of what was at stake, the Ghanaian delegate said:

It was in the interest of the Governments not to take shelter behind a narrow conception of their sovereignty and behind the principle of non-intervention in order to escape the obligation to preserve the civil and political rights of man. There was, in fact, such a close relationship between human rights and peace and stability that any State which sought to inhibit the rights of its nationals was creating the conditions for its own overthrow.[86]

There were other states who also saw the bigger picture regarding the right to petition. The Canadian delegate described how this right had been included in the *Declaration on the Granting of Independence to Colonial Countries and Peoples* and in the Convention on racial discrimination. This was again a precedent argument. The Canadian delegate used this as a foundation for an argument in favor of the right to petition as human rights:

had become an accepted part of twentieth-century thinking . . . It was essential to continue moving the concept of human rights from the purely moral and ethical level to the world of law, politics and reality.[87]

This was an accurate assessment of what was at stake. The UN human rights project had barely evolved since the Universal Declaration of Human Rights had been adopted in 1948. It was the responsibility of the legal instruments to take the aims of the UN Charter and the Universal Declaration to a different plane in terms of legal accountability and

---

[85] Mr. Dombo (Ghana), UN General Assembly, Third Committee, 21st session, 1438th meeting, November 29, 1966, p. 365.

[86] Mr. Dombo (Ghana), UN General Assembly, Third Committee, 21st session, 1418th meeting, November 7, 1966, p. 245.

[87] Mr. Macdonald (Canada), UN General Assembly, Third Committee, 21st session, 1439th meeting, November 30, 1966, p. 371.

state responsibility. The Convention on racial discrimination from 1965 had been the first step toward this.

The Communist Bloc reacted strongly against introducing the right to petition in the Covenant. It was a response clearly on the defensive. It left little space for a dynamic interpretation of the Covenants or evolution of human rights by developing practice in the field. It was also a highly opportunistic and incoherent admission after the strong support for the Convention on racial discrimination expressed by all Communist states in 1965. This did not go unnoticed. The U.K. delegate quoted a Polish statement from the 1965 negotiations. Here, Poland had made a strong statement on the political importance of the Convention on racial discrimination. It "marked a new stage" in the history of the United Nations as the Convention "established a system of control and implementation which could serve as a precedent for the drafting of further conventions and for the settlement of international disputes in general."[88] It was an appropriate and well-timed reminder from the United Kingdom. It also showed how closely states were monitoring each other's positions as part of the evolving human rights diplomacy. The Communist opposition was an indication of the difficulty of securing universal endorsement of the Covenant. The Convention on racial discrimination had included an optional clause on the right to petition inside the Convention itself. This was proposed again in 1966 but there was still opposition and others argued – as in 1965 – for the right to petition to be included in a separate protocol. The debate continued but it was difficult to resolve the issue. Lebanon then called for a vote whether the right to petition should be in a separate protocol.

In a rather arbitrary and confused procedure, a vote suddenly took place, and with forty-one states in favor and thirty-nine states against (16 abstentions), a new international instrument had been introduced. After more wrangling, it became the Optional Protocol to the Covenant on Civil and Political Rights and its right to petition provision was modeled on the optional clause in the Convention on racial discrimination. The problem was solved but it did not leave many happy as the split vote indicated. It also offered an escape clause as regards accountability.

---

[88] Quoted by Lady Gaitskell (UK), UN General Assembly, Third Committee, 21st session, 1415th meeting, November 7, 1966, p. 223. Gaitskell was quoting from statement by Mr. Resich (Poland), UN General Assembly, Third Committee, 20th session, 1373rd meeting, December 14, 1965, pp. 499–500.

It was not on all accounts that the Convention on racial discrimination served as precedent. There were two areas where there was a noteworthy difference between the Convention on racial discrimination and the Covenants, namely regarding the number of ratifications required for entry into force of the Covenants and the referral of state disputes to the International Court of Justice.

The Convention on racial discrimination required ratifications from twenty-seven countries before it would enter into force. This number was deemed appropriate to allow a critical mass to recruit members for the eighteen-person Committee since the members would be nominated from State parties to the Convention. The same procedure could have been applied for the Covenants – indeed it would have been logical as an eighteen-person Committee was to be established for the Covenant on Civil and Political Rights. France undermined this potential precedent. It proposed that "the ideal universality" would require fifty ratifications of the Covenants, since "it would not be reasonable to go below a figure which was already less than one half of the number of States Members of the United Nations."[89] It was a rather arbitrary line of reasoning and can, in light of other French interventions in the debate, be seen as a spoiler argument to restrict the entry into force of the Covenants. The delegate from Chile was among the very critical respondents to this proposal, stating that a requirement of fifty ratifications "if adopted, it might well doom the instrument to failure." Others shared this sentiment but the overbidding from France still had effect since the compromise reached was to require thirty-five ratifications for the Covenants to enter into force.

The deletion of referral to the International Court of Justice was the other significant area where the precedent of the Convention on racial discrimination was not followed. The International Court of Justice was part of the 1965 Convention but was heavily criticized and omitted from the draft Covenants. The reason was its ruling on the South West Africa case against South Africa issued in July 1966 after "seven months of deliberation and five years of litigation."[90] It was widely expected that the ruling would go against South Africa. Both the United States and the United Kingdom had discussed their contingency plans for dealing

[89] Mr. Paolini (France), UN General Assembly, Third Committee, 21st session, 1407th meeting, October 28, 1966, p. 170.
[90] Irwin (2010), "Apartheid on Trial," p. 636.

with a decision where the rule of law would have to be upheld against the interests of the "White man in Southern Africa." The surprise came with the ruling – an 8–7 verdict – that claimed that the applicants did not have sufficient legal interest in the South West Africa mandate. It let South Africa off the hook of international justice and the "decision not only reversed the logic, content and implication of the Court's 1962 ruling [where the Court accepted the merits of the case]; it shattered the idea that the Court would act as an agent of transitional justice."[91] The Senegalese Foreign Minister leveled a particularly critical assessment of the Court, stating that "The only interest deemed worthy of legal protection, according to the logic of the Court – a logic that was not formulated, but logic just the same – is the interest of South Africa."[92] It was a shameful moment for international law that would affect the Court's reputation for years to come.

The ruling also meant that the International Court of Justice came under severe attack in the Third Committee, with its authority and credibility being challenged. The first time this criticism was used directly in the negotiations was in the attacks over establishing a Committee of experts for the Covenant on Economic, Social and Cultural Rights where the critique of the International Court of Justice played a role in undermining this proposal. The Tanzanian delegate was rather blunt in stating that "the peoples of Africa had recently seen an example of what 'experts' were capable of, and they would never forget what the Judges of the International Court of Justice had done to the people of South West Africa."[93]

The critique reappeared in the negotiations over the conciliation components and state-to-state disputes for the Covenant on Civil and Political Rights. The Soviet Union again used the ICJ ruling in their arguments to weaken the implementation measures and claimed that the Court "had

---

[91] Ibid., p. 636. For an insightful account on the problematic internal process at the Court that led to the controversial ruling, see Victor Kattan (2015), "Decolonizing the International Court of Justice: The Experience of Judge Sir Muhammad Zafrulla Khan in the South West Africa Cases," *Asian Journal of International Law*, vol. 5, no. 2, pp. 310–355.

[92] Mr. Thiam (Senegal), UN General Assembly, 21st session, 1414th meeting, September 23, 1966, p. 25.

[93] Mrs. Malecela (Tanzania), UN General Assembly, Third Committee, 21st session, 1401st meeting, October 1, 1966, p. 140. The Soviet Union also used the status of the International Court of Justice Judges as supposedly "a body of experts" to undermine the Committee proposal for the Convention on Economic, Social and Cultural Rights. See 1399th meeting, p. 127.

jeopardized its reputation for all African and Asian states."[94] The Soviet Union and many other critics wanted all references to the International Court of Justice to be deleted. Among the normal supporters of the International Court of Justice there was also strong criticism; however, they were able to separate the specific ruling from the Court's purpose and function. Uruguay stated that even though the Court "had handed down a regrettably mistaken decision, that was no reason to eliminate all reference to it, especially since its prestige could be restored through the election of better judges."[95] Two different viewpoints crystallized over the International Court of Justice. One viewpoint saw merit in its inclusion and regarded it as a "retrograde step to remove a reference to the principal judicial organ of the United Nations from a document which owed its very existence to the United Nations."[96] The other viewpoint targeted the failings of the International Court of Justice ruling over South West Africa to argue the case that "the human rights committee should not be judicial in character."[97] It was the latter viewpoint, most strongly argued by the Communist Bloc and some African countries, that prevailed. The judges of the International Court of Justice had played a significant role in undercutting the efforts to give juridical clout to the UN human rights machinery. This was not a failing of the Convention on racial discrimination as a precedent vis-à-vis the Covenants. It was an external factor that greatly affected the faith in international justice as a means of securing reasonable legal and political outcomes. The disillusionment affected not just global race politics but also the UN human rights diplomacy and that trumped the precedent from the Convention on racial discrimination.

On December 7, 1966, after lengthy negotiations, the Third Committee voted and adopted unanimously both Covenants. This was followed by another unanimous vote in the General Assembly on December 16.[98] A number of statements following the vote reflected on the

[94] Mr. Nasinovsky (the USSR), UN General Assembly, Third Committee, 21st session, 1429th meeting, November 21, 1966, p. 303.
[95] Mr. Gros Espiell (Uruguay), UN General Assembly, Third Committee, 21st session, 1429th meeting, November 21, 1966, p. 305.
[96] Mr. Macdonald (Canada), UN General Assembly, Third Committee, 21st session, 1434th meeting, November 25, 1966, p. 335.
[97] Mr. Nasinovsky (the USSR), UN General Assembly, Third Committee, 21st session, 1434th meeting, November 25, 1966, p. 335.
[98] On Monday, December 19, 1966, both Covenants opened for signature. On the first day, they were signed by Jamaica, the Philippines, Costa Rica, Honduras and Israel. It was a very different group of countries to those who had been the first two sign the

deeper meaning of the achievement. Cyprus assessed the significance most poignantly:

We are perhaps too close to the event to be able to evaluate its full significance. There can be no doubt, however, that the international instruments which we adopt today will open up a new era in the history of man. A new, an additional, charter will come into existence, bringing the field of human rights within the concept of the rule of law. The moral obligations for respect of human rights will become a legal duty.[99]

He continued by looking forward to the 1968 human rights year:

We earnestly trust that the International Conference on Human Rights, scheduled for 1968 to commemorate the twentieth anniversary of the proclamation of the Universal Declaration of Human Rights, will duly recognize the significance and importance of the adoption of the Covenants on Human Rights as marking a new era, a new epoch, in the development of positive international concern for human rights.[100]

It was not unreasonable to express a sense of hope in December 1966. The First World Conference on Human Rights in 1968 would be a noteworthy event but the many challenges faced in getting to the completed Covenants did not subside. The jury was still out on whether the 1968 International Year for Human Rights would signify a new era or whether it would just be the end of a very long beginning.

The UN negotiations from 1962 to 1966 that led to the first three major human rights conventions being adopted reflect the creation of new legal meaning – what Robert Cover calls *jurisgenesis*. This happened as two normative universes represented by the Cold War and decolonization converged. Human rights came into existence as binding international law as a result of the rapidly evolving political dynamics between East–West and North–South. In the context of decolonization, the meeting of race and human rights became an intersection between past, present and future in world affairs. The process elevated the concept of human rights from one that had been on the fringe of international affairs to one that could not be ignored. It was a process that the superpowers – so dominant in the military and economic spheres – could not control. It was a triumph of meaning over might and exemplifies the point made

Convention on racial discrimination. Cyprus signed the Covenant on Civil and Political Rights on this day, while Colombia signed both on December 21.

[99] Mr. Rossides (Cyprus), UN General Assembly, 21st session, 1495th meeting, December 16, 1966, p. 16.

[100] Ibid., p. 16.

by Robert Cover that "the uncontrolled character of meaning exercises a destabilizing influence upon power."[101]

This recognition is important to the diplomatic processes and to the overall human rights story. Neither the two superpowers nor countries such as the United Kingdom and France were very interested in the expansion of human rights into international law but it happened anyway – despite their unease and lack of political readiness when the process took off in 1962. Human rights would gradually become a parameter in the Cold War competition and the big powers would have to adapt to this new reality. The important point is that they were pushed forward to this situation by smaller states, especially from the Global South. It is perhaps a poignant illustration of the importance of the United Nations at this time.

It is, however, necessary to emphasize that this story was not only shaped by racial discrimination, although this served as an important foundation. Religion was a very significant companion to this transformation. Religion played a major part in the human rights breakthrough of the 1960s – although this story ended with a different outcome. If the focus on race had been a challenge to the United States, the focus on religion turned the tables and shed a revealing light on the realities of life in the Soviet Union.

[101] Robert Cover (1995), "Nomos and Narrative," *Narrative, Violence and the Law. The Essays of Robert Cover.* Edited by Martha Minow, Michael Ryan and Austin Sarat, Ann Arbor, MI, p. 112.

5

"The hymn of hate"

The failed convention on elimination of all forms of religious intolerance, 1962–1967

"Who would decide where the dividing line between a believer and a fanatic lay?"

Mr. Jamal Baroody (Saudi Arabia), UN General Assembly,
Third Committee, November 2, 1962[1]

Race and religion together transformed the role of human rights in international affairs during the 1960s. They were political Achilles' heels for the two superpowers. The global struggle for racial equality challenged the legitimacy of United States leadership on the world stage because of the system of racial segregation across the Southern states. This dynamic had an impact on domestic political reform in the United States in the 1960s.[2] The issue of religious freedom was a direct challenge to Communist societies and their capacity for reform proved significantly lower. There were states that had an interest in raising these issues in the international system and each of the superpowers could use them as pressure points against their Cold War adversary. From 1964 to 1965, the United Kingdom made the Convention on Elimination of All Forms of Religious Intolerance the major priority in their human rights strategy, seeing it as part of their Cold War diplomacy.[3] It played an important role in the U.K. policy change that from 1966 would recognize human

---

[1] Mr. Baroody (Saudi Arabia), UN General Assembly, Third Committee, 17th session, 1171st meeting, November 2, 1962, p. 193.
[2] Mary Dudziak (1988), "Desegregation as a Cold War Imperative," *Stanford Law Review*, vol. 41, pp. 61–120; Mary Dudziak (2002), *Cold War Civil Rights. Race and the Image of American Democracy*. Princeton, NJ; Thomas Borstelmann (2001), *The Cold War and the Color Line*. Cambridge, MA.
[3] See British National Archives (Kew), Box FO 61/226, "Human Rights: Religious Intolerance."

rights as an issue of legitimate international concern. They were soon followed by the United States and other Western states. They were not, however, the initiators of this process.

The initiative came from the Global South and illustrates how race and religion intersected both with the Cold War and decolonization. The nature of the Cold War conflict called for a new theology.[4] This inspired change in religious doctrines, institutions and in interreligious relations such as ecumenical work. Decolonization provided a North–South dimension. If we are able, as Matthew Connelly has proposed, to take off the "Cold War lens," race and religion emerge in a different light during the same period. The racial and religious differences that could emerge with the new system of states raised political concerns from the 1950s as "international conflict along racial and religious lines was an appalling prospect even if the communists kept out of it."[5]

Negotiated during the 1960s, the Convention on Elimination of All Forms of Religious Intolerance was arguably the most ambitious attempt in the twentieth century to make religion a subject of international law. The story of this process, however, has never been adequately told and the draft Convention appears largely to have been forgotten in contemporary research on religion, human rights and international affairs.[6] On

---

[4] See William Inboden (2009), *Religion and American Foreign Policy 1945–1960*. Cambridge, pp. 21–22. See also Andrew Preston (2012), *Sword of the Spirit, Shield of Faith: Religion in American War and Diplomacy*. New York.

[5] Matthew Connelly (2000), "Taking off the Cold War Lens: Visions of North-South Conflict during the Algerian War for Independence," *American Historical Review*, vol. 105, no. 3, p. 742.

[6] See its absence from the four-volume *Religion and Human Rights: Critical Concepts in Religious Studies* (2010), edited by Nazila Ghanea, vols. I–IV, London. The only article dealing specifically with the content of the draft Convention is John Claydon (1972), "The Treaty Protection of Religious Rights: UN Draft Convention on the Elimination of All Forms of Intolerance and of Discrimination Based on Religion or Belief," *Santa Clara Law Review*, vol. 12, pp. 403–423. Claydon's article offers limited analysis of the political process behind the draft Convention. See also Cornelis D. de Jong (2000), *The Freedom of Thought, Conscience and Religion or Belief in the United Nations (1946–1992)*. Antwerpen. Otherwise, the Convention has, on a few occasions, received a passing reference in a footnote or with only a very short and simplified comment. This literature dates back about three decades. See Roger S. Clark (1979), "The United Nations and Religious Freedom," *New York University Journal of International Law and Politics*, vol. 11, pp. 197–225; Natan Lerner (1981), "Toward a Draft Declaration against Religious Intolerance and Discrimination," *Israel Yearbook on Human Rights*, vol. 2, pp. 82–105; Donna J. Sullivan (1988), "Advancing the Freedom of Religion or Belief through the UN Declaration on the Elimination of Religious Intolerance and Discrimination," *American Journal of Law*, vol. 82, no. 3, pp. 487–520; and Brice Dickson (1995), "The United Nations and Freedom of Religion," *International and Comparative Law Quarterly*, vol. 44, no. 2, pp. 327–357. Some contemporary writings close to the events provide a useful

the one hand, it dealt with religious freedom and nondiscrimination for religious believers. On the other hand, it dealt with protection of atheist and secular beliefs as well as the relationship of the State and society to these phenomena and to freedom of thought and conscience. The term "religious intolerance" was later deemed to have a weaker legal meaning than the term "discrimination," but its political significance was evident and that informed the negotiations.

Mark Edwards has argued that diplomatic historians must "give attention to the multiplicity of religious incarnations in foreign affairs."[7] The story of negotiating the convention is at its core a story about the scope of the normative transformations, reflected in the sphere of international law, which could be achieved during this period. The context, however, is also much wider. In a study of religion since the 1960s, the sociologists Robert E. Putnam and David E. Campbell identify two parallel, sometimes mutually reinforcing, trends that have been important drivers of developments in this field, namely religious pluralism and polarization.[8] One trend has led to greater acceptance and tolerance as part of religious faith. Another trend has been increasing polarization and conflict around religious belief. Their work focuses on the United States but their observations appear equally relevant on a global scale. The balance between religious pluralism and polarization might have developed differently if international legal principles on religion, backed by monitoring and reporting mechanisms, had been completed in a binding human rights convention in the 1960s that could then have shaped international debates in the

but still only limited account of the political dynamics behind this process. See Sidney Liskofsky (1968), "Eliminating Intolerance and Discrimination Based on Religion or Belief: The UN Role," *Reports on the Foreign Scene*, February, no. 8, pp. 1–12; and Morris Abram (1967), "Die Gedanken-, Gewissens- und Religionsfreiheit," *Journal of the International Commission of Jurists*, vol. 8, pp. 49–62. A more recent reference to this Convention, although for a distinctly contemporary purpose, can be found in: Mark Limon, Nazila Ghanea and Hilary Power (2014), *Combating Global Religious Intolerance: The Implementation of Human Rights Council Resolution 16/18*. Versoix. The Convention has also received limited attention in a recent article: Ofra Friesel (2014), "Race versus Religion in the Making of the International Convention Against Racial Discrimination, 1965," *Law and History Review*, vol. 32, no. 2, pp. 351–383.

7 Mark Edwards (2009), "'God Has Chosen Us': Re-Membering Christian Realism, Rescuing Christendom, and the Contest of Responsibilities during the Cold War," *Diplomatic History*, vol. 33, no. 1, p. 94. See also Andrew Preston (2006), "Bridging the Gap between the Sacred and the Secular in the History of American Foreign Relations," *Diplomatic History*, vol. 30, no. 5, pp. 783–812; and Preston (2012), *Sword of the Spirit, Shield of Faith*.

8 Robert E. Putnam and David E. Campbell (2010), *American Grace: How Religion Divides and Unites Us*. New York, pp. 4–6.

following decades. It almost came to pass, but instead, it became a missed opportunity of some significance. Today's international community has found itself in dire need of legal standards and procedures like those being negotiated for this Convention to counter religious persecution and conflict.

Religion and the Draft Covenant on Civil and Political Rights, 1960

The UN human rights project was reconfigured around race and religion in 1962. It is, however, in this context necessary to start in 1960 in order to capture an important point about agency in the relationship between religion and human rights standard setting. It was at the 1960 General Assembly session that the article on religion in the Covenant on Civil and Political Rights was negotiated.[9] This debate determined the basis for the contemporary standards on freedom of religion. Many states were involved in this debate, which in full dealt with freedom of thought, conscience and religion (Article 18).[10] The controversies were over whether the article favored religious belief or favored atheism and the individual's right to freely decide on his religious faith, including the right to change religion. The task was explained by a Latin American delegate as follows, "It was not for the Third Committee to hold forth upon God and religion; its duty was simply to establish a liberal principle recognized by all civilized nations."[11]

[9] There was another significant development in 1960 in the field of religion and human rights, namely the launch of Arcot Krishnaswami's noteworthy study on "Discrimination in the Matter of Religious Rights and Practices." The study was initiated in 1956 with Krishnaswami being appointed as Special Rapporteur of the Sub-Commission on Prevention of Discrimination and Protection of Minorities. His study remains a reference point for research today, but its impact inside the United Nations is less clear. The study was discussed at length by the Sub-Commission in 1960 and by the Commission on Human Rights in 1961 and 1962. In 1962, the work on religion under the agenda item based on Krishnaswami's study was completely overtaken by the Liberian initiative analyzed in this chapter. It was an approach that made religion a more central issue in the diplomatic debates and that would define the UN debates on religion and human rights for the remainder of the decade. I have therefore not focused on his study in this chapter. The study was reprinted in Ghanea, *Religion and Human Rights*, Vol. IV, pp. 9–73.

[10] Article 18 of the 1948 Universal Declaration of Human Rights states: "Everyone has the right to freedom of thought, conscience and religion; this right includes freedom to change his religion or belief, and freedom, either alone or in community with others and in public or private, to manifest his religion or belief in teaching, practice, worship and observance."

[11] Mr. Rey (Venezuela), UN General Assembly, Third Committee, 15th session, 1026th meeting, November 18, 1960, p. 221.

The draft article established that everyone should have the right to freedom of thought, conscience and religion. It also gave the individual the "freedom to maintain or to change his religion or belief..." This proposal was challenged by Saudi Arabia, arguing that the provision on the right to change religion was unjustified and it could enable a situation where "a powerful State with a proselytizing State religion, if it had mass media of information at its disposal, might well use them to cast doubt in the minds of members of other faiths."[12] Saudi Arabia proposed to delete the provision on the right to change religion completely.

In what would prove a dress rehearsal for the larger United Nations debate on religion and human rights in the 1960s, Liberia was the most outspoken opponent of the Saudi proposal, arguing that "a man who could not change his religion in fact had a religion imposed on him." Religious freedom was an established principle in the Liberian constitution. The second strongest and heated opposition to Saudi Arabia came from Pakistan, whose delegate stated their "unhesitating and unequivocal support for the freedoms set out in the article... [which] was not merely a matter of policy or expediency for the question was one which in some of its aspects involved the honour of Islam."[13] In a direct critique of the Saudi position, the Pakistani delegate went on to explain that "Islam was, furthermore, a missionary religion and it therefore yielded to other faiths the free right of conversion... it would be the greater evil to deny the freedom of exchange of belief or faith."[14]

There was an attempt at compromise. Brazil and the Philippines submitted an amendment that would replace the words "freedom to maintain or to change his religion or belief" with new wording, namely "freedom to have a religion or belief of his choice." It removed the emphasis on "change" and was a weaker provision. A number of delegations preferred the original draft article and wanted to maintain its wording. The new wording was accepted by Saudi Arabia and Afghanistan. Western countries were largely not engaged in the debate on freedom of thought, conscience and religion.[15] The outspoken defenders of adequate human

---

[12] Mr. Baroody (Saudi Arabia), UN General Assembly, Third Committee, 15th session, 1021st meeting, November 14, 1960, p. 198.

[13] Mr. Ahmed (Pakistan), UN General Assembly, Third Committee, 15th session, 1024th meeting, November 16, 1960, p. 211.

[14] Ibid., p. 211.

[15] The United Kingdom did make one important intervention late in the debate by submitting an amendment that included the words "to adopt." This meant that the proposal by Brazil and the Philippines would read "freedom to have and to adopt a religion or

rights standards in this field were in fact Liberia, Pakistan, Sri Lanka, Venezuela and others from the Global South. Among these states, Liberia would play the leading innovative role at the United Nations for promoting freedom of religion in international human rights law during the 1960s.

The debate on religious intolerance, 1962

At the 1962 General Assembly, Liberia proposed that a Declaration and a human rights Convention on Elimination of All Forms of Religious Intolerance should be developed in parallel to those proposed on racial discrimination. The proposal sparked a debate, with controversies over Israel and the situation in the Middle East and discrimination against Jews in the Soviet Union. Strong pressure was put on Liberia by Communist states and Saudi Arabia to withdraw the proposal as they strongly opposed the idea. Liberia stood firm.

The issues raised during the debate set a pattern for the negotiations in the years that followed. Saudi Arabia was among the most restrictive countries and part of the small minority of member states that had abstained when the Universal Declaration of Human Rights was adopted in 1948. Saudi Arabia was particularly uneasy when the debate turned to religion and human rights and initiated an attack with a thinly veiled critique directed at both Israel and the Communist bloc. Jamal Baroody, the Saudi delegate, warned that:

religion could be used as a pretext for the birth of political movements, as the United Nations itself had shown by establishing within Islam a State which was a dangerous political weapon. The various ideologies which in many countries had displaced religion could equally serve as a pretext for discrimination.[16]

The latter point was exactly what convinced many states to turn to international law-making as it was deemed necessary to define standards for religious freedom to be upheld in Communist states and elsewhere. For Saudi Arabia, it was a further argument to abandon any effort to establish human rights standards regarding religious intolerance. Other states, including France, who strongly objected to the Saudi statement, felt it

---

belief of his choice." This restored to some extent the emphasis on the individual right to change religion. The article was approved as such and appears with this language as Article 18 in the International Covenant on Civil and Political Rights from 1966.

[16] Mr. Baroody (Saudi Arabia), UN General Assembly, Third Committee, 17th session, 1166th meeting, October 29, 1962, p. 161.

appropriate to highlight the discrimination that affected many different persons and that "the question of religious intolerance covered equally well the case of agnostics and atheists."[17] The other Saudi point of criticism, the one directed against Israel, drew supporters from the Middle East region. The United Arab Republic (Egypt) targeted the motives of Israel and lifted the controversy to a global scale, as they claimed that:

no one in the Committee spoke as the representative of Islam, Christianity or Buddhism, and by the same token Israel was not entitled to speak for all the Jews in the world. Israel clearly sought to claim the double allegiance of Jews wherever they were, and to convince the world that all States were accountable to it for acts committed against Jews.[18]

Israel was not the only state concerned with the plight of the Jews. The situation for Jews in the Soviet Union was raised by other member states who challenged the Soviet human rights record. Australia expressed concern over the treatment of Jews and cited media attacks by Soviet authorities and restrictions placed on the religious observances of the Jewish community, turning it into a principled critique that would resonate even more in the 1970s:

If the USSR had difficulty in giving Jews full freedom to practice their religion, it had a moral obligation, under article 13 paragraph 2 of the Universal Declaration of Human Rights, to permit them to leave the country.[19]

The United Kingdom echoed this and criticized how education and media were employed in the Soviet Union as "weapons against religion." The United States also spoke about the Soviet Jews when they themselves were criticized on their record related to racial segregation. It illustrated the reciprocal nature of the race and religion equation and how it fitted into the political dynamics of Cold War diplomacy at the UN.

The Soviets responded by questioning the motives of their opponents and denied that any domestic problem existed:

There was not a shred of truth in his [Australian delegate] charges, which were intended not to seek out areas of discrimination but merely to blacken the name of the USSR. There was in the USSR no discrimination against Jews or any other nationality or group, and no fact to prove the contrary could possibly be

---

[17] Mr. Bouquin (France), UN General Assembly, Third Committee, 17th session, 1167th meeting, October 30, 1962, p. 166.

[18] Mr. Ghorbal (Egypt), UN General Assembly, Third Committee, 17th session, 1168th meeting, October 31, 1962, p. 172.

[19] Mr. White (Australia), UN General Assembly, Third Committee, 17th session, 1170th meeting, November 1, 1962, p. 186.

presented. Charges of anti-semitism in the USSR stemmed either from ignorance or from a rabid hatred of communism.[20]

The battle lines were drawn sharply between East and West in the debate on religious intolerance. In his attempt at putting religious intolerance on the international law-making agenda, the Liberian delegate had several supporters among the Afro-Asian states, for example Tanzania, Congo and Pakistan.[21] Pakistan expressed an interesting legal vision for the UN human rights diplomacy, linking the proposed Convention on religious intolerance to the larger purpose of the United Nations in the field of international law-making:

Admittedly the Charter of the United Nations already proclaimed the principle of non-discrimination; but it did so in a general way, so that a convention on the subject would in no way be superfluous. It might be said that United Nations conventions were to the Charter what a country's laws were to its constitution.[22]

For the African group, their main concern was to ensure that there would be two separate declarations and conventions on race and religion, respectively. Their first priority was to eliminate racial discrimination and they wanted to avoid that it fell victim to wider ideological Cold War struggles. The unification of race and religion into one convention could easily lead to this – whereas a division into two would separate the problems. Liberia submitted a revised resolution with fifteen cosponsors.[23] The resolution called for urgent action as a draft Declaration was to be submitted to the 1963 General Assembly and a draft Convention to the 1964 General Assembly, if possible, and no later than the 1965 session. The making of legally binding standards on racial discrimination and religious intolerance was to be fast-tracked.

[20] Mrs. Nikolaeva (the USSR), UN General Assembly, Third Committee, 17th session, 1170th meeting, November 1, 1962, p. 186.

[21] Pakistan had a few months earlier recommended to the Commission on Human Rights that a Convention should be prepared on "Principles on Freedom and Non-Discrimination in the Matter of Religious Rights and Practices." This recommendation had not been successful, but it gave Pakistan all the more reason to support the Liberian proposal at a critical stage during the Third Committee debate. See document E/CN.4/832/Rev.1 – Commission on Human Rights, Report of the Eighteenth Session (March 19 – April 14, 1962), ECOSOC Official Records, 34th session, Supplement no. 8.

[22] Mrs. Khatoon (Pakistan), UN General Assembly, Third Committee, 17th session, 1171st meeting, November 2, 1962, p. 192.

[23] They were twelve African countries (Congo Brazzaville, Congo Leopoldville, Ghana, Guinea, Madagascar, Mali, Mauritania, Niger, Nigeria, Tanganyika, Togo and Upper Volta) as well as Iraq, Pakistan and Syria.

Reflecting on the debate, the Liberian delegate explained his country's action in bringing South Africa before the International Court of Justice over the question of apartheid in South West Africa. The two initiatives on race and religion were linked because Liberia argued for action against all forms of discrimination. In a skilful diplomatic maneuver, Liberia delivered a coup de grâce to its critics and opponents, especially the Soviet Union, in its final reflection on the debate:

> Since many delegations had stated that no religious discrimination existed in their countries, it was his desire to believe that they would not find it difficult to vote for his amendment.[24]

This was an eloquent and paradoxical use of denial. By turning the habit of denial against its proponents, Liberia had outsmarted opposition from the Communist Bloc and from Saudi Arabia – at least for now. It illustrated that the emphasis on "race, creed and colour" in the 1960 debate on ending colonialism for some states carried real meaning and these states shaped decision-making at the United Nations.

Race versus religion, 1963–1964

Race and religion were now on the agenda for the UN bodies responsible for human rights. However, battles ensued over the priorities of the UN human rights program. In reality, it was a tug of Cold War over the meaning and centrality of race and religion in international affairs. At the March 1963 session of the Commission on Human Rights, it led to a battle over the agenda. Racial discrimination quickly became the top priority and it was decided that it should be the first item to be discussed. The question was what priority should be given to religion. The Soviet Union and Ukraine tried to include several agenda items between race and religion. This was the first expression of a strategy of filibustering that would take different forms up until 1967. Western delegates argued that they were parallel issues and religion should follow immediately after the debate on the Declaration on racial discrimination.

René Cassin argued most strongly for the dual track where race and religion were the two main priorities. Cassin contended that "the legacy of history was so heavy that the separation of the two forms of

---

[24] Mr. Yancy (Liberia), UN General Assembly, Third Committee, 17th session, 1171st meeting, November 2, 1962, p. 192. For more on Liberian foreign policy during this period, see D. Elwood Dunn (2009), *Liberia and the United States during the Cold War*. London, pp. 59–72.

discrimination was unacceptable both intellectually and morally." His second argument focused on more recent developments that placed the emerging debates on religious intolerance and international law in a wider contemporary context.

Cassin explained that the Commission on Human Rights "should remember that for the past year or more the leaders of religious movements with hundreds of millions of members had been protesting against religious intolerance." Cassin referred to the Second Vatican Council that had opened in October 1962, generating worldwide interest. If the Commission on Human Rights gave a lower "order of priority to a problem which was a matter of present and universal concern, it would be lagging behind world public opinion and would be laying itself open to criticism."[25] The Second Vatican Council, arguably the most significant church event in the twentieth century, would lead to a theological and strategic renewal of Catholic teachings and their relation to the modern world. Human rights were a central element in this transformation. This was already evident a month after Cassin's statement to the Commission on Human Rights.

On April 11, 1963, Pope John XXIII issued the encyclical *Pacem in Terris (Peace on Earth)*.[26] *Pacem in Terris* did not just endorse the Universal Declaration of Human Rights. It went as far as calling it "An act of the highest importance . . . [and] an important step towards the juridical-political organization of all the peoples of the world."[27] The encyclical also endorsed constitutional government, the division of powers and the rule of law and defined three requisites for the juridical organization of a State. The first requisite was "that a charter of fundamental human rights be drawn up in clear and precise terms and that it be incorporated in its entirety in the constitution."[28] This was a new vision of the State by the Catholic Church. The Church was embracing constitutional law. It also gave new prominence to the dignity of the individual person in the Church's teachings by emphasizing that "The human individual, far

---

[25] Mr. Cassin (France), Commission on Human Rights, 19th session, 739th meeting, March 12, 1963, p. 3.

[26] The full title was *Pacem in Terris: On Establishing Universal Peace in Truth, Justice, Charity and Liberty*.

[27] See *Pacem in Terris*, paras. 143–144. See also comments on the significance of this endorsement of the Universal Declaration of Human Rights by John P. Humphrey, who was the UN Director for Human Rights at the time. John P. Humphrey (1984), *Human Rights & the United Nations: A Great Adventure*. New York, p. 76.

[28] See *Pacem in Terris*, paras. 75–77.

from being an object and, as it were, a merely passive element in the social order, is in fact, must be and must continue to be, its subject, its foundation and its end."[29]

The opening sections of *Pacem in Terris* read almost as a Papal Bill of Rights and as a blueprint for promoting rights and duties, equality, social justice with the additional element of providing space for the spiritual well-being of the individual. It was a societal vision that clearly distinguished itself from the Communist system. This was evident from a statement highlighting that "some political regimes which do not guarantee for individual citizens a sufficient sphere of freedom within which their souls are allowed to breathe humanly; in fact, under those regimes even the lawful existence of such a sphere of freedom is either called into question or denied."[30] The Pope gave legitimacy to codification of religious liberty in international human rights law.

Pacem in Terris also addressed the escalation of the arms race, nuclear deterrence, the conditions for peace and the consequences of the use of force and violence within states and on a global scale. The encyclical attacked racism and racial discrimination and identified decolonization as balancing out inferiority complexes among some peoples and superiority complexes among others, leading to general acceptance of "the conviction that all men are equal by reason of their natural dignity."[31] It was not only attacking unjust hierarchies. It was also arguing a causal connection between decolonization and the emergence of human rights. The Encyclical was a remarkable expression of the aspirations that human rights were starting to evoke in the early 1960s. It helped define the legacy of the Second Vatican Council as one focused on religious renewal.[32]

The launch of the Second Vatican Council in itself had been a cause for controversy on the Eastern side of the Iron Curtain. According to canonic law, all Catholic bishops were required to participate in an event of this nature. In Poland, a country with sixty-three bishops, this created special problems for the leadership of the Communist Party in the period leading up to the opening of the Council. The Polish authorities had among other steps initiated forced closures of Catholic schools and there would be little

---

[29] *Pacem in Terris*, para. 26.
[30] *Pacem in Terris*, para. 104.
[31] *Pacem in Terris*, para. 44.
[32] See Matthew L. Lamb and Matthew Levering (eds.) (2008), *Vatican II: Renewal within Tradition*, Oxford. See also Bernard Haring (1966), *Road to Renewal. Perspectives on Vatican II*. New York; Preston (2012), *Sword of the Spirit, Shield of Faith*, pp. 508–513, 522.

doubt about the sympathies of the Vatican Council regarding Communist policies on religious affairs. The party allowed thirty-five bishops to travel to Rome. It was an uneasy compromise that revealed a conflict between hardliners and more tolerant segments in the Polish Communist Party as well as between the party and the Church.[33]

At the United Nations, René Cassin fought to secure priority regarding the issue of religious intolerance on the Commission's agenda. Immediately before the vote on the agenda for the 1963 Commission on Human Rights session, Cassin explained that the "procedural vote was really a vote on substance."[34] It was an acute observation. Cassin's position prevailed and religious intolerance became the second item on the Commission's agenda. The victory was short-lived. The debate on racial discrimination occupied almost the whole session and confirmed the fears of the Liberian delegate, who had initiated the process. He explained that he had advocated equal importance of race and religion and that the General Assembly had endorsed his view. He made it clear that the Commission had to give priority to the Declaration on Elimination of All Forms of Religious Intolerance at the next session.[35] Lebanon, who had also supported Liberia in the General Assembly, drew the same conclusion. They believed it was of the greatest importance for the United Nations to prepare universal standards on elimination of religious intolerance.[36]

Only two meetings on religion were held out of a total of thirty-five meetings during the 1963 session of the Commission on Human Rights and they allowed only for a brief general discussion. The Western countries focused on violations of religious freedom in order to elevate the importance of the issue of religious intolerance to the same level as racial discrimination. The United States attacked legal formalism whereby states denied the existence of religious discrimination by referring to

[33] Danish National Archives (Rigsarkivet), "Forholdet mellem Stat og Kirke i Polen," Notat fra den danske ambassade i Warszawa, October 17, 1962, Danish UN Mission in New York Archive, 119.L.13, Box 63.

[34] Mr. Cassin (France), Commission on Human Rights, 19th session, 739th meeting, March 12, 1963, p. 3.

[35] Mr. Doe (Liberia), Commission on Human Rights, 19th session, 768th meeting, April 2, 1963, p. 10.

[36] The Lebanese self-image played a significant part in Lebanon's support to the Liberians. As the Lebanese delegate explained, "there were many religious communities in Lebanon, and had they not lived in harmony, Lebanon could not have survived as a State respecting religious freedom and providing a refuge for persons seeking religious freedom." The 1960s were for some clearly still a decade of hope in what their statehood would entail. See statement by Mr. Hakim (Lebanon), Commission on Human Rights, 19th session, 768th meeting, April 2, 1963, p. 11.

constitutional provisions that guaranteed freedom to practice religion while in actual fact "religious minorities were subjected to systematic political, religious and cultural deprivation."[37] Chile pointed to the broad scope that was required in this process of international legal standard setting, arguing that "Liberty of conscience had also to cover external manifestations of belief, where it was related with the right of peaceful assembly and association." The discrimination against Jews in the Soviet Union was referred to several times, including the prohibitions imposed on them by Soviet authorities even on apparently minor issues – but religiously significant – such as baking unleavened bread.

The Soviet Union again denied the existence of any problems, claiming that they had "no difficulties in implementing the relevant articles of the Universal Declaration . . . and no discrimination was practiced against anyone on grounds of religion." The difference to the United States' position on racial discrimination was evident. Throughout the 1960s, the United States did acknowledge the existence of racial problems and took time to explain, often in some detail, what the Federal Government was doing to address these. The two superpowers had different strategies on how to handle these delicate domestic issues before the United Nations.

That the Soviet Union faced domestic challenges over religion was obvious. On March 31, 1964, an hour-long program "Questions and Answers on Religion at a Workers Club" was broadcast on Soviet television. It featured questions from the audience to a panel of four state experts. A member of the audience asked:

Question: Why do they say religion contradicts Communism? For it is said that Communism is 'paradise on earth.'

Answer: Formerly, theologians called Communism Satanic; now they are trying to disguise the basic antagonism between religion and scientific Communism. But Communism seeks to create a happy earthly life; religion calls this life transitory and falsely focuses on a supposed life after death.[38]

Another audience member asked why certain religious groups were prohibited since freedom of conscience was supposedly recognized in Soviet

---

[37] Mrs. Tree (USA), Commission on Human Rights, 19th session, 768th meeting, April 2, 1963, p. 5.

[38] "Questions and Answers on Religion on Moscow Television," Airgram, U.S. Embassy, Moscow, April 14, 1964, U.S. National Archives (College Park, MD), RG 59/250/7/20/7, Soc14, Box 3252.

law. The experts struggled with providing adequate answers to the questions from the audience. This difficulty represented a deeper challenge to Soviet ideology and the Soviet system itself when faced with religion.

The U.S. Embassy in Moscow monitored religious developments in the Soviet Union closely. In their assessment of the TV program, the Embassy wrote that it shed light "on average Russians' attitude toward religion some decades after the inception of the Soviet anti-religious campaign."[39] The Embassy had already written to the State Department a month before the March 1964 broadcast, analyzing an article written by the Head of the Ideological Commission of the Central Committee, L. F. Ilyichev. The article indicated a hardening of the Communist Party's approach to religion and made the remarkable claim that "Stalin had been 'soft' on religion."[40] According to the U.S. Embassy, the article reflected the party leadership's disquiet over the "population's loss of enthusiasm for official Soviet ideology." The analysis continued:

Although the regime has, in fact, damaged organized religion to the point that it has little hold over most of the population, religion offers a distinctly non-Communist world view to believers (. . .) and as such is feared by the regime.[41]

In the aftermath of the Second World War, religious communities in the Soviet Union had experienced a less oppressive regime. In 1956, the state allowed publication of the Bible for the first time since 1917. In the preceding years, churches and theological seminaries had been allowed to reopen.[42] This changed around 1959–1960 during Nikita Khrushchev's leadership. Between 1959 and 1964, thousands of churches were closed, theological education was restricted and leaders of Christian communities were persecuted for conducting religious teaching and for resisting the new measures that were imposed.[43]

The Jewish Community was the religious group whose conditions of existence in the Soviet Union received most international attention. In April 1964, the International Socialist Study Group, which united intellectuals from a number of European countries, conducted a fact-finding mission to the Soviet Union to examine the situation. They claimed to

---

[39] Ibid., pp. 1–2.
[40] "Religion and the Regime: Article by Ilyichev in Kommunist," Airgram, U.S. Embassy, Moscow, February 4, 1964, U.S. National Archives (College Park, MD), RG 59/250/7/20/7, Soc14, Box 3252, p. 1.
[41] Ibid., p. 1.
[42] Michael Bourdeaux (1975), "Religion," *The Soviet Union Since the Fall of Khrushchev.* Edited by Archie Brown and Michael Kaser. London, p. 158.
[43] Ibid., p. 158.

be not unsympathetic to the Soviet Union and did not want "to stimu-
late anti-Soviet feeling," but they felt impelled to address the situation
of the Soviet Jews, which they viewed "in the context of détente."[44]
From this perspective, it was clear that discrimination against Jews in
the Soviet Union had "the same far-reaching importance as, for example, that of discrimination against Negroes in the United States." The
Study Group's fact-finding mission documented "discrimination against
the Jewish population of the Soviet Union as a national minority group,
as a religious community and as individuals."[45] Their report called for the
Soviet authorities to act against the discriminatory practices as the Soviet
policy toward the Jews, they argued, threatened international détente.
There was plenty to negotiate over at the United Nations.

The 1964 session of the Commission on Human Rights was a repeti-
tion of the 1963 session. Racial discrimination remained the main priority, and on procedural grounds, the Communist states managed to filibuster debate on religious intolerance. However, one thing had changed.
The Sub-Commission on Prevention of Discrimination and Protection of
Minorities had prepared a preliminary draft Declaration for the consideration of the Commission on Human Rights.

The draft contained a preamble and fourteen substantive articles. It
elaborated in some detail the possible content of a Declaration. The
preamble stated that one of the fundamental objectives of the United
Nations was to build a world society free from all forms of religious intolerance. The articles specified the freedoms and protections that should be
in effect and responsibilities that states had in upholding them. Among
its strongest provisions was that everyone had "the right to adhere, or
not to adhere, to a religion or belief and to change in accordance with
the dictates of his conscience – without being subjected to any pressure,
inducement or undue influence likely to impair his freedom of choice or
decision in this matter." This would provide protection for believers and
nonbelievers alike.[46]

---

[44] "The Situation of the Jewish Community," Report from International Socialist Study
Group Fact-Finding Mission, April 1964, Danish National Archives (Rigsarkivet),
Danish UN Mission in New York Archive, Box 271.

[45] Ibid.

[46] The draft Declaration included as a right freedom to worship, in public or in private,
without suffering any discrimination as well as equal legal protection to all forms of
worship. This was a significant point in light of the pressures placed on faith communities
behind the Iron Curtain. It was not the only article clearly addressed to the Communist
states. Article 6 explained that "Where the State controls the means of production and
distribution," the State would have a responsibility to make materials available for the

Apart from this preliminary draft, there had been no real progress between 1963 and 1964 with codifying human rights standards on eliminating religious intolerance. The opponents of the normative work on religion and human rights had used a variety of procedural means to postpone the debate. However, with the draft Convention on racial discrimination now on its way to the General Assembly, this could no longer be used to obstruct other work. From 1965, the member states would have to engage in the substantive and potentially binding aspects of religious intolerance in a way they had not done before – not even during the drafting of Article 18 of the Universal Declaration in the 1940s or the Draft Covenant on Civil and Political Rights in 1960.

Drafting the convention: the Commission of Human Rights, 1965–1967

The most constructive phase in developing the Convention on Elimination of All Forms of Religious Intolerance was the period from 1965 to the beginning of 1967. There were practical and strategic reasons for this situation. In the Commission on Human Rights, the Communist states in Eastern Europe were outnumbered as members from all other regions were sympathetic, for various reasons, toward the work on religious intolerance. The Soviets therefore sought a temporary truce with the United States.

There was also a strategic balance to strike between race and religion. At the March 1965 session of the Commission on Human Rights, the Convention on racial discrimination had not yet been completed and adopted by the General Assembly. This invited to a degree of restraint as a full-fledged attack on the Convention on religious intolerance might well lead to a counterreaction, delaying the completion of the Convention on racial discrimination. The latter Convention was a priority for the Communist states as part of their anticolonialist campaign and their angling for support from Third World countries. There were reasons for not rocking the diplomatic boat too much.

The January 1965 session of the Sub-Commission produced an elaborate draft Convention with a preamble, thirteen articles and a recommended set of measures of implementation that became the basis for the

religious communities so they could observe their religious rituals – dietary practices being one example. Freedom of movement was also included as pilgrimages to holy sites should be a right no matter whether these sites were within or outside the territory of a given State.

discussions over the next years. It had been decided to focus on the Convention over the Declaration and the draft confirmed that the Convention would deal with religion and belief, which included theistic, nontheistic and atheistic beliefs. The draft called on all states to ensure freedom of thought, conscience and religion for everyone. States should implement policies aimed at ensuring religious tolerance. The guarantees were to include freedom to manifest a religion or belief, freedom to worship, freedom to teach, disseminate and learn about religion and belief, freedom to practice, freedom to observe rituals, equal legal protection and freedom from compulsion.

Article 8 in the draft Convention mirrored one of the most controversial articles in the Convention on racial discrimination, namely the article whereby promotion or incitement to racism and racial hatred or violence should be punishable by law. The controversy had been about balancing this with freedom of expression. The United Kingdom, the United States and India had each submitted wording for Article 8, addressing this in the context of religious intolerance. They tried in various ways to maintain a delicate balance. The Soviet Union also submitted a draft. This proposal avoided making an offence punishable by law by stating that "All states shall take effective measures to prevent and eliminate discrimination based on religion or anti-religious belief in all fields of civil, political, economic, social and cultural life."[47] It was an interesting admission – but also not very concrete and mainly aiming to maintain a balance between religion and antireligious beliefs. The Polish delegate added a proposal that would determine that "Religious institutions, ministers of religion and other authorities"[48] were also to be held responsible for any incitement to discrimination or violence based on religion or belief. The aim was to emphasize legal accountability for preachers and religious actors. At the end, a consensus was achieved and included in the draft Convention submitted to the Commission on Human Rights. It read:

States Parties shall ensure equal protection of the law against promotion or incitement to discrimination on the ground of religion or belief. Any incitement to hatred or acts of violence against any religion or belief or its adherents shall be

---

47 E/CN.4/882: Report of the 17th Session of the Sub-Commission on Prevention of Discrimination and Protection of Minorities to the Commission on Human Rights, Geneva, January 11–29, 1965, p. 57.
48 Ibid., p. 57. Proposal from Mr. Ketrzynski (Poland).

considered an offence punishable by law, and all propaganda designed to foster it shall be condemned.[49]

The Western states were walking a thin line. The standards they criticized in the Convention on racial discrimination due to concerns over freedom of expression were not very different to the standards they were willing to accept in the sphere of religion. The scope of legal limitations to freedom of expression relied on the precise interpretation of what incitement and propaganda entailed.

The Commission on Human Rights now had a substantive draft to work on at the 1965 session.[50] Article 1 provided the legal definition to guide the whole Convention. It stated that "For the purpose of this Convention: (a) the expression "religion or belief" shall include theistic, non-theistic, and atheistic beliefs."[51] The discussion focused on the nature of atheism, with the United States representative Morris Abram initiating the debate. The Americans wanted to distinguish religion from atheism, believing that the purpose of the Convention was to address beliefs of a religious nature. The United States therefore proposed wording that made a negation of atheism as a form of belief. The wording focused on "theistic and non-theistic religion, or belief concerning religion, including rejection of any or all such religion or belief." The American diplomats knew that if the Convention mentioned atheism or provided protection for this form of belief, it would meet opposition domestically.[52] Accepting freedom of thought for atheists in this Convention could become a political problem in the United States, most notably with the U.S. Congress.

Morris Abram's intervention alluded to the significance of the Second Vatican Council before making the position of United States clear:

---

[49] Ibid., pp. 59, 79.

[50] The Commission held twenty-one meetings on the draft Convention. The draft from the Sub-Commission was well received. Ukraine even went as far as saying "that the Sub-Commission text was a remarkable achievement, the outcome of lengthy discussions, and provided a balance which it was desirable should not be disturbed," Mr. Nedbailo (Ukraine SSR), Commission on Human Rights, 21st session, 820th meeting, March 24, 1965, p. 8.

[51] E/CN.4/882: Report of the 17th Session of the Sub-Commission on Prevention of Discrimination and Protection of Minorities to the Commission on Human Rights, Geneva, January 11–29, 1965, p. 77.

[52] "Memo on Commission on Human Rights, 21st Session, Geneva, March 22–April 15, 1965 – Draft Convention on the Elimination of all Forms of Religious Intolerance," U.S. National Archives (College Park, MD), Central Foreign Policy Files, RG 59/250/7/20, Soc 14, Box 3202, p. 5.

At a time when religions were becoming more tolerant of the rights and freedoms of others, attacks against religions by public bodies were becoming more frequent. Acts of intolerance committed in the name of scientific atheism were as reprehensible as religious persecution.[53]

There was no wait for the response. The Soviet delegate objected to the attack by the United States, and felt that the purpose of the unclear wording was to introduce "into the draft convention a degree of discrimination against atheists."[54] According to the Soviet response, the proposal of the United States would prevent "a very large number of countries from acceding to the future convention, which should after all, be universal."[55] The battle was whether the Convention would focus mainly on religious freedom or whether the Convention would provide an equal legal standing between religion and nonreligious beliefs.[56] It was a confrontation between two very different agendas because the political worldviews behind these agendas were so different.

The United States responded in a way that highlighted the different strategies that the two superpowers had. Morris Abram quoted Lyndon B. Johnson's famous Voting Rights Speech held in front of a Joint Session of Congress a week before, on March 15, 1965. With the Voting Rights

---

[53] Mr. Abram (USA), Commission on Human Rights, 21st session, 819th meeting, March 24, 1965, p. 7. According to his autobiography, Abram had, as Chairman of the American Jewish Committee, been close to the process where the Catholic Church changed its age-old teachings and reconciled with the Jews. Morris Abram (1982), *The Day Is Short – An Autobiography*. New York. Abram had an interesting profile. He was something as rare as a Jewish rural southerner raised in Georgia, a civil rights lawyer in Atlanta and a former staff member at the Nuremberg Trials. He served on the Sub-Commission from 1962 to 1965 and used this role and his links to Atlanta to try and nuance the Sub-Commission members' views on race relations in the United States by inviting them on a study tour to Atlanta in January 1964; see H. Timothy Lovelace Jr. (2014), "Making the World in Atlanta's Image: The Student Nonviolent Coordinating Committee, Morris Abram, and the Legislative History of the United Nations Race Convention," *Law and History Review*, vol. 32, no. 2, pp. 385–429. Abram was appointed by Lyndon B. Johnson as the U.S. representative to the Commission on Human Rights, where he served from 1964 to 1968.

[54] Mr. Abram (USA), Commission on Human Rights, 21st session, 819th meeting, March 24, 1965, p. 7.

[55] Ibid., p. 8.

[56] Both Israel and Italy entered the discussions describing the transformations taking place in the Catholic Church toward unprecedented ecumenical efforts and theological reform and that this represented a distancing from intolerance that the ideological atheism had not equaled. Israel exemplified this by detailing the intolerance shown toward Christians, Jews and Muslims in the Soviet Union. Mr. Cohn (Israel), Commission on Human Rights, 21st session, 819th meeting, March 24, 1965, p. 9 and Mr. Ferretti (Italy), Commission on Human Rights, 21st session, 819th meeting, March 24, 1965, p. 11.

Act, President Johnson had decided to end a century of failed Civil War reconstruction that had not secured the African Americans their right to vote. Johnson readily admitted his nation's failings. In a way that was finely tuned to the policy of the Johnson administration, Morris Abram turned this self-critique into an attack on the Soviet Union:

The President of the United States had recently stated that there was no part of the United States where the promise of equality had been fully kept, and he was sure that that was true of every country and society...If anyone regarded any society as perfect, then obviously that society was going to be frozen in its existing mould and there would never be any improvement.[57]

The United States, according to Abram, had no problems providing legal protections for atheists, but the purpose of the Convention was to "prevent governments from launching ideological campaigns against any religion or belief."[58] His Soviet opponent was not impressed and accused the United States of wanting to take a step back to the "age of intolerance" when heretics and nonbelievers had been burnt alive. The Soviet and the Ukrainian responses expressed full support to the Sub-Commission's definition. This meant that Morris Abram could at least draw a tactical legal concession, namely that the Communist states thereby accepted the protection of religious belief and Abram decided to withdraw his amendment that had deleted atheism from the draft Convention. It was an exchange that revealed – similar to the debates on racial discrimination – the ideological underpinnings of Cold War diplomacy and how this had its own dynamics.

Jamaica brought the debate on religion and atheism back on track. With a clear-sighted intervention that received widespread praise, the Jamaican UN Ambassador Egerton Richardson clarified what the task was all about:

The purpose of the convention was to say that religion and belief were matters for the conscience of the individual and that every individual should be free to decide whether he wished to believe or not, to worship or not, and to observe or not to observe any particular religion. In short, it was the purpose of the convention to declare that, in such matters, the State had no authority to interfere with the individual and to urge every State to grant equal freedom to all individuals.

---

[57] Mr. Abram (USA), Commission on Human Rights, 21st session, 820th meeting, March 24, 1965, p. 3.
[58] Ibid.

It was the individuals who were thus placed on an equal footing, not the religions or beliefs themselves.[59]

It was clearly directed at the Soviet Union and the United States and was another example that the most visionary leadership on human rights in the 1960s came from voices of moderation from the Global South. The Jamaican Ambassador's intervention was an astute reflection on one of the major problems that the Commission faced, recognizing the individual as a subject of international law, but in doing so, he had opened up for another debate, namely on the role and nature of the State.

The debate was again between the two superpowers. Halfway into the debate, Morris Abram identified two schools of thought in the Commission on Human Rights. There were the United States and the United Kingdom, who argued that the State had no right to impose limits on freedom to adhere or not to adhere to a religion or belief. The other school consisted of the USSR and Ukraine, which believed that no part of the Convention would be immune from State supervision "for reasons of public order, morality or health." It was according to Abram "inconceivable that such a thesis could be defended in 1965 ... The very idea that the State might be empowered to delve into the conscience of man should make everyone recoil from any proposal which would have that effect."[60]

As the negotiations over the articles continued, the debate on the role of the State was reflected in discussions over freedom of worship and freedom of movement, where the issue of travel to the Second Vatican Council in Rome was debated. It fell outside the provision on pilgrimages but fitted a provision that added "other journeys" to this. At the end, the United States summed up its position on the overall matter by emphasizing that it was the State that was required not to be discriminatory. The Soviets disagreed, stating that "States should be required to ensure freedom from compulsion from any quarter." Few members of the Commission believed that aspiration had relevance to the Soviet reality. However, the U.S. position was also regarded as too restrictive in its outlook. It was again a voice from the South that expressed the principled purpose that could unite many states while the superpowers fought their own internal battles.

---

[59] Mr. Richardson (Jamaica), Commission on Human Rights, 21st session, 820th meeting, March 24, 1965, p. 10. My italics.

[60] Mr. Abram (USA), Commission on Human Rights, 21st session, 829th meeting, March 31, 1965, pp. 3–4.

The Indian delegate eloquently defined the larger strategic aim behind states negotiating an international convention by highlighting universality and tolerance as requirements for a liberal order. The statement grew out of a discussion on protecting mixed marriages where the Indian delegate noted that the Catholic Church was now considering this and then reflected on the scope of responsibility for the Commission:

> The Commission should not shy away from such a provision because of the difficulties and differences of opinion which still existed, for the very purpose of the convention was to establish liberal standards to help to remove those difficulties and differences... If social cohesion was to be achieved, all peoples must learn to tolerate religious differences, even to the extent of permitting mixed marriages. The aim was not uniformity, but tolerance of the belief of others; mixed marriages of necessity involved the breaking down of barriers. The world was shrinking fast and all countries were becoming neighbours.[61]

The point made was that the increasing interdependence globally called for universal approaches and an international legal order. It was similar to the point made by Jamaica about the need for an international legal order if the United Nations was to function as an organization for collective security. The Indian statement was among the last words spoken on the draft Convention on religious intolerance at the 1965 session. The work on the Convention had expanded in scope and depth. The Commission had adopted the preamble and four articles but had not completed its work. It would receive priority at the next session of the Commission on Human Rights. The 1966 Commission session took place at an important juncture. The first major human rights convention had been adopted – the Convention on Elimination of All Forms of Racial Discrimination – in December 1965. The Commission debate in March 1966 reflected on the legal significance of the right to freedom of thought, conscience and religion in light of developments at the Second Vatican Council.

The Second Vatican Council ended on December 8, 1965. It ended by approving the Declaration on Religious Liberty – *Dignitatis Humanae* – which was among the most significant statements from the Council during its three years of deliberation. *Dignitatis Humanae* – like *Pacem in Terris* – was a major development in how the Catholic Church situated itself in the wider political world and on ecumenical matters.[62] In October 1965, the

---

[61] Mr. Pant (India), Commission on Human Rights, 21st session, 839th meeting, April 7, 1965.

[62] F. Russell Hittinger (2008), "The Declaration on Religious Liberty, Dignitatis Humanae," *Vatican II: Renewal within Tradition*. Edited by Matthew L. Lamb and Matthew Levering. Oxford, pp. 375–376.

Council had issued the Declaration on the Relationship to Non-Christian Religions. It stated that the Catholic Church rejected nothing that was holy to non-Christian religions. The Council had debated its relationship to the Jewish faith and this was reflected in the Declaration.[63] The Council's concluding months was a high point in the Catholic Church's move toward renewal.

The World Council of Churches was mainly positive in their reception of these Declarations. The World Council of Churches had been established in 1948 to unite Protestant and Orthodox communities in ecumenical work around the world. It faced some of the same challenges as the Catholic Church vis-à-vis the Communist bloc, but even so, they had not had an easy relationship with each other. In their detailed assessment of the Declaration on Religious Liberty, the World Council of Churches emphasized that the Catholic Church had for the first time in many centuries proclaimed the universality and inviolability of religious liberty for all. It was to be ensured through effective legal safeguards and with "international authorities, whose influence, especially in matters of religious liberty, we very much hope to see grow."[64] The World Council of Churches assessment did not explain what type of international authority could fulfill this role, but it did endorse the UN standards on religion as expressed in the Universal Declaration of Human Rights. It recognized that the theological realignment within the Catholic Church was likely to have consequences "on the world level. And here we enter into a completely new and unexplored land, of which no one has the slightest experience."[65] It was certainly an endorsement of the UN's normative work in this field.

The significance of anti-Semitism in eliminating religious intolerance became a major topic at the 1966 session of the Commission on Human

---

[63] The Council's early emphasis on Jewish religion was controversial. It was criticized by several Arab leaders as a political act and as support for the state of Israel. Bishops in countries with large Muslim population were concerned about a specific declaration. The Vatican became involved in diplomatic efforts in the Middle East to explain that it was not a political matter but about a religious relationship. See Arthur Kennedy (2008), "The Declaration on the Relationship of the Church to Non-Christian Religions, *Nostra Aetate*," *Vatican II: Renewal within Tradition*. Edited by Matthew L. Lamb and Matthew Levering. Oxford, pp. 397–400.

[64] Angel Francisco Carrillo de Albornoz (1966), "The Ecumenical and World Significance of the Vatican Declaration on Religious Liberty," *Ecumenical Review*, vol. 18, no. 1, pp. 65, 81.

[65] Ibid., p. 82.

Rights.[66] The debate was about whether anti-Semitism was such a histor-ically distinct example of intolerance that it deserved special mention in the convention. Chile, Israel and the United States favored inclusion and the latter two made references to the recent developments at the Vatican Council.[67] It was not a new debate. The inclusion of anti-Semitism had been discussed during the development of the Convention on Elimination of All Forms of Racial Discrimination. The majority of UN member states had rejected the inclusion. There was opposition to mentioning specific examples of discrimination as it was seen as privileging anti-Semitism over other examples. It was deemed inappropriate to single out one spe-cial case when the Convention was universal in scope. Some among the opposition also had other reasons. During the 1965 session, the Iraqi representative to the Commission had already stated "that the represen-tative of the Zionist State in the Commission could not be referring to religious intolerance without an ulterior motive."[68] The tense situation in the Middle East was a backdrop to these negotiations. It had not had a decisive influence – yet.

The same argument was used by other member states but without the ideological suspicions held by Iraq. India, Jamaica and the Philip-pines opposed inclusion. They saw themselves in a mediating role in their efforts to secure progress with both the Convention and wider interna-tional human rights law. They knew that the proposal was unlikely to succeed in the Third Committee and did "little to serve the aims of the Convention."[69] The Philippines argued the case of universality with a degree of self-acknowledgment that was rare in the UN human rights debates. The Philippines argued that:

anti-Semitism was essentially European; it was uncommon in Asia and non-existent in the Philippines so it could not be said to be universal in character. The

---

[66] The Commission held fourteen meetings and adopted another five articles of the Con-vention. There were two major topics of debate at the 1966 session. The other topic, which can be seen as a continuation of the 1965 debate on the role and nature of the state, was about religious versus secular education of children and whether the state should secure a separation between schools and religious institutions.

[67] See Mr. Cohn (Israel), Commission on Human Rights, 22nd session, 860th meeting, March 14, 1966, p. 11; Mr. Abram (USA) Commission on Human Rights, 22nd session, 861st meeting, March 15, 1966 p. 5.

[68] Mrs. Afnan (Iraq), Commission on Human Rights, 21st session, 820th meeting, March 24, 1965, p. 5.

[69] Miss King (Jamaica), Commission on Human Rights, 22nd session, 861st meeting, March 15, 1966, p. 11.

majority of the Philippine people were Catholic, and any religious intolerance was more likely to be directed against Moslems and atheists.[70]

The Philippines and Jamaica wanted to follow the precedent established by the Convention on elimination of racial discrimination. This was a coherent strategy to neutralize proposals that were pursued with a political agenda intended to derail proceedings or undermine the human rights principles that the conventions were supposed to define and uphold. Their arguments did not prevail and the reference to anti-Semitism was approved by the Commission in a split vote and included in Article 5. It was hard to see it as a significant victory for the human rights project. The Saudi delegate warned that "The Commission should not force the Assembly into another controversial and futile debate on that issue." In this case, the Saudi delegate had a point, but futile and controversial had been what a majority of Commission members, led by Israel, the United States and Chile, had voted for.[71] This they would get. In the meantime, the Commission had not completed its work and would have to return to the draft Convention at its session in 1967.

By February 1967, the Commission on Human Rights had expanded to twenty-eight member states and had become more representative of

---

[70] Mr. Lopez (the Philippines), Commission on Human Rights, 22nd session, 861st Meeting, March 15, 1966, p. 15.

[71] Within the World Jewish Congress (WJC), there was skepticism about this approach. In a letter dated November 5, 1965 – four months before the Commission's 1966 vote on the inclusion of anti-Semitism – Maurice Perlzweig, who was active at the UN on behalf of WJC, wrote that several key allies had shown "signs of impatience and irritation" with what they regarded as an effort merely for "the opportunity of Cold War purposes." The proposal for inclusion of anti-Semitism had been made in the 1965 Commission debate by the United States and Brazil. Perlzweig described what he regarded as credible opposition to the idea. The legal scholar Natan Lerner had prepared an analysis of UN summary records showing that "half of those who voted to eliminate references to ideologies were quite honestly convinced that they were technically out of place in the text under consideration." Perlzweig had spoken with a Ghanaian diplomat, who explained that the Americans had done nothing to consult with the Afro-Asian group on the matter to seek support. The group had instead settled on the noninclusion of ideologies as their position. Perlzweig identified New Zealand, Jamaica, Denmark and Chile among those who opposed inclusion but "cannot be accused of being friendly to anti-Semitism." He had spoken with Angela King, the Jamaican representative to the Third Committee, who had a Jewish grandmother. She was therefore "somewhat embarrassed to have to vote against the condemnation of anti-Semitism but in the view of her delegation it was completely out of place." See letter from Maurice Perlzweig, World Jewish Congress, New York, to A. L. Eastermann, World Jewish Congress, London, November 5, 1965, "Re: Debate on Zionism-anti-Semitism-Nazism at UN." I would like to thank Nathan Kurz for bringing this source to my attention.

the changed United Nations. Nigeria, Dahomey (Benin), Senegal, Iraq, Pakistan and France all called for giving the highest priority to the Convention on religious intolerance to secure its completion at the 1967 session.

The major part of the debate was whether incitement to hatred or violence based on religion or belief should be punishable. The United States suggested deleting "incitement to hatred" from Article 8 to protect freedom of speech and freedom of information. Israel opposed this proposal. They wanted an obligation on states to enact legislation against intolerance and discrimination. Israel criticized the United States for having "an unjustified lack of confidence in the judiciary."[72] Several delegations agreed with Israel and stated their misgivings about the United States proposal and criticized the United States for only wanting to uphold its own Constitution's negative rights and its broad interpretations of freedom of speech and freedom of the press.[73] The United States received little support in the Commission even from West European countries. There was broad agreement that it was reasonable to include a provision that made incitement to hatred a punishable offence. The views varied widely from the Soviet Union's problematic and unclear assertion that freedom of speech should serve the interests of the community to other states who argued in favor of making incitement to hatred a "civil wrong" in accordance with the Western legal tradition.[74] It was the latter position that held sway.

The American delegate, Morris Abram, responded to the critique with a long statement on American history and contemporary affairs, arguing that the United States had arrived at a new stage in its history with a new synthesis on human rights reflected in Roosevelt's Four Freedoms from 1941 and the policies of President Johnson's administration. Abram believed everybody had to adopt the new international synthesis:

If his countrymen, brought up in a tradition of negative rights and freedoms, had accepted and assimilated imperatives of economic and social rights, surely other

---

[72] Mr. Cohn (Israel), Commission on Human Rights, 22nd session, 897th meeting, February 22, 1967, p. 9.
[73] It was again Jamaica that provided the most erudite legal explanation against the United States proposal while emphasizing the need to follow the standards outlined in the Covenant on Civil and Political Rights adopted two months earlier. Austria, Tanzania, Iraq and others supported the Jamaican analysis.
[74] Egerton Richardson (Jamaica), Commission on Human Rights, 22nd session, 903rd meeting, September 8, 1967, p. 6.

States could accept and assimilate the civil, political and religious rights of the Universal Declaration.[75]

It was the same equilibrium that the negotiations over the two Covenants had strived to maintain. The synthesis was significant because it was about defining the role of the state. The transformation of the international state system in the 1960s posed new questions to the international community about the nature of statehood. The elaboration of standards on the rights of individuals and the duties of states was about the functional homogenization of a State's responsibilities, which essentially was a further aspect of negotiating universality.

The Commission concluded its debate on the draft Convention by deciding on the remaining substantive articles but did not have time to discuss the measures of implementation. The Commission transmitted a revised draft Convention along with the Sub-Commission's draft on implementation measures to the upcoming session of the UN Economic and Social Council (ECOSOC) in order to have the draft Convention passed on for completion at the 1967 General Assembly session. It was done with some hope for success.

The fall of religion: the convention and the 1967 UN General Assembly

With the significant achievements of the 1965 and 1966 General Assembly session, where the Convention on racial discrimination and the two Covenants had been completed and adopted, the Convention on religious intolerance was set to continue this positive trend at the 1967 General Assembly. The debate was well positioned between the new precedent where the United Nations completed its major tasks on human rights and the upcoming International Year for Human Rights in 1968 that for several years had served as a target and had helped drive progress on human rights principles becoming international legal standards. The debate reflected this position between new precedent and aspiration before 1968.[76]

---

[75] Mr. Abram (USA), Commission on Human Rights, 22nd session, 899th meeting, February 23, 1967, p. 6.

[76] In the 1967 Third Committee debate, the Convention on Elimination of All Forms of Racial Discrimination was referred to thirty-six times (mainly as a positive precedent). There were twenty-seven references to the International Year for Human Rights. The latter was evoked as an argument for completing the Convention on religious intolerance at the 1967 General Assembly session and to focus the proceedings on achieving this goal.

Unfortunately, international relations had deteriorated dramatically since the two previous General Assembly sessions and even since the 1967 Commission session in February–March. This change was felt acutely inside the United Nations. The first step had been the ruling by the International Court of Justice in 1966 over apartheid in South West Africa where the Court had denied to rule on the legality of South Africa's mandate. It was a victory for South Africa and a controversial ruling that led many to lose faith in international law as a positive force for justice. By the time of the 1967 General Assembly, the situation had become much worse. The Six-Day War in the Middle East in June 1967 dominated the political atmosphere at the General Assembly session that started in September 1967. It was in the context of this international crisis that the Convention on religious intolerance was to be completed.[77] The crisis became the perfect alibi for the Communist bloc.

The deterioration in the international political climate was also reflected in another more symbolic way that highlights the schism between religious pluralism and polarization. Throughout the years 1962–1966, there had been numerous references during the debates on the convention to events in Rome, where the Second Vatican Council took place. The reference to the contemporary events in Rome symbolized a liberalization of faith and a modernization of religion in terms of greater acceptance of other religions and of religious endorsement of human rights as guiding principles for the practice of state power.

The geographical location most frequently referred to during the 1967 Third Committee debate was Jerusalem. In the aftermath of the Six-Day War, Jerusalem symbolized war, religious conflict, Zionism, displacement and battles over sovereignty. These symbolic meanings were exploited for political reasons by the Communist states as an attack on the Convention itself. They wanted to destroy the Convention and delegitimize its supporters. Bulgaria accused the Israeli Government of planning to destroy Islam's sacred places in Jerusalem and continued, "Israel's religious fanaticism was supported by precisely those who claimed to favor the elimination of religious intolerance."[78] These attacks on the

---

[77] Arthur Goldberg, the U.S. Ambassador to the UN, informed the Secretary of State prior to the debate that "It increasingly apparent Arabs intend use this item as forum for major attack on Israel, claiming Israeli treatment of Arabs basic violation of human rights and, in particular, example of religious discrimination." Telegram dated October 12, 1967, "US Mission UN New York to Secretary of State – Subject Committee 3 – Religious Intolerance Convention," U.S. National Archives (College Park, MD), Central Foreign Policy Files RG59/150/Soc 14, Box 3128, p. 1.

[78] Mr. Bahnev (Bulgaria), UN General Assembly, Third Committee, 22nd session, 1490th meeting, October 20, 1967, p. 135. While Egypt did mention Jerusalem in two critical

Convention were only a beginning. The shift in geographical reference symbolized a larger political closure for human rights norm-making at the United Nations.

Other states brought forward grievances or bitterness over religious conflicts with neighboring states. Ireland referred to Northern Ireland, and Pakistan and India had a tense exchange after Pakistan spoke of the grievances faced by Muslims in India over two centuries. The Indian delegate could not recognize this description of events and opposed the notion "that religion was the basis of nationality" and then went on to describe the elimination of religious minorities – Hindus and Sikhs – in West and East Pakistan. In what could have been an epitaph for the situation in the Middle East, the Indian delegate complained about "The hymn of hate that was continuously sung from across the border."[79] There were underlying tensions between states that the diplomatic tone of the proceedings could no longer hide. They were coming forward and the postcolonial world with its dispersion of national sovereignty was bursting at the seams.

The place of religion in national and international affairs as well as in contemporary law was one of the challenging issues. The fact that the Convention was an instrument drafted to cover both religion and atheism and protect believers and nonbelievers alike was important. The broad perspective had made the Convention a significant document not just on religious intolerance but on the broader meaning of freedom of conscience.

Bulgaria, one of the higher-profiled Communist countries in the human rights debates, argued that international law derived its force from universal recognition and that only the principles which were not in conflict with the "ideology of any particular legal system" could receive universal recognition. This was an attack on the whole Convention project as this position meant a veto on the ground of ideology rather than on principles of sound law-making.[80] This was not an unknown approach to

statements, they were more moderate than the statements from Bulgaria and Ukraine. Ukraine stated that "Israel had violated the Charter of the United Nations and its resolutions on the City of Jerusalem. What Israel was doing to the Arabs could be compared to what the Nazis had done to the Jews in Europe." Mr. Kachurenko (Ukraine SSR), UN General Assembly, Third Committee, 1489th Meeting, October 19, 1967, p. 129. Syria made a similar comparison by using lebensraum rhetoric to describe Israeli intentions.

79 Mr. Hasan (India), UN General Assembly, Third Committee, 1493rd Meeting, October 24, 1967, p. 155. The Pakistani statement was from the same meeting (p. 152).

80 Mr. Bahnev (Bulgaria), UN General Assembly, Third Committee, 22nd session, 1490th meeting, October 20, 1967, p. 134.

international legal diplomacy from the Communist states. Belarus took the critique even further. From their perspective, "Religion had played a sorry role in history" and the problem was that "The instrument would have the effect of strengthening religion and enlarging its sphere of influence."[81]

The Communist states' main problem was that the process of codifying elimination of religious intolerance in international law by definition meant that standards for religious tolerance were codified and the duties of states herein were defined. This challenged their state ideology, which allowed only a very minimal space for religion. This explains the opposition from the Communist countries as well as the strategies for filibustering that had been applied since the earliest stages of the negotiations. The Communist states did engage actively when the focus was on protecting atheism as a belief or protecting the rights of nonbelievers, but any attempt at privileging religion or advancing religious freedom was challenged.

The major problem for the United States was a weakened negotiating position. The unwillingness by the U.S. Congress to ratify international agreements – even against slavery and genocide – gave a problem of credibility. It limited the United States' ability to promote religious liberty – at least through the mechanisms of international norms and lawmaking. It deeply frustrated Arthur Goldberg, the U.S. Ambassador to the United Nations, who wrote to the Secretary of State Dean Rusk. Goldberg explained that the United States instead had to seek support from the recognized leaders within the UN human rights diplomacy to table strong proposals, including on the measures of implementation. These states were identified as Jamaica, Ghana and Mexico.[82] They, however, did not need any prompting by the United States.

The most elaborate responses to the attacks from the Communist states came from countries in the South. They varied in content but focused on explaining why addressing religious intolerance was important. They also presented a broader vision for the human rights project where religion was a natural subject for international law-making. Ghana regarded the Convention on religious intolerance as one of the main documents that would ensure respect for the UN Charter, believing that "the adoption of a

---

[81] Mr. Loshchinin (Belarus SSR), UN General Assembly, Third Committee, 22nd session, 1493rd Meeting, October 24, 1967, p. 153.

[82] See Telegram dated October 12, 1967, "US Mission UN New York to Secretary of State – Subject Committee 3 – Religious Intolerance Convention," U.S. National Archives (College Park, MD), Central Foreign Policy Files RG59/150/Soc 14, Box 3128, p. 3.

convention would provide *a guarantee for the future.*"[83] Ghana envisaged a strong set of implementation measures for the Convention, including a reporting system with inter-State complaint mechanisms, a conciliation system for disputes between states, a system with petitions for individuals and, finally, recourse to the International Court of Justice.[84]

Jamaica agreed with Ghana, believing that implementation measures should parallel those agreed in 1965 for the International Convention on Elimination of All Forms of Racial Discrimination. The two Conventions were seen as comparable legal instruments. Jamaica also took on another criticism from the Communist states, namely that the West used religion for expansive purposes and interference in the affairs of other states and equaling it to imperialism. Jamaica did not shy away from separating legal principle from political opportunism and had little patience for Communist maneuvers that they had been for several years regularly opposing in other debates, most notably in the preparations for the human rights year. First, the Jamaican delegate Marcella Martinez made it clear that:

In Jamaica God had never been considered as an agent of Western imperialism. Slavery, that brutal practice which had left so deep a mark on the country, had been combated by the non-conformist clergy.[85]

Jamaica went a step further and proposed an additional paragraph to the Convention. Having witnessed the attacks on the Convention that had taken place during the general debate, even before the negotiations over the preamble and articles had started, combined with the general political atmosphere in the Third Committee, Jamaica sensed that there was a risk that the Convention might be hijacked. This meant that provisions might be adopted that were not about individual human rights but about limiting religion and religious liberty. The Jamaican proposal stated that none of the provisions of the Convention should require or authorize any derogation from any provision in the Covenants. This step can best be described as a safety clause to protect standards of international law from political abuse.

The Jamaican response was also an anticipation of the second wave of attacks from the Communist states. It was an attack that created

---

[83] Mr. Lamptey (Ghana), UN General Assembly, Third Committee, 22nd session, 1495th meeting, October 26, 1967, p. 167. My italics.

[84] Ibid., p. 167.

[85] Miss Martinez (Jamaica), UN General Assembly, Third Committee, 22nd session, 1492nd Meeting, October 23, 1967, p. 147.

new divisions in the Third Committee and played a significant part in the downfall of the Convention. The attack started with revisions to the preamble and a Soviet announcement of "holy war against colonialism."[86] That the ideologically atheist state of the Soviet Union was declaring a "holy war" illustrates well the political opportunism that was driving their negotiation strategy. The Soviet proposal contained two elements, namely that religion should not serve as a pretext for intervention in a State's domestic affairs and should not be an obstacle to the fight against colonialism. The Soviets believed that religion had often served the purposes of colonialism and wanted to use this to curtail religious organizations. They added to this their own polemic assertion that religion was not really a fundamental part of an individual's conception of life.

The proposal was part of a divide and rule strategy, in which the heated topic of colonialism was mobilized to create divisions to help undermine the Convention. The Soviet Union added that anyone opposed to the proposal had to be opposed to ending colonialism. The proposal met with strong opposition but was also successful in dividing the countries from the Global South. A number of countries from the Afro-Asian Bloc supported its inclusion in the Convention and several Middle Eastern countries supported it in light of the Six-Day War, which they believed had a colonialist agenda.[87]

The opposition observed that those countries that had most recently suffered from colonialism had not themselves suggested a mention of colonialism in the Convention. Several countries also noted that the Third Committee had already – in a vote over the mention of anti-Semitism – decided not to include any "isms" or specific references to forms of religious intolerance. The states that had pushed for this vote now ignored its broader implications when colonialism was on the table. The fact that the Soviet Union claimed a role as spokesperson for those countries that had experienced colonialism was not well received by a number of states. Jamaica fought back against what they perceived as Soviet arrogance and objected to the Soviet statement that delegations which were against its proposal "were secretly in sympathy with the champions of colonialism.

---

[86] Mr. Nasinovsky (the USSR), UN General Assembly, Third Committee, 22nd session, 1499th Meeting, October 31, 1967, p. 184.

[87] The experience of displacement and the aftermath of war in the Middle East lay behind a proposal from Egypt to add a paragraph to the convention guaranteeing everyone the right not to be expelled from one's country for reasons of religion and belief.

Jamaica, which had been a colony for 453 years, could not be suspected of pro-colonialist sentiments."[88]

The Soviet strategy to undermine the Convention thrived on these controversies. The Soviet Union also proposed that the issue of religion should not be used to interfere in the domestic affairs of states. It was without doubt an attempt to protect them from criticism of their human rights record. It was difficult not to be suspicious of Soviet motives and these suspicions were aired. The Communist states were criticized for their "dogmatic assertions" in the UN debates and their:

tendency... to picture atheism as the highest form of devotion to the welfare of society and to the progress of States. Given the social and economic injustice which was being suffered by the peoples, especially those of developing countries, what needed to be done was to help them emerge from their poverty rather than to deprive them of their religion, for atheistic science would be of little avail in the absence of a spirit based on respect for human rights and of effective means for exercising those rights.[89]

The high hopes visible in the Third Committee in the preceding years were fading and little had been achieved. It was further evidence that the negotiation process was falling apart in the strained political atmosphere. The Soviet Union continued to fuel this and, among other things, compared the use of napalm in Vietnam with the Crusades.[90] The vote on each paragraph of the preamble was often split – at times close to equal or with a large number of abstentions – and the Soviet proposal on colonialism was adopted.[91] It was a bad omen for any attempt at universality. As frustrations grew, it became increasingly clear that the draft Convention would not be completed and adopted at the 1967 General Assembly session and would not be ready for the International Year of Human Rights in 1968. There were efforts to ensure the Convention would be given priority at the 1968 General Assembly session but they were more habits of UN procedure than determined aspirations from a significant number of member states. International relations were at a low after the war in the Middle East and the Convention on religious intolerance was part of the collateral damage.

[88] Miss Martinez (Jamaica), UN General Assembly, Third Committee, 22nd session, 1506th meeting, November 6, 1967, p. 218.

[89] Mr. Siri (El Salvador), UN General Assembly, Third Committee, 22nd session, 1500th meeting, October 31, 1967, p. 188.

[90] Mr. Nasinovsky (the USSR), UN General Assembly, Third Committee, 22nd session, 1503rd meeting, November 2, 1967, p. 206.

[91] This happened in a slightly reworded version that the Soviet Union agreed with Nigeria.

The Convention that Ghana had hoped would become "a guarantee for the future" had, in the words of the Netherlands, become a text that was "turned towards the past and was purely negative." The disillusion was expressed most directly by Iraq, who had cosponsored the Liberian resolution in 1962 that started the whole effort at codifying religious intolerance into international human rights law. Iraq concluded that "Perhaps the experts should have admitted that it was not possible to draw up a draft Convention on religious intolerance."[92] After a remarkable breakthrough period, UN human rights diplomacy now faced major crisis.

By November 1967, the effort to prepare the human rights Convention on elimination of religious intolerance had collapsed. By April 1968, when the first world conference on human rights took place over three weeks in Tehran, religion was not even on the United Nations agenda. With little interest in debating the issue at the 1968 General Assembly, the issue was left to linger for several years. It would not reappear until the early stages of the Conference on Security and Cooperation in Europe (CSCE) process. In 1972, the General Assembly decided to revive the idea of a Declaration. It lingered until the end of the 1970s. The Iranian revolution in 1979 spurred renewed interest. The United Nations finally adopted the Declaration on the Elimination of All Forms of Intolerance and of Discrimination Based on Religion or Belief in 1981. It had originated in the 1960s, but the 1981 Declaration was of much less significance compared with the aspirations of the earlier era.

The 1960s Convention was not far from completion and adoption. There was a full draft Convention in existence prepared on the back of several other successful human rights conventions during the mid-1960s. The precedent for completion was there within grasp. It will remain uncertain what impact a Convention on eliminating intolerance and discrimination on the grounds of religion or belief would have had if it had been completed. A successful Convention could have established international legal and normative standards, international monitoring and reporting procedures, and obligations on states to adopt and change laws related to various aspects of freedom of religion and belief. It could have nurtured far greater legal attention in addressing religious intolerance in international affairs over a period of four decades. There might perhaps have been a different trajectory for the relationship not just between

---

[92] Mrs. Afnan (Iraq), UN General Assembly, Third Committee, 22nd session, 1508th meeting, November 8, 1967, p. 230.

religion and international law but also between religion and global society.

This last point is connected to contemporary discussions on political theology. Political theology can help shape a peaceful constitutional order but also help to legitimize political violence. The concept has been explained as "the set of ideas that a religious actor holds about what is legitimate political authority."[93] It raises questions like: "What is the right relationship between religious authorities and the state? What are the obligations of religious believers toward the political order?"[94]

It was questions of this nature that the UN member states addressed during the period of negotiating the Convention on Elimination of All Forms of Religious Intolerance. They approached these questions from the perspective of states and from different traditions of religion and belief. The challenge was articulated most eloquently during the 1962 General Assembly debate when Liberia put religious intolerance on the international human rights agenda. The Saudi delegate Jamal Baroody asked the international community with chilling poignancy: "Who would decide where the dividing line between a believer and a fanatic lay?"[95]

Jamal Baroody's statement was actually a profound question about the legitimacy and authority of international law in relation to religion. The question struck at the core of the challenge to codify religious intolerance into international human rights law. Religion and international law would never have a straightforward relationship. They are built on different foundations of meaning and represent different social imaginaries. The irony is that the most comprehensive attempt at making elimination of religious intolerance a subject for international law was undermined by states that were ideologically atheist. The Communist states had tried to undermine this attempt since 1962. They filibustered and obstructed the process, but in the long run, it is uncertain whether they would have been able to undermine it completely. They were helped by international developments and the gradual unmaking of the hopes for a liberal world order sustained by faith in the ability of international institutions to secure international peace and security. These hopes had been among the great

93 Monica Duffy Toft, Daniel Philpott and Timothy Samuel Shah (2011), *God's Century. Resurgent Religion and Global Politics*. New York, p. 27.
94 Ibid, p. 27.
95 Mr. Baroody (Saudi Arabia), UN General Assembly, Third Committee, 17th session, 1171st meeting, November 2, 1962, p. 193.

aspirations in the United Nations in the 1960s but they had faded dramatically. A new crisis in the international state system emerged that shaped the remainder of the Cold War.

War was clearly a determinant for human rights. The Six-Day War was the direct cause of the collapse and was exploited to the fullest. At the moment when human rights became international law in the mid-1960s, religion experienced its fall. It would never find its place among the major international human rights conventions. The Israeli representative to the 1967 session of the Commission on Human Rights offered one diagnosis to describe this failure when he explained that "All religions taught love, and all had failed to put their teachings into practice."[96] From the perspective of the failed Convention on Elimination of All Forms of Religious Intolerance and the aspirations behind it, the chanting of the hymn of hate soon became a symphony of sorrow.

---

[96] Mr. Cohn (Israel), Commission on Human Rights, 23rd session, 903rd meeting, February 27, 1967, p. 5.

6

"So bitter a year for human rights"

1968 and the UN International Year
for Human Rights

"When moral posturings are employed to conceal a contrary truth, the danger is that cynicism may become universal."

Michael Manley, Lecture at University of West Indies, Kingston, Jamaica, February 29, 1968[1]

"It is not a matter of preferring one category of human rights against another, but putting emphasis on their interdependence... One of our greatest contributions to the implementation of human rights would be if we succeeded in awakening the conscience of men and thus give new impetus and stimulation to the protection of human rights by the people themselves."

Rudolf Bystricki (Czechoslovakia), International Conference on Human Rights, Tehran, April 29, 1968[2]

On December 10, 1968, Rene Cassin was awarded the Nobel Peace Prize. In her nomination speech, the Norwegian Chairwoman of the Nobel Peace Prize Committee looked back at the year that had passed and

---

[1] Michael Manley (1968), *The Angry Egalitarian: Roger Mais and Human Rights*. Lecture at the Creative Arts Centre, University of the West Indies, February 29, 1968. National Library of Jamaica (Kingston). Michael Manley was a leading member of the opposition People's National Party.

[2] A/CONF.32/SR.12: Statement by Mr. Bystricky (Czechoslovakia), International Conference on Human Rights, April 29, 1968, pp. 184–185. Both the United States and the British delegations wrote memos on the Czechoslovak statement back to their Foreign Ministry. It was the only speech from Teheran that they filed apart from their own. See, for example, British National Archives, FCO 95/380, Speech by Professor Rudolf Bystricky, April 29, 1968. See also Archie Brown (2009), *The Rise and Fall of Communism*. London, pp. 368–397.

described 1968 as "so bitter a year for human rights."[3] It was a somber assessment and one that deserves further examination.

Much has been written about the famous year 1968. Most of the literature deals with the new youth culture and with student and New Left politics. It focuses on May 1968 in Paris and student revolts around the world: on the Prague Spring and the Soviet invasion of Czechoslovakia in August; on the Vietnam War, the assassinations of Martin Luther King Jr. and Robert Kennedy and the dramatic 1968 Democratic Party Convention with violent clashes between police and protesters in the streets of Chicago and other political contestations elsewhere during 1968.

It is not well known that 1968 was also the UN International Year for Human Rights.[4] The story of this eventful year has rarely been explored from the perspective of this emerging field in international politics.[5] The 1968 revolts rarely relied on human rights language but drew on other political traditions and ideas to articulate their own versions of emancipatory politics. If the upheavals of 1968 did not pay much attention to the existence of the new international human rights debates, the wider meaning of these upheavals were reflected upon during events related to the human rights year. The vision of law and human rights as a stabilizer and civilizer of societal conflicts was a companion to "1968." It may

---

[3] Presentation speech by Mrs. Aase Lionaes, Chairman of Nobel Committee, December 10 (1968). Aase Lionaes was President of the Lagting (a Parliamentary chamber) and a former member of parliament. In this capacity, she had been a Norwegian representative to the United Nations from 1946 to 1965. She was part of the negotiations of the Universal Declaration and had served as Chairman for the UN General Assembly Third Committee in 1957 during the negotiations of the two Covenants. The speech is available at: www.nobelprize.org/nobel_prizes/peace/laureates/1968/press.html (accessed on September 16, 2015).

[4] The international human rights developments – or the fact that 1968 was an international human rights year – has not been a topic in the literature about the famous year. See George Katsiaficas (1987), *The Imagination of the New Left. A Global Analysis of 1968*. Boston; Ronald Fraser (ed.) (1988), *1968. A Student Generation in Revolt*. New York; Arthur Marwick (1998), *The Sixties*. Oxford; and Martin Klimke and Joachim Scharloth (2008), *1968 in Europe: A History of Protest and Activism, 1956–1977*. New York. There is a brief passing reference to the International Human Rights Year in the following "1968" book: Mark Kurlansky (2004), *1968 – The Year That Rocked the World*. New York, p. 14.

[5] For the few exceptions, see Roland Burke (2008), "From Individual Rights to National Development: The First UN International Conference on Human Rights, Tehran 1968," *Journal of World History*, vol. 19, no. 3, pp. 275–296; Daniel J. Whelan (2010), *Indivisible Human Rights. A History*. Philadelphia, PA; and Andrew S. Thompson (2015), "Tehran 1968 and Reform of the UN Human Rights System," *Journal of Human Rights*, vol. 14, no. 1, pp. 84–100.

appear a peripheral one but it was not absent. Human rights have their own 1968 story.

The main human rights developments in 1968 should be viewed from two perspectives. The first perspective sees the Human Rights Year as the planned culmination of the process initiated in 1962. The second perspective assesses 1968 as a bridge between the international human rights efforts of the 1960s and 1970s. There are undoubtedly many connections and a larger historiographical argument that can be made which places the 1960s as a strategic landmark – both reaping the initial work of the 1940s and sowing its own seeds to be harvested in the 1970s. It was countries from the Global South that had driven the human rights agenda forward during the 1960s, but new political trajectories started to crystallize in 1968, with the human rights engagement of the Global South on the decline while Western interest in international human rights was in the ascendant. It would take a few more years for this development to be clearly visible, but 1968 became a crossroads for these two trends.

Before Tehran, January–April 1968

The situation across Southern Africa remained of great concern as the final preparations for the Tehran Human Rights Conference took place in the early months of 1968. In 1967, the Commission on Human Rights had, upon African initiative, established for the first time a working group that was to deal with "consistent patterns of human rights violations." In the following years, a working group examined prison conditions and practices of torture in South Africa, Namibia and Rhodesia and its reports provided some of the initial evidence for the debates on torture that from 1973 were to become an increasingly central part of UN human rights debates.

The situation in Rhodesia was particularly high on the political agenda at the UN. The international community was witness to repeated executions of political prisoners involved with the independence struggle. These executions were perpetrated by the Iain Smith regime without any trial or due process. In early March 1968, the Commission on Human Rights issued a strong statement, both to Iain Smith's regime and to the United Kingdom, demanding the restoration of constitutionality, law and order and that the lives of the remaining prisoners, of which there were more than one hundred, be saved. Rhodesia and apartheid in South Africa occupied thirty-five of the fifty meetings of the 1968 session of the Commission on Human Rights held in February–March.

When Keith Johnson, the new Jamaican Ambassador to the United Nations,[6] attended the UN commemoration of the International Day for the Elimination of Racial Discrimination on March 21, 1968, he heard great disillusionment with the United Nations from the chairman of the UN Special Committee on Apartheid. The latter – the UN Ambassador from Guinea – spoke about the situation in Southern Africa and stated that war had broken out across the subregion, making any peaceful solution to the racial conflict increasingly unlikely. He indicted "the culpable impotence of the international community" and continued:

It is distressing to conclude today that a problem which could have been solved peacefully by negotiations between the oppressed and the oppressors must henceforth be resolved by force of arms, by fire and blood. This is a proof of our common failure and unfortunately augurs difficult days ahead for our Organization and for all Member States.[7]

This was a widely shared concern one month before the International Human Rights Conference in Tehran. Difficult days were ahead for the United Nations. It was not the best omen for the conference.

There were other more positive trends. The conference was stimulating interest in signing and ratifying the human rights conventions. The two Covenants had been approved by the General Assembly on December 16, 1966 and had opened for ratification. By the beginning of 1968, the Convention on racial discrimination had received eighteen ratifications.[8] The signatures and ratifications were policy statements. Initially, they had a more symbolic value, but even so they played directly into the dynamics of the multilateral process. Increasingly, if a member state wanted to speak with credibility during the human rights debates, the signatures and ratifications of the legal instruments became a requirement. It was symbolic competition or peer pressure that could deliver real policy outcomes when a sufficient number of ratifications were achieved. The International

---

[6] Egerton Richardson had in 1967 been appointed Ambassador to the United States.

[7] "Statement by Chairman (Achkar Marof) of Special Committee on Policies of Apartheid at Special Commemorative Meeting, 21 March." The Danish UN Ambassador attended the meeting and reported that Ambassador Marof's speech was "symptomatic for the frustrations that exist among the majority of the UN's Afro-Asian member states due to the UN lack of ability to have any influence over the development in Southern Africa" (my translation from Danish). Danish National Archives (Rigsarkivet), Danish UN Mission in New York Archive 119.L.22.a/9.2, Box 264.

[8] A/CONF.32/7: Status of Multilateral Agreements in the Field of Human Rights Concluded under the Auspices of the United Nations – Report of the Secretary-General, January 31, 1968.

Human Rights Year and the Tehran Conference provided a platform for this peer pressure to be effectively applied.

In the month leading up to the Tehran Conference, the pattern of signatures on both Covenants is interesting. The Soviet Union was among the states that signed both Covenants in the period between late March and late April 1968 when the conference began.[9] The signatures were timed to gain symbolic authority for the debates in Tehran. But this also meant that the Soviet Union had formally endorsed both Covenants, including the one on Civil and Political Rights. The integrity of their motives can be questioned, but the effect on the multilateral dynamics in the human rights field was not an unintended consequence. It was part of the purpose behind the international human rights year. The Jamaica-initiated process was a skilful and strategic use of United Nations diplomacy.

The potential strategic value did not go unnoticed. The United Kingdom immediately analyzed the possible implications of the Soviet Union's signatures. By early April 1968, the British Foreign Office had prepared a background report for the Tehran Conference, entitled "Civil Liberties in the USSR." The report highlighted that the Soviet authorities had "always devoted great care to the cultivation of a good image abroad" and their signing of the human rights Covenants continued this tradition. The Soviet system had always relied on its ability to control domestic protest, but the Soviet signatures on the two Covenants meant an internationalization of human rights that could have wider implications. The Foreign Office report argued that when:

it comes to the flouting of international conventions, the Soviet authorities may find it extremely difficult to counter the disgust felt by foreign public opinion. Even foreign Communist Parties are finding it increasingly difficult to side with the Soviet Union on a wide range of issues affecting human rights.[10]

It would be an overstatement to argue that there was a direct causal link between this strategic recognition by a key Western player and the Helsinki process of the 1970s. What is clear is that the International Human Rights Year and the Tehran Conference as diplomatic processes were crystallizing the potential political meanings and utilization of human rights in international relations. In this sense, these events served as part of the foundation for the human rights politics of the 1970s.

This same report analyzed the concept of "Socialist Legality" and the nature of repression in the Soviet Union directed at writers, national

---

[9] These countries also included Ukraine, Belarus, Denmark, Norway and Iran.
[10] British National Archives (Kew), FCO 95/380, "Civil Liberties in the USSR," April 1968, p. 16.

minorities, religious believers, labor camp inmates and those in mental hospitals. In December 1967, the newly appointed head of the KGB, Yuri Andropov explained in Pravda that with Socialist Legality, "The distortions in the work of the State security bodies were liquidated... reliable political and legal guarantees of Socialist law and order were introduced."[11] The concept of "Socialist Legality" was the Communist Party's version of the rule of law in Soviet society. It was a concept rife with contradictions, lies and self-deception, as events in January 1968 would make evident.

The Soviet authorities had in 1966 prosecuted the writers Yuli Daniel and Andrey Sinyavsky in a secret trial for publishing "anti-Soviet material." Their crime was to have written fiction. The case led to an international outcry over their treatment and the violation of their freedom of expression. In January 1968, only weeks after Andropov's statement on reliable legal guarantees, four other "dissident" writers were tried in court, including Alexander Ginzburg, who had published a report on the Daniel–Sinyavsky trial. This led to a large number of protests inside the Soviet Union and from abroad. The case helped further expose the legal veneer of the Soviet system and inspired the dissident movement to engage more systematically with international human rights norms. According to the historian Benjamin Nathans, the dissidents' strategy shifted, drawing its inspiration from a combination of factors, namely their experience with domestic rights violations in the Soviet Union, the aspirations connected to the Prague Spring as well as the existence of the UN International Human Rights Year.[12] The Human Rights Year gave an international backdrop to their domestic struggles – a backdrop that the Soviet regime itself had endorsed at the United Nations. It also signified that human rights as a language and a set of ideals was starting to unfold more widely, linking the local and the global in new ways.

The clearest expression of this came with a new noteworthy samizdat publication *Chronicle of the Human Rights Year* prepared by Soviet dissidents. The publication became better known under the title *Chronicle of Current Events* and was one of the most important publications by Soviet dissidents. The first issue of this underground publication came in April 1968 and its masthead carried the words "Human Rights Year

---

[11] British National Archives (Kew), FCO 95/380, Quoted from "Civil Liberties in the USSR," April 1968, p. 1.

[12] See Benjamin Nathans (2012), "Die Entzauberung des Sozialismus: Sowjetische Dissidenten, Menschenrechte und die neue globale Moralität," *Moral für die Welt?* Menschenrechtspolitik in den 1970er Jahren. Edited by Jan Eckel and Samuel Moyn. Göttingen, pp. 104–105.

in the Soviet Union." This was the platform the dissidents built on and would carry into 1969, where the revised masthead read "Human Rights Year in the Soviet Union Continues" before they came up with a new formulation "The Movement in Defence of Human Rights in the Soviet Union Continues" in 1970.[13] The very first words in the first issue from April 1968 referred to the Universal Declaration of Human Rights and that:

On December 10th, 1967, Human Rights Year began all over the world. On December 11th the trial was due to begin in the case of Yury Galanskov, Alexander Ginzburg, Aleksei Dobrovolsky and Vera Lashkova. The trial was, however, postponed and did not begin till January 8th 1968.[14]

It was a very deliberate connection between international context and commitments with local realities, which would become a mainstay of human rights advocacy. It is striking to note that these Soviet dissidents were so inspired by and explicitly built their political platform on the Jamaican political initiative and invention that had developed in response to conversations which had taken place during the independence celebrations in Kingston in August 1962 as this country was in the process of defining its foreign policy and which they had carried forward with great determination at the United Nations.[15] The idea had traveled far.

The Jamaican initiative was also inspiring thinking elsewhere. In April 1968, the American Bar Association (ABA), fierce opponents of the Universal Declaration of Human Rights in the 1940s, held a special symposium on human rights. This initiative reflected their new response to societal developments in which human rights law was highlighted for having "both a stabilizing and an energizing influence." It also reflected a more profound historical experience as 1968 was the centennial of the 14th Amendment to the U.S. Constitution. This post–Civil War Reconstruction Amendment contained equal protection and due process

---

[13] Peter Reddaway (ed.) (1972), *Uncensored Russia: Protest and Dissent in the Soviet Union.* New York, pp. 24–25.

[14] Quoted in Reddaway (ed.) (1972), *Uncensored Russia*, pp. 53–54. In what appears as a convergence in thinking, another prominent Soviet dissident Andrei Sakharov published at the end of April 1968 his important essay "Reflections on Progress, Co-existence and Intellectual Freedom," which included a strong endorsement of human rights and a call for their safeguarding in the Soviet Union. For Sakharov's essay, see Council of Europe (2011), *Andrei Sakharov and Human Rights.* Strasbourg, p. 46.

[15] For a comparable account on the role of the International Year for Human Rights in East Germany, in particular as a platform for religious communities to protect their rights, see Ned Richardson-Little (2014), "Dictatorship and Dissent: Human Rights in East Germany in the 1970s," *The Breakthrough. Human Rights in the 1970s.* Edited by Jan Eckel and Samuel Moyn, Philadelphia, PA, p. 57.

clauses that had been revived with the civil rights struggles in the 1950s. With the urban crisis at home keeping race and poverty firmly on the agenda and with the Vietnam War abroad, the United States faced severe political challenges in 1968. The Chairman of ABA's rights section saw human rights in 1968 in a light that reflected this reality:

We could, if we would, make the occasion one for much pomp and ceremony, and engage in no end of celebration. For is not 1968 International Human Rights Year? Is it not the centennial of the adoption of the fourteenth amendment? The blunt answer is that this is no time for easy ceremonial. The problems of society are too great, too urgent. The call is for hard commitment and action, not embellished lip service. The challenge is to the human spirit. Do we have the qualities of heart to make ours a truly just society? It is a time for soul-searching about human rights and social responsibility, a time for massive action.[16]

The new embrace of human rights took place not just out of idealism or political calculation but also from a sense of being overpowered by the scale of societal challenges. The ABA had moved far from its stance on human rights back in the 1940s. It now exemplified the shift in understanding and relevance the field of human rights had for those seeking justice. This much-wider NGO engagement with human rights would be one of the outcomes of the 1968 human rights year.

This response was borne out of the conflicts of the decade. A liberal "politics of change" was increasingly shaping U.S. human rights diplomacy, which in turn was propelling itself away from the self-imposed limitations of the Eisenhower years.[17] The national human rights legislation of the 1960s had set in motion a transformation of American society, which, in spite of it shining a light on massive domestic social and economic problems, also emboldened the Johnson administration to take more of a forthright position on international human rights. The 1966 debate on the Covenants, in which the United States had been the leading champion of implementation measures for economic, social and cultural rights, and the work on the draft Convention on Elimination of All Forms of Religious Intolerance had showed a more ambitious U.S. approach to UN human rights diplomacy.

Another example took place in March 1968. In one instance, it was a trial run of the 1977 Belgrade Conference on Security and Cooperation in Europe (CSCE) follow-up meeting where aggressive American human

---

[16] Jefferson B. Fordham (1968), "Introduction: Human Rights – 1968: A Symposium," *University of Pennsylvania Law Review*, vol. 116, no. 6, p. 967.

[17] G. Calvin Mackenzie and Robert Weisbrodt (2008), *The Liberal Hour: Washington and the Politics of Change in the 1960s*. New York.

rights advocacy endorsed by the Carter administration challenged the survival of the Helsinki Process. The March 1968 incident involved an interesting overlap of characters compared with the 1977 Belgrade debate, namely American UN Ambassador Arthur Goldberg and Soviet dissident Alexander Ginzburg alongside other dissidents against Soviet diplomats. The occasion was the same 1968 session of the Commission on Human Rights where Rhodesia had been high on the agenda.

A conflict had been brewing over several weeks in the Commission on Human Rights. The Soviet Union strongly criticized the United States over Vietnam. This led to a rebuttal by Morris Abram, the U.S. Representative. He began with a formal explanation of U.S. views on Vietnam – partly based on Abram's own experiences from a recent visit to South Vietnam. He then went on to speak of being able to freely criticize one's own country on its government's policies. In the United States, Abram explained, intellectuals and clerics could place an ad in the newspaper – which had been done in the *New York Times* on January 31, 1968 – stating their critical views about the conduct of the Vietnam War without fearing a secret trial. Abram asked, "Can anyone imagine an ad in *Pravda* or *Izvestia* condemning the policy of the Soviet Union, even in International Human Rights Year?"[18]

Abram expanded his critique by asking everyone to compare what they knew of Soviet practices with relevant articles of the Universal Declaration of Human Rights. Abram highlighted Article 13 on the right to leave and return to one's country; Article 18 on the right to freedom of thought, conscience and religion; Article 19 on freedom of opinion and expression, mentioning the trial against Sinyavsky and Daniel; and Article 21 on the right to take part in the government of his country directly or through freely chosen representatives. This was more than the regular tit-for-tat rhetorical Cold War diplomatic exchange. There was at this stage, shortly before the Tehran Conference, more at stake.

It was a battle over the content and scope of future international human rights work. The progress in the preceding years was changing the human rights work from focusing mainly on standard-setting to a yet uncertain balance between implementation, addressing specific human rights violations and further standard-setting. Morris Abram addressed this problem at the 1968 Commission of Human Rights session in an attack mainly directed against the Communist states. Abram explained the U.S. position as follows:

---

[18]   U.S. National Archives (College Park, MD), RG/43/250/C/76/05/Box 15 – Statement by Morris B. Abram to Commission on Human Rights, February 20, 1968.

We acknowledge with some sorrow and regret that some of the most gross and persistent violations of human rights have never come under scrutiny or study in this Commission. We believe that the double standard should give way to the single standard. We believe that the United Nations should be evenhanded in the use of its powers of study and reporting, that no area should be exempt, and that no government should be unjustly condemned by a United Nations body without due process, involving fact-finding by fair representatives.[19]

The United States commitment to expanding this system had over the years been highly questionable, but as policies shifted, the differences between the major powers on international human rights became starker. This expansion of the UN human rights system was exactly what the Communist states had feared that the Tehran Conference could promote and they had fought against it through all the preparatory stages – except when it was related to race and apartheid. In the build-up to the Tehran Conference, the stakes for this expansion were being raised by a number of other states.

Ambassador Arthur Goldberg entered the fray at the Commission on Human Rights in early March 1968 with a statement about freedom of information, freedom of opinion and expression, and the treatment of Soviet dissidents. His statement also addressed the relationship between law and literature. Goldberg spoke about the 1966 trial of Sinyavski and Daniel, followed by the recent trial against four other writers Alexander Ginzburg, Yuri Galanskov, Aleksei Dobrovolsky and Vera Lashkova in January 1968. Goldberg explained how Communists in the West had publicly opposed the Soviet persecution of these writers. For his most stinging critique, Goldberg used the words of the author Alexander Solzhenitsyn, who had openly condemned the 1966 secret trial and had described how extreme measures of censorship had been forced on Soviet writers as a condition if they wanted their works to be published. Through this reference, Goldberg described the Soviet Union as a "mutilated" society, quoting Solzhenitsyn:

What is best in our literature appears in a mutilated form . . . Literature which does not breathe the same air as contemporary society, which cannot communicate its pain and fears, which cannot warn in time against moral and social dangers, does not deserve the name of literature, but merely of cosmetics.[20]

---

[19] Ibid., p. 5.
[20] U.S. National Archives (College Park, MD), RG/43/250/C/76/05/Box 15 – Statement by Arthur J. Goldberg, March 6, 1968. The quote comes from Solzhenitsyn's open letter to the Fourth Soviet Writers' Congress dated May 16, 1967. Goldberg drew the quote from a version that had appeared in *Le Monde* later in May 1967. Before Goldberg's citation

The Soviet response to this was unprecedented. There had been a heated exchange between Goldberg and his Soviet counterpart Morozov in the Commission on Human Rights, but the Soviets moved to have the debate struck from the Commission report. The U.S. delegates were distressed when this move was successful and the exchange was outright censured.[21] The fact that the Soviets got away with it was a further indication of the rapid deterioration of the UN human rights debates in the period since the Six-Day War.

Goldberg's statement and the use of Solzhenitsyn's letter in the Czechoslovakian context did point toward an important development. Closer links between human rights, the literary imagination and artistic expression had begun to emerge. These two imaginaries – the legal and the literary – found a mutual affinity that would shape both domestic dissident politics and international support for human rights. It was not that the connection had never been made before, but it now took on a more powerful political meaning and became part of the political and intellectual landscape of the late 1960s and the 1970s.

Seen together, Goldberg's and Morris Abram's contributions point to another link to the 1970s. The articles on human rights they had emphasized were the same articles that became the central human rights provisions in the Helsinki Final Act (Baskets I and III). The link again is not causal – partly because U.S. foreign policy under President Richard Nixon was much less concerned with human rights – but it shows the contours of what became the key issues when human rights were integrated into the framework of European détente.

The Soviet Union had its own agenda for the International Human Rights Year. As the Tehran Conference approached, an article appeared in the April 1968 edition of the Soviet foreign policy journal *International Affairs* that presented the official view on the International Human Rights

---

of Solzhenitsyn at the Commission on Human Rights, the Czechoslovak author Pavel Kohout read out loud Solzhenitsyn's letter at a spirited debate during the 4th Congress of the Union of Czechoslovak Writers held in June 1967 – a debate that can be seen as anticipating the developments in that country in 1968, particularly around issues related to human rights and freedom of expression. See Michael Zantovsky (2014), *Havel: A Life.* New York, p. 98. Solzhenitsyn's open letter can be found in: Alexander Solzhenitsyn (1974), *Solzhenitsyn: A Documentary Record.* Edited by Leopold Labedz. London, pp. 110–116. The version here differs slightly from the translated version that Goldberg quoted in the Commission on Human Rights in March 1968.

[21] U.S. National Archives (College Park, MD), RG/43/250/C/76/05/Box 15 – Telegram from U.S. Department of State to UN Mission, New York, March 15, 1968.

Year.[22] It wrongfully claimed that the Soviet Union had been a champion of the 1948 Universal Declaration but otherwise focused on the developments during the 1960s, namely decolonization and racial discrimination and the documents that had been adopted in 1960, 1963 and 1965. These should now serve to stop the "widespread and exceedingly grave" violations of human rights taking place, whether it was napalm bombing in Vietnam, the alleged NATO support to the 1967 military coup in Greece, or in the Middle East, Rhodesia, South Africa and domestically in the United States. The article finished by pointing an accusing finger at the United States for its lack of commitment to the international human rights agreements.

The Soviets criticized the United States for having never signed any agreements, saying the United States "has assumed no obligations under any of the international agreements relating to the defence of fundamental human freedoms and rights elaborated in the United Nations."[23] The Soviet Union was using the U.S. failure to sign and ratify specific agreements as grounds for doubting their political credibility. The lack of U.S. ratification was a problem that had concerned both the Kennedy and the Johnson administrations and continued to frustrate American UN diplomats, not least Ambassador Goldberg. The Soviet journal took special satisfaction in quoting its American counterpart *Foreign Affairs*, which had pointed to the company that the United States was keeping by not having ratified a single human rights treaty, namely South Africa and General Franco's Spain.[24]

The intention behind the article was clear. It laid out the Soviet agenda for the Tehran Conference while presenting itself as a flawless champion of human rights. In this self-deceived worldview, the creation of the much discussed UN High Commissioner for Human Rights or the involvement of NGOs was seen as a distortion of the UN human rights work and not as moving it forward. In the Soviet view, human rights were a matter merely for governments. It was easy to propagate such inconsistencies in a party-controlled journal. The official bravado was, however, not quite matched by the Soviet approach in Tehran. This approach revealed Soviet concerns and difficulties with UN human rights diplomacy. This became

[22] Y. Arkadyev (1968), "International Human Rights Year," *International Affairs*, April, no. 4, pp. 8–11, p. 26.
[23] Ibid., pp. 8–11, 26.
[24] Ibid., p. 11.

clear despite several elements appearing, at least on the surface, to be to Soviet advantage.

The First International Human Rights Conference, Tehran, April–May 1968

It can be seen as ironic that the first international human rights conference was held in Iran where the Shah brutally suppressed democratic opposition and expressions of dissent. The Conference opened with a statement by the Shah, who talked about social justice and economic democracy and about adjusting the principles of the Universal Declaration "to the requirements of our time." It praised economic and social rights in the international human rights discourse. With a strong dose of hypocrisy, the Shah added that "real progress" was "breaking daily some more of the chains which privileged minorities have for centuries imposed on the less fortunate masses."[25] The speech had an element of the surreal.

In his opening statement, the UN Secretary-General U Thant struck a somber tone. The Secretary-General knew well that the conflicts escalating around the world did not bode well for the conference. The "pattern of history," he said, was that "preoccupations for the life and well-being of the individual give way to requirements of military imperatives. Violence breeds violence. Fear breeds fear. Restraints of those who possess force disappear in situations where the use of force is openly encouraged."[26] The UN Secretary-General recommended that the international community should place particular emphasis on addressing torture and cruel, inhuman and degrading treatment. He was not alone in calling for such emphasis to deal with massacres, summary executions and detention practices. The emphasis on these principles – Article 5 of the Universal Declaration – was gaining momentum in 1968.

Unfortunately, things quickly turned sour. A proposal by the Arab states for an additional agenda item on the "Occupied Territories" led to a lengthy discussion on the work of the conference, which took a large part of the first week. The Soviets sided with the Arab states and presented harsh attacks on Israel, allegedly calling their delegation "persons who

---

[25] Address by Shahinshah Aryamehr: United Nations (1968), *Final Act of the International Conference on Human Rights: Teheran, 22 April to 13 May.* Geneva, p. 34.

[26] Address by U Thant: United Nations (1968), *Final Act of the International Conference on Human Rights*, p. 36.

arrive with blood-soiled hands."[27] It was a debate full of bitter accusations with no resolution in sight but helpful for anyone inclined toward obstructing the proceedings.

Then suddenly, the Prague Spring made its presence felt in Tehran in front of the delegates from eighty-four countries and the NGO representatives. It would be the highlight of the three-week International Conference on Human Rights. The Czechoslovakian government delivered its statement on April 29, explaining that their country was currently undergoing a process of direct relevance to the conference as the reformist aspirations entailed a national discussion on determining "new standards in the field of human rights and civil liberties." The Czechoslovak delegate even argued that the Prague Spring was Czech society's "spontaneous contribution towards the International Year of Human Rights." The statement admitted the failings of the regime, adding that it had been a mistake that "human rights and political freedom" had not been reintroduced after the revolutionary changes of the late 1940s. The new Government declared a commitment to "the rights and freedoms of the citizens, first of all of the political rights and freedom together with personal rights, as a cornerstone of the socialist state."[28]

The Czechoslovakian speech caused a "mild sensation." The speech illustrated what an endorsement of human rights could offer when the willingness to reform was greater than that of following the dictates of a state ideology protected by force. A large number of delegates were surprised by what they had just heard and "heavy applause in which Russians barely participated" broke out in the conference hall.[29] The Soviet delegation was not pleased. It was as if a ray of light had seeped through the confines of the Iron Curtain. The moment did not last long, but for one key observer, it was "a moment of truth."

---

[27] "Report from Danish Embassy in Teheran regarding Human Rights Conference," May 21, 1968. Danish National Archives (Rigsarkivet), Danish Mission to the UN in New York Archive, 119.L.22a/3.2, Box 260.

[28] A/CONF.32/SR.12: Statement by Mr. Bystricky (Czechoslovakia), International Conference on Human Rights, April 29, 1968, pp. 184–185. Both the United States and the British delegations wrote memos on the Czechoslovak statement back to their Foreign Ministry. It was the only speech from Teheran that they filed apart from their own. See, for example, British National Archives, FCO 95/380, Speech by Professor Rudolf Bystricky, April 29, 1968. See also Archie Brown (2009), *The Rise and Fall of Communism*. London, pp. 368–397.

[29] U.S. National Archives (College Park, MD), RG 59/Subject Numeric File 1967–69, Soc 14, Box 3127, "Telegram 4428: From AM Embassy Teheran to Sec State Washington, April 1968."

There can be no doubt that the speech had been endorsed by the Czechoslovak Foreign Minister and thereby expressed the reformist government's evolving policy. It actually had an even stronger foundation as it reflected the policy positions that had been declared earlier the same month by Alexander Dubcek's government in *The Action Programme of the Czechoslovak Communist Party*. The Action Programme from early April 1968 was a blueprint for the "socialism with a human face."[30] This policy may have been crushed in August 1968, but in 1977, the deposed Foreign Minister from the Prague Spring, Jiri Hajek, was one of the main spokespersons for Charta 77 along with Vaclav Havel. Charta 77 was one of the most important documents produced by Eastern European dissidents and shaped the international political discourse on human rights in the late 1970s and 1980s. It shows again how human rights discourses in 1968 were connected to the human rights politics of the 1970s.[31]

In hindsight, the speech could be viewed merely as an expression of the brief window of hope that the Prague Spring offered, only to have that hope crushed with the Soviet invasion in August 1968. In this view, the speech would be reduced to a mere coincidence, namely that the timing of the Prague Spring and the International Human Rights Conference overlapped. This is too narrow an understanding of its significance.[32] There were lessons learned from the 1968 events and there were individual and political trajectories that were connected to the later events.

After the lengthy plenary debate on the Middle East during the first week, the work of the conference was split into two Committees. The first Committee dealt with apartheid, racial discrimination, colonialism and slavery. It became an unconstructive series of debates that meant that the

---

[30] Central Committee of the Communist Party in Czechoslovakia (1968), *The Action Programme of the Czechoslovak Communist Party*. Prague, April 5. (English version published by the Bertrand Russell Peace Foundation, Nottingham, 1970).

[31] On Jiri Hajek's involvement in Charta 77 and the links to the 1968 reformist agenda, see Zantovsky (2014), *Havel*, pp. 171–174, p. 311. For his memoirs of the Prague Spring presented from his perspective of a Communist reformer, see Jiri Hajek (1970), *Demokratisierung oder Demontage? Ein Prager Handbuch*. Munich. Hajek writes briefly on *Havel*'s role in the public debates in 1968 on pages 112–114. For an excellent study on the relationship between dissent in Czechoslovakia and Charta 77, see Jonathan Bolton (2012), *Worlds of Dissent: Charter 77, The Plastic People of the Universe and Czech Culture under Communism*. Cambridge, MA.

[32] See, for example, the brief but informative timeline on the expansion of freedom of expression in 1968 before censorship returned after the Soviet invasion: International Commission of Jurists (1969), "Reimposition of Censorship in Czechoslovakia," *The Review*, September, no. 3, pp. 5–9.

outcome, reflected in six resolutions, would prove of little value. The Arab states kept the item on the occupied territories on the plenary agenda well into the third week and bogged down the work of the conference. The second Committee covered women's rights, family planning, freedom from arbitrary arrest, freedom of expression, freedom of information, illiteracy, human rights education, war crimes, implementation of human rights and more. It was a heavy agenda, and not without its controversies, but the outcomes were better. The Committee helped, for example, to lay a foundation for future work on family planning with a human rights dimension. It also gave impetus to a new development in international law.

Throughout the Tehran Conference, the Jamaican delegation tried to keep attention focused on the overarching purposes – evaluation of past human rights efforts and defining a new international human rights program. In their plenary statement, they highlighted the fact that the UN had recently started to place greater emphasis on two techniques in the human rights field, namely fact-finding and dissemination of these facts. The UN had been impelled to take these steps to deal with the conditions in Southern Africa.[33] The Jamaican government was concerned with expanding these techniques and strengthening their foundations in international law. As a result, Jamaica focused on securing approval of several key resolutions. They proposed resolutions focusing on human rights and armed conflict, on treatment of persons who oppose racist regimes and on the establishment of a new, additional UN program on racial discrimination. The latter proposal, which appeared very constructive and relevant given the focus of the conference agenda, was opposed by many African states as a protest over the policies of one of Jamaica's cosponsors – the United Kingdom. With this key exception, all of Jamaica's other resolutions were approved. The approval of a resolution on human rights and armed conflict was testimony to Egerton Richardson's outreach and the network he had developed as the leading UN diplomat in the human rights field during the 1960s.

In March 1968, the Assembly for Human Rights, an NGO gathering of diplomats and legal experts from around the world, met in Montreal to assess the condition of human rights at a time of international crisis. They wanted to explore new ways to ensure protection of human rights. It was timed to influence the Tehran Conference. Their final statement focused on well-known areas, including discrimination and apartheid,

---

[33] A/CONF.32/SR.3: Mr. Williams (Jamaica), International Conference on Human Rights, 3rd Meeting, p. 22.

FIGURE 5. The official UN poster for the 1968 International Year for Human Rights. *Source*: United Nations Photos

but also introduced a new area of concern: human rights in armed conflict. The Assembly was disturbed by a variety of brutal practices used in violent conflicts around the world and highlighted shortcomings such as the failure to update international humanitarian law. The International

FIGURE 6. The Jamaican diplomat Marcella Martinez (seated left) worked at the UN mission in New York. Working with Richardson, she was an eloquent proponent of the vision that drove Jamaica's human rights diplomacy during these years. Here she is with Joyce Robinson, Chairwoman of Jamaica's National Committee for the Human Rights Year at the Tehran Conference. *Source*: United Nations Photos

Committee of the Red Cross had written to all governments in early 1967 to draw attention "to the need for more up-to-date and comprehensive international safeguards for civilian populations and other victims of violent conflict."³⁴ The Red Cross appeal had been ignored by governments.

The Assembly appointed a Standing Committee to implement its recommendations, consisting of John Humphrey, the UN Director for Human Rights from 1946 to 1966; Sean MacBride, Secretary-General of the International Commission of Jurists; and Egerton Richardson. During the Tehran Conference, Egerton Richardson took this assigned role very seriously. He secured international approval for a resolution that addressed the concerns raised by the Montreal Assembly. The resolution aimed to expand legal protections to apply in conflicts inside a state border – international humanitarian law focused on international

---

³⁴ Montreal Statement of the Assembly for Human Rights, March 22–27, 1968.

FIGURE 7. View of the International Conference on Human Rights in Tehran, April–May 1968. During the opening plenary on April 22, a moment of silent tribute was held for Martin Luther King Jr. who had been assassinated in Memphis, TN, earlier that month. *Source*: United Nations Photos

conflicts – and to extend protection to civilians and others. It stated that in all armed conflicts the inhabitants and belligerents should be protected in accordance with "the principles of the law of nations derived from the usages established among civilized peoples, from the laws of humanity and from the dictates of the public conscience." The resolution would have quite an afterlife as this initiative formally linked international human rights law with international humanitarian law. It illustrated that the Tehran Conference was not only a lost cause as many believed.

The Americans had aimed to "gain whatever psychological benefits"[35] possible from the conference, but they ended up keeping a relatively low profile.[36] President Johnson appointed Roy Wilkins, the Executive Director of the National Association for the Advancement of Colored People, to head the U.S. delegation. The selection of an African American helped reduce the risk that the Conference would be used as a platform to

---

[35] LBJ Library (Austin, TX), Office Files of Ernst Goldstein, Box 15.
[36] LBJ Library (Austin, TX), Personal Papers of Ramsay Clark, Box 79.

FIGURE 8. The International Committee of NGOs for the Human Rights Year meeting at the Palais des Nations in Geneva in January 1968. The process leading up to the Human Rights Year had witnessed extensive planning and coordination efforts to mobilize NGOs. The year was instrumental in defining a clearer focus for NGOs work on human rights, which highlighted the need for more operational and specialized types of human rights NGOs such as Amnesty International and the International Commission of Jurists. *Source*: United Nations Photos

attack the United States. The choice of Roy Wilkins carried some poetic justice. He had been part of the Jamaican independence celebrations and his message there about the need for a moderate but progressive "black" member state in the United Nations had struck a chord with the Jamaican government in 1962. It had helped inspire the Jamaican initiative in the human rights field. Wilkins capably handled the situation in Tehran, but ironically, it is likely that he was unaware of his own initial contribution to the process that had brought him there. In his speech at the Conference, Wilkins balanced his own perspectives with the views of the Johnson administration, emphasizing the interdependence between civil, political, economic, social and cultural rights similar to what Morris Abram had done at the United Nations.

Just as the Czechoslovakian statement had embraced the necessity of furthering civil and political rights, Wilkins' statement in reference

FIGURE 9. The Prague Spring reached the Tehran Conference when Czechoslovak representative Rudolf Bystricky on April 29 delivered the message on behalf of the reformist government. The content and the frankness of the speech were a highlight of the three-week conference and something of an embarrassment for the Soviet delegation. Rene Cassin is seated behind Bystricky who is seen delivering Czechoslovakia's statement. *Source*: United Nations Photos

to Johnson's emphasis of the American promise – the title of the 1965 Voting Rights speech – embraced economic and social rights as a new national purpose. "We Americans are merely beginning to implement a full panoply of economic and social rights which will validate the promise of American life." These two examples show that the new synthesis of the indivisibility of human rights cannot be reduced to a Third World demand for development aid and economic democracy.[37] It had a wider appeal and is also too reductive of Third World views. Wilkins' statement was restrained but not without a target. Clearly directed at the Communist states, Wilkins argued that "No state in any system will be able to fence out ideas or fence in people."[38]

The Soviet Union took the offensive on issues such as racial discrimination, colonialism and in the debate over the occupied territories.[39] The Soviets, however, were troubled by the independence of some of the European Communist states, most notably Czechoslovakia. They also grew concerned with the many proposals that were brought forward on expanding the international human rights work, including suggestions for an International Court of Human Rights and wider measures of investigation within the United Nations. The Soviet delegates became increasingly concerned with the events in Tehran. They therefore approached the Americans to establish some kind of common understanding that could curtail the "small nation prima donnas" that the Soviets felt were causing problems.[40] U.S. State Department sources indicate that the Soviets proposed to the Americans that the two countries could reach an agreement on the Tehran Final Act and, thereby to a large extent, determine the conference outcome.

Behind the scenes, the Soviet delegation had struggled with pressure from Moscow to escalate their attacks on colonialism and imperialism, but in Tehran, they were now seeking an alliance with the other great power so that the "small powers would be put in place" in the interest of "subduing rambunctious reps from small nations who get quite

---

[37] See Whelan (2010), *Indivisible Human Rights*, pp. 136–154.
[38] U.S. National Archives (College Park, MD), RG 220/650/34/14 – Box 3: Records of Temporary Committees, Commissions and Boards, "Implementing Human Rights – New Understanding, New Attitudes and New Will," Statement by Roy Wilkins, April 24, 1968, The UN International Conference on Human Rights, Tehran.
[39] See, for example, the Soviet statement to the plenary: Mr. Chikvadze (the USSR), 15th meeting, May 1, 1968, A/CONF.32/SR.15.
[40] Burke, Roland (2010), *Decolonization and the Evolution of International Human Rights*. Philadelphia, PA, p. 108.

intoxicated at these conferences."[41] The American diplomats were not displeased with seeing the Soviet Union in difficulties but had themselves an interest in shaping the final statement. They wanted to bring the Iranian hosts on board to promote the conference document. From May 6 and the following days, drafts were being worked out and an agreement was reached on the Tehran Final Act. Nevertheless, on the final day, the Soviet Union distanced itself from the adopted Proclamation. It was most likely due to criticism received from Moscow over the final result.[42] The Soviet strategy had proven rather erratic. The Americans were satisfied with their own performance and the outcome.

After three difficult weeks, the conference approved a Final Act with a Proclamation and twenty-nine resolutions. The noncommittal nature of the Proclamation resonates. International human rights work had been energized by Afro-Asian countries at the beginning of the decade, but these countries were now deeply divided over its relevance. The human rights project was in crisis despite agreement on a final statement.[43] The outcomes from Tehran were uncertain. Any results from Tehran required formal endorsement and follow-up by the UN General Assembly. This meant repeating the debates from Tehran in New York later in the year. It was not a tempting proposition.

"Our moment of truth": NGOs and the International Human Rights Year

In the aftermath of Tehran, more than 125 NGOs gathered in Paris in September 1968 for a five-day International NGO Conference on Human Rights. The purpose was to formulate an NGO strategy for human rights promotion and protection. It was again organized as part of the International Year for Human Rights. The Conference brought together a number of distinguished speakers, including the Zambian President Kenneth Kaunda, Rene Cassin, S. S. Ramphal (the former Jamaican-based lawyer and now Attorney General of British Guyana) and Charles

---

[41] U.S. National Archives (College Park, MD), Soc 14: Subject numeric file 1967–1969, Box 3127, "Telegram from U.S. Embassy Tehran to Secretary of State Washington DC."

[42] A/CONF.32/SR.27: Statement by Mr. Chikvadze (the USSR), 27th plenary meeting, May 13, 1968, pp. 160–161. See also the Soviet assessment of the conference full of self-praise over the achievements: V. Chikvadze and Y. Ostrovsky (1968), "International Human Rights Conference," *International Affairs*, August, no. 8, pp. 16–21.

[43] Burke (2010), *Decolonization and the Evolution of International Human Rights*, pp. 92–111.

Malik, the Lebanese codrafter of the Universal Declaration. UN Secretary-General U Thant gave the opening statement.

Among the group of speakers, Ambassador Richardson delivered his assessment of the Tehran Conference. He had been reflecting on its value. Had his goals of conducting an international review of the UN's human rights efforts and laying down an international program for the succeeding period been the right approach? He believed they had been. But he believed that the conference had deliberately neglected to examine the causes behind the lack of progress on human rights since the Universal Declaration. He made it abundantly clear that:

Tehran was our moment of truth, when we came face to face with the nature of our beast — when we saw what it means to be promoting the cause of Human Rights by working mainly through governments. Surely no one would have been taken by surprise at the results in Tehran.[44]

Richardson explained that the way forward for international human rights work had to involve a much greater role for NGOs and a focus on the national level. The Paris NGO meeting was a first step in this direction since its outcome outlined the elements of the first international NGO strategy for human rights.

The International Human Rights Year had inspired NGOs to give new emphasis to human rights. The International Commission of Jurists (ICJ) had most fully embraced the Jamaican agenda for the year and had worked closely with Egerton Richardson.[45] It was no coincidence that at the Paris NGO meeting, the ICJ Secretary-General Sean MacBride highlighted the resolution from Tehran on human rights in armed conflicts as maybe "the most valuable concrete result of Human Rights Year."[46] It had been a joint effort between Jamaica and the ICJ and one of the few major achievements from Tehran. However, their hopes of addressing the defects of the UN human rights implementation machinery that was "piecemeal, disjointed and . . . political rather than judicial" had faded.[47]

---

[44] Egerton Richardson (1968), "The Perspective of the Tehran Conference," *Toward an NGO Strategy for the Advancement of Human Rights* [Conference Report], The International NGO Conference on Human Rights, Paris, September 1968, p. 25.

[45] See Editor (1967), "Introduction: The Meaning of Human Rights Year," *Journal of the International Commission of Jurists*, vol. 8, no. 2, pp. III–VIII. The Journal's editor was Sean MacBride. This issue included articles by Rene Cassin, the American Law Professor Louis B. Sohn, Morris Abram and T. O. Elias from Nigeria.

[46] Sean MacBride (1968), "New Avenues of Implementation," *Toward an NGO Strategy for the Advancement of Human Rights* [Conference Report], The International NGO Conference on Human Rights, Paris, September 1968, p. 65.

[47] Editor (1967), "Introduction," p. IV.

The ICJ was a major NGO actor in the human rights field. At the Paris NGO meeting, alongside Amnesty International, the ICJ was the most articulate organization to define the priorities of the international NGO human rights strategy. Amnesty International had also used the human rights year strategically. They had mobilized their national branches into a stronger coordinated international organization. The new International Council of Amnesty International held its first meeting in Stockholm in August 1968 – a month before the Paris NGO meeting. Amnesty International had been established in 1961 and had immediately mobilized widespread public interest, achieved consultative status with the Council of Europe and the United Nations in 1962 and had experienced some early success with releases of prisoners of conscience. By the mid-1960s, it was caught between the original founder Peter Benenson's more impulsive approach and a desire for a more organized way of campaigning and running the organization.[48]

It was in Stockholm that Amnesty formalized the move toward a more coherent and professional human rights organization. It adopted a formal statute for the organization that included a new priority that would help define its work in the 1970s. The major theme for the 1968 gathering was torture. This had been decided by November 1967 as part of Amnesty's plan of activities for the International Human Rights Year.[49] It reflected the new developments at the UN, where the 1967 session of the Commission on Human Rights had initiated a fact-finding process to investigate torture and inhuman and degrading treatment in Southern Africa.[50]

Amnesty International held an international conference on torture on August 23, 1968. It was organized in close collaboration with the Swedish Committee for the Human Rights Year, which consisted of more than thirty Swedish NGOs. It was a turning point for Amnesty's work on torture. The draft statute approved in July 1968 by Amnesty's Executive Committee – chaired by Sean MacBride from the ICJ – defined the focus of Amnesty International as being composed of the following three principles: (i) freedom from arbitrary arrest and detention, (ii) freedom of opinion and (iii) freedom of thought, conscience and religion (Universal

---

[48] Tom Buchanan (2004), "Amnesty International in Crisis, 1966–67," *Twentieth Century British History*, vol. 15, no. 3, pp. 267–289.

[49] International Institute of Social History (IISH), Amnesty International Archive, International Executive Committee, Folder 41.

[50] Felix Ermacora (1968), "International Enquiry Commissions in the Field of Human Rights," *Human Rights Journal: International and Comparative Law*, vol. 1, no. 2, pp. 180–218.

Declaration of Human Rights Articles 9, 18 and 19, respectively).[51] The statute adopted by the International Assembly on August 25, 1968 by the representatives from Amnesty's national sections included a fourth principle, namely Article 5 on torture or cruel, inhuman or degrading treatment.[52] It did not just bring greater clarity to Amnesty's identity as a human rights NGO; it was also a starting point for the campaign against torture that was launched in 1972 and was a major reason for their being awarded the Nobel Peace Prize in 1977. That was Amnesty's own achievement. The decision in 1968 to make Article 5 part of the organization's mandate, however, happened in the context of the human rights year. It was the result of a collaboration with a sizeable national NGO Committee for the Human Rights Year that had grounded torture as a major human rights issue in Swedish civil society and no doubt helped shape the Swedish government's commitment to the issue.[53]

The NGO strategy outlined in Paris focused on three elements: ratification, fact-finding/advocacy and human rights education. The first element meant that NGOs should focus efforts on securing state ratification of the international human rights instruments. The second and most innovative element determined that NGOs should provide information that put the spotlight on "serious violations in a disastrous world situation."[54] This would imply fact-finding, advocacy and strategic information to be fed into relevant public forums through diplomatic channels or through "world public opinion" – an approach that NGOs would refine with great effect during the 1970s. It implied a professionalization of human rights NGOs and a greater focus on public campaigning and activism. One outcome from the Paris meeting supported this, namely the creation of a permanent human rights subcommittee among the Conference of NGOs that was to be a consultative body to the United Nations.[55] The third

[51] International Institute of Social History (IISH), Amnesty International Archive, International Executive Committee, Folder 42, "Revised Draft Statute as Finally Approved by the International Executive," July 23, 1968.

[52] International Institute of Social History (IISH), Amnesty International Archive, International Council Meeting, Folder 8, "Statute of Amnesty International. Adopted by the Sixth International Assembly, Stockholm, August 25, 1968."

[53] The Swedish Government was a driving force behind the UN Declaration on Torture, Cruel, Inhuman and Degrading Treatment from 1975.

[54] Germaine Cyfer-Diderich (1968), "Report of the General Rapporteur," *Toward an NGO Strategy for the Advancement of Human Rights* [Conference Report], The International NGO Conference on Human Rights, Paris, September 1968, p. 6.

[55] Howard Tolley (1989), "Popular Sovereignty and International Law: ICJ Strategies for Human Rights Standard Setting," *Human Rights Quarterly*, vol. 11, no. 4, p. 565.

element concerned itself with human rights education focused on "international ethics inspired by the principles of the Universal Declaration."[56]

These three priorities show a convergence of NGO thinking but they do not capture the significant interest that also existed for specific measures, such as the creation of a World Court on Human Rights, an International Criminal Tribunal to prosecute those responsible for crimes against humanity, creation of an international body charged with inspecting prisons and detention camps, a UN registry and records office to keep records of all acts and charges of crimes against humanity to be submitted to a relevant criminal jurisdiction, or the idea for national mechanisms such as commissions for human rights. The commonality was that they all represented ideas on how to move away from the "often ill-equipped part-time United Nations committees or sub-committees, selected on a political basis."[57] The NGO perspective was fixed well beyond the confines of the United Nations processes, although many of these ideas would require just that, namely UN action. The outline of the strategy did not detail how this would be done. It would be necessary to find solutions to overcome this if the NGOs were to play a role in finding answers to the major questions of the era of "world crisis" as the Paris NGO delegates phrased it.

Egerton Richardson provided concrete examples of this crisis and placed them in the context of the International Human Rights Year:

Is it any wonder, ladies and gentleman, that you found Tehran disappointing? Czechoslovakia, Biafra and the Middle East. Can anyone dare to believe that the climate of international understanding is improving or that a better basis of cooperation between nations is likely to be found before long?[58]

Richardson could have added Vietnam, South Africa and numerous other examples. It was again a somber conclusion – one that resonated well beyond the NGO meeting. Richardson pinpointed the fact that the aspirations that had inspired many earlier in the 1960s had come undone.[59] The outcomes of the decolonization process were, however, never predetermined. They were made in a multiplicity of political, economic and social processes at local, national, regional and global levels. As the emphasis on human rights grew stronger, it shed more light on the gap between ideals and reality.

---

[56] Cyfer-Diderich (1968), "Report of the General Rapporteur," p. 6.
[57] MacBride (1968), "New Avenues of Implementation," p. 64.
[58] Richardson (1968), "The Perspective of the Tehran Conference," p. 26.
[59] Ryan Irwin (2012), *The Gordian Knot. Apartheid and the Unmaking of the Liberal World Order*. Oxford.

Richardson lamented a crucial factor that he believed had been most directly illustrated by the failed Convention on Elimination of All Forms of Religious Intolerance, namely that the whole human rights project was still in trouble because:

member states are not agreed as to what we are concerned to protect; that it is the individual's freedom of conscience and worship and not the state's claim to know what is best for its citizens.[60]

His hope was that NGOs would start stepping in where governments had failed. He briefly defined four elements that might help overcome his pessimistic outlook. Each focused on shifting attention to the national level. First, he believed that it was the weight of domestic and not international opinion that would move the governments, and NGOs needed to mobilize this. Second, work was needed by NGOs at the country level to influence society and "humanize its functioning." Thirdly, the national-level emphasis should be underpinned by national institutions focused on protecting human rights alongside numerous NGOs working to protect these rights. This was similar to the idea of mandated national human rights commissions that Jamaica had been advocating within the United Nations for at least two years. Finally, governments and NGOs should share representation in the national delegations to regional and international forums inspired by the International Labour Organization (ILO) model. The "moment of truth" carried its own lessons pointing forward and Richardson and others were trying to salvage some success from the disappointments. The challenge was that the momentum provided by the human rights year was rapidly disappearing and it was uncertain how this momentum could be revived.

"The shadows should be moving the other way"

This trend was also visible in Jamaica. The human rights year had been met with great expectation and stimulated manifold activities around the country. The media coverage was extensive, with one leading newspaper publishing more than 190 articles on the human rights year in the course of 1968.[61] It shaped public debate on human rights. However, the challenges of independent statehood and social and economic crisis had also taken its toll on Jamaican politics. It had led to a brutalization of

[60] Richardson (1968), "The Perspective of the Teheran Conference," p. 26.
[61] The *Jamaica Gleaner* newspaper card registry (human rights), National Library of Jamaica. Kingston.

law enforcement and the entrenchment of discrimination based on party affiliation, especially in housing and employment, which created deep divisions in Jamaican society that would escalate into large-scale violence in the 1970s. It bred self-doubt, disillusionment and political indifference. In this, Jamaica was representative of trends affecting a large number of the decolonized states where those in power increasingly turned abusive and the project of independent statehood turned sour.

The brutalization of Jamaican society was detailed by the new NGO, the Jamaican Council for Human Rights, in a well-documented report. They cited Prime Minister Hugh Shearer, the same person who had spoken alongside Lyndon B. Johnson during the 1962 independence celebrations and had delivered Jamaica's first speech to the United Nations where the proposal for the human rights year was made, for legitimizing increased brutality with his announcement that "the police force under this Government is not reciting Beatitudes to anybody." The report published in May 1968, at the height of the human rights year, called the government "the chief perpetrator of violence in Jamaica" and concluded that "It is this attitude of authority for authority's sake that is sapping the moral fibre of our young nation."[62]

Two months later, the Jamaican government made a decision that meant abandoning the global leadership role that Jamaica had taken upon itself since 1962. The significance went unnoticed but a debate in the Jamaican parliament on July 31, 1968 sealed this fate. The prominent opposition politician Michael Manley, son of Norman Manley and himself a future prime minister, presented in March 1968 a motion in parliament proposing the establishment of a National Human Rights Commission in Jamaica.[63] The Commission should be mandated to investigate allegations of discrimination in, for example, housing and the workplace. As Manley argued in the July debate, such powers were necessary for the Commission because it could not "function effectively as the

---

[62] Jamaican Council for Human Rights (1968), *Government, the Police and Personal Freedom.* Kingston, p. 11.

[63] Michael Manley announced on March 28, 1968 in the Jamaican House of Representatives that he would present a resolution on this matter, "recognizing the supreme importance of maintaining public confidence in our institutions urges the Government to establish a Human Rights Committee for the purpose of ensuring prompt investigation of all allegations of discrimination, in employment, allocation of housing, award of Government contracts, issue of passports and all other matters involving the rights of the individual in relation to Government action," *Jamaica Hansard: Proceedings of the House of Representatives Session, 1968–1969*, vol. 1, no. 1, March 28, 1968–October 22, 1968, p. 5, National Library of Jamaica (Kingston).

safeguard and watch guard of individual liberties and human rights if it does not have the power to conduct investigations into allegations."[64]

The idea of a Human Rights Commission had been promoted by Jamaica at the UN since 1966 – including their proposal to have it included as an article in the Covenant on Civil and Political Rights[65] – and it had been a major recommendation from the UN seminar on civil and political rights held in Kingston in 1967, a meeting widely reported by the Jamaican media. The government of Hugh Shearer now strongly opposed the idea. Michael Manley argued that such a Commission was necessary because of "Jamaica's international posture . . . and by conditions in the country itself" and argued that it was a relevant action in response to the UN human rights Covenants and the human rights year.[66] Prime Minister Shearer responded that there was "nothing to justify" its creation and did not accept "that any citizens are being deprived of their rights."[67] It was far removed from the vision that had guided Jamaica into independence. The Shearer Government's opposition to the Human Rights Commission was the moment that Jamaica abandoned its global pioneering role. The creation of such a commission would have been a novel creation for any UN member and would clearly have placed Jamaica at the forefront of national implementation measures in the human rights field for several years to come.[68] The Shearer government's decision also symbolized a stage in human rights history, namely the passing of leadership in the human rights field from a group of key actors from the Global South.

Michael Manley had perhaps seen this coming. Earlier in 1968, he had delivered a remarkable lecture at the University of the West Indies on human rights and the Jamaican experience. It was as eloquent as his father's speeches on human rights and the rule of law, but Norman Manley's earlier aspirations were now tempered by Michael Manley's

---

[64] Ibid., p. 366.

[65] For their proposal, see A/C.3/L.1407: Draft International Covenants on Human Rights, Jamaica: Amendment to the Draft Covenant on Civil and Political Rights, UN General Assembly, Third Committee, November 23, 1966.

[66] "Proposal for Human Rights Commission Rejected by House," *The Jamaica Gleaner*, August 2, 1968, p. 10.

[67] Ibid., p. 10. See also the full record of the debate in the House of Representatives on July 31, 1968, *Jamaica Hansard: Proceedings of the House of Representatives Session, 1968–1969*, vol. 1, no. 1, March 28–October 22, 1968, pp. 365–370, National Library of Jamaica (Kingston).

[68] It took another twenty-five years before the idea of National Human Rights Commission was inscribed in a UN agreement, namely the Vienna Programme of Action, which was the outcome document of the 1993 World Conference on Human Rights, with their mandate elaborated in the so-called Paris Principles in 1994.

great concern about the future. It was a sentiment that in many ways reflected the realities and the disillusionment of the postcolonial era and thereby had global relevance. He said:

In many ways we now see Human Rights consciously subverted. Every time a man has to join a political party to get a house or a job, Human Rights have been undermined. The partisan requirement ascends the death knell of equality as surely as did the colonial situation before. We still have to find a level where Jamaicans accept equality – that kinship of all living beings as the foundation on which all else rests. Instead, if we look about us we see the lengthening shadows of a thousand small corruptions creeping across the landscape of our nation. But this is monstrous. It is not the evening of our history; it is the morning and the shadows should be moving the other way.[69]

Manley continued with a moment of self-doubt, raising a much greater challenge extending well beyond the borders of Jamaica:

Now in the face of all that should we not examine ourselves? Should we not ask ourselves the question – Did we really have the right to propose a Human Rights Year at the United Nations? It may be that the question is idle – but I fear hypocrisy: For when moral posturings are employed to conceal a contrary truth, the danger is that cynicism becomes universal.[70]

It was a profound – almost poetic – assessment of the status for the global human rights project at the end of the 1960s. The sentiment seemed to be reflected at the 1968 UN General Assembly.

The Tehran Proclamation had international stature but all of its twenty-nine resolutions needed the endorsement of the UN General Assembly to carry weight. The 1968 General Assembly debated at length the human rights year, the conference outcome and the follow-up. The debate was an anticlimax. At its end the British delegate aptly pronounced, "at no time during this session could anyone have described our Committee as what the hippies call 'a Love in'."[71] The debate was focused on Israel and the Middle East, the outburst of anti-Semitism in Poland and the invasion of Czechoslovakia by a member state "who, only three months earlier, had endorsed the Proclamation of Tehran, in which they had reaffirmed the rights laid down in the Universal Declaration of Human Rights."[72]

---

[69] Manley (1968), *The Angry Egalitarian*, p. 16.
[70] Ibid., pp. 16–17.
[71] British National Archives (Kew), FCO 61/200, Human Rights British Interests in Third Committee: Speech by Lady Gaitskell (UK), Third Committee, December 15, 1967.
[72] Lady Gaitskell (UK), UN General Assembly, Third Committee, 23rd session, 1626th meeting, December 2, 1968, p. 5.

In their speech to the General Assembly two weeks after the NGO meeting in Paris, the Jamaican government expressed its disappointment with the slow pace of progress since the Universal Declaration and that the Tehran Conference had not fulfilled any of its tasks. "It may well be," it was noted with a tone of resignation, "that given the political realities of 1968, we could not have done so."[73] The Netherlands were harsher in their verdict of the human rights year, "1968 had been a year in which the realization of fundamental human rights had to a disappointing degree remained in the realm of fantasy."[74] A number of states highlighted the new NGO efforts and mentioned the Montreal Assembly and the Paris NGO meeting as examples that did provide some hope.

Something had changed due to the Soviet invasion of Czechoslovakia. The former colonial powers had never been at ease with the right to self-determination but France now presented itself as a supporter of this principle in the context of détente. France had been rather obstructive during the decisive human rights negotiations in 1965 and 1966 but now changed their tone. Their statement focused on the Soviet invasion in August and they called for a stronger application of the UN Charter principles, "in particular the self-determination of peoples and non-intervention in the internal affairs of States, and also the principles of the Universal Declaration of Human Rights, not only universally accepted but universally applied, so that mankind might continue its progress along the road of détente and cooperation."[75] This was a significant shift in thinking on human rights by the most foot-dragging of the democratic states in Western Europe. It appears that the events of 1968 may have started to yield new government policy.[76] This change is directly linked to the early negotiations of the Helsinki Process that began in 1972. After two decades of having widely discarded the right to self-determination as a human right, the Western states now used this principle in the East–West negotiations, where they gave it significant weight. The invasion of

---

[73] Mr. Allen (Jamaica), UN General Assembly, 23rd Session, 1679th meeting, October 3, 1968, p. 15.

[74] Miss Ferringa (the Netherlands), UN General Assembly, Third Committee, 23rd session, 1628th meeting, December 4, 1968, p. 5.

[75] Mr. Paolini (France), UN General Assembly, Third Committee, 23rd session, 1622nd meeting, November 27, 1968, p. 6. On French responses to the invasion, see Georges Henri Soutou (2008), "Paris und der 'Prager Frühling'," *Prager Frühling: Das Internationale Krisenjahr 1968*, vol. 1. Edited by Stefan Karner *et al.* Graz, pp. 355–364.

[76] Jeremi Suri has argued that the protests of 1968 were directly linked to the rise of détente politics. See Jeremi Suri (2003), *Power and Protest. Global Revolutions and the Rise of Détente.* Cambridge.

Czechoslovakia helped frame this new thinking and gave it credence in Europe-wide politics.

There was one resolution that did meet with wide consensus. It was the resolution on human rights in armed conflicts inspired by the situation across Southern Africa where executions had become a regular occurrence. The resolution stated that the persons struggling against these regimes "should be protected against inhuman or brutal treatment and also that such persons if detained should be treated as prisoners of war or political prisoners under international law."[77] Their legal status was unclear because these conflicts were within state borders and hence not an international conflict, which the Geneva Conventions were concerned with. The resolution called for an improved application of international humanitarian law and rules in armed conflicts and highlighted the need for new international conventions in this field "to ensure the better protection of civilians, prisoners and combatants in all armed conflicts and the prohibition and limitation of the use of certain methods and means of warfare."[78]

The proposal from Tehran received strong support. In a joint Nordic assessment of the Tehran Conference, the Norwegian representative called the resolution "a positive exception and deserving support."[79] At the 1968 General Assembly, it was approved as a resolution and in 1969 became part of the legal debates at the International Conference of the Red Cross. In 1977, it became part of international humanitarian law as the second additional protocol to the Geneva Conventions. The significance of this development in international law is well documented. Jamaica's driving role in this process – and how it relates to the wider 1960s human rights agenda and the human rights year – is not. Jamaica championed this agenda at Tehran and also at the 1968 UN General Assembly and were remarkably clear about the outcome they envisaged. They wanted to address the gaps in the rules governing the law of war. The Geneva Conventions did not contain any provision for their revision, so it would be a problematic strategy to try and change these. It would likely imply a new and cumbersome ratification process. The Jamaicans

---

[77] See Resolution XXIII: United Nations (1968), *Final Act of the International Conference on Human Rights*, p. 18.

[78] Ibid., p. 18.

[79] Danish National Archives (Rigsarkivet), Danish UN Mission in New York Archive, 119.L.22.a/3 – Box 260: Statement by Ulf Underland (Norway), Memo from meeting with Nordic Ministries of Foreign Affairs, September 30, 1968 on legal matters before the 23rd UN General Assembly.

therefore requested that the UN Secretary-General prepare a study to determine whether "additional, new or supplementary conventions, or protocols to the existing conventions" should be developed.[80] It was the latter model that was subsequently adopted.

As Egerton Richardson had stated in 1966, the most constructive approach for international diplomacy would be to explore the "possible application of human rights techniques" to curtail the actions of apartheid-style governments in Southern Africa. The resolution was an expression of this focused approach and illustrated how it could serve the purposes of international law-making. The impact of this development in international law has been assessed in the following way:

In 1968 the International Conference on Human Rights, which convened in Tehran under the auspices of the United Nations, marked an important turning point by establishing the relationship between human rights and international humanitarian law. By adopting a resolution on human rights in armed conflicts which encouraged the development of new rules, the Conference qualified humanitarian law as an extension of human rights and included it amongst the matters of concern for the United Nations.[81]

The establishment of the link between International Human Rights Law and International Humanitarian Law was another development that connects the 1960s human rights diplomacy with the development of international legal norms in the 1970s. The vision behind these norms was shaped by the failed decolonization processes and the violent birth of the postcolonial order. The norms would have a long-lasting effect on international legal discourse, although it is uncertain if the process initiated by Jamaica in 1968 changed much on the ground in the short and medium term. The Southern African region would continue to be riddled with apartheid and violent conflicts throughout the 1970s and 1980s.

There was, however, one area that saw continued progress throughout the human rights year. It was the signing and ratification of the international human rights instruments by states. By the end of 1968, there were nineteen signatures on each of the Covenants. The Human Rights Day commemoration on December 10 provided a final round of signatures. The Human Rights Covenants also received their first ratification

---

[80] Miss Martinez (Jamaica), UN General Assembly, Third Committee, 23rd session, 1633rd Meeting, December 9, 1968, p. 5.
[81] International Committee of the Red Cross (1987), *Commentary on the Additional Protocols of 8 June 1977 to the Geneva Conventions of 12 August 1949*. Edited by Yves Sandoz, Christophe Swinarski and Bruno Zimmermann. The Hague, p. 1327.

submitted by Costa Rica on November 29, 1968. It coincided with their statement to the Third Committee debate on the International Human Rights Year.[82] In early December 1968, when India and Poland became the 26th and 27th countries to ratify the Convention on Elimination of All Forms of Racial Discrimination, it entered into force.[83] The first human rights treaty body would now be established, signifying a new phase in the UN human rights work. 1968, labeled a "bitter year for human rights," did end with something to show for itself. Human rights had formally become international law.

---

[82] Mr. Barish (Costa Rica), Third Committee, 1623rd meeting, November 29, 1968, p. 5.

[83] At a planning meeting for NGOs in November 1966 – in which Egerton Richardson participated – the entry into force of the Convention on Elimination of All Forms of Racial Discrimination was promoted as a specific objective for the international human rights year. See paper by Peter Benenson from Amnesty International, "The Opportunity of Human Rights Year," presented at the seminar "Planning for the International Human Rights Year," Winspread, Racine, WI, November 14–15, 1966. Box 43: International Year for Human Rights, Papers of the International League for the Rights of Man/Human Rights, New York Public Library.

7

"To cope with the flux of the future"

Human rights and the Helsinki Final Act, 1962–1975

"The United Nations is the only loom on which the western world and the Southern Hemisphere can 'weave the fabric of common interests' so wide and so strong that it can someday contain – and then suffocate – the East–West struggle."

U.S. Assistant Secretary of State Harlan Cleveland, August 1961[1]

"It is hard to swallow a situation in which apartheid has become a major issue in international relations with the Soviet Union leading the pack, while their own shortcomings are allowed to pass."

U.K. Ambassador John Killick (Moscow) to British Foreign Minister
Alec Douglas-Home, September 1973[2]

The International Human Rights Year was more than a culmination of the 1960s human rights story. It was part of an historical period lasting from 1962 to 1968 where some of the most important foundations were laid for contemporary international human rights work. These foundations did not merely originate with the so-called human rights revolution in the 1970s. While the emphasis on the latter may fit into a Western-oriented historical interpretation, it is a too limiting view and interpretation. We must allow for a more varied chronology as we are operating with different elements and factors that shaped the rise of human rights. This makes

---

[1] "United States Strategy at the Sixteenth General Assembly, August 3, 1961 (Harlan Cleveland)," U.S. National Archives (College Park, MD), RG59/150/71/15/4, Records Pertaining to UN General Assembly, 1962–1965, Box 4.

[2] Letter from U.K. Ambassador John Killick to Alec Douglas-Home, September 5, 1973, "The Conference on Security and Cooperation in Europe 1972–1975," *Documents on British Policy Overseas Series III, Vol. II*. London, 1997, p. 179.

it important to look at how the human rights developments of the 1960s and the 1970s are linked. What has become an authoritative source of international norms or law in one era can be based on a surprising historical trajectory that is significant in itself. This should be kept in mind when dealing with legal diplomacy and wider normative politics.

It is fair to say that Jamaica and its nearest Global South partners delivered the human rights project onto the doorstep of the 1970s. It was a decade where the Helsinki Process, Amnesty International, Chile, Alexander Solzhenitsyn and the campaigns against torture and enforced disappearances would further define the meaning of human rights. It is reasonable to ask what state the human rights project was in at the turn of the decade. In a conflicted world, the project was very much in need of a new lease on life after the human rights year had passed. However, it cannot be denied that the 1970s human rights efforts did build on lessons and achievements from the 1960s.

The 1960s developments in the human rights field helped define what state obligations entailed in a postcolonial world. It also changed how leading actors involved with European détente approached human rights internationally. These connections deserve consideration because the human rights diplomacy of key states from the Global South in the 1960s is linked with the 1975 Helsinki Final Act, which was negotiated and adopted by the Conference on Security and Cooperation in Europe (CSCE). The Final Act would come to play a transformative role in Cold War politics, especially because of its human rights provisions.[3] It beckons the questions: How and why did human rights become part of the 1975 Helsinki Final Act? This has actually been something of an enigma for the research on the CSCE and the Cold War. Against the existing trend in the literature, I would argue that this cannot be adequately understood without bridging the human rights stories of the 1960s and 1970s.

Legal diplomacy and the UN road to Helsinki, 1962–1970

One key development linking the 1960s and the 1970s and the Helsinki Final Act with the wider human rights history is the 1970 *UN Declaration*

---

[3] Paul Goldberg (1988), *The Final Act. The Dramatic, Revealing Story of the Moscow Helsinki Watch Group*. New York; Daniel C. Thomas (1999), *The Helsinki Effect. International Norms, Human Rights and the Demise of Communism*. Princeton, NJ; Snyder, Sarah (2011), *Human Rights Activism and the End of the Cold War. A Transnational History of the Helsinki Network*. Cambridge.

on *Principles of International Law Concerning Friendly Relations and Cooperation among States*. Developed between 1964 and 1970, it was the most elaborate statement of principles guiding international law since the UN Charter. It would subsequently serve as a foundation for the CSCE negotiations. While the negotiation process started in 1964, it was again the UN General Assembly in 1962 that was the turning point for this renewed engagement with international law. In previous chapters, we have looked at what made 1962 a turning point by focusing on a leading actor (Jamaica) and the two major themes (race and religion) that had the political traction to carry the international human rights work forward. A third perspective is offered here, namely the place of human rights in broader legal diplomacy and the politics of international norm-making.

In 1962, the UN General Assembly began debating a proposal to further elaborate principles of international law. The disintegration of the colonial system and the creation of many new states had substantially increased the subjects of international law. The Danish delegate Hermod Lannung noted that there had been a "change in the geography of international law."[4] It was a reality that could no longer be ignored and it became a recurring theme that international law was too underdeveloped to fulfill the requirements of a new era. "Juridically speaking," the delegate from Dahomey observed, "international society was primitive in character."[5]

There was wide agreement on the importance of further developing the principles of international law but there were strong doubts as to the motives driving the process. The debate, which took place in the General Assembly's Sixth Committee, started two weeks after the end of the Cuban Missile Crisis.[6] The Communist states did not hide the fact that this initiative was part of Khrushchev's international campaign on peaceful coexistence. The Western states were adamant that the elaboration should happen within the framework of the UN Charter and not veer into new, politically uncertain territory. Even this limited ambition could be problematic. In preparing a U.S. Working Paper in 1963 as this process

---

[4] Mr. Lannung (Denmark), UN General Assembly, Sixth Committee, 17th session, 756th meeting, November 9, 1962, p. 111.

[5] Mr. Pessou (Dahomey), UN General Assembly, Sixth Committee, 17th session, 759th meeting, November 14, 1962, p. 125.

[6] The Sixth Committee is the UN General Assembly's main forum for dealing with legal questions, although the human rights questions belonged to the Third Committee.

was slowly getting underway, the U.S. Ambassador Jonathan Bingham laid out the risks and requirements from a U.S. perspective:

What is needed in international relations today is not an attempt to rewrite or restate the Charter. What rather is required is a sustained and searching effort to use international institutions and opportunities in the reinforcement of peace... An attempt to codify its growing law might result more in ossification than codification, more in the acceptance of the least common denominator of the recent past than the promotion of a law fit to cope with the flux of the future.[7]

The politics of developing international norms and law did not receive the same attention as the conflicts and controversies that were dealt with at the UN Security Council but they carried their own significance, which required careful consideration. There were multiple political agendas and uncertainties involved as these processes could take on a life of their own or fall victim to short-term needs or political expediency. The ideal was that this type of normative politics would help the international community "to cope with the flux of the future" but unhelpful distortions were an inherent risk – especially with the rapidly evolving United Nations of the early 1960s.

The states from the Global South were concerned with being part of the process of defining international law and having their viewpoints reflected. The 1962 General Assembly debate became an exploration of universality as a legal concept. Decolonization had made this concept central to the debate. It meant that the ideological battles and complexities of the Cold War and the North–South relations – and the intersections between the two – became part of the elaboration of international law. Human rights were a regular feature in the 1962 debate. They were seen as part of the evolving field of international law but their exact place was uncertain. It was clear that they sat uneasily with more sovereignty-focused notions, but that they were also seen as a requirement for an international community trying to base itself on the principles of law. As the debate developed throughout the 1960s, it would be one of the most central and challenging normative areas to contend with. The debate drew heavily on the developments in the Third Committee taking place in parallel with the broader work on international law.

---

7 U.S. National Archives (College Park, MD), RG/150/71/15/4 – Box 6: "Records Pertaining to the United Nations General Assembly, 1962–1965," Telegram 1343, October 12, 1963, "Friendly Relations," from U.S. UN Mission New York to Secretary of State, Washington, DC.

The General Assembly decided to establish a Special Committee on Principles of International Law to continue the work. The Assembly agreed on four well-known principles that would be the starting point for the Committee's work, namely: (i) States shall refrain from the threat or use of force; (ii) Peaceful settlement of disputes; (iii) Non-intervention in matters within domestic jurisdiction and (iv) Sovereign equality of states.[8] Human rights were not among these core principles but they were part of the debates in the Special Committee from the outset. In the context of the Sixth Committee debate on the international principles, a resolution cosponsored by Jamaica, Liberia and the Netherlands put fact-finding and international commissions of inquiry on the UN agenda. This would have broader applicability, for example, in the context of conflicts, but there is little doubt these countries had human rights protection in mind when they launched this proposal. It became subject to strong criticism from the Soviet Union and the other Communist states.[9] The resolution called, among other things, for the UN Secretary-General to conduct a study of fact-finding as an international procedure.[10] The report, launched in May 1964, was the first significant product from this new process of exploring legal principles to ensure friendly relations among states.[11] The report became a reference point for the debates in 1966 and 1967 on creating fact-finding mechanisms in the human rights field that led to the creation of the first Ad Hoc Working Group to investigate human rights violations in Southern Africa.[12]

The Special Committee on Principles of International Law gathered for the first time in September 1964 and reflected on the importance of the Universal Declaration of Human Rights, the 1960 Declaration on Ending

---

[8] Antonio Cassese (2001), *International Law*. Oxford, pp. 86–116.

[9] See Mr. Tammes (the Netherlands), UN General Assembly, Sixth Committee, 18th session, 831st meeting, December 9, 1963, p. 279; Mr. Francis (Jamaica), UN General Assembly, Sixth Committee, 18th session, 832nd meeting, December 10, 1963, p. 285; Mr. Morozov (the USSR), UN General Assembly, Sixth Committee, 18th session, 831st meeting, December 9, 1963, p. 283. The adopted resolution is available in A/5671: Consideration of Principles of International Law Concerning Friendly Relations and Co-operation among States in Accordance with the Charter of the United Nations – Report of the Sixth Committee, December 13, 1963, pp. 34–35.

[10] UN General Assembly Resolution 1967/18 adopted at 1281st meeting, December 16, 1963.

[11] A/5694: Report of the Secretary-General on Methods of Fact-Finding, May 1, 1964.

[12] Felix Ermacora (1968), "International Enquiry Commissions in the Field of Human Rights," *Human Rights Journal: International and Comparative Law*, vol. 1, no. 2, p. 181.

Colonialism and the 1963 Declaration on Elimination of All Forms of Racial Discrimination. They were viewed by a number of states as areas where the UN Charter was incomplete but formed "part of the common law of mankind."[13] It was reiterated again that the most important element in "the process of evolving international law was universality."[14] The arc that positioned human rights in these wider discussions on international law linked the Universal Declaration with decolonization and racial discrimination. It provided a platform on which a wider contestation over the significance of human rights was fought.

The Special Committee on Principles of International Law continued its debates and in 1966 it settled on the seven principles that would define the 1970 UN Declaration. In addition to the four principles already established, it also included: "(v) The duty of states to co-operate with one another in accordance with the Charter; (vi) The principle of equal rights and self-determination of peoples and (vii) The principle that States shall fulfil in good faith the obligations assumed by them in accordance with the Charter."[15] The Committee did not make much progress on the specific contents of the seven principles. The Committee was divided – especially between East and West – but what was noteworthy was the fact that it was these three additional principles that included the strongest human rights content in the 1970 Declaration. The Soviet push for defining peaceful coexistence as a principle in international law was meeting a more organized push-back as human rights were simultaneously becoming international law. The debate on the meaning of universality also drew on the human rights language in the UN Charter's Article 55(c).[16] This trend continued at the 1967 session of the Special Committee. Progress was still slow, and the Western states were in no rush to land agreements that veered away from the UN Charter provisions. They had reason to doubt the legal principles that the Communist states were espousing. At the same time, several Global South delegates were looking to develop the principles so they could legitimize military intervention in the context of colonialism and the situation in Southern Africa.

The Western countries were, however, achieving noteworthy concessions. In 1967, the Committee reached agreement on the principles

---

[13] A/5746: Report of the Special Committee on Principles of International Law concerning Friendly Relations and Co-operation among States, November 16, 1964, p. 17.

[14] Ibid., p. 18.

[15] A/6230: Report of the 1966 Special Committee on Principles of International Law, June 27, 1966, p. 18.

[16] Ibid., p. 190.

regarding the duty of states to cooperate "in the maintenance of peace and security . . . and in the elimination of all forms of racial discrimination and all forms of religious intolerance."[17] It was a defeat for the Communist states and it would remain there for the CSCE negotiations to build upon.[18] The Western states that were fighting to balance a sovereignty- and anticolonial-focused process with human rights commitments knew this was an important achievement. No doubt referring to the language on religious intolerance, the United States called it a "strong human rights provision which expressed the relevant provisions of the United Nations Charter without detracting from them."[19] France called it "a substantial improvement."[20]

The whole process was a normative tug of war. When the Communist states promoted a provision aimed to ban what they labeled as "war propaganda," Western delegates were concerned about the impact on freedom of expression. It was not an issue whether propaganda was harmful but, as some Western states argued, was about finding "a golden mean between respect for individual freedom of expression and the social necessity for protection against dangerous incitement to violence." The response from Italy and the Netherlands, aimed at countering the Communist call for a ban, was to introduce language under the principle on the use of force, which stated that UN members "should favour the free exchange of information and ideas essential to international understanding and peace."[21] It is difficult not to see a normative link between this proposal and the strategies pursued by the nine members of the European Economic Community – the EEC "Nine" – during the CSCE negotiations five years later.

The dynamics in the Special Committee changed in 1968. The Committee session started two weeks after the Warsaw Pact invasion that ended the Prague Spring. It situated the Soviet efforts to promote the right to self-determination in a very different light. The Soviet Union had always regarded this as a matter relevant only for colonial settings, but European politics had changed after the invasion of Czechoslovakia. The

---

[17] A/6799: Report of the Special Committee on Principles of International Law, September 26, 1967, p. 83.
[18] Ibid., p. 85.
[19] Ibid., p. 84.
[20] Ibid., p. 85.
[21] A/7326: Report of the Special Committee on Principles of International Law Concerning Friendly Relations and Co-operation Among States, UN General Assembly, 33rd session, Agenda Item 87, 1968, p. 13.

U.K. and the U.S. submitted a proposal calling for every state to respect the principle of equal rights and self-determination of peoples.[22] It was a debate that also brought renewed attention to the Universal Declaration and its Article 21, which emphasized that "the will of the people should be the basis of the authority of the Government."[23] The debates were tense and progress was slow. The Special Committee session did not have time to discuss the principle of nonintervention, much to the regret of the Canadian and Romanian delegate – the latter representing a Communist state opposed to the invasion of Czechoslovakia.[24] The concept of peaceful coexistence had been delegitimized and the process was not providing the gains for which the Soviet Union had been hoping at the outset of these debates on international law earlier in the decade.

In 1969, the Soviet Union tried to launch an offensive by shifting attention toward colonial settings. As drafting finally progressed, the Soviet delegate declared that "the main obstacle now standing in the way of completion of the Committee's work was the question of whether international law should legalize the liberation struggle of colonial peoples."[25] The Soviets were hoping to secure political gains in the Third World but the response from the West was firm. The West may not have had a majority on this position but they were determined not to provide a large loophole legalizing violence. They made it clear that "no system of law could establish a legal right of revolution."[26] The Western states stood firm on the principle of universality in agreement, playing this to their advantage, thereby securing a final document that did not declare this far-reaching principle.

The Special Committee reached agreement in 1970 on a final draft of the Declaration. It had been a struggle between sovereignty-based provisions and human rights and between universal principles and politically opportunistic exceptions. It was not an ideal text but a compromise with which the West could live despite some misgivings. These were voiced by the two most active Western delegations that would soon also be among the active CSCE states. Italy concluded that "a number of delegations had applied themselves more than was necessary to attaining short-term political objectives, thus losing sight of the more permanent needs of the international community."[27] At the UN General Assembly,

---

[22] Ibid., p. 59.
[23] Ibid., p. 65.
[24] Ibid., p. 69.
[25] A/7619: Report of the Special Committee on International Law, 1969, p. 43.
[26] Ibid., p. 60.
[27] A/8018: Report of the Special Committee on International Law, 1970, p. 85.

the Netherlands argued that "the draft Declaration contained too much of national sovereignty and too little of international responsibility of States."[28] However, they had learned some important lessons for the CSCE process.

In the existing scholarship, the links between the 1960s and the 1970s have been artificially separated. In his influential book *The Helsinki Effect*, Daniel C. Thomas writes that the 1970 Declaration did not contain "any mention of human rights."[29] The assessment that human rights were not at all part of the outcome is a surprising oversight for a book on international norms since there are clear references to human rights in four different parts of the UN Declaration. They had become part of the evolving principles of international law as human rights appear in the Preamble and in two of the seven principles established by the Declaration. The Declaration even contains language that was adopted in the core human rights principle (Principle 7) of the Helsinki Final Act. The human rights language in the 1970 Declaration is actually a synthesis of the human rights developments of the 1960s, starting with the *Declaration on the Granting of Independence to Colonial Countries and Peoples* from 1960. In the most elaborate reference under the principle "The duty of States to co-operate with one another in accordance with the Charter" – a section that reads almost as a blueprint for the structure of the Helsinki Final Act – it is stated that:

(b) States shall co-operate in the promotion of universal respect for, and observance of, human rights and fundamental freedoms for all, and in the *elimination of all forms of racial discrimination and all forms of religious intolerance.*[30]

The 1970 Declaration thereby placed special emphasis on the two issues that, to a large extent, had defined the 1960s human rights diplomacy, namely race and religion. Racial discrimination was never going to be a central issue in the CSCE because when the scene shifted from the United Nations to the CSCE, the colonial context and the race issue would not have relevance. Religious intolerance, however, was a different matter. Religion and human rights came to the foreground when the principles

---

[28] Mr. Houben (the Netherlands), UN General Assembly, 35th session, 1183rd meeting, September 28, 1970, p. 37.

[29] Thomas (2001), *The Helsinki Effect*, p. 52. Jean H. Quataert makes the same point in Jean H. Quataert (2009), *Advocating Dignity. Human Rights Mobilizations in Global Politics*. Philadelphia, PA, p. 94.

[30] My italics. See United Nations (1970), *Declaration on Principles of International Law Concerning Friendly Relations and Co-operation Among States in Accordance With the Charter of the United Nations*. Document A/8082 available at: www.unmultimedia.org/searchers/yearbook/search.jsp?q=A%2F8082 (accessed on September 16, 2015).

for détente and cooperation in Europe were being elaborated. This points toward an important historical point about the human rights linkages between the 1960s and the 1970s.

During the CSCE negotiations, Western states were benefiting from the Liberian initiative that in the 1960s had placed freedom of thought, conscience and religion high on the agenda for international human rights diplomacy. The 1970 Declaration consolidated this normative development for the process that unfolded in Helsinki and Geneva from 1972 to 1975. The point is not that Europe and the United States did not have its own history of engaging with freedom of thought, conscience and religion in political and constitutional thinking. They clearly did. The point is that they had not had the foresight or ability to elevate it as a core principle in the evolving global human rights framework that shaped how international principles on cooperation and friendly relations among states were defined. Liberia's initiative in 1962 provided a missing link in this process at a time when both the United States and the major European powers were skeptical about the international human rights framework.

Liberia's challenge to the Communist political order reflected some deeper historical roots. Liberia represented a negation of the American historical experience but an affirmation of its constitutional values. The Liberian state was created in the 1820s by the American Colonization Society and by former slaves believing that the United States offered no future. Hence, the country was created because of American slavery by people who were forced to escape to remain free from slavery and racism. This was the negation of the American historical experience, but the new country based itself on the American Constitution almost ad verbatim. A cornerstone of this document was religious freedom and this became part of Liberian multilateral diplomacy. Liberia was a founding member of the United Nations and their promotion of elimination of religious intolerance at the United Nations with their remarkable 1962 initiative can be seen as a projection of their constitutional values onto the multilateral scene and the new international world in the making. By the time of the CSCE a decade later, the Western European states were embracing this human rights thinking and were building on 1960s developments in which they had been, at best, reactive. In reality, they were reaping the Liberian dividend. This was a somewhat contradictory outcome compared with the realities of life in Liberia itself.[31]

---

[31] Liberian foreign policy was Western-oriented, anti-Communist and strived to be a moderating voice in African politics also engaging actively with international institutions.

The wider international developments in the human rights field were definitely on the radar of CSCE diplomats as one influential British diplomat highlighted the link to the international apartheid debates, saying, "it is hard to swallow a situation in which apartheid has become a major issue in international relations with the Soviet Union leading the pack, while their own shortcomings are allowed to pass."[32] The period after the 1968 International Human Rights Year had given the British additional cause for frustration as the Soviet Union had filibustered and effectively undermined UN debates on the creation of a UN High Commissioner for Human Rights and on individual petition.[33] This backdrop illustrates why the European political context alone is too narrow a framework to explain how and why the human rights provisions became part of the Helsinki Final Act. The process was drawn out on a larger political and strategic canvas than that of European politics. The United Nations was an important forum for channeling global political changes into normative developments. The United Nations served as a useful parallel forum during the CSCE negotiations that were initiated in November 1972.

Negotiating the human rights provisions, 1972–1975

The 1975 Helsinki Final Act is widely regarded as a turning point in European politics that helped broker a peaceful end to the Cold War.[34] As mentioned, it was an outcome of the CSCE, which from 1972 brought together almost all European states and the United States and Canada to negotiate the conditions for a possible détente in Europe. The Final Act

Domestic life revealed a more complex reality under the rule of William W. S. Tubman – six-term President from 1944 until his death in 1971 – whose autocratic style of leadership and monopolizing of power was detrimental to democratic development and could not hide the sense of exclusion felt by large groups in society. This would become a source of future violent conflict. See D. Elwood Dunn (2009), *Liberia and the United States during the Cold War*. London, pp. 31–45.

[32] Letter from U.K. Ambassador John Killick (Moscow) to Alec Douglas-Home, September 5, 1973, *Documents on British Policy Overseas Series III, Vol. II*, Document 45. London, 1997, p. 179.

[33] British National Archives (Kew), FCO 95/1118, "The Soviet Union, the UN and Human Rights," May 1971.

[34] Poul Villaume and Odd Arne Westad (eds.) (2010), *Perforating the Iron Curtain: European Détente, Transatlantic Relations and the Cold War, 1965–1985*. Copenhagen; Oliver Bange and Gottfried Niedhart (eds.) (2008), *Helsinki 1975 and the Transformation of Europe*. New York; Andreas Wenger, Vojtech Mastny and Christian Nuenlist (eds.) (2008), *Origins of the European Security System: The Helsinki Process Revisited, 1965–75*. London; Sarah Snyder (2011), *Human Rights Activism and the End of the Cold War: A Transnational History of the Helsinki Network*. Cambridge.

covered a wide range of issues from overarching principles of interstate relations to concrete measures related to military security, economic collaboration, trade, environmental concerns, cultural exchanges, technical collaboration, confidence-building measures, tourism, travel and family reunification. The process also helped to settle territorial issues that had been left unresolved in the aftermath of the Second World War and which left East Germany without formal recognition as a state and hence without political representation in international forums. This settlement was the major policy objective behind the Soviet Union's desire to engage in a European peace conference. The CSCE was only possible after West Germany, through the *Ostpolitik* implemented by the former Mayor of West Berlin, and from 1969, German Chancellor Willy Brandt had entered into a number of bilateral agreements with Eastern states aimed at normalizing relations. The West, however, never closed the door on the possibility for future German reunification.[35]

The Western European states believed that any CSCE agreement should be based on principles of international law. They did not want the Soviet Union to achieve an agreement that would appear to constitute separate regional European law. There was always a risk of the latter happening as it suited Soviet designs and ambitions. It had been a struggle not to allow such designs to shape the 1970 *UN Declaration on Principles of International Law*. This was also the reason why the Western states, being deeply skeptical of Soviet intentions, did not accept that the Final Act would have a legally binding status. It was to be a political agreement with built-in follow-up procedures to monitor implementation by the participating states. The negotiation process could justifiably limit its attention to European issues and the realities facing a continent divided on military and ideological grounds, but it remained a struggle over which version of détente would prevail. In this process, the 1970 UN Declaration was a frequent reference point and was influential in shaping the design of the Helsinki Final Act – especially Basket I. It is therefore relevant to take a closer look at the process from 1972 to 1975 to understand how human rights became such a central component of the Final Act of the CSCE.

The CSCE was a complex and controversial undertaking. In the early stages, it was criticized for legitimizing Soviet control in Eastern Europe

---

[35] Ratti, Luca (2008), *Britain, Ost- and Deutschlandpolitik, and the CSCE (1955–1975)*. Bern; Romano, Angela (2009), *From Détente in Europe to European Détente. How the West Shaped the Helsinki CSCE*. Bruxelles.

due to its emphasis on inviolability of frontiers – seen as ensuring the status quo of a divided Europe. The Helsinki Final Act also included some of the most far-reaching human rights commitments contained in any international agreement up to this point. These commitments were initially subject to much skepticism, but they would create a platform for East European dissidents and human rights monitoring groups that, combined with international scrutiny, further challenged the legitimacy of the Communist regimes. The human rights commitments were embedded in a larger set of political agreements but were a critical component of the strategy pursued by the members of the European Community, known as the "EEC Nine," who showed a hitherto unseen level of political coordination during the CSCE negotiations from 1972 until the summer of 1975 when the Helsinki Final Act was signed.[36] The "Nine" transformed the Soviet desire for a new political settlement in Europe, which included limiting U.S. influence in Western Europe, into something that was much more in Western favor than most observers had expected would be achievable.[37] The Soviet Union had wanted a European security conference for a long time before the negotiations finally started in 1972. It turned out differently from what they had wanted.

The Helsinki Final Act was a new beginning for human rights politics. The human rights components of the Helsinki Process have been the subject of much scholarly interest. It is striking that the existing research on human rights and the Helsinki Process narrates the story as if there were no prehistory. It is well known that the idea for a European security conference predated the actual beginning of the CSCE negotiations by almost two decades. This two-decade-long approach to landing the CSCE negotiations has been studied. It is known that the notion of a human dimension, including more direct communications between the peoples of the divided Europe, was aired by Western states as early as the 1950s.[38] The significant contribution made by the *Ostpolitik*, including the West German bilateral cooperation agreements with several Eastern European countries, developed by Willy Brandt, who after serving as Foreign Minister had become German Chancellor in 1969, has also

---

[36] See Daniel Moeckli (2009), *European Foreign Policy during the Cold War: Heath, Brandt, Pompidou and the Dream of Political Unity.* London.

[37] Romano, Angela (2010), "The Main Task of the European Political Cooperation: Fostering Détente in Europe," *Perforating the Iron Curtain: European Détente, Transatlantic Relations, and the Cold War, 1965–1985.* Edited by Poul Villaume and Odd Arne Westad. Copenhagen, pp. 123–142.

[38] Romano (2009), *From Détente in Europe to European Détente,* p. 62.

been well studied and rightly so. However, when it comes to studying the human rights components, it is presented very differently – most often as a self-contained story where the starting point for human rights is situated somewhere within the Helsinki Process itself.[39] This is a problem both of research design and of scholarly imagination, which means we do not have an adequate understanding of why "Respect for human rights and fundamental freedoms, including the freedom of thought, conscience, religion or belief" became the core human rights principle (also known as Principle 7) of the Helsinki Final Act and how it entered the agreement. The human rights principle combined generic language with the specific language of Article 18 of the Covenant on Civil and Political Rights, which had also informed the work on the Convention on Elimination of All Forms of Religious Intolerance. This outcome is worth exploring in greater detail.

On July 3, 1973, the Soviet Foreign Minister Andrei Gromyko spoke before the Foreign Ministers gathered in Helsinki. After six months of negotiations, they had gathered to discuss the CSCE process and reaffirm their agreement of the outcome of the early negotiations – known as the *Multilateral Preparatory Talks* (MPT). On June 8, 1973, the CSCE diplomats had agreed on the *Final Recommendations of the Helsinki Consultations* that established the framework for the process. In his speech, Gromyko stated that "respect for human rights and fundamental freedoms, including the freedom of religious beliefs" was among the generally recognized norms of relations among states and reflected the specific political features of Europe.[40] Gromyko's choice of words was noteworthy. That the Soviet Union appeared to speak in favor of religious freedom was certainly a surprising development. There is little doubt that, on one level, the statement can be seen as a Soviet "sweetener" – a tactic that was a regular feature of the Soviet negotiation strategy during the CSCE.[41] On

---

[39] The first mention of human rights in the preparatory phase appears to have been a document by the French that in April 1970 made reference to the Universal Declaration of Human Rights. By September 1971, human rights had a more consolidated presence in background notes. Romano (2009), *From Détente in Europe to European Détente*, p. 106, 114.

[40] Speech by Soviet Foreign Minister Andrei Gromyko, July 3, 1973, quoted from *Human Rights, European Politics and the Helsinki Accord: The Documentary Evolution of the Conference on Security and Co-operation in Europe 1973–1975*, Vol. 1. Edited by Igor Kavass, Jaqueline Granier and Mary Frances Dominick. Buffalo, NY, 1981, p. 55.

[41] For an elaboration of the Soviet "sweetener" strategy, see John Maresca (1987), *To Helsinki: The Conference on Security and Cooperation in Europe 1973–1975*. Durham, NC, pp. 25–33.

another level, this type of statement reflected something more significant, namely that human rights provisions were potentially on offer, raising Western expectations and ambitions for what could be achieved through the CSCE process. It would not be a simple process going forward, but that there was something to hold out for was confirmed in the *Final Recommendations* from June 1973. It was in this document that Principle 7 on "Respect for Human Rights and fundamental freedoms, including the freedom of thought, conscience, religion and belief" was first established as part of the CSCE framework.[42]

This was an outcome of the earliest stage of negotiations. In November 1972, as the CSCE diplomats gathered at the Dipoli Conference venue just outside Helsinki for preparatory talks, they worked to establish the framework for the whole process. The process had gained momentum since the late 1960s, initiated at least in part in response to the unsettled European situation within the military blocs and after the Soviet invasion of Czechoslovakia in August 1968.[43] The process was initially envisaged to have a relatively narrow focus. The Warsaw Pact wanted to focus on the renunciation of force and on expanding trade, while the early Western draft proposals also had a limited scope.[44] Proposals were more advanced by the time the preparatory talks started, and by December 1972, a proposal for an elaborate three-stage CSCE process guided the discussions. Human rights became a part of the negotiations in mid-January 1973 with an initial proposal by Italy. This coordinated move could be viewed as part of a dual-track strategy involving the United Nations.

In November 1972, after five years, the UN General Assembly re-opened the discussion on making freedom of thought, conscience and religion into an international human rights instrument. It was Sweden and the Netherlands who most actively promoted this move. The USSR and Belarus tried to sideline the effort on procedural grounds. References to the 1960s debates appeared frequently and the title of the proposed instrument was the same, namely a Declaration or Convention on Elimination of All Forms of Religious Intolerance. The promoters of the

---

[42] "Final Recommendations from the Helsinki Consultations," *Human Rights, European Politics and the Helsinki Accord*, Vol. 1, p. 10.

[43] Jussi M. Hanhimäki (2003), "'They Can Write It in Swahili': Kissinger, The Soviets, and the Helsinki Accords, 1973–1975," *Journal of Transatlantic Studies*, vol. 1, no. 1, p. 39.

[44] "Britain and the Soviet Union 1968–1972," *Documents on British Policy Overseas Series III, Vol. I*. London, 1997, p. 196.

proposal, supported by Liberia and Morocco among others, secured a resolution that placed the drafting of an instrument on freedom of religion on the agenda for the 1973 UN General Assembly.[45] These debates illustrate that the Western emphasis on religion in the CSCE context was related to the normative process that had previously been set in motion at the United Nations.

The Italian proposal to the CSCE was presented in Helsinki on January 15, 1973. It was launched on the same day as a Danish proposal on "Development of Human Contacts, Broadening of Cultural and Educational Exchanges and Wider Flow of Information" which would become Basket III.[46] The Italian proposal was the first elaboration of what would become the guiding principles. It outlined nine of the ten principles that were included in the June 1973 document. In the Italian proposal, the language was "respect for human rights, for fundamental freedoms and for equal rights and self-determination of peoples." It also highlighted "fulfillment in good faith of obligations under international law."[47]

In a proposal from January 17, 1973, two days later, one of the neutrals, Switzerland, elaborated on this proposal, separating "respect for human rights and fundamental freedoms" from the principle on equal rights and self-determination of peoples. In the following months, debate would ensue over the exact language. The other principles were relatively fixed but the human rights principle was repeatedly challenged. The Soviet Union was working to make the principle of nonintervention in domestic affairs a principle that ranked over the principles of human rights and self-determination.[48] The human rights language was only settled in late May when the full wording with "freedom of thought, conscience, religion or belief" became part of the list of the ten guiding principles in the Final Recommendations document from June 8. This was why Gromyko made the statement he did at the July Helsinki Conference, glossing over Soviet obstructions. It was this principle that created the foundation for the specific human rights provisions during the second stage of the CSCE.

---

45 See UN General Assembly Resolution 3027/27 adopted at the 2114th meeting, December 18, 1972.

46 See CESC/HC/19 from January 15, 1973 – Denmark, OSCE Archive, Prague.

47 CESC/HC/18 from January 15, 1973 – Italy, OSCE Archive, Prague.

48 Thomas Fischer (2009), *Neutral Power in the CSCE. The N+N States and the Making of the Helsinki Accords 1975*. Vienna, p. 193.

There was an attempt at the July 1973 Helsinki Conference, known as Stage I, to change the meaning of Principle 7. It was a move that revealed the true nature of Gromyko's "sweetener." The Soviet Foreign Minister's speech from July 3 was followed by a Soviet proposal dated July 4, entitled "General Declaration on the Foundations of European Security and the Principles Guiding Relations between States in Europe." The Soviet proposal was based on the framework provided by the ten principles, but by providing specific content, they could try and influence their meaning as they would try with Principle 4 on "Inviolability of Frontiers."[49]

The only principle that had a changed title in the Soviet proposal was the human rights principle. The wording "respect for human rights and fundamental freedoms" remained but the latter part "including the freedom of thought, conscience, religion or belief" had been deleted. In the explanation of Principle 7, the Soviet proposal read "the participating States will respect human rights and fundamental freedoms, including freedom of religious belief." What sounded like a Soviet acceptance of recognizing and protecting religious freedom was in essence an effort to eradicate freedom of thought and conscience from the guiding principles of the CSCE. It was a battle over political meaning and it might well have proved to be a very sour "sweetener" if the Soviet move had succeeded. It did not.[50] The formula that combined thought, conscience and religion and which had been determined as a unified human rights standard during the drafting of the 1948 Universal Declaration of Human Rights had proven its worth as an established international principle.

Several of the foreign ministers touched upon the relationship between the different baskets. The British Foreign Secretary Alec Douglas-Home did so most eloquently when he pushed for a practical approach. He argued that "The principles are valueless without the practice. In the language of Helsinki, Basket I will be empty unless there are plenty of eggs in Basket III."[51] Douglas-Home did not specifically mention human rights, preferring instead to quote an earlier statement by Andrei Gromyko that the Conference should deliver "a code of conduct for Europe," but by

---

[49] Gottfried Niedhart (2008), "Peaceful Change of Frontiers as a Crucial Element in the West German Strategy of Transformation," *Helsinki 1975 and the Transformation of Europe.* Edited by Oliver Bange and Gottfried Niedhart. New York, pp. 43–45.

[50] The text of the *Final Recommendations* from June 8 became the outcome from the July 1973 Stage I meeting.

[51] CSCE/I/PV.5: Speech by Alec Douglas-Home (UK), Helsinki, July 5, 1973, pp. 200–201.

highlighting freedom of movement and freer exchange of information and ideas, the British Foreign Minister's statement was an expressed commitment to the human rights components of the CSCE.[52]

From the beginning of October 1973, in what was known as Stage II of the negotiations, the Netherlands and the United Kingdom pushed the human rights agenda with a strategy to broaden it beyond Principle 7. On October 3, 1973, both countries submitted new proposals to the CSCE to elaborate on the meaning of the guiding principles. They also linked the Declaration in Basket I with progress on the more detailed provisions in Basket III. If Western states had throughout the 1950s and 1960s expressed qualms when developing countries promoted self-determination as a human rights issue, they had learned to "suppress" their old discomforts. Times had changed and the Netherlands, the former colonial power, now sought to include the principle from Article 1 of the International Covenants on self-determination into the Helsinki Principle 8 on "Equal rights and self-determination of peoples" in a slightly reworded version.

The Dutch approach had been outlined by their Foreign Minister Max van der Stoel in his speech in Helsinki on July 6, 1973.[53] The October 1973 proposal argued that the CSCE states should recognize the inalienable right of every people with respect for human rights and fundamental freedoms to choose or change its own system (whether political, economic, social or cultural), without facing any kind of interference from another state or a group of states.[54] The shadow of the invasion of

---

[52] The British were clearly active in securing strong human rights provisions in the Helsinki Final Act. The nature of this engagement has been subject to scholarly debate. I side with the "proactive" interpretation argued in Kai Hebel (2014), "Propaganda Tools and Idealistic Goals: Britain and the Cold War Politics of Human Rights in the CSCE Context, 1972–1973," *Human Rights in Europe during the Cold War*. Edited by Rasmus Mariager, Karl Molin and Kersti Brathagen, London, pp. 113–135, as opposed to a British "indifferent" view on human rights argued by Martin D. Brown (2012), "A Very British View of Détente: The United Kingdom's Foreign Policy during the Helsinki Process, 1969–1975," *Visions of the End of the Cold War in Europe, 1945–1990*. Edited by Frédéric Bozo *et al.*, New York, pp. 121–133.

[53] CSCE/I/PV.7: Speech by Mr. Van der Stoel (the Netherlands), Helsinki, July 6, 1973, pp. 312–313. For a more detailed account of the Dutch focus on human rights in the CSCE process during this period, see Floribert Baudet (2008), "It Was Cold War and We Wanted to Win": Human Rights, "Détente" and the CSCE," *Origins of the European Security System: The Helsinki Process Revisited, 1965–75*. Edited by Andreas Wenger, Vojtech Mastny and Christian Nuenlist, Abingdon, pp. 183–198.

[54] CSCE/II/A/8, Geneva, October 3, 1973, "Explanatory Document Submitted by the Delegation of the Netherlands: Equal Rights and Self-determination," Vol. 2, OSCE Archives, Prague.

Czechoslovakia loomed large over this language. Self-determination as a human right had traditionally been strongly criticized by Western states while the Communist states had promoted it because of decolonization. The tables had turned.

The U.K. proposal was a first draft of what became the specific content of Principle 7. It recommended that NGOs and individuals should participate in efforts to promote human rights. There would be no reference to NGOs in the Helsinki Final Act but the reference to individuals would be strengthened. The U.K. proposal also emphasized that all states would be bound by the UN Charter and all other international human rights conventions and instruments. It was an invitation to continue the elaboration of these principles in the United Nations. This was done at the 1973 UN General Assembly in New York later the same month.

On October 25, 1973, the Netherlands opened the UN debate and presented a new draft Declaration on the Elimination of All Forms of Religious Intolerance. Their statement was followed by another active CSCE state, Denmark, who made it clear that the purpose was "to give more substance to article 18 of the Universal Declaration of Human Rights" – the article on freedom of thought, conscience and religion. With Italy making the third statement, it looked like a coordinated strategy. They all wanted a declaration ready before the end of the 1973 General Assembly session to mark the 25th anniversary of the Universal Declaration. The counterreaction came from Belarus using procedural issues to delay the work.

The debate proceeded with arguments for and against preparing an international declaration. The debate also dealt with protection of believers and atheists, and the "silent church" behind the Iron Curtain. Poland advocated what was a novel approach to sidelining progress with the instrument on religious intolerance. They argued that an effective effort to strengthen human rights and fundamental freedoms should instead focus on "the greatest possible number of states," acceding to the, "most important" international human rights instruments, namely the Covenants on Civil and Political Rights and on Economic, Social and Cultural Rights. It seemed like the goal posts in the international human rights debate had shifted within very few years. Had ratification of the Human Rights Covenants become a strategy by the Communist states to shift focus away from new human rights instruments? There certainly was an intimate timing between the Helsinki Process and the ratification and entry into force of the two Covenants. It was another example of the mutually reinforcing processes occurring in the human rights field by the mid-1970s. The

Polish position may also reflect that they believed that the enforcement provisions in the two Covenants were sufficiently weak to not cause them any domestic problems, whereas new normative and legal developments incurred a risk.

During the 1973 UN General Assembly session, the Third Committee worked on the preamble and eight articles for the draft Declaration. The draft was met with counterproposals. As time ran out, a consensus resolution was tabled in early November.[55] It was not as ambitious as the promoters of the agenda item had hoped but it did reaffirm Article 18 as the basis for a new international instrument and enabled the work to continue within the United Nations beyond the 1973 General Assembly. If the initiative had not been wholly successful, it did help draw concessions of relevance for the CSCE negotiations.

The first CSCE debate on the specific content of Principle 7 started a few weeks later and took place between November 26 and December 4, 1973. The EEC "Nine" further consolidated their joint commitment to human rights in December 1973 by issuing the *Copenhagen Declaration on European Identity*. It was useful for the purpose of the CSCE negotiations to emphasize a commitment by the members of the EEC:

based on a determination to build a society which measures up to the needs of the individual, they are determined to defend the principles of representative democracy, of the rule of law, of social justice – which is the ultimate goal of economic progress – and of respect for human rights. All of these are fundamental elements of the European Identity.[56]

The CSCE was not just an ongoing process of consolidating the work of the "Nine" but also a process of West European identity-making.[57]

On January 25, 1974, it was decided that the drafting of the principles should begin by starting with the first principle and then work its way through to Principle 10.[58] It was only in July 1974 that the Stage II negotiations reached Principle 7. The negotiations on Principle 7 would continue for the remainder of 1974 while the other baskets took

---

[55] Mr. Karassimeonov (Bulgaria), UN General Assembly, Third Committee, 28th session, 2014th meeting, November 1, 1973, p. 198.

[56] European Community (1973), *Declaration of European Identity (Copenhagen, December 14, 1973)*. Available at: www.cvce.eu/content/publication/1999/1/1/02798dc9-9c 69-4b7d-b2c9-f03a8db7da32/publishable_en.pdf (accessed on September 16, 2015).

[57] Romano (2010), "The Main Task of the European Political Cooperation," pp. 123–142.

[58] See Journal no. 55, January 25, 1974, Committee I: Sub-Committee 1. Edited by Igor Kavass, Jaqueline Granier and Mary Frances Dominick, Vol. 2: Stage 2 – Geneva 1973–1975.

form.[59] By November 20, 1974, the provisional text for Principle 7 was registered. Officially, its place in the final document and the overall agreement on the text was still to be confirmed, but this draft became the wording included in the Helsinki Final Act.[60]

The Western states wanted the negotiations on each area to develop in parallel to ensure balance and interdependence between the different baskets. It also made it more possible to hold out for concessions. The principle of human rights in Basket I needed to find concrete expression in Basket III on human and cultural contacts. The ambition was that Basket III should cover provisions related to freedom of movement and ideas, including family reunification, travel and cultural exchanges. The Soviet Union saw agreement on Basket III provisions linked to concessions on other Basket I principles, namely the principles regarding the inviolability of frontiers and nonintervention in internal affairs.[61] It was this multidimensional and integrated approach that brought a lot of the complexity into the negotiation process. It was, however, also the cornerstone for any successful outcome.[62]

Human rights in the 1975 Helsinki Final Act

The Helsinki Final Act reflected a peculiar balancing act regarding international law. This Europe-wide agreement applied a set of legal principles without making them binding. The human rights provisions extended to all three Baskets. To understand the meaning of this, a closer reading of the 1975 Final Act is required.

Basket I contained the "Declaration on Principles Guiding Relations between Participating States," which was inspired by the 1970 UN Declaration. It consisted of ten main principles, where number 7 was "Respect for human rights and fundamental freedoms, including the freedom

---

[59] The negotiations took place from July 5 to July 26, 1974 (Journal nos. 139–152), September 9 to October 14, 1974 (Journal nos. 153–175), October 22 to November 14, 1974 (Journal nos. 180–196) and on November 20 (Journal no. 200).

[60] CSCE/II/A/136 – Principle 7. See also Letter from Mr. Hildyard (UKMIS Geneva) to John Killick, November 29, 1974, *Documents on British Policy Overseas Series III, Vol. II* (Document 105). London, 1997, p. 359.

[61] Thomas (1999), *The Helsinki Effect*, pp. 75–76. On Basket III, see also Poul Villaume (forthcoming), "Anticipating European Détente: Denmark, NATO and the Struggle for an All-European Security Conference in 'The Long 1970s'," *The Long 1970s. New Perspectives on the Epoch-Making Decade: Human Rights East-West Détente and Transnational Diplomacy*. Edited by Poul Villaume, Helle Porsdam and Rasmus Mariager, Farnham.

[62] Richard Davy (2009), "Helsinki Myths: Setting the Record Straight on the Final Act of the CSCE, 1975," *Cold War History*, vol. 9, no. 1, pp. 1–22.

of thought, conscience, religion or belief."[63] This principle was elaborated in eight paragraphs – making it the most detailed principle in the Declaration. It reaffirmed in paragraph 1 the nondiscriminatory measures as extending to "race, sex, language and religion." The second paragraph of Principle 7 established a commitment to promote the broad range of rights – civil, political, economic, social and cultural. The special significance awarded to religious freedom was visible in paragraph 3, which focused on freedom of religion and determined that states would respect "the freedom of the individual to profess and practice, alone or in community with others, religion or belief acting in accordance with the dictates of his own conscience." This was, at least on paper, a significant concession gained from the Soviet Union and the Communist bloc. The content was well aligned with the revised *Draft Declaration on the Elimination of All Forms of Intolerance and Discrimination based on Religion or Belief* that Sweden and the Netherlands had submitted to the UN General Assembly in November 1974.[64]

Paragraphs 5–8 expanded the meaning and application of human rights as a set of obligations and, by design, grounded these in the framework of the whole Final Act. First, human rights were determined as "an essential factor for the peace, justice and well-being" necessary for friendly relations and cooperation among all states. The Final Act built explicitly on the 1970 UN Declaration on Principles of International Law. Paragraph 6 contained a commitment to "constantly respect these rights and freedoms in their mutual relations" and to promote universal respect for them "jointly and separately," including at the UN and thereby acknowledged the relevance of the United Nations to the CSCE. It also indicated that the UN setting could be used to evolve principles that could then be built upon in the CSCE process. In this context, it was not coincidental that 1972, 1973 and 1974 witnessed a renewed interest in religious freedom as part of the UN General Assembly human rights debates. Paragraph 6 was a call for states to act on human rights in their domestic setting.

Paragraph 7 presented a simple but profound and potentially far-reaching obligation as the CSCE states "confirm the right of the individual to know and act upon his rights and duties." It was a direct challenge to the Communist system and one that would subsequently inspire dissidents behind the Iron Curtain. Finally, paragraph 8 committed states to "act in

---

[63] See text of Helsinki Final Act – Basket I, Principle 7.
[64] A/C.3/L.2131: Elimination of All Forms of Religious Intolerance, Working Paper by the Netherlands and Sweden, November 11, 1974.

conformity" with the human rights elements of the UN Charter, the Universal Declaration of Human Rights and to "fulfill their obligations" of international agreements, including the 1966 International Covenants on Human Rights. The language here varied between softer wording relating to the 1940s documents and stronger wording related to the obligations emanating with the 1960s documents that had transformed human rights into international law and that states would be bound by upon ratification. The language represented a historical evolution that demonstrated how the 1960s were central to the political, diplomatic and semilegal ambition that the "Declaration on Principles Guiding Relations between Participating States" in Basket I represented.

Basket II extended the Declaration on Principles, including the principle on human rights, to all areas under its heading "Co-operation in the Field of Economics, of Science and Technology and of the Environment." It rather discreetly included some elements with a human rights dimension to them, namely the areas dealing with health and migrant workers. The wider theme of "Science and Technology" also included provisions that supported freedom of information through increased collaboration and exchanges in these areas. Nevertheless, Basket II focused on ways to increase technical collaboration and exchange on a range of issues. It is usually not considered for its human rights content. It is noteworthy, however, that the environmental issues included in Basket II would later become an area used by Eastern European dissidents for mobilizing for human rights.[65]

Basket III included provisions related to freedom of movement and freedom of information, reflecting a desire from the Western countries for freer movement of peoples and ideas. These were areas that had received long-standing attention in UN human rights debates but with limited progress. Both freedom of movement and freedom of information were part of the 1948 Universal Declaration of Human Rights and the 1966 Covenants on Human Rights. They had also – although to little effect – been subject of elaboration as specific instruments as part of the Cold War struggle at the United Nations. There had been unsuccessful attempts to develop a Convention on Freedom of Information in the 1940s through to the 1960s.[66]

---

[65] Kacper Szulecki (2011), "Hijacked Ideas: Human Rights, Peace and Environmentalism in Czechoslovak and Polish Dissident Discourses," *East European Politics and Societies*, vol. 25, no. 2, pp. 272–295.

[66] Eckel, Jan (2014), *Die Ambivalenz des Guten. Menschenrechte in der Internationalen Politik seit den 1940ern*. Göttingen, pp. 123–135.

It was therefore not the novelty of the human rights standards promoted during the Helsinki negotiations that was the source of its success. It was the timing, established precedent and the new political context for applying human rights that made this strategy possible and part of the Western European negotiating position. The status of human rights had matured with the UN diplomacy during the 1960s and a major barrier for a fuller engagement with human rights by the leading Western European states had subsided. European values had gradually been transformed through the process of decolonization.

Helsinki 1975

As the thirty-five Heads of State from CSCE countries gathered in July–August 1975 for the signing ceremony, each leader spoke and expressed their official views on the Final Act. The speeches were exercises in highlighting achievements while managing disappointments. Many statements focused on what should be expected from the Helsinki Final Act. In the speeches by the Communist countries, there was not one single reference to human rights or fundamental freedoms. In the speeches by the EEC Nine and the West European neutrals, it was a recurring theme. It was emphasized that a new principle had been established. Several Western statements highlighted the specific importance of the human rights provisions on freedom of religion or the wider freedom of thought, conscience and religion. A number of these statements also referred to the United Nations as a wider forum for human rights promotion and universality. The West European states were fully aware that the Council of Europe and the European Convention on Human Rights had contributed little to the process. The Council of Europe offered a legal and political institutional framework that was too geographically restrictive in scope, focusing as it did on Western Europe and Greece and Turkey, to help deliver a wider normative foundation for human rights in this more expansive pan-European setting.

The divisions between East and West were expressed most clearly on human rights, with the former emphasizing the principles on inviolability of frontiers and territorial integrity of states. Swedish Prime Minister Olof Palme combined the new meaning of human rights with a strong expression of policy intent. Palme first explained that "the respect for human rights has been accepted as a norm of equal rank with other principles of international relations. We recognize thereby that flagrant violations of these rights cannot but affect the climate of détente," but he went further and stated, "frank criticism must be allowed to make itself heard in the face of phenomena such as the oppression of dissidents, torture and racial discrimination."[67] It was a clear-sighted statement. The plight of dissidents behind the Iron Curtain became one of the areas where the Helsinki Final Act would play its most significant role. Palme pointed to this already in the summer of 1975. His point on torture was one of clear policy intent since shortly after Sweden launched a human rights initiative on torture at the UN General Assembly that resulted in the 1975 *Declaration on the Protection of All Persons from Being Subjected to Torture and Other Cruel, Inhuman or Degrading Treatment or Punishment* – the basis for the 1984 Convention against Torture. It reflected a position pointing back to the 1968 Amnesty International meeting in Stockholm on torture that had mobilized both Swedish civil society and the government on this issue. Palme's reference to racial discrimination was recognition of the foundation on which the new human rights system was built. In his Helsinki speech, Palme thereby captured the past, present and future of international human rights diplomacy and activism.

It was an indication that the status of human rights in international affairs was broadening and consolidating. The Western human rights strategy does deserve a comment. The Western countries were calling for adherence to international standards and binding instruments to which they themselves had not committed. The Helsinki Final Act calls for fulfilling "obligations as set forth in the international declarations and agreements in this field, including inter alia the International Covenants on Human Rights."[68] By August 1, 1975, when the Heads of States signed the Helsinki Final Act, it was only Denmark and West Germany among the EEC Nine that had ratified the Covenant on Civil and Political Rights and the Covenant on Economic, Social and Cultural Rights. Beyond the EEC Nine, it was only Sweden and Norway among the West European countries that had ratified these Covenants. Not even Finland – in whose capital the gathering took place and gave name to the Final Act – had done so. Within three weeks, on August 19, 1975, Finland ratified both Covenants at the United Nations, probably realizing they needed to "catch up." Other states that had been active promoters of the human rights provisions in the Final Act would only ratify later

---

[67] Mr. Palme (Sweden), pp. 104–105.
[68] See Helsinki Final Act, Basket I, Principle 7, paragraph 8.

(e.g., U.K. in 1976; the Netherlands and Italy in 1978). The irony was that the Communist states had, to a wide extent, ratified the Covenants before the signing of the Helsinki Final Act. Eight of them had ratified the Covenants (Bulgaria 1970; Yugoslavia 1971; the USSR, East Germany, Belarus and Ukraine in 1973; Hungary and Romania in 1974) before the CSCE negotiations were completed, and when Czechoslovakia in December 1975 as the 35th country ratified the Covenant on Civil and Political Rights, it entered into force.

These data reveal the rather tentative status for human rights as an area of international politics and law in the mid-1970s. The rationale and timing for the formal ratifications by Communist states deserve further study. It is likely they believed they were in full control of the domestic situation, so ratification would not be a political problem at home but could provide a tactical advantage abroad. It is also possible that normative goal posts had changed and the ratifications expressed similar to ratifying the Convention on racial discrimination necessary international commitments. It is also possible that signing the Covenants was a strategy to restrain the development of new instruments on freedom of thought, conscience and religion; however, by making respect for human rights a condition for détente, the significance of human rights was raised to a new level. It is perhaps most logical to see the delayed ratification by Western European states as a legacy of the problems these countries had had with the international human rights diplomacy of the 1960s. They had not fully adapted – at least outside Scandinavia – to new values and new sources of meaning in international affairs. In this context, Helsinki became a lesson for everyone and this had a wider impact on international human rights.

The process of ensuring inclusion of the human rights provisions in the Helsinki Final Act was a political struggle over defining the specific meaning of détente and defining the elements of European cooperation and security. These definitions were not stable categories. The 1975 Final Act was a significant achievement but also a provisional one. The process that followed would entail a continued struggle of political interpretation. There were criticisms voiced against the 1975 agreement from several quarters. Others such as Olof Palme saw with greater clarity what the commitments made could entail and intently pursued these goals. It is interesting to note that these promoters were simultaneously heavily involved in the expansion of the international human rights system at the United Nations.

The human rights components of the CSCE process were part of a larger normative universe that had developed dramatically in the decade prior to the Helsinki Final Act. The American legal scholar Robert Cover talks of *jurisgenesis* – the creation of legal meaning. The making of the Helsinki Final Act was such an example – while it did not present itself as a formal legal process. The continued CSCE process would be a further development of this as individual dissidents, monitoring groups and committees, writers, intellectuals, academics and many more would start interpreting the meaning of the Helsinki agreement and act on it. It became part of a larger system of reciprocity and exchange between East and West that would fundamentally alter the political and military situation, ultimately leading to the largely peaceful transformation of Europe in 1989.[69] Human rights played a transformative role but it came about within a larger system of reciprocity and exchange. This should not be ignored. A detailed description of the human rights aspects during the 1972–1975 negotiations is highly relevant, but a fair assessment of the Helsinki process must acknowledge that human rights were not a stand-alone project. Human rights were embedded in larger political, security and economic frameworks and narratives.[70]

If we pursue the context of the human rights narratives from which the Final Act drew its meaning, we can also observe a world on which the basis of contemporary Europe exists. It is a world where actors from the Global South elevated human rights during the 1960s, making them ripe for appropriation in a European political process in the 1970s. The CSCE and the decolonization process are hence linked at a normative and political level. Europe in the 1970s emerges in a slightly different light when viewed through this lens. The subtle but particular emphasis on religion and Article 18 on freedom of thought, conscience and religion links back to the Liberian initiative from the early 1960s and the political developments this initiated. The presence of human rights in the Helsinki Final Act therefore has an important background history. It was a further

---

[69] On societal systems of exchange and reciprocity and their importance for avoiding violent conflict, see Marcel Mauss (1925), *The Gift: Forms and Functions of Exchange in Archaic Societies*. London.

[70] An intriguing perspective on economic issues and Eastern financial debts is provided in Stephen Kotkin (2010), "The Kiss of Debt: The East Bloc Goes Borrowing," *The Shock of the Global – The 1970s in Perspective*. Edited by Niall Ferguson *et al.* Cambridge, MA, pp. 80–96.

iteration and not merely a *Stunde Nul* for human rights. It did, however, help move human rights toward a more central role in global politics. The year 1975 witnessed an important consolidation and expansion of these efforts as well as significant controversy over the meaning and application of human rights.

8

The presence of the disappeared, 1968–1993

"People were seized by images of physical suffering and donated generously to such organizations as Oxfam. But it was more difficult to make the leap of imagination into the cell of a political prisoner or to understand mental repression."

Statement at Human Rights Seminar, British Foreign Office,
June 1978[1]

As President of the 1975 UN General Assembly, Luxembourg's Foreign Minister Gaston Thorn would rapidly shift his attention from Helsinki to New York and oversee new developments in the human rights field. The Conference on Security and Cooperation in Europe (CSCE) had become the major forum for negotiating political détente and the Helsinki Final Act was presented at the United Nations as an important political development. At the UN General Assembly, European states reflected on the wider international meaning of the CSCE outcome. The Communist states highlighted their contributions to securing détente and stabilizing relations between states and claimed responsibility for the results while again ignoring the human rights provisions.[2] The West European states specifically highlighted the human rights provisions in the Helsinki Final Act that had made "the implementation of human rights a major subject"

---

[1] FCO 58/1421: Human Rights Seminar, June 22, 1978, Summary of afternoon session, p. 5.
[2] The Soviet Union called the Final Act "one of the most outstanding documents of our time," Mr. Gromyko (the USSR), UN General Assembly, 30th session, 2357th meeting, September 23, 1975, p. 106.

and emphasized their universality.[3] It was clear that human rights had achieved a new prominence in European diplomacy.

During the Helsinki Conference, where the Final Act was signed, Gaston Thorn had delivered a determined assessment of the human rights project in 1975, stating that "the time for verbal niceties and legalism has passed. We cannot camouflage reality. The meaning of words must be restored."[4] The CSCE was an important development, but Chile, torture, enforced disappearances and racial discrimination were the issues that would define the 1975 Assembly debate. Here, the work of restoration could not make the disappeared return to their families, their lives already taken and their bodies brutally disposed, but there was a restoration of sorts in terms of meaning; the disappeared were made present in the global conscience through their relatives' memory activism. This was supported by detailed human rights reporting and campaigning, which had a significant impact on international opinion. The reactions – especially to the practices of torture and enforced disappearances – helped change important aspects of the global moral imagination. The 1975 UN debates also revealed a more complicated reality.

Human rights were becoming a form of storytelling about the global human condition. There were plenty of stories to tell. In September 1976, ten Argentinean schoolchildren were kidnapped because they had signed a petition that called for reduced rates for students on buses. The regime responded by arresting, starving and torturing them. Seven of the schoolchildren never reappeared.[5] The Argentinean schoolchildren were victims of the military junta that took power in 1976. Their story was among hundreds, if not thousands, of stories about human rights violations being brought to public attention during the 1970s. Latin America, a region that had in previous decades made important contributions to international human rights standards, now found itself the unpleasant center of attention because of the gross violations taking place on the continent. Chile and Argentina were the most significant cases where the actions of the military dictatorships were measured against international

---

[3] Mr. Genscher (West Germany), UN General Assembly, 30th session, 2359th meeting, September 24, 1975, p. 141.

[4] Speech by Gustav Thorn (Luxembourg), CSCE/III/PV.6 – Helsinki, August 1, 1975, *Human Rights, European Politics and the Helsinki Accord: The Documentary Evolution of the Conference on Security and Co-operation in Europe 1973–1975*, Vol. 6. Edited by Igor Kavass, Jaqueline Granier and Mary Frances Dominick. Buffalo, NY, p. 168.

[5] Iain Guest (2000), *Behind the Disappearances: Argentina's Dirty War against Human Rights and the United Nations*. Philadelphia, PA, p. 31.

human rights standards. El Salvador and Guatemala followed around 1980. The Argentinean schoolchildren were among the 90,000 persons in Latin America who became victims of enforced disappearances from 1973 to 1983 – one third of these happening in Argentina during "the dirty war" from 1976 to 1982.[6]

The United Nations response to these atrocities was painfully slow and severely curtailed every step of the way. Powerful interests wanted it this way. Leading up to the 1968 Human Rights Year, the establishment of a range of new mechanisms to address human rights violations had been under negotiation, including a High Commissioner for Human Rights, a human rights council, regional courts and human rights mechanisms, national commissions on human rights, but none of these proposals had materialized. It was only a few fact-finding mechanisms that had come into existence. They did represent steps toward introducing some level of implementation measures, but their actual mandates were weak and they had a very limited geographical focus. It would take twenty-five years to reconstruct most of what had been aspired to, negotiated and subsequently lost between 1965 and 1968. The system would be exposed to significant criticism during the intervening decades up to the early 1990s when the post–Cold War human rights program was defined in 1993 at the first World Conference on Human Rights since the 1968 Tehran Conference. One of the most persistent criticisms – apart from inaction – was that the approach taken was the opposite of human rights universality. The accusations were that the system was extremely selective for political and ideological reasons. The story of human rights after 1968 and up until 1993 very much appears as one of a slow, staggered development of an international human rights system – a scramble for universality.

A major change between the 1960s and the 1970s was that external actors to the UN increasingly shaped the human rights field. They still lobbied and challenged the international organization, but to a large extent, they determined the focus of the debates. The strategy to give priority to human rights fact-finding developed by NGOs in 1968 had by 1973 led to a number of international NGOs presenting evidence on specific countries to the Commission on Human Rights. The leading organizations in this work were Amnesty International and the International Commission of Jurists. Both developed new types of human rights reporting,

---

[6] Jean Quataert (2009), *Advocating Dignity. Human Rights Mobilizations in Global Politics*. Philadelphia, PA, p. 129.

worldwide surveys and campaigning strategies linking country situations with international mass media publicity. Amnesty International's influential 1973 *Report on Torture*, the first world survey of its kind, dealt with more than sixty countries around the world at a time when the United Nations was only examining two cases.[7] Human rights found an identity through these representations. The fact that these violations were happening worldwide was in itself an affirmation – albeit in a very negative form – of the universality that underpinned human rights claims. People were victims of torture all over the world.

The surveys also helped the UN to face one of its major shortcomings. During the 1970s "UN selectivity" was increasingly highlighted as a major problem of credibility. Since the late 1960s, the UN's human rights focus had been on Israel and Southern Africa. In 1975, this expanded to Chile. Initially, it seemed as if the UN's very narrow focus had only expanded from two to three cases, but in reality, the controversies over Chile helped to shift the UN from selectivity to a much wider approach to human rights violations. This process took several years and the Argentinean case, with the many enforced disappearances, also played a role in the more concerted attack on selectivity that was launched in 1978. The disappeared achieved a presence in political terms because the campaigning of their relatives challenged the straitjacket of selectivity and expanded another aspect of universality, namely greater international attention to human rights violations wherever they happened. Local organizations, including the Mothers of the Disappeared in Argentina, were profoundly influential in this regard.

System in limbo, 1968–1973

The relationship between the moral and the legal imagination took on a new and more expansive form in the 1970s compared with the 1960s but also built on developments from the latter decade. There were preliminary discussions in 1973 about expanding the UN human rights work both geographically as well as with a stronger focus on torture. The military coup in Chile in 1973 would catapult these nascent developments into a much larger and decisive debate. Chile was both a rupture and the case that gave new shape to the different human rights efforts. UN implementation in the human rights field had little to show for itself at this point. The fact that the human rights Covenants were suspended

---

7 Amnesty International (1973), *Report on Torture*. London.

in legal limbo between their adoption in 1966 and the lack of sufficient ratifications that would allow them to enter into force did not help in the situation. By the beginning of 1973, only half of the necessary thirty-five state ratifications had been obtained. It left a degree of uncertainty about how the UN human rights system could develop further – despite the fact that the treaty body for the Convention on Elimination of All Forms of Racial Discrimination had started its work in 1971.

The Soviet Union continued with filibustering. During this period, the Communist states successfully used every procedural means to undermine efforts to create a position as UN High Commissioner for Human Rights and to deal with individual petitions that revealed "a consistent pattern of gross human rights violations." As more information was coming forward about dissident protests behind the Iron Curtain – against the backdrop of the Communist states' resistance to human rights – the relevance and necessity of human rights was coming into stark focus. Public opinion on foreign policy was changing in Western countries due to the Vietnam War, Czechoslovakia, South Africa and Biafra and was moving toward a greater appreciation of human rights and humanitarian concerns. Politicians were starting to consider the implications. Furthermore, various strands of human rights work had actually been developing since 1968. Their parallel development slowly reshaped the human rights field as these different forums started to provide each other with a set of political feedback mechanisms that each of them could use to expand their own contribution. The system was in limbo after 1968 but a range of initiatives had been taken that would contribute to a greater convergence in the 1970s.

In early 1967, the Commission on Human Rights established its first Ad Hoc Working Group. It came as a response to the failed South West Africa case before the International Court of Justice. As the bitterness at this outcome was expressed in no uncertain terms at the UN General Assembly, members of the Commission sought a new approach to point the spotlight at the situation in Southern Africa. The proposal for a fact-finding group was pushed by Commission members from the Global South and was the subject of intense negotiations at the important 1967 session of the Commission on Human Rights. Subsequently, the Economic and Social Council approved the new UN fact-finding mechanism on June 6, 1967 – the day after the Six-Day War in the Middle East had started. The Ad Hoc Working Group of Experts was given a mandate to focus on South Africa, Namibia, Southern Rhodesia, Angola and Mozambique. Over the next years, the group provided detailed evidence on a whole range of issues, including torture, imprisonment, executions, freedom of movement, freedom of expression and assembly, right to work and right to health. In 1974, the debate on the Working Group's report served as a means to focus on wider issues, especially Chile. On June 6, 1967, the UN passed also resolution 1235 that allowed the Commission on Human Rights to look beyond South Africa and look at cases where "a consistent pattern of gross violations similar to apartheid" occurred.[8] It was evidence of the steps forward being taken in the build-up to the human rights year. These initial steps were the result of some interesting debates inside the UN and had some momentum with countries like Jamaica, Senegal and Dahomey carrying the torch against more rigidly inclined states. These steps would also suffer the impact from the fallout after the Six-Day War – a major cause of the ensuing limbo.

In other political forums, efforts were stepped up. In late 1967, Norway, Sweden, Denmark and the Netherlands decided to use the state-complaint mechanism in the Council of Europe system against the Greek Junta that had staged a military coup in April 1967 and thereafter initiated a campaign of political repression and torture. It culminated with a report from the European Human Rights Commission and a judgment of the situation in Greece that led the military regime to withdraw from the Council.[9] The case sent a signal but it was not really a successful outcome. Despite this, the Council of Europe's human rights work was energized after 1968. The assessment after their participation in the Tehran Conference on Human Rights in 1968 was that the European human rights system had never received such international attention and interest.[10] This experience in Tehran was assessed very positively and the Council of Europe followed up by developing a program of work in response to decisions taken during the international human rights year. It shaped the internal debates, and in January 1971, the Consultative Assembly of the Council of Europe took the initiative to seek a more systematic approach to furthering human rights in Europe, recognizing

[8] Guest (1990), *Behind the Disappearances*, p. 97.

[9] Kristine Kjaersgaard (forthcoming), "Human Rights in Europe between Law and Politics. The Scandinavian Complaints against Greece to the European Commission of Human Rights, 1967–1970," *The Long 1970s. New Perspectives on the Epoch-Making Decade.* Edited by Poul Villaume, Helle Porsdam and Rasmus Mariager. Farnham.

[10] Until this point, the Council of Europe had actually developed very little human rights practice and jurisprudence. See, for example, Jan Eckel (2014) *Die Ambivalenz des Guten. Menschenrechte in der internationalen Politik seit den 1940ern.* Göttingen, pp. 167–168.

FIGURE 10. New fact-finding mechanisms in the human rights field were introduced during the International Year for Human Rights. The Ad Hoc Working
Group of Experts dealing with the treatment of prisoners in Southern Africa are
seen interviewing a witness from Namibia (South West Africa) during a session
in Dar-es-Salaam, Tanzania. Around ninety witnesses were questioned during
the first round of investigations that took place in London, Geneva and several neighboring African countries from late June to early September 1968.
Source: United Nations Photos

that "twenty years after the conclusion of the [European] Convention
new ideas are emerging and new techniques are being developed, creating situations which were unforeseeable a short time ago."[11] The Legal
Committee of the Council pointed to omissions in the European system
compared with the UN Covenants. The European system was the most
advanced regional system, but the comparison did not say much. Instead,
the European system was trying to catch up with global developments. By
the end of October 1971, a Parliamentary Conference on Human Rights
had stressed that the parliamentary and governmental machinery of the
Council of Europe should be strengthened to further human rights in

[11] Council of Europe Archive, "Report of the Committee of Experts on Human Rights to
the Committee of Ministers," September 12, 1974, Box 1808, Committee of Experts on
Human Rights, 1974–1976, Folder 1218, p. 3.

Europe. It is difficult not to see some influence from here on preparing the ground for the debates on strategy for the future CSCE negotiations in Helsinki.

Across the Atlantic, the new attention to international human rights and concerns over U.S. foreign policy inspired Congress to take more coherent action. On August 1, 1973, a month before the coup in Chile, the House International Relations Sub-Committee on International Organizations and Movements under the Chairmanship of Representative Donald M. Fraser (D-MN) began an unprecedented set of hearings dealing with the international protection of human rights. These hearings led to the report *Human Rights in the World Community: A Call for US Leadership* published in March 1974. It marked a turning point in the U.S. Congress engagement with human rights.[12] Just before the release of the report, Fraser spoke before the 1974 session of the Commission on Human Rights, announcing the publication of the Congressional report. He spoke assertively about the need for action, clearly inspired by Amnesty International, as he highlighted their 1973 report on torture and called for the Commission to begin "developing international machinery which would prevent the practice of torture."[13] He also witnessed how the Commission was struggling to come up with a concerted response to the Chilean crisis. Fraser was a leading figure in pushing Congress into becoming active in making human rights concerns part of U.S. foreign policy by challenging an intransigent Secretary of State Henry Kissinger, who did not believe that human rights and foreign policy should be combined. Kissinger did not want to have his hands tied in any way. With the Vietnam War and the Watergate scandal looming large, Congress did not take Kissinger's negative reaction lightly and looked toward a wider transformation of U.S. foreign policy that would take human rights into consideration.[14] The Nixon–Kissinger views on foreign policy meant

---

[12] William Michael Schmidli (2012), "Human Rights and the Cold War: The Campaign to Halt the Argentine 'Dirty War'," *Cold War History*, vol. 12, no. 2, p. 348; Sarah Snyder (2013), "A Call for US Leadership: Congressional Activism on Human Rights," *Diplomatic History*, vol. 37, no. 2, pp. 372–397. See also William Michael Schmidli (2013), *The Fate of Freedom Elsewhere: Human Rights and the U.S. Cold War Policy Toward Argentina.* Ithaca, NY.

[13] Donald Fraser (USA), Commission on Human Rights, 30th session, 1279th meeting, March 1, 1974, pp. 171–172.

[14] Barbara Keys (2010), "Congress, Kissinger and the Origins of Human Rights Diplomacy," *Diplomatic History*, vol. 34, no. 5, pp. 823–851. For a rich and comprehensive account of these political changes, see Barbara Keys (2014), *Reclaiming American Virtue. The Human Rights Revolution of the 1970s.* Cambridge, MA.

that the United States had not been committed to secure the inclusion of human rights in the Helsinki Final Act. It had very much been a European project, but the foreign policy debates in the United States were gradually shifting.

As illustrated by Fraser's statement to the Commission on Human Rights, Amnesty International featured more and more frequently as a source of reference as well as an initiator of developments. In December 1972, Amnesty launched its international Campaign for the Abolition of Torture. It was an outcome of the decision made by the International Council in Stockholm in 1968 where torture was made a key part of the Amnesty mandate. At that time, Amnesty International had been deeply involved with documenting the abuses in Greece. The campaign against torture was based on the publication of systematically compiled data on the widespread use of torture and the collection of more than a million signatures worldwide in support of an antitorture resolution at the United Nations. It had immediate effect.[15] In early 1973, torture was placed on the UN agenda, and before the end of the year, the General Assembly had passed a resolution calling on governments to ratify the international instruments that contained prohibitions of torture and other inhuman or degrading treatment. It was a remarkable success for the campaign, but the passing of the resolution could not hide a more dubious aspect of how the United Nations also operated. As Amnesty International was preparing for an International Conference on the Abolition of Torture in Paris opening on December 10, 1973 – the 25th Anniversary of the Universal Declaration – they were informed shortly before that the meeting facilities provided to them by UNESCO would be withdrawn due to pressure placed on UNESCO by governments mentioned in Amnesty's report on torture.[16] However, the momentum behind the campaign showed that the state of limbo was now being challenged. The following years would see this accelerate.

The Chilean case, 1973–1974

Until 1973, Chile was a relatively strong proponent of elaborating international legal standards, including human rights. In 1972, Chile had ratified both human rights Covenants, following Sweden and Denmark but

---

[15] Amnesty International (1975), *Report on Torture*, p. 8.
[16] International Institute of Social History (IISH), Amnesty International Archive, "Documents concerning the Conference for the Abolition of Torture, Paris," Folder 972.

coming before Norway on the list of ratifying states. In early April 1973, the Chilean member of the Commission on Human Rights was appointed to be part of the five-person Ad Hoc Working Group of Experts on Southern Africa. It was the last time that Chile would be at the vanguard of international human rights protection during the Cold War. The coup in Chile in September 1973 placed renewed emphasis on torture and a range of other human rights issues. The tables had turned in a dramatic way as Chile became the newest cause for concern at the United Nations.

On September 11, 1973, Chilean President Salvador Allende was ousted in a military coup led by General Augusto Pinochet. The Pinochet regime took control of most aspects of public life in Chile, instigating torture, disappearances and killings on a significant scale. These crimes immediately sparked an international outcry, with Chile now viewed as a major perpetrator of gross human rights violations. It led to a transnational solidarity campaign that became an important engine for human rights activism. The campaign united exiled Chileans, international human rights NGOs, concerned citizens and politicians from various countries. The International Commission of Inquiry created in late 1973 was one such example. Its first meeting in March 1974 brought together delegates from twenty-seven countries.[17] Interestingly, the first Secretary-General of the Commission was the Swedish lawyer Hans Göran Franck, who had been the main organizer of the 1968 Amnesty International Stockholm Conference on torture. Organizational and personal trajectories were combined in new transnational networks as the expanding human rights activism responded to international events with new momentum. In this, the United Nations served as a forum that provided transnational connections, and frustrations, among those engaged in human rights advocacy. The UN could not be ignored. The problem was that the UN occupied an international political space it did not fill.

In March 1973, the Commission on Human Rights combined debate on the report findings by the Ad Hoc Working Group of Experts on Southern Africa with a debate on situations with "a consistent pattern of gross violations of human rights."[18] It was still not possible to secure support for action beyond the Working Group's mandate, but the latter item allowed international NGOs to deliver statements on specific

---

[17] Patrick William Kelly (2013), "The Chilean Coup and the Origins of Transnational Human Rights Activism," *Journal of Global History*, vol. 8, no. 1, p. 178.

[18] E/CN.4/SR.1217–1242: Commission on Human Rights, 29th Session, March 20–April 6, 1973, Vol. 2. See especially 1229th, 1232nd and 1233rd meetings.

situations but without naming the country in question. It was a controversial procedure that faced state opposition but it showed that NGOs had mobilized around fact-finding and advocacy. Delegates from the Anti-Slavery Society and the International Student Movement for the United Nations, speaking on behalf of thirteen youth NGOs, delivered detailed statements about the situation in six unnamed countries. The confidential procedure, known as 1503 after the 1970 resolution establishing it, was a façade as it was often possible to guess the country in question. The procedure faced strong resistance and showed how difficult it was to expand attention beyond that mandated for the Ad Hoc Working Group. Greece, among those six countries, wanted the confidential procedure struck down. They argued that the Commission on Human Rights was not competent to deal with these human rights violations.[19]

The Commission member from the Netherlands, Theo van Boven, reacted strongly against the Greek statement. van Boven denied the accusations made against the competence of the Commission and defended the NGOs' right to bring these cases before the Commission as he argued that "the various non-governmental organizations spoke for themselves and the Commission would lose all prestige if it remained silent."[20] He specifically praised Amnesty International and the International Commission of Jurists and criticized the Soviet practice of placing detained individuals in psychiatric institutions. It was a practice that Alexander Solzhenitsyn had described in his 1970 Nobel Lecture as "Lunatic asylums for the sane."[21] It was a practice that emerged with the rise of the Soviet dissident movement – a type of Gulag of the mind. From this point, Theo van Boven emerged as the driving force for expanding the UN work in the human rights field. In the following decade, from 1977, as Director of the UN Division for Human Rights, he played a major role in the efforts to overcome UN selectivity by placing a special emphasis on enforced disappearances.

Chile became van Boven's next major diplomatic battle in an almost decade-long process. The process took off at the 1974 session of the Commission on Human Rights – the first session after the coup in Chile.

---

[19] Mr. Velissaropoulos (Greece), Commission on Human Rights, 29th session, 1233rd meeting, March 30, 1973, p. 275.
[20] Theo van Boven (the Netherlands), Commission on Human Rights, 29th session, 1233rd meeting, March 30, 1973, p. 276.
[21] Alexander Solzhenitsyn (1974), *Solzhenitsyn: A Documentary Record*. Edited by Leopold Labedz. London, pp. 317–318. On the Soviet "psychoprisons," see also Darius Rejali (2007), *Torture and Democracy*. Princeton, NJ, pp. 394–395.

The Soviet Union had led the Communist states' resistance to NGO involvement in UN human rights work but the Soviet Union was never reluctant to apply a procedural double standard when it was in their favor. During the 1974 session of the Commission on Human Rights, the Soviet Union, in a rare show of support of NGOs, gave their speaking rights to the representative from the Women's International Democratic Federation to bring attention to the situation in Chile. The representative was President Allende's widow Hortensia. On December 30, 1973, Mrs. Allende had written to the UN Secretary-General Kurt Waldheim, calling for a UN investigation in Chile. On February 25, 1974, she spoke before the Commission and called again for an "official intervention" by the United Nations.[22]

The Communist states lined up to praise Hortensia Allende and condemn the Chilean regime. The Bulgarian delegate even stated that "the Commission should be the spokesman of the world's conscience and must act to condemn flagrant violations of human rights and fundamental freedoms wherever they occurred."[23] Theo van Boven was not impressed by any of the sides. He criticized members of the Commission for acting not in the interest of human rights but only in the "direct interests of their Governments."[24] van Boven condemned the Chilean military regime and challenged the Commission by calling for an investigation of the situation in Chile. The Communist states did not support van Boven's proposal because they were opposed to expanding the UN's investigative role in the human rights field. They thereby ignored the heartfelt request from Allende's widow – the person they themselves had placed on a pedestal at the Commission. They did want the UN to condemn Chile and call for the release of prisoners but they did not want UN action on the ground to monitor the actions of the Pinochet regime because of the precedent it might establish. The Communist states were all bark and no bite. Instead, it was other countries, with van Boven in the lead, who heeded Mrs. Allende's plea.

Theo van Boven presented a carefully crafted argument in favor of a UN investigation in Chile. He first spoke about the work of the

[22] Mrs. Allende (Women's International Democratic Federation), Commission on Human Rights, 30th session, 1271st meeting, February 25, 1974, p. 54, 58.

[23] Mr. Pentchev (Bulgaria), Commission on Human Rights, 30th session, 1272nd meeting, February 25, 1974, p. 62.

[24] Mr. van Boven (the Netherlands), Commission on Human Rights, 30th session, 1272nd meeting, February 25, 1974, p. 67.

FIGURE 11. Hortensia Allende, widow of the former Chilean President Salvador Allende, speaking before the Commission on Human Rights on March 25, 1974, during a debate on Chile following the 1973 military coup. The debate, which took place two weeks after Soviet writer Alexander Solzhenitsyn was forced into exile for publishing *The Gulag Archipelago*, sparked controversy. The situation in Chile led the UN to take renewed steps in terms of investigating gross human rights violations. *Source*: United Nations Photos

Ad Hoc Working Group on Southern Africa – a relevant precedent initiated in 1967 – before describing the situation in Chile. He referred to the summary executions, torture and the secret detainment of thousands of people and the failure by the military regime to protect the right of due process and the right to freedom of thought, conscience and religion before proposing an investigation of the human rights situation in Chile. From there, van Boven argued for UN action on the question of torture before concluding his statement with a critique of regimes that suppressed the freedom to express dissenting views. It was directed both at Chile and at the Soviet Union. He was careful not to promote selectivity, although he called for specific action. The Chilean delegate ignored Theo van Boven and claimed it was all a Soviet-controlled campaign against his country. The Soviet delegate responded that the Chilean delegate could hardly include "the Netherlands among the countries which carried out the directives of Moscow."[25]

The new Chilean member of the Commission acted with arrogance. The Chilean strategy attempted to characterize the criticism directed at them as a Cold War duel between the Chilean regime and the Soviet regime. The Chilean made repeated mention of the treatment of Alexander Solzhenitsyn, who with widespread international publicity two weeks previously – following the publication of his book *Gulag Archipelago* – had been arrested and forced into exile by the Soviet authorities. For a short while, the Commission debate became a literary shootout by proxy between Nobel Prize Laureates Alexander Solzhenitsyn and Pablo Neruda conducted by diplomats. The Chilean poet Neruda – a Communist himself – had died twelve days after the military coup from illness but in conditions that have been shrouded in suspicion. Both sides used their literary ammunition against each other. It was ideological grandstanding from both sides that provided plenty of drama but neither party wanted to resolve anything.

The Chilean strategy behind this approach was clear. They relied on the fact that the Cold War divisions would provide them with impunity against any human rights investigative action by the United Nations. Chile believed that by attacking the Soviet Union on its record while ignoring the criticism voiced by others, they would avoid interference from the outside. The Chilean delegate – Ambassador Raul Bazan Davila – may also have relied on the UN track record's inability to introduce any strong measures to counter human rights violations. In response to concerns about summary executions, he argued that "the death penalty was laid down in Chilean law and since none of the international conventions on human rights prohibited it, Chile could not be accused of violating human rights by applying it." It was an extreme argument to place before the Commission. Thereafter, he stated that "The Commission could learn from the events in Chile a useful lesson for promoting respect for human rights."[26] When the Chilean delegate the second time provoked the Commission into action by claiming "The fact was, however, that Chile had nothing to hide... Anyone could go to Chile to see the situation for himself,"[27]

[25] Mr. Kolosovsky (the USSR), Commission on Human Rights, 30th session, 1272nd meeting, February 25, 1974, p. 70.

[26] Mr. Bazan Davila (Chile), Commission on Human Rights, 30th session, 1272nd meeting, February 25, 1974, p. 82.

[27] Mr. Bazan Davila (Chile), Commission on Human Rights, 30th session, 1278th meeting, February 28, 1974, p. 163.

the bravado did not go unnoticed. Theo van Boven made it clear that "the statement made by the representative of Chile at the previous meeting to the effect that the allegations were due to lack of information was in itself a strong argument in favour of an investigation or a study."[28] At the 1974 session of the Commission on Human Rights, Chile did more to bring investigatory action upon itself than all the Communist states put together.

The proposal for the Working Group received the strongest backing from Antonio Cassese from Italy, Ghulam Allana from Pakistan and the Chairman of the 1974 Commission session Felix Ermacora from Austria. Amnesty International also spoke in support. They had reacted immediately following the September 1973 coup, compiling information about the situation. In November 1973, less than two months after the coup, they launched a human rights fact-finding mission to Chile led by the Berkeley Law Professor Frank Newman.[29] Newman also served as the Amnesty spokesperson at the 1974 session of the Commission on Human Rights. Amnesty International's participation thereby offered the authority of an expert witness. Newman made it clear that "Chile had become a symbolic case of the defense for human rights" and called it "a momentous test for the Commission on Human Rights."[30] It was a test that the Commission failed. The proposal for a working group on Chile withered away as time passed. The British and French did not support such action. It was, however, the unwillingness of the otherwise outspoken Communist states to back Hortensia Allende's request that meant that there was a lack of backing for the proposal.

Instead, the Commission agreed on a much weaker action, namely to send a telegram to the Chilean government asking them to formally respond to the accusations concerning the human rights violations.[31] The response was outright denial. The Chileans responded they could not comment on things that had not occurred. At the ECOSOC meeting a few months later, the United Kingdom had changed their position. As in 1964, a change of U.K. government from the Conservatives to a

---

[28] Mr. van Boven (the Netherlands), Commission on Human Rights, 30th session, 1279th meeting, March 1, 1974, p. 167.

[29] Kelly (2013), "The 1973 Chilean Coup and the Origins of Transnational Human Rights Activism," p. 172.

[30] Frank Newman (Amnesty International), Commission on Human Rights, 30th session, 1275th meeting, February 27, 1974, p. 125.

[31] Text of telegram is contained in E/CN.4/L.1275/Add.1, Commission on Human Rights, March 6, 1974.

new Harold Wilson Labour government in early March 1974 brought
a new approach to human rights – especially concerning the situation
in Chile. At the ECOSOC session in May 1974, the United Kingdom
submitted a resolution also on behalf of the Netherlands and Sweden that
outlined their joint dissatisfaction of Chile's response to the Commission
on Human Rights. This new development paved the way for the decision
that had not been possible to secure sufficient support for during the
1974 Commission on Human Rights session. As the evidence against
the Pinochet regime mounted, also from persons who had been openly
critical of the Allende government's political maneuverings,[32] the 1975
Commission on Human Rights decided to take action.

By the time of the 1975 Commission session, Theo van Boven secured
consensus for a resolution on the Chilean case prepared with backing
from Ghana and Senegal among others. It was an alliance that forced the
Communist countries to accept the same proposal they had not supported
the previous year. It established an Ad Hoc Working Group mandated
to undertake a fact-finding mission to Chile and report to the 1975 UN
General Assembly. It was the first step forward in several years and
it placed fact-finding at its core. The Chilean delegate had to accept
the Working Group and promised that the group would be accepted
into Chile. The promise was delivered in front of the 1975 Commission
Chairman Ghulam Allana from Pakistan. Allana would remember this
promise of collaboration and of entry into Chile as he was appointed
Chairman of the Ad Hoc Working Group on Chile, but as the group's
work began, the controversies continued.

The 1975 UN General Assembly

In 1975, the United Nations celebrated its 30th anniversary. The moment
called for critical self-assessment at the UN General Assembly. Where did
the United Nations stand? The question shaped the debates on human

---

[32] One example was a powerful letter from Eugenio Velasco, a former Dean of the Law Faculty at the University of Chile, Santiago, and a leading critic of President Allende, written to Council of the College of Advocates on August 30, 1974. He detailed the violations, indicted the Council for its failure to speak out against the disappearances and even "the detention, torture and killing of its own colleagues." The result was that the regime took legal action to prosecute Velasco. The letter was included in the International Commission of Jurists' 1974 mission report to Chile and had a clear impact on the members of the Commission on Human Rights. See Velasco letter in International Commission of Jurists (1974), *Report on Mission to Chile*, Appendix A, Document E/CN.4/1166/Add. 6. Geneva.

rights and the 1975 Assembly session gave mixed answers. The Danish Foreign Minister, K. B. Andersen, explained that the "United Nations was never intended to be an organization of like-minded States."[33] In that, it was certainly proving successful. The Dutch Foreign Minister, Max van der Stoel, believed that "mankind more than ever had become conscious of the interrelationship between peace and security, economic and social development, human rights and the rule of law. If the United Nations fails in one, the negative effect will spread to other areas."[34] The Dutch Foreign Minister acknowledged that the stakes for the international organization had increased dramatically in the postcolonial era. The interconnectedness of global issues had deepened. The risk of falling short in the ability to deliver solutions was evident and a greater sense of skepticism affected how the UN was viewed. As Max van der Stoel also pointed out, "a creeping irrelevancy has emerged, interest in the United Nations has decreased and there is a tendency to deal with vital problems outside the United Nations."[35]

The Ad Hoc Working Group on Chile presented their report to the 1975 General Assembly. Its preparation had been controversial. The invitation to visit Chile was soon withdrawn by the regime and other hurdles were inserted. The Working Group progressed by interviewing numerous witnesses outside the country. They compiled a comprehensive report detailing torture and disappearances and estimated that the number of arrests since September 1973 had reached 100,000. They provided a set of recommendations aimed at ensuring the restoration of the rule of law and respect for human rights and that explanations were to be provided regarding the fate of the disappeared. They also called for the disbandment of DINA, the central organ of the intelligence services of the Army, Navy, Air Force and Police, whom they held responsible for the crimes they detailed. The Working Group asked that the leader of DINA, Oswaldo Romo, be tried for crimes against humanity.[36]

It was a more assertive approach than usual for the United Nations. The General Assembly debate reflected that an important procedure with

---

[33] Mr. Andersen (Denmark), UN General Assembly, 30th session, 2360th meeting, September 24, 1975, p. 149.

[34] Mr. van der Stoel (the Netherlands), UN General Assembly, 30th session, 2362nd meeting, September 25, 1975, p. 193.

[35] Ibid., p. 192.

[36] Mr. Allana (Chairman of the Ad Hoc Working Group), UN General Assembly, Third Committee, 30th session, 2144th meeting, October 29, 1975, p. 178.

potential for much wider application "was being put to the test."[37] The assertive approach was supported by developments in Southern Europe. The military dictatorships in Portugal and Greece had fallen in 1974 and they were now represented by governments trying to build democratic societies.[38] They found themselves entering a political landscape in Europe where human rights had become more central to Western-oriented states. The CSCE and the Council of Europe were cases in point. In the preceding years, Greece and Portugal had been severely criticized for their human rights record. They had been authoritarian perpetrator nations but were now asserting a new democratic identity expressed through support for human rights. Both countries spoke forcefully against the situation in Chile, knowing only too well from their own experience the types of violations that were documented before the General Assembly.[39] It was a critical shift. On November 20, 1975, Chile did little to help their image when they called for the Third Committee to pay tribute to the memory of General Franco of Spain, the last fascist dictator in Western Europe, on the occasion of his passing.[40]

The Chilean regime lacked credibility at the United Nations. They did, however, receive support from several Latin American states, some with repressive military regimes, which argued that the principle of nonintervention applied to Chile. It was a well-known argument that placed sovereignty over human rights. In this instance, it had limited support in the Third Committee. In the government-controlled Chilean press, the Working Group had been accused of being "part of an international Marxist–Leninist plot." It was one of many unfounded accusations from Chile. The Chairman of the working group Ghulam Allana came from a wealthy business family in Pakistan and had belonged to a right-wing

---

[37] Mr. Campbell (Australia), UN General Assembly, Third Committee, 30th session, 2150th meeting, November 5, 1975, p. 210.

[38] Tony Judt (2006), *Postwar. A History of Europe since 1945*. London, pp. 504–534.

[39] See Mr. De Faria (Portugal), UN General Assembly, Third Committee, 30th session, 2146th meeting, October 31, 1975, p. 182; Mr. Kalliga (Greece), UN General Assembly, Third Committee, 30th session, 2150th meeting, November 5, 1975, p. 205. The price for Portugal's transformation, which included a sudden decolonization, was paid heavily in the former colonies as the Indonesian invasion of East Timor and escalating civil wars in Mozambique and Angola proved. The fall of the colonial power in the two latter also meant a brutalization of the South African security apparatus as the apartheid system felt more exposed without the buffer of Portuguese rule in Southern Africa. Jamie Miller (2012), "Things Fall Apart: South Africa and the Collapse of the Portuguese Empire 1973–74," *Cold War History*, vol. 12, no. 2, pp. 183–204.

[40] Mr. Diez (Chile), UN General Assembly, Third Committee, 30th session, 2165th meeting, November 20, 1975, p. 299.

political party. The Austrian Felix Ermacora was a professor of international law and a member of parliament for a Conservative Christian Democratic Party. They served alongside a retired Ecuadorian UN diplomat and a Supreme Court Judge from Senegal.[41] None really fit the profile of a Marxist–Leninist stalwart. In addition, the Communist states had not promoted the creation of the Working Group.

There was more merit in the debate that arose about selectivity or universality in UN human rights work. The critique of selectivity was the best argument that Chile used in its defense. Their problem was that they were – as a major violator – not regarded as a credible proponent of the critique. The record of violations in Chile was too strong and the regime's behavior so erratic and arrogant that it made them an untrustworthy proponent of a more universal approach. They did try. They criticized the fact that torture and human rights violations were never investigated or denounced in larger countries. They cited Amnesty International reports that claimed that human rights were violated in more than hundred countries and countered that "the Third Committee was concerning itself with only one of them."[42] They found the UN action against them a "shameful case," but acknowledged without any sense of appreciation or irony that "The 'Chilean case' would perhaps lead the way towards establishing a non-discriminatory system to ensure respect for human rights throughout the world."[43]

The 1975 debate on torture, which led to adoption of the UN Declaration on Torture and Other Cruel, Inhuman or Degrading Treatment or Punishment, showed that this observation had merit. It was clear that many states now equated Chile with torture.[44] It was Sweden and the Netherlands who proposed the Declaration. They were outspoken critics of the Chilean regime. In this debate, they were careful to present a broader case for this normative work and that it was the starting point for the work on an international Convention against torture.[45] The groundwork had already been made to pave the way for the Declaration's

---

[41] Mr. Allana (Chairman of the Working Group on Chile), UN General Assembly, Third Committee, 30th session, 2154th meeting, November 11, 1975, p. 231.

[42] Mr. Diez (Chile), UN General Assembly, Third Committee, 30th session, 2153rd meeting, November 10, 1975, p. 228.

[43] Ibid., p. 228.

[44] See statements by Norway, West Germany, Sri Lanka (2160th meeting), Belarus (2161st meeting), the USSR and East Germany (2162nd meeting).

[45] Mr. Larsson (Sweden), UN General Assembly, Third Committee, 30th session, 2166th meeting, November 21, 1975, p. 306.

approval. The draft had been prepared at the 5th *UN Congress on the Prevention of Crime and the Treatment of Offenders* held in September 1975 and had involved more than hundred states.[46] The Third Committee debate showed that international human rights advocacy against torture was having an effect at the United Nations. It was noteworthy that support for the Declaration was based on "the increasing reports of torture in several parts of the world."[47] The argument here was not necessarily about an increase in torture itself. It was that the international human rights reporting increasingly brought public attention to a widespread problem that needed a response.

The question of torture invited a more general focus that could transcend the Cold War divide. This approach featured in the interventions by many of the West European states that, backed by the Helsinki Final Act, were presenting a more coherent approach on human rights. This general focus helped to shape human rights as a wider moral and political critique and to build a case against selectivity. The United Kingdom reflected this in the debate when they emphasized that "Torture was thus common to repressive regimes, whether of the right or the left."[48] The British Foreign Office was, in their internal strategy debates on human rights, beginning to discuss how to overcome UN selectivity.

It was an issue that the U.S. Ambassador to the United Nations Daniel Patrick Moynihan took on forcefully during the 1975 General Assembly. In the debate on Chile, he criticized the UN's "selective morality" on human rights, asking whether there was any reason "to limit concern to only two of the 143 States Members of the United Nations?"[49] Moynihan was preparing a larger critique of the UN's human rights work, which he launched during the controversial debate on resolution 3379, which equated Zionism with racism.

The attack on Zionism was launched by the Arab states. As before, they could rely on the Communist states and a number of African countries for

---

[46] Mr. Schreiber (Director, UN Human Rights Division), UN General Assembly, Third Committee, 30th session, 2159th meeting, November 14, 1975, p. 266.

[47] Mr. Nothomb (Belgium), UN General Assembly, Third Committee, 30th session, 2160th meeting, November 14, 1975, p. 270. This was also reflected in a draft resolution A/C.3/L.2187 presented by Greece that included the words "because of the increase in the number of alarming reports on torture."

[48] Mr. Broad (UK), UN General Assembly, Third Committee, 30th session, 2167th meeting, November 24, 1975, p. 317.

[49] Mr. Moynihan (USA), UN General Assembly, Third Committee, 30th session, 2156th meeting, November 12, 1975, p. 249.

support. This particular debate created a deep divide among the African states. The resolution severely undermined the more reasonable aims that formed part of the "Decade for Action to Combat Racism and Racial Discrimination." It alienated more moderate states, including Liberia, Senegal, Ghana and Sierra Leone, and completely overshadowed their priorities such as the continuing crisis in Southern Africa. They unhappily witnessed that "eliminating Zionism" was becoming one of the objectives of the program against racism.[50] The Liberian delegate delivered a sharply worded rebuttal to the Arab states and their supporters, who by shifting the focus to the controversial debate on Zionism had undermined the planned General Assembly debate on a wider program for the Decade to Combat Racism and Racial Discrimination, stating that "If a member of the racist regime of South Africa had been present . . . he would probably have danced with joy."[51]

In reality, the resolution contained little that was new. Its main accusation had been aired in UN human rights debates on a number of occasions dating back to the early 1960s. At the 1975 General Assembly, it evolved again into a bitter debate about the nature of Zionism and the situation in the Middle East. Critics called it morally, legally and conceptually flawed and the contents an attack on the principles of the UN Charter. Western European states withdrew support for the program against racism but Ambassador Moynihan launched a more direct attack. It was an attack against what Moynihan saw as a hijacking of the United Nations by dictatorships and other dubious regimes.

Moynihan was right in challenging the United Nations because of grave concerns with the nature of the proceedings. There were, however, also several problems with Moynihan's approach. There was no acknowledgment of more moderate Third World states that had fought against the resolution – some rather eloquently. Moynihan had also condescendingly presented decolonization as something gracefully awarded by the colonial powers because of their belief in human rights. He stated that "Many of the members of the United Nations owe their independence in no small part to the notion of human rights, as it has spread from the domestic sphere to the international sphere and exercised its influence over the old

---

[50] Mrs. Mutukuwa (Zambia), UN General Assembly, 30th session, 2400th meeting, November 10, 1975, p. 785.
[51] Mr. Wilson (Liberia), UN General Assembly, 30th session, 2400th meeting, November 10, 1975, p. 780.

colonial Powers."[52] A large number of states had a reasonable case to claim that it did not reflect their experience of decolonization.

Another problem was a critique from a close ally, the United Kingdom, who believed that Moynihan had himself promoted selectivity. The British UN Ambassador Ivor Richard, who was not unsympathetic to Moynihan's concern about the West being on the defensive at the UN, voiced this rather strongly in an internal memo to the Foreign Office in London, "Ambassador Moynihan's cardinal and, in my view unforgivable error, was to attack the developing countries while ignoring the East Europeans."[53] The human rights debates at the UN should, according to the British Ambassador, build on the new foundations from the CSCE process, and from there, a wider effort against selectivity could be launched. Moynihan overlooked the Helsinki Final Act – the platform upon which Western European states were building their human rights diplomacy. The British Ambassador was not unjustified in pointing to this flaw in Moynihan's approach.

There was one development during the 1975 General Assembly that offered a possible way forward. On October 6, 1975, the UN Director of Human Rights, Marc Schreiber, announced that the 35th state ratification of the Covenant on Economic, Social and Cultural Rights had taken place and that it would now enter into force. He expected that the Covenant on Civil and Political Rights would soon follow. Schreiber believed it was a momentous occasion worthy of special praise. Schreiber had followed UN human rights work closely since the early 1960s. It was in this context Schreiber saw this historic achievement and he felt inclined – in a rather unique gesture – to single out one country for special praise. Schreiber asked the Committee members to acknowledge the legacy behind the achievement by joining him in "expressing appreciation to the Government of Jamaica, whose representatives had played such an important role in the adoption of the Covenants" in 1966.[54] The memory of their role had withered as the Jamaican representative, although grateful for the kind words, failed to grasp the depth of meaning in Schreiber's reference to Jamaica's importance. They seemed to have forgotten their

---

[52] Mr. Moynihan (USA), UN General Assembly, 2400th meeting, November 10, 1975, p. 797.

[53] British National Archives (Kew), FCO 58/1009, Ivor Richard, "Human Rights at the United Nations: No Armistice in the War of Ideas, undated confidential memo from U.K. UN Mission to British Foreign Office (early 1976).

[54] Marc Schreiber (Director, UN Human Rights Division), UN General Assembly, Third Committee, 30th session, 2122nd meeting, October 6, 1975, p. 57.

own pivotal role. The world of the 1970s was a very different place from the world of the 1960s. The locus of human rights had changed with it.

Challenging UN selectivity, 1976–1984

The 35th ratification of the International Covenant on Civil and Political Rights followed in December 1975. The Covenants' entry into force was an important new development for the United Nations as it gave human rights a stronger stature in international law. It meant a new UN institutional mechanism for the monitoring of human rights and provided a stronger basis for NGOs to call for state accountability on human rights. This potential progress was, however, still facing one major hurdle – UN selectivity.

The question of torture was from 1975 part of the Assembly agenda and received greater political attention, although without breaking much new ground in legal terms. More states did call for a Convention against torture and for a comprehensive UN program to deal with torture, inhuman and degrading treatment. The response by the Communist states was to continue to focus on South Africa, Israel and Chile and to appear concerned by the existence of torture while entrenching the restrictive and selective approach of the United Nations. The UN had to live with constant questions about its credibility in the field.

There had been changes. The dictatorship had fallen in Spain following General Franco's death and Spain followed in the footsteps of Portugal and Greece and asserted its emerging democratic identity during the human rights debates. At the 1977 UN General Assembly, Spain aligned itself with the Western European approach – a change from the Helsinki negotiations. In a powerful description of authoritarian and oppressive rule, they labeled the states and government bodies who practiced torture "structural refuges of terror and cruelty."[55] It was an indictment of what national sovereignty had come to entail and the impunity that went with it. There was an element of lived experience involved here and it indicates the role human rights played in the democratic political transitions in the three Mediterranean states, which again broadened the basis for Western European human rights policies. Western Europe was reforming itself away from its dictatorial legacy. Eastern Europe was not.

[55] Mr. Garcia Tejedor (Spain), UN General Assembly, Third Committee, 32nd session, 36th meeting, November 1, 1977, p. 9.

In the United States, Jimmy Carter took office in January 1977. He made human rights a cornerstone of U.S. Foreign Policy, arguing for a moral rejuvenation of the American nation.[56] It was a determined policy move that was both concrete and complex. One of its first visible expressions came at the CSCE Follow-up Conference in Belgrade in 1977 where Arthur Goldberg (UN Ambassador from 1965 to 1968) represented Carter and put significant pressure on the Soviet Union over the fate of named Soviet dissidents, including Alexander Ginzburg. Another expression was its effect on Latin America. In 1975, Henry Kissinger had told the Chilean Foreign Minister that human rights and foreign policy should not be connected. The message from the Carter Administration was very different. The U.S. Deputy Secretary of State, Warren Christopher, explained the new diplomacy to members of Congress:

> The primary ingredient in this human rights diplomacy has a seeming simplicity: We frankly discuss human rights in our consultation with foreign diplomats and leaders. This may seem an obvious technique. But it is a diplomatic change from past diplomatic practice. In the past, our diplomats tended to shy away from high-level dialogue on sensitive human rights issues such as the fate of political prisoners. Now those issues are raised in face-to-face conversation. They are brought to the center of the diplomatic interchange, where they must be addressed, rather than being conveniently ignored.[57]

Human rights was gradually becoming a more central ingredient in the contents of international diplomacy. The new approach was a significant challenge to a number of American allies. It complicated the bilateral relations as human rights was made part of considering eligibility for U.S. financial and other support to countries and the beneficiaries had to consider the implications of this change in policy. The Carter administration's emphasis on human rights did produce an interesting result that consolidated the establishment of a regional human rights system in the Americas. The Inter-American Convention on Human Rights had been adopted in 1969, requiring eleven ratifications before it would enter into force. When Carter took office in 1977, only two countries had ratified. Eighteen months later, twelve countries had ratified and the Convention entered into force during one of the most violent periods in Latin

---

[56] Keys (2014), *Reclaiming American Virtue.* See also David F. Schmitz and Vanessa Walker (2004), "Jimmy Carter and the Foreign Policy of Human Rights: The Development of a Post-Cold War Foreign Policy," *Diplomatic History*, vol. 28, no. 1, pp. 113–143.

[57] See document record in British National Archives (Kew), FCO 58/1708, Human Rights: USA Policy.

American history. The timing had a lot to do with the new human rights diplomacy pursued by the Carter administration.

It was not a coincidence that Warren Christopher's example was about political prisoners. In December 1977, Amnesty International was awarded the Nobel Peace Prize for its work on behalf of prisoners of conscience and on torture. Their acceptance speech combined the well-known formula of legal analysis and moral appeal. They highlighted the disappearances of "almost uncontrollable proportions." They spoke about violations around the world and specifically mentioned Latin America, where "Emergency laws have been misused to legalize brutal repression – even when by objective standards there are no emergencies."[58] The conclusion of the speech illustrated the strength of the moral appeal of human rights that Amnesty International had done so much to promote. In their Nobel acceptance speech, they quoted an Amnesty prisoner's letter, a communication form that Amnesty had nurtured to shine a light on forgotten prisoners of conscience:

> "Soon the night will fall and they will
> close the doors of the cell.
> I feel lonely.
> No . . . I am with the whole of mankind.
> And the whole of mankind is with me."[59]

In the decade that saw the rise of identity politics, Amnesty offered a different approach, namely identification politics. The plight of individuals around the world who were imprisoned and tortured for their beliefs by repressive regimes captured the attention of a wide international audience. Amnesty was effective in mobilizing this awareness and channeling it into simple forms of political engagement and action, like letter writing to specific prisoners or to the heads of states in countries where violations occurred. This form of activism identified strongly with persecuted individuals. This was part of the strength of the organization's appeal to a Western public and it played a significant role in shaping the human rights imagination of the 1970s.

By 1978, human rights appeared to be in ascendance. It now had to become apparent at the United Nations. At this point, the United Kingdom took steps to give the issue of enforced disappearances special

---

[58] See Amnesty International 1977 Acceptance Speech. Available at: http://www.nobelprize .org/nobel_prizes/peace/laureates/1977/amnesty-lecture.html (accessed on September 16, 2015).
[59] Ibid.

significance. For some time, the British had worked to integrate human rights into their foreign policy. The initial steps came after the Helsinki Final Act. In 1978, with the backing of Foreign Minister David Owen, the Member of Parliament and UN delegate Evan Luard organized a series of human rights seminars in the Foreign Office with NGOs and academic experts. Human rights were part of détente but the British approach was also a concerted effort against selectivity. In a major policy speech from March 1977, the British Foreign Minister made it clear that "We will apply the same standards and judgements to Communist countries as we do to Chile, Uganda and South Africa . . . The Communist countries must recognize that concern for human rights is not a diversionary tactic but an integral part of foreign policy in the Western Democracies."[60]

The attack against UN selectivity had been brewing but the UN focus was still mainly on Southern Africa, Chile and Israel. There was great concern over the developments in Argentina, where the disappearances were much more widespread than they had been in Chile. The Argentinean UN Ambassador Gabriel Martinez was much more skilful at countering UN criticism than his Chilean counterparts before him. Fighting his own diplomatic "dirty war" at the United Nations, Martinez manipulated all available procedures and possible alliances to avoid investigation and undermine his opponents.[61]

The 1978 British initiative to take on the alleged UN selectivity was twofold. It focused on securing a UN resolution on enforced disappearances and securing a UN investigation of the atrocities taking place in Cambodia. The scale of the atrocities was so extreme that it called for action. It also broke a barrier, being the first time a Communist country was investigated by UN human rights machinery. The initiative started at the session of the Commission on Human Rights in March 1978, where Evan Luard delivered a statement focusing on the large-scale executions and disappearances taking place in Cambodia.[62] After presenting evidence for the case, Luard offered to circulate a U.K.-prepared dossier containing many more reports, enabling the Commission to examine the Cambodia case. It was a well-prepared challenge to the Commission. Luard backed it up with a direct critique, stating "All those atrocities had

---

[60] British National Archives (Kew), FCO 33/3317, Human Rights and Foreign Policy. "Foreign Secretary on Détente," speech by Secretary of State David Owen, March 3, 1977, p. 6.

[61] See Guest (1990), *Behind the Disappearances*, pp. 103–110, 122–134, 357–380.

[62] Evan Luard (UK), Commission on Human Rights, 34th session, 1466th meeting, March 8, 1978, pp. 2–4.

aroused the conscience of the world, but the Commission had disregarded them for political reasons."[63] The British were forcing the Commission to act or expose itself as impotent.

The United Kingdom continued their efforts at the 1978 UN General Assembly when they tabled a resolution on enforced disappearances. The resolution aimed at applying a thematic approach to the UN's human rights monitoring instead of a single-country approach. As a Foreign Office memo later explained, the resolution aimed to be "a useful contribution to debate widespread abuses of human rights. It is relevant to conditions in Latin America, Uganda, Cambodia and in the Eastern European countries."[64] The resolution highlighted the scope of the violations and placed responsibility with law enforcement agencies, security authorities and governments. The General Assembly called on the Commission to address the enforced disappearances with the aim of "making recommendations for the investigation and prevention of such occurrences."[65] The Commission had so far failed to act, but with approval of the resolution on December 20, 1978, the General Assembly gave the Commission a strong mandate to scale up its efforts.[66]

As Director of the UN Human Rights Division since 1977, Theo van Boven had also pushed this agenda forward but opposition had been fierce from Argentina, who had been in line for investigation since the military junta had launched its "dirty war" in 1976. At the 1978 Commission on Human Rights session, and before Luard's intervention, he had highlighted that the Commission "appeared to ignore many cases of killing . . . torture and disappearance."[67] The General Assembly resolution gave him a better platform to pursue the goal of some level of UN monitoring of the situation in Argentina and elsewhere. The whole debate reflected the presence of the disappeared as the Mothers of the Disappeared and other groups were in Geneva to share their stories with the delegates. At the Commission session, seven Western delegations put

---

[63] Ibid., p. 4. Cambodia was debated at the 1979 Commission session.

[64] British National Archives (Kew), FCO 58/1689, British Resolution on Missing Persons: "Background Note: UN General Assembly Resolution 33/173 – Disappeared Persons, August 1979."

[65] UN General Assembly Resolution 33/173: "Disappeared Persons," December 20, 1978.

[66] For a critical take on the state of the 1978 UN human rights debate, see Roland Burke (2015), "Human Rights Day after the 'Breakthrough': Celebrating the Universal Declaration of Human Rights at the United Nations in 1978 and 1988," *Journal of Global History*, vol. 10, no. 1, pp. 147–170.

[67] Theo van Boven (UN Division of Human Rights), Commission on Human Rights, 34th session, 1428th meeting, February 7, 1978, p. 4.

forward a resolution that went considerably further than the General Assembly resolution from December 1978. It mentioned Argentina by name and called for a direct investigation.[68]

In 1970, the UN adopted resolution 1503 containing a procedure to investigate countries where gross human rights violations were taking place. The condition for approval was that the procedure was confidential in its dialogue between the UN and the government in question. For three years, Ambassador Gabriel Martinez had spent considerable efforts to keep Argentina off the list, but with pressure rising, he changed his strategy. He now ensured that Argentina was placed under the confidential 1503 procedure instead of facing a working group that investigated and reported in the open. The Soviet delegate was instrumental in saving the right-wing military dictatorship in Argentina from public exposure. The Mothers of the Disappeared were shocked and Western delegations embittered. They mobilized support for the 1980 session and as a result a Working Group on Enforced or Involuntary Disappearances was finally established. With the work on the Torture Convention still unfinished, it was instead the more specific issue of disappearances that broke the deadlock and set the precedent for the first thematic mechanism set up by the Commission on Human Rights.[69] The idea was that the UN could be "examining violations by category," and not only examining a single country at a time.[70] The UN selectivity that had restrained the UN's human rights work for so long had finally suffered a significant defeat. A precedent had been established for monitoring violations wherever they occurred, whenever they occurred. The two first reports from the Working Group were comprehensive and reported on disappearances in fifteen and twenty-two countries, respectively, on four continents.[71] They also contained detailed evidence provided by local human rights' defenders, who for years had been gathering evidence on killings and disappearances. This work was now endorsed by the United Nations and those

[68] Guest (1990), *Behind the Disappearances*, p. 136.

[69] Theo van Boven (2004), "UN Commission on Human Rights and Freedom of Religion or Belief," *Facilitating Freedom of Religion or Belief: A Deskbook*. Edited by Tore Lindholm *et al.* Leiden, p. 177.

[70] Mr. Giustetti (France), UN General Assembly, Third Committee, 35th session, 77th meeting, December 2, 1980.

[71] E/CN.4/1435, "Report of the Working Group on Enforced or Involuntary Disappearances," January 26, 1981; E/CN.4/1492, "Report of the Working Group on Enforced or Involuntary Disappearances," December 31, 1981. The Working Group also took action with governments on individual cases when information about a disappearance was brought to their attention.

who had disappeared went on record. The negotiation of universality had taken a belated but noteworthy step forward.

The diplomatic battles did not end here however. Argentina fought back, this time going after Theo van Boven. With a new presidential administration in the United States, there was a more receptive audience to the interests of the military junta than there had been during the Carter administration. The Soviet Union had never liked van Boven as he had been firm in airing criticism of them, for example, when the issue of Chile arose in the Commission in 1974. He had worked for the expansion of UN human rights monitoring, something that the Soviets vehemently opposed. It was, however, the alliance between Argentina and the Reagan administration that led to Theo van Boven's downfall as UN Director for Human Rights. van Boven had secured UN action concerning the atrocities in Latin America. Despite a public record to the contrary, he was rather ironically accused of "selectivity."[72] The Argentinean Ambassador was happy to pursue this accusation since van Boven had been a continued target for his diplomatic efforts. The U.S. officials wanted to shift the UN's attention away from Latin America toward Eastern Europe and disliked van Boven's approach; the UN leadership in New York had also grown weary of him. In February 1982, they succumbed to pressure and dismissed van Boven during the Commission of Human Rights session a few days after he had delivered his opening statement where he strongly condemned Cambodia, Uganda, Chile, Iran, El Salvador and Guatemala. The Europeans were left deeply angered by his dismissal.[73]

The selectivity debate had taken on a more sinister form since its beginnings in the 1980s. The United Nations was starting to focus on mass killings and summary executions being committed in El Salvador and Guatemala by government security forces.[74] These governments not only denied that there was a basis for these accusations, which were well documented, but even presented themselves as universalists in the cause of human rights at the United Nations, "This system, the keystone of which is universality, has been betrayed through selective criticism of three countries in Latin America... singled out for this new hypocritical Inquisition."[75] The UN's response was rather more nuanced. There

---

[72] Guest (1990), *Behind the Disappearances*, p. 324.
[73] Ibid., pp. 321–329.
[74] On Guatemala, see Jonathan Power (2001), *Like Water on Stone. The Story of Amnesty International*. London, pp. 45–76.
[75] Mr. Rosales-Rivera (El Salvador), UN General Assembly, 38th session, 100th meeting, December 16, 1983, pp. 1620–1621. This echoed a similar criticism from 1982.

was a specific focus on El Salvador, Guatemala and Chile, but these and other examples had also inspired the UN to follow the broader thematic approach instigated with the Working Group on Enforced Disappearances. In 1982, the UN created a Special Rapporteur on Extrajudicial, Summary or Arbitrary Executions.[76] The universalistic approach had another mechanism to build on.

These developments took place while the larger normative work on the international Convention against torture was going on. The Commission on Human Rights had started working on this in 1978 based on a Swedish draft but progress was slow. The two major challenges were on implementation measures and on universal jurisdiction for the sake of prosecutions. The latter, known as Article 5, focused on removing safe havens for perpetrators of torture.[77] It added a new component to the negotiation of universality in the international human rights system. The UN had for a long time worked on universal standards and since the 1960s on universal approaches to investigating violations. Now universal jurisdiction to secure prosecution of the perpetrators of torture was being negotiated. It was a challenging proposition but a necessary one for the Convention against Torture to have real effect.[78]

The drafting work was assigned to a working group meeting before the Commission on Human Rights session. In 1982, parallel to the Argentineans undermining of Theo van Boven's position as Director of the UN Human Rights Division, Argentina declared strong opposition to the notion of universal jurisdiction. Alongside Uruguay, they argued against the notion because they claimed the crime of torture was not international in nature despite the victims in Argentine and Chile having a variety of nationalities; it was improbable that a torturer would leave a state where he enjoyed impunity, and because if another state prosecuted an individual, it could be interpreted by the state where the crime had originated "as a demonstration of lack of trust in its judicial system, a violation of its sovereignty and even as an interference in its internal affairs."[79]

See El Salvador and Guatemala's statements to UN General Assembly, 110th meeting, December 17, 1982.

[76] van Boven (2004), "UN Commission on Human Rights and Freedom of Religion or Belief," p. 177. For a general study of developments during this period, see Howard Tolley (1983), "Decision-Making at the United Nations Commission on Human Rights, 1979–82," *Human Rights Quarterly*, vol. 5, no. 1, pp. 27–57.

[77] Jan Herman Burgers and Hans Danelius (1988), *The United Nations Convention against Torture*. Dordrecht, p. 58.

[78] On the universal jurisdiction debate, see Ahcene Boulesbaa (1999), *The UN Convention on Torture and the Prospects for Enforcement*. The Hague, pp. 177–204.

[79] Ibid., p. 78.

The United States delegate took issue with this position, arguing strongly in favor of universal jurisdiction and explaining to Argentina that the expanded jurisdiction was mainly intended to address situations where torture was state policy, the state therefore not being likely to prosecute torturers, "For the international community to leave enforcement of the convention to such a State would be a formula for doing nothing."[80] There were other more moderate concerns about the article on universal jurisdiction and how to manage this within certain domestic legal systems but these concerns were far removed from the Argentinean position, which was all about securing impunity. The other UN member states had become accustomed to this line of arbitrary reasoning from Argentina but things were about to change – and with some effect.

The negotiations staggered along throughout 1982 and 1983. In 1983, the Soviet Union attacked the implementation measures and demanded that these were moved to an optional protocol. This risked undermining the Convention or delaying the negotiations into the distant future. Argentina was in favor of this proposal. A new draft set of measures was introduced that were modeled on the 1965 Convention on Elimination of All Forms of Racial Discrimination but the issue was not settled. Then in 1984, things changed. After the fall of the military junta in Argentina in 1982, a new government was trying to establish a new and democratic system. The junta was out of power but still powerful enough to protect its own. The new President Raul Alfonsin, who was inaugurated on December 10, 1983, had to perform a balancing act to solidify democracy in Argentina and that meant making compromises with members of the old regime. At the United Nations, the Argentinean government had a freer hand to pursue the human rights agenda on which it had partly been elected.

At the 1984 negotiations on the Convention against Torture, the new Argentinean government informed the Committee that it supported universal jurisdiction and would make every effort to ensure that the Convention was finalized. There was no longer the same opposition to universal jurisdiction, but the Soviet Union maintained its opposition against the implementation measures. The Commission on Human Rights could not reach agreement and decided to submit the draft Convention with this matter unresolved to the 1984 General Assembly. The negotiations proved to be difficult in the Assembly. It was uncertain whether final agreement and adoption would be achieved. It became clear that certain delegations were planning to submit a resolution calling for the work

[80] Ibid., pp. 78–79.

on the Convention to be postponed until the 1985 session, which meant throwing the whole process up in the air. In opposition to this development, Argentina, the Netherlands and Sweden decided that the waiting time should end. They joined together and submitted a proposal that the Third Committee should adopt the Convention against Torture.[81] Their joint proposal led to tense negotiations in late November and early December but finally their pressure paid off. The Convention was adopted first by the Third Committee and subsequently by the General Assembly on December 10, 1984. Apart from the 1979 Convention on the Elimination of All Forms of Discrimination against Women, it was the first major convention to be adopted since 1966.

It was a remarkable coalition and turn of events that had secured this. The two most consistent promoters of the work against torture at the United Nations had been joined by their bitter foe that had until this point done everything in its power to undermine the UN human rights system. The new democratically elected Argentinean government could benefit from helping to secure the breakthrough for this international convention that included universal jurisdiction. It was not the most elegant maneuver but it was one that, with the completion of the Convention against Torture, carried an important truth. The adoption of the Convention had benefited greatly in the last vital stages from the activism and moral sentiments that had given the disappeared a presence in international diplomacy. Sweden and the Netherlands had consistently been dedicated to making public their plight. The new Argentinean government acknowledged their existence by taking this action at the United Nations in 1984. It may not have had immediate results but it was an investment for the future. The prohibition of torture and the issue of universal jurisdiction would be intertwined with larger debates around international law and politics in the 1990s and 2000s. The presence of the disappeared was no longer only a matter for the relatives' memory activism or the subject of a bitter human rights debate in a UN meeting room. It was inscribed in international human rights law.

The silent shoes, 1986–1993

The second half of the 1980s showed that human rights were coming of age. The legal and social imagination that had inspired the turn toward human rights as international law and politics had matured to the extent

---

[81] Ibid., pp. 103–106.

where human rights became a factor in how the Cold War came to an end, in shaping the peaceful nature of the political transformations in most of East and Central Europe and for the values that would guide European reunification in the 1990s. This meant that human rights carried new significance into the post–Cold War era with high hopes about the new world in the making. These developments would, however, be accompanied by darker clouds on the horizon as constant warnings for those harboring illusions about the new era. The war in Bosnia and the 1994 Rwandan genocide were not far removed in time from the peaceful transformations in 1989. These two genocides showed how feeble the humanitarian rhetoric of "Never Again" could be.

The dramatic changes that would take place before the end of the decade were not in sight in 1985. The CSCE process had only yielded limited results, although the diplomatic engagement continued. Four years later, it looked very different. In her book *Human Rights Activism and the End of the Cold War*, Sarah Snyder suggests that January 19, 1989 could appropriately be regarded as an end date for the Cold War. It was the day when CSCE delegates agreed on the Vienna Concluding Document.[82] It was a result of the long and complex process of CSCE negotiations. The CSCE had, after the first follow-up meeting in Belgrade in 1977, continued during the 1980s with a series of multiyear meeting processes and thematic expert conferences with mixed success. While there was a setback in the early 1980s, relations between East and West from 1985 and onward entered a different mode, with Mikhail Gorbachev's leadership in the Soviet Union being a major contributing factor. Another factor was the protracted economic and political crisis behind the Iron Curtain that necessitated collaboration with the West. When the Vienna meetings started in 1986, there was a new impetus for collaboration. While it took time to mature, it did lead to the January 1989 Vienna agreement that Snyder argues was a turning point in the Cold War. It contained commitments to a more systematic strengthening of human rights and human contacts in Europe. It was clear that human rights thinking in European affairs had matured considerably since the mid-1970s. Beginning in January 1989, the Human Dimension was the theme that guided the work of the CSCE. It was the focus of three major conferences: Paris in June 1989, Copenhagen in June 1990 and Moscow in September 1991. The Copenhagen meeting was one high point in this evolution

[82] Sarah Snyder (2011), *Human Rights Activism and the End of the Cold War. A Transnational History of the Helsinki Network*. Cambridge, p. 244.

since former dissidents now represented the Czechoslovakian and Polish governments.

At the Copenhagen meeting, West Germany and East Germany jointly presented a resolution on human rights reflecting on Europe's historical experience with totalitarianism and tyranny. To address this painful past, the two German states proposed that human dignity should be at the center of all politics and that states must uphold this as a firm principle.[83] The resolution stated that if Europe was to overcome its divisions, the future had to be based on the rule of law, with a focus on democratic and pluralist institutions and policies of nondiscrimination, for example, on race and religion.[84] The resolution was a powerful symbol indicating that the Cold War was ending and a different Europe was in the making. The resolution by the two German states showed that human rights were part of the imaginary that was to guide the European transformation from the Cold War into a new era. The transformation had happened with remarkable speed. It had only been seven months since the fall of the Berlin Wall. Since then, there had been frantic political maneuvering to define a new political settlement in Europe. The settlement that was chosen was that of German reunification and greater European integration. It was not the only possible outcome of big power diplomacy (known as "4 + 2") during these transformative months in 1989 and 1990, but by June, the issue of reunification was settled.[85] The joint West and East German CSCE resolution was an outcome of this intense process. In October 1990, the two states became one when reunification formally took place.

At the third Human Dimension meeting in Moscow in September 1991, clouds were visible on the horizon. After the attempted Soviet military coup in August 1991, it was clear from his speech to the CSCE that Mikhail Gorbachev was fighting for his political survival.[86] The remarkable progress in the preceding two years could not be denied but signs of political instability and uncertainty – and hence greater political risk in relation to the European transition process – were now apparent.

---

[83] CSCE/CHDC.12: Proposal Submitted by the Delegations of FRG and GDR, June 7, 1990, CSCE, Second Conference of the Human Dimension, Copenhagen Meeting, OSCE Archive, Prague.

[84] Ibid.

[85] Mary Elise Sarotte (2009), *1989: The Struggle to Create Post-Cold War Europe.* Princeton, NJ.

[86] Mikhail Gorbachev speech, CSCE, Third Conference on the Human Dimension, Moscow Meeting, September 10, 1991, OSCE Archive, Prague.

The United Nations reacted to these changes that naturally affected the wider world. In early November 1989, a proposal for a World Conference on Human Rights was put before the General Assembly two days before the fall of the Berlin Wall.[87] Human rights were not an afterthought. As changes rapidly unfolded in Eastern Europe in November and December, the conference idea gained significance and was approved in mid-December 1989.[88] Human rights had a role to play in the post–Cold War transformations. The United Nations was the only organization that could make this a global process. It was only the second time that the international community had agreed on a World Conference on Human Rights as the way forward. There were numerous references to the Tehran Conference in 1968 as a precedent during the preparations for the 1993 Conference.[89]

The aim for the 1993 World Conference was to define international human rights work in an era freed from Cold War restrictions. There was a foundation to build on – established in past decades – but the aspiration was also to start afresh or, as one Russian diplomat argued, "to clean the ideological rust of the past."[90] The preparation process involved extensive regional consultations and engagement with civil society around the world from 1991 through 1993 on new human rights priorities. The original proposal was for the World Conference to take place in Berlin – a highly symbolic location since this would be the first major UN conference to be held in the formerly divided city and even in Germany. Berlin was a compelling choice of city to host the World Conference on Human Rights and German Foreign Minister Hans-Dietrich Genscher was a strong advocate for this outcome.[91]

---

[87] Mr. Martenson (UN Under-Secretary General for Human Rights), UN General Assembly, 44th session, Third Committee, 34th meeting, November 7, 1989, p. 12.

[88] Resolution 44/156: "World Conference on Human Rights," 82nd Plenary Meeting, December 15, 1989.

[89] See, for example, A/CONF.157/PC/12: "Opening Statement at the First Session of the Preparatory Committee for the World Conference on Human Rights by the Secretary-General of the World Conference," September 9–13, 1991, p. 2; A/CONF.157/PC/57: "Report of the Regional Meeting for Africa on World Conference on Human Rights," Tunis, November 2–6, 1992.

[90] A/CONF.157/PC/MISC.3: Serguey Kossenko (1993), "Common Move Towards Universal Culture of Human Rights," p. 2.

[91] A/CONF.157/PC/4: World Conference on Human Rights, "Letter dated May 22 from the Permanent Representative of the Federal Republic of Germany to the United Nations addressed to the Secretary-General of the United Nations," June 28, 1991. For a while, Berlin looked to be the likely location, but with the cost of German reunification becoming clearer, German Chancellor Helmut Kohl overruled his Foreign Minister's aspiration

Just as decolonization had been accompanied by great aspirations, the fall of Communism and the end of the Cold War raised hopes for a better world, with changes proceeding remarkably peacefully. There were exceptions to this though and the inability of the international community to stop violent conflicts would once again be exposed by the outbreak of a bloody war. The delegates at the World Conference on Human Rights in Vienna in June 1993 could not avoid being aware of this. As they approached the Plenary Hall to listen to speeches from Boutros-Ghali and others, they would walk alongside pairs of worn-out shoes set out and scattered around the floor of the conference area. They were the silent shoes of Bosnians – belonging to victims of the ongoing ethnic cleansing and genocide where many had disappeared into mass graves.[92] It represented a continued insistence – following on from the Latin American activism from the 1970s – that the disappeared should be present when international human rights policy-making processes took place. It was also a reminder of a world where peaceful change and human rights were struggling to assert themselves. It was not the only poignant reminder of what that world might entail.

Another reminder came the same week that Boutros-Ghali spoke of human rights as absolute, timeless and historically defined, when subscribers to *Foreign Affairs* received the journal's summer issue. It contained what became the most controversial article in four decades – since George Kennan's famous Mr. X article on the Soviet Union from 1947 – namely Samuel Huntington's piece "The Clash of Civilizations."[93] Huntington argued that in the future "the dominating source of conflict will be cultural" and "the clash of civilizations will dominate global politics."[94] Huntington's diagnosis interpreted the state of the world in which human rights would have to operate. The battle since the drafting of the UN Charter for human rights principles and measures to transcend the prerogatives of state sovereignty and domestic jurisdiction was still ongoing. Now an even more toxic political ingredient – a clash of civilizations – was being thrown into the mix of international affairs.

for a Berlin World Human Rights Conference. Vienna was eventually selected as host city.

92 Richard Reoch (1993), "The Silent Shoes of Bosnia," *Terra Viva*, June 25, 1993, printed in *Human Rights – The New Consensus* (1994), London.

93 The chronology is based on Yale Law School Library's receipt of the issue stamped June 11, 1993.

94 Samuel Huntington (1993), "The Clash of Civilizations," *Foreign Affairs*, vol. 72, no. 3, pp. 22–49.

In Vienna, the diplomats were almost simultaneously negotiating an agreement to declare that human rights were universal, interdependent and indivisible. Just as Egerton Richardson and his peers had done twenty-five years earlier, they were trying to find the formulas and legal techniques that would be able to curtail the world's propensity toward violence, war and discrimination and define a new international legal order based on human rights. The contrast was stark and the fault lines of international relations were drawn up dramatically – universality versus the clash of civilizations. The war in Bosnia, which loomed large over the Vienna Conference, revealed an uncertain response to that challenge.

Agreement was reached on the Vienna Declaration and Programme of Action after lengthy negotiations. The Declaration reaffirmed an international commitment to human rights and broke the backlog on several issues that had been circulating in the UN for more than four decades. There was a breakthrough for establishing a UN High Commissioner for Human Rights and national human rights commissions to monitor national-level implementation of human rights – both were issues that had been intensely debated in the run up to the 1968 conference in Tehran. They became two of the major institutional innovations that emerged from the Vienna Conference. Agreement was also reached on the wording for a renewed human rights commitment. The Vienna Declaration clearly stated that "the universal nature of these rights and freedoms is beyond question" and that "All human rights are universal, indivisible and interdependent and interrelated . . . it is the duty of States, regardless of their political, economic and cultural systems, to promote and protect all human rights and fundamental freedoms."[95] These formulas were fought for intensely during the negotiations. The backdrop was a cultural relativist view highlighting "Asian Values." It emphasized "national and regional particularities and various historical, cultural and religious backgrounds" in a way that ran counter to the idea of the universality of human rights.[96] The negotiation of universality had encountered a normative victory with the document that defined the international program for post–Cold War human rights work but it was a victory that contained some problematic shadows.

The "Asian Values" debate was not lost on Samuel Huntington. As he responded to the many critics of his theory at the end of 1993, he

---

[95] Articles 1 and 5, Vienna Declaration and Programme of Action, June 1993.
[96] The language was included in Article 5 of the Vienna Declaration as part of a compromise.

used the Vienna Conference as evidence for his civilizational paradigm, believing that "the confrontation at the Vienna Human Rights Conference between the West, led by US Secretary of State Warren Christopher, denouncing 'cultural relativism,' and a coalition of Islamic and Confucian states rejecting 'Western Universalism'" had proven him correct.[97] It was not the most nuanced representation of the dynamics at the Vienna World Conference but there was a divide over human rights that the United Nations would not be able to ignore in the years that followed.

The world had come a long way since 1945 – and then in some ways maybe not. The Vienna Conference and the Programme of Action proved very clearly that human rights remained an "invention to remake"[98] in a new world and a new era where a structural political change was taking place after the fall of Communism but where religious conflicts and intolerance were also on the rise. Human rights still had to operate in a world where, as the American Anthropological Association had claimed in 1947, "power carried its own convictions." This realization had, to a large extent, shaped the human rights trajectory throughout the Cold War and it would determine the onward journey for human rights through the 1990s until present day.

---

[97] Samuel Huntington (1993), "If Not Civilizations, What? Paradigms of the Post-Cold War World," *Foreign Affairs*, vol. 72, no. 5, p. 187.
[98] Samuel Moyn (2010), "Human Rights in History," *The Nation*, August 11.

Conclusion

In his classic 1958 novel *Things Fall Apart*, the Nigerian writer Chinua Achebe makes a dramatic change of narrative perspective in the very last paragraph of the book. To this point, the novel is a rich and complex evocation of tribal life in Western Africa before and during the arrival of colonialism. The book captures with nuance the strength and vanity, the compassion and the brutality of its characters and how this is reflected in the social life of the tribe.

In the very last paragraph however, the narrator suddenly becomes the British colonial administrator who during the book's passage has come to control the territory where the story is set. From his view, the complex characters we have encountered fit a much simpler description. He describes them as "The Primitive Tribes of the Lower Niger" – a label that is the closing sentence of the book.[1]

With this, Chinua Achebe presented a challenge to his Western reader. In the changing world of the late 1950s, readers could either continue viewing the colonized peoples from the lens they had been conditioned to see them through – namely as primitives in need of saving – or they could learn to appreciate the dignity, the richness and the struggles of the people of the Third World. Achebe tells us that how we perceive, how we label and how we narrate the stories of our fellow human beings shapes our fates and is telling of who we really are.

Achebe's challenge remains relevant for how we construct narratives today, including how we write histories of human rights. Narrative perspectives matter; labeling and perceptions matter; and our imagination

---

[1] Chinua Achebe (1958), *Things Fall Apart*. London.

as scholars and readers matter. I would contend that most contemporary human rights work operates with a significant gap in knowledge about its own historical evolution. The paradox is that the human rights movement has been at the vanguard of making claims about the universality of human rights – and then gone ahead and presented a discounted version of the universality story. The movement has been aided in the process by human rights skeptics and cultural relativists as well as by actors with a range of political interests who were involved in human rights diplomacy.

The cause hereof has a lot to do with how historical narratives have been constructed and reproduced originating with the United Nations in the 1940s when a specific template for the evolution of human rights was proposed through the International Bill of Rights. The way the dominant historical narratives have been construed and reproduced in the ensuing decades has, to a large extent, reflected relations of power – especially the powers of definition in the global domain. It has left not just significant gaps of knowledge but also a remarkable exclusion of pivotal transnational historical processes and connections in twentieth-century history. There is a richer and more complex story that deserves to be brought forward.

The 1960s involved a major reframing of the human rights project underpinned by an emphasis on racial discrimination and religious intolerance. This dual emphasis was so significant for the breakthrough of human rights that it is relevant to question whether the normative foundations for modern human rights are so clearly built around civil, political, economic, social and cultural rights as standard interpretations – such as those basing themselves on the International Bill of Rights narrative – would have it. From 1962 until around 1975, race and religion were defining for the legal and political breakthrough in the human rights field that took place during these years that a reassessment – or at least nuancing – seems appropriate. After 1975, it was again civil, political, economic, social and cultural rights that formed the most significant basis for human rights developments and controversies, although these were accompanied by topics such as women's and children's rights. The continuum that originated in 1948 was not an unbroken one and it is necessary to acknowledge the discontinuities and ruptures within the larger post-1945 timeframe.

In hindsight, it is rather surprising how international human rights research has been able to sustain itself with such ignorance about the 1960s developments in the human rights field. This decade linked the 1940s and the 1970s. More importantly, human rights underwent a fundamental transformation for reasons outlined in the preceding chapters. It is hard to sustain the elevated focus on the 1970s in the human rights literature without acknowledging the contributions of the previous decade. The point is that new historical connections and causalities emerge in our understanding of the twentieth century when these elements are brought together, with an eye for the transnational dynamics involved in international human rights politics.

The book has offered a reinterpretation of the evolution of international human rights, with an eye for both structure and agency in the postcolonial moment that the 1960s represents. Decolonization was – through its structural transformation of international politics – a decisive factor that actually enabled human rights to emerge despite significant opposition to become a significant factor for international diplomacy and politics in the past decades. The importance of agency has been represented in two main ways. First, through the role Jamaica, especially Egerton Richardson, and other key states from the Global South played as innovators and initiators of several major initiatives in the human rights field. Second, through some of the myriad of processes this inspired over decades as a varied cast of actors responded to these diplomatic and political initiatives.

The human rights story has too readily been understood as a story of Western values but a rather different version has been presented here. In reality, what happened in the 1960s was that the states of Jamaica, Ghana, the Philippines and Liberia and others gave a master class in international human rights diplomacy to both the Eastern and the Western actors embroiled in the Cold War. They were at the vanguard of universality – despite all the contradictions between their international diplomacy and the domestic experiences of independent statehood. It was from this point that human rights much more fully began their trajectory toward becoming a legal, normative and ethical concept of universal scope and significance. In this sense, the 1940s was a false start politically – even in the light of the imaginative drafting of the Universal Declaration.

The vanguard role of these Global South countries did not perhaps last long – due to a whole range of issues – but it was pivotal. These countries brokered the breakthrough of international human rights law and laid foundations for what has been called "the human rights revolution" in the 1970s. In the quest for universality, a number of states from the Global South made not just an important but a transformative contribution that would influence the shaping of European détente through the Helsinki

Final Act. This reflects a point that Frederick Cooper has articulated in a related context, namely the fact that these actors from the Global South "were not simply entrapped in a framework of European beliefs; they profoundly changed what Europeans thought they believed."[2]

This realization should challenge how human rights are perceived and also how we approach the study of human rights. There is a strong need for more imaginative approaches to the study of human rights – past and present – as their evolution has too often been narrated from a Western perspective or based on a certain construct of what the West represents. There is both an important methodological and substantive issue at stake, as Jean Quataert has eloquently pointed out:

> What validates a notion of Eurocentrism in human rights debates about origins is more precise, specific, and readily documented: It is about evidence and sources – who the agents in the study are and whose voices the historian consults and allows to be heard. International human rights history cannot be written credibly from sources that are exclusively and narrowly limited to Western thought and thinkers.[3]

My aim has been to adequately document how different an historical narrative emerges when the approach that Quataert argues for is applied. This approach should be considered both when studying what shaped human rights developments and when assessing who and what processes made an impact regarding human rights in international affairs. The shaping part should bring greater attention to the political imaginaries that, for example, led to the turn toward international law, human rights and the engagement with "negotiating universality" in the mid-twentieth century. When exploring these political worlds, some of our findings may seem counterintuitive from the vantage point of today but that is our problem – and not that of the historical record. Historical anachronism should be avoided – a risk that is certainly present in human rights research – but so should too readily ignoring contestations of the past like those who have been uncovered here. They are important to understand transnational historical processes like the evolution of international human rights.

To take one example, the vision that guided Jamaican human rights diplomacy reflected an appreciation of the relationship between law and

---

[2] Frederick Cooper quoted in Ryan Irwin (2012), *The Gordian Knot. Apartheid and the Unmaking of the Liberal Order*. Oxford, p. 182.

[3] Jean Quataert (2014), "A Review of 'The International Human Rights Movement: A History'," *Journal of Human Rights*, vol. 13, no. 4, p. 538. The review is of a book written by Aryeh Neier (2012).

civilization rarely attributed to a country from the Global South. Law as a civilizer was an important theme in the period under study and it cannot be reduced to a merely hegemonic notion. There was greater nuance and more at stake than merely seeing the development of international law as part of the West's civilizing mission.[4] If we do want to remain within this framework of thinking about civilizing, it would be timely to acknowledge the ways that the Global South civilized the West.

One of the most eloquent proponents of this idea was the Jamaican politician and lawyer Norman Manley, who was an important figure in the Cold War human rights story and also somewhat of a mentor to Egerton Richardson in his career. As a political leader in Jamaica, Manley introduced a sanctions policy against Apartheid South Africa in the late 1950s – the first country in the world after India – to do this. As a legal practitioner and thinker, Manley was linked to global debates on human rights and the rule of law. Manley explained:

The fact is that there is a close relationship between law and civilization, between law and all the concepts of human rights... What is unique about the ideas that are common among lawyers is the fact that those ideas and ideals are intimately concerned with human relationships – with the authority of the State as against the rights of the individual and with the rights of men as between themselves. And it is that fact that makes it inevitable that the lawyer should reach out in this anxious and troubled world to find a basis for thought and action which can apply the wide world over.[5]

It was an idealistic understanding of the universality in human relationships and the potentiality of law to serve the international community and secure peace. It was an understanding that would be difficult to sustain over time – but it did have political impact. It may well be that the struggle for nondiscrimination as a universal idea and practice – and a key component of human rights – was the most important twentieth-century representation of this notion of law as part of the civilizing process.[6] While this intersected with other global political and economic processes that most certainly were powerful determinants in shaping the postcolonial

---

[4] The notion of law as a civilizer was frequently referred to in UN human rights debates. See, for example, Senegal defining "civilized society" as equaling the principles of the Universal Declaration on Human Rights in Chapter 4, "The Making of a Precedent." There are numerous other examples from the Global South.

[5] Norman Manley (1971), "Human Rights: An Idea in Law," *Norman Manley and the New Jamaica. Selected Speeches and Writings 1938–1968*. Edited by Rex Nettleford, London. p. 348. The quoted speech by Manley was delivered in 1966.

[6] Norbert Elias (2000) (original in 1939), *The Civilizing Process*. London.

world, these notions of law and justice and what nurtured them cannot be easily discarded. There is very important and complex legal, ethical and political territory to navigate here that should lead us to consider different histories about the post-1945 era – including further transnational histories about the world decolonization made.

The impact of human rights diplomacy by key Global South states now appears more tangible to assess. One major strategic contribution was that they – at the height of the Cold War in 1962 – redefined the field of international human rights diplomacy as a central part of the contestations over international law and forced the Communist states to engage with it. The Communist states could not reject being part of this – due to the nature of the Cold War as a global conflict – no matter how much they opposed its expansion. In this process, Jamaica and the other states shaped international norms and international politics far more than has been hitherto understood. In effect, they delivered the human rights project onto the doorstep of the 1970s when the Helsinki Final Act, Chile, Amnesty International, torture and further issues defined what human rights meant in international affairs. The West European states picked up the mantle and carried human rights to the center of European détente. It was not a given that they would do this or that they would succeed. The Europeans might well have dropped the project for a variety of reasons – not least as the United States government in the early 1970s was widely opposed to the nexus between foreign policy and human rights – but they did not. Human rights did however gain political traction in Western foreign policy from the mid-1970s and thereby became increasingly significant as a political strategy and a set of international principles. These developments were invariably linked to the normative and legal transformations of the 1960s and processes located outside Europe and the United States.

There were marked differences between the worlds of the 1960s and the 1970s. Global South diplomacy came to reflect the new reality where escalating national debt, increasing poverty and violent conflicts came to define life in a large number of the postcolonial states. These factors shaped ideas about global politics, and the international economic order and human rights were viewed rather differently in this context. The unforgiving realities of the 1970s have overshadowed the potentialities offered during the 1960s and have situated the nexus between the Global South and human rights in a too narrow perspective. The latter decade did shape later developments in remarkable ways. Even if these impacts were too limited – especially seen in a much broader context than merely the human rights field – they still have relevance today for the visions and aspirations regarding equality, justice, freedom and dignity that they expressed. What was so eloquently expressed by Jamaica in October 1962 upon launching their human rights initiative, that "the total world would be concerned with the total world," today still rings true and necessary.[7]

When assessing the impact of universal human rights, the issue is often reduced to a question as to whether the glass is half full or half empty. This metaphor is misguided because it reduces the human rights story to a singular image – a singular way of explaining the world. This was what Huntington was striving to do but it is the wrong prescription for scholarship and for understanding the world in which we live.[8] Robert Cover explained this relationship eloquently:

> No set of legal institutions or prescriptions exists apart from the narratives that locate it and give it meaning. For every constitution there is an epic, for each decalogue a scripture. Once understood in the context of the narratives that give it meaning, law becomes not merely a system of rules to be observed, but a world in which we live.[9]

Our historical narratives have not been representative of how human rights actually gained significance as a legal, political and moral imagination in the increasingly interdependent world from the 1940s and onward. Our narratives have not matched the world in which we lived and live.

What is needed is a pluralist account that sees a cabinet full of human rights glasses; some half full, some half empty, some drained dry and some filled to the top; for some, the contents have fizzled out and, for others, they are boiling; and then there are those glasses smashed beyond repair. From such a pluralist narrative, we may start to fully understand and assess the role of human rights in international affairs – and indeed better understand international affairs itself more widely. This more nuanced approach situates human rights in a different light and places the negotiation of universality – with its many contestations and contradictions – as one of the significant historical processes of the twentieth and the twenty-first century. Our historical narratives must aim to capture with greater richness how and why this story unfolded.

---

[7] Mr. Shearer (Jamaica), UN General Assembly, 17th session, 1145th meeting, October 8, 1962, p. 379.

[8] Huntington (1993), "If Not Civilizations, What?," p. 186.

[9] Robert Cover (1995), "Nomos and Narrative," *Narrative, Violence and the Law. The Essays of Robert Cover*. Edited by Martha Minow, Michael Ryan and Austin Sarat. Ann Arbor, MI, p. 96.

Archives and References

Archives

Czech Republic

Organization for Security and Cooperation in Europe, Prague

- CSCE Archive Collection, 1972–1991

Denmark

Rigsarkivet (Danish National Archives):

- Foreign Ministry, Danish UN Mission (New York)

France

UNESCO Archives, Paris

- In-house collection and UNESDOC

Council of Europe Archives, Strasbourg

- 121: Human Rights (policy and general matters)
- Various other thematic files
- Papers of the First Session of the Committee of Ministers, August 8–13, 1949.

Italy

EU Historical Archives, Florence

- Papers on Early Preparation for CSCE, 1970–1971

Jamaica

National Archives, Spanish Town

- Norman Manley Papers

National Library of Jamaica (NLJ), Kingston

- *Jamaica Gleaner* Newspaper Archive
- *Jamaica Hansard: Proceedings of the House of Representatives*
- NLJ Library and Archive Collection

The Netherlands

International Institute of Social History (IISH), Amsterdam

- Amnesty International Archive Collection

Switzerland

UN Library, Geneva

- UN General Assembly (including Committees)
- Commission on Human Rights
- Sub-Commission on the Prevention of Discrimination and Protection of Minorities
- Preparation for International Human Rights Conference, 1968
- Preparation for World Conference on Human Rights, 1993
- Special Committee on Principles of International Law concerning Friendly Relations and Co-operation among States, 1964–1970

World Council of Churches (WCC), Geneva

- WCC Archive Collection, Human Rights

Trinidad and Tobago

National Archives, Port of Spain

- Materials related to Trinidad and Tobago's independence negotiations, 1958–1962

United Kingdom

British National Archives, London (selected archive groups listed)

- General Human Rights and Foreign Policy: FO 371, FCO 58, FCO 61, LAB 13
- Jamaica: DO 200, CO 1031

United States

U.S. National Archives, College Park, MD (selected archive groups listed)

- RG 59, RG 84, Soc 14, Subject numeric files, 1961–1963, 1964–1966, 1967–1969

Lyndon B. Johnson Library and Archive, Austin, TX (selected archive groups listed)

- White House Central Files, Human Rights
- NSF Country File
- Vice-Presidential Papers 1961–1963
- Personal Papers (various)

John F. Kennedy Library, Boston, MA

- White House Central Subject Files, Human Rights
- Personal Papers
- Country Files (Jamaica)
- Oral History Files

Papers of the International League for the Rights of Man/Human Rights, New York Public Library Archives and Manuscript, New York

- Country Files (Jamaica)
- International Human Rights Year
- UN Seminars on Human Rights

Collection of Sources

British Foreign Policy

"The Conference on Security and Cooperation in Europe 1972–1975," Documents on British Policy Overseas Series III, Vol. II. London, 1997.

Conference on Security and Cooperation in Europe

Human Rights, European Politics and the Helsinki Accord: The Documentary Evolution of the Conference on Security and Co-operation in Europe 1973–1975, Vols. 1–7. Edited by Igor Kavass, Jaqueline Granier and Mary Frances Dominick. Buffalo, NY, 1981.

United Nations

1948 Universal Declaration of Human Rights: Drafting and Negotiation Process, 1946–1948. Available at: www.un.org/Depts/dhl/udhr/ (accessed on September 16, 2015).
Yearbook of the United Nations (1946–2007). Available at: http://unyearbook.un.org/ (accessed on September 16, 2015).

United States Foreign Policy

Foreign Relations of the United States (FRUS), 1961–1963, Organization of Foreign Policy; Information Policy; United Nations; Scientific Matters, Vol. 25.

Foreign Relations of the United States (FRUS): 1964–68, Energy Diplomacy and Global Issues, Vol. 34.

References

Abram, Morris (1967), "Die Gedanken-, Gewissens- und Religionsfreiheit," *Journal of the International Commission of Jurists*, vol. 8, pp. 49–62.

Abram, Morris (1982), *The Day Is Short – An Autobiography*. New York.

Achebe, Chinua (1958), *Things Fall Apart*. London.

Afshari, Reza (2007), "On Historiography of Human Rights Reflections on Paul Gordon Lauren's The Evolution of International Human Rights: Visions Seen," *Human Rights Quarterly*, vol. 29, no. 1, pp. 1–67.

Albornoz, Angel Francisco Carrillo de (1966), "The Ecumenical and World Significance of the Vatican Declaration on Religious Liberty," *Ecumenical Review*, vol. 18, no. 1, pp. 58–84.

Alfredsson, Gudmundur and Asbjørn Eide (eds.) (1999), *The Universal Declaration of Human Rights: A Common Standard of Achievement*. The Hague.

Alomar, Rafael Cox (2009), *Revisiting the Transatlantic Triangle: The Constitutional Decolonization of the Eastern Caribbean*. Kingston.

Alston, Philip (2013), "Does the Past Matter: On the Origins of Human Rights," *Harvard Law Review*, vol. 126, no. 7, pp. 2043–2081.

American Anthropological Association (1947), "Statement on Human Rights," *American Anthropologist*, vol. 49, no. 4, pp. 539–543.

Amnesty International (1975), *Report on Torture*. London.

Amrith, Sunil and Glenda Sluga (2008), "New Histories of the United Nations," *Journal of World History*, vol. 19, no. 3, pp. 251–274.

Anderson, Carol (2003), *Eyes off the Prize. The United Nations and the African American Struggle for Human Rights 1944–1955*. Cambridge.

Arkadyev, Y. (1968), "International Human Rights Year," International Affairs, April, no. 4, pp. 8–11, 26.

Baldwin, Roger N. (1949), "The International Bill of Rights," *Great Expressions of Human Rights*. Edited by R. M. MacIver. New York, pp. 201–210.

Bange, Oliver and Gottfried Niedhart (eds.) (2008), *Helsinki 1975 and the Transformation of Europe*. New York.

Bates, Ed (2010), *The Evolution of the European Convention on Human Rights: From Its Inception to the Creation of a Permanent Court of Human Rights*. Oxford.

Baudet, Floribert (2008), "'It Was Cold War and We Wanted to Win': Human Rights, 'Détente' and the CSCE," *Origins of the European Security System: The Helsinki Process Revisited, 1965–75*. Edited by Andreas Wenger, Vojtech Mastny and Christian Nuenlist. Abingdon, pp. 183–198.

Bell, Wendell (1964), *Jamaican Leaders. Political Attitudes in a New Nation.* Berkeley, CA.

Bender, Gerald J. (1978), *Angola under the Portuguese. The Myth and the Reality.* London.

Black, Allida (2012), "Are Women 'Human'? The UN and the Struggle to Recognize Women's Rights as Human Rights," *The Human Rights Revolution: An International History*. Edited by Akira Iriye, Petra Goedde and William I. Hitchcock. Oxford, pp. 133–155.

Bolton, Jonathan (2012), *Worlds of Dissent: Charter 77, The Plastic People of the Universe and Czech Culture under Communism.* Cambridge, MA.

Borgwardt, Elizabeth (2005), *A New Deal for the World: America's Vision for Human Rights.* Cambridge, MA.

Borgwardt, Elizabeth (2012), "'Constitutionalizing' Human Rights: The Rise and Rise of the Nuremberg Principles," *The Human Rights Revolution: An International History*. Edited by Akira Iriye, Petra Goedde and William I. Hitchcock. Oxford, pp. 73–92.

Borstelmann, Thomas (2001), *The Cold War and the Color Line.* Cambridge, MA.

Boulesbaa, Ahcene (1999), *The UN Convention on Torture and the Prospects for Enforcement.* The Hague.

Bourdeaux, Michael (1975), "Religion," *The Soviet Union Since the Fall of Khrushchev*. Edited by Archie Brown and Michael Kaser. London, pp. 157–180.

van Boven, Theo (2004), "UN Commission on Human Rights and Freedom of Religion or Belief," *Facilitating Freedom of Religion or Belief: A Deskbook*. Edited by Tore Lindholm *et al.* Leiden, pp. 173–188.

Brandt, Willy (2003), *Erinnerungen.* Munich.

Brown, Archie (2009), *The Rise and Fall of Communism.* London.

Brown, Martin D. (2012), "A Very British View of Détente: The United Kingdom's Foreign Policy During the Helsinki Process, 1969–1975," *Visions of the End of the Cold War in Europe, 1945–1990*. Edited by Frédéric Bozo *et al.* New York, pp. 121–133.

Buchanan, Tom (2002), "'The Truth Will Set You Free': The Making of Amnesty International," *Journal of Contemporary History*, vol. 37, no. 4, pp. 575–597.

Buchanan, Tom (2004), "Amnesty International in Crisis, 1966–67," *Twentieth Century British History*, vol. 15, no. 3, pp. 267–289.

Burgers, Jan Herman (1992), "The Road to San Francisco: The Revival of the Human Rights Idea in the Twentieth Century," *Human Rights Quarterly*, vol. 14, no. 4, pp. 447–477.

Burgers, Jan Herman and Hans Danelius (1988), *The United Nations Convention Against Torture.* Dordrecht.

Burke, Roland (2006), "'The Compelling Dialogue of Freedom', Human Rights at the Bandung Conference," *Human Rights Quarterly*, vol. 28, no. 4, pp. 947–965.

Burke, Roland (2008), "From Individual Rights to National Development: The First UN International Conference on Human Rights, Tehran 1968," *Journal of World History*, vol. 19, no. 3, pp. 275–296.

Burke, Roland (2010), *Decolonization and the Evolution of International Human Rights*. Philadelphia, PA.

Burke, Roland (2015), "Competing for the Last Utopia? The NIEO, Human Rights, and the World Conference for the International Women's Year, Mexico City, June 2015," *Humanity: International Journal of Human Rights, Humanitarianism and Development*, vol. 6, no. 1, pp. 47–62.

Burke, Roland (2015), "Human Rights Day after the 'Breakthrough': Celebrating the Universal Declaration of Human Rights at the United Nations in 1978 and 1988," *Journal of Global History*, vol. 10, no. 1, pp. 147–170.

Byrne, Jeffrey James (2009), "Our Own Special Brand of Socialism: Algeria and the Contest of Modernities in the 1960s," *Diplomatic History*, vol. 33, no. 3, pp. 427–447.

Cabrita, Joao M. (2000), *Mozambique – The Tortuous Road to Democracy*. London.

Caro, Robert (2012), *The Passage of Power. The Years of Lyndon Johnson*. New York.

Cassese, Antonio (2001), *International Law*. Oxford.

Chkhikvadze, V. (1966), "The Nations Repudiate Racism," International Affairs, May, no. 5, pp. 49–54.

Chikvadze, V. and Y. Ostrovsky (1968), "International Human Rights Conference," International Affairs, August, no. 8, pp. 16–21.

Clark, Roger S. (1972), *A United Nations High Commissioner for Human Rights*. The Hague.

Clark, Roger S. (1979), "The United Nations and Religious Freedom," *New York University Journal of International Law and Politics*, vol. 11, pp. 197–225.

Clark, Roger S. (1981), "The International League for Human Rights and South West Africa 1947–1957: The Human Rights NGO as Catalyst in the International Legal Process," *Human Rights Quarterly*, vol. 3, no. 4, pp. 101–136.

Clavin, Patricia (2013), *Securing the World Economy. The Reinvention of the League of Nations 1920–1946*. Oxford.

Claydon, John (1972), "The Treaty Protection of Religious Rights: UN Draft Convention on the Elimination of All Forms of Intolerance and of Discrimination Based on Religion or Belief," *Santa Clara Law Review*, vol. 12, pp. 403–423.

Connelly, Matthew (2000), "Taking off the Cold War Lens: Visions of North-South Conflict During the Algerian War for Independence," *American Historical Review*, vol. 105, no. 3, pp. 739–769.

Connelly, Matthew (2002), *A Diplomatic Revolution. Algeria's Fight for Independence and the Origins of the Post-Cold War Era*. Oxford.

Cooper, Frederick (2002), *Africa since 1940. The Past of the Present*. Cambridge.

Cooper, Frederick (2005), *Colonialism in Question: Theory, Knowledge, History*. Berkeley, CA.

Cooper, Frederick (2014), *Citizenship between Empire and Nation. Remaking France and French Africa, 1945–1960*. Princeton, NJ.

Council of Europe (2011), *Andrei Sakharov and Human Rights*. Strasbourg.

Cover, Robert (1995), "Nomos and Narrative," *Narrative, Violence and the Law. The Essays of Robert Cover*. Edited by Martha Minow, Michael Ryan and Austin Sarat. Ann Arbor, MI, pp. 95–172.

Cyfer-Diderich, Germaine (1968), "Report of the General Rapporteur," *Toward an NGO Strategy for the Advancement of Human Rights* [Conference Report], The International NGO Conference on Human Rights, Paris, September 1968, pp. 1–6.

Darwin, John (1984), "British Decolonization Since 1945: A Pattern or a Puzzle?," *Journal of Imperial and Commonwealth History*, vol. 12, no. 2, pp. 187–209.

Davy, Richard (2009), "Helsinki Myths: Setting the Record Straight on the Final Act of the CSCE, 1975," *Cold War History*, vol. 9, no. 1, pp. 1–22.

de Jong, Cornelis D. (2000), *The Freedom of Thought, Conscience and Religion or Belief in the United Nations (1946–1992)*. Antwerpen.

Dickson, Brice (1995), "The United Nations and Freedom of Religion," *International and Comparative Law Quarterly*, vol. 44, no. 2, pp. 327–357.

"The Conference on Security and Cooperation in Europe 1972–1975," *Documents on British Policy Overseas Series III, Vol. II*. London, 1997.

Donert, Celia (2014), "Whose Utopia? Gender, Ideology, and Human Rights at the 1975 World Congress of Women in East Berlin," *The Breakthrough. Human Rights in the 1970s*. Edited by Jan Eckel and Samuel Moyn. Philadelphia, PA, pp. 68–87.

Dubow, Saul (2008), "Smuts, the United Nations and the Rhetoric of Race and Rights," *Journal of Contemporary History*, vol. 43, no. 1, pp. 45–74.

Dubow, Saul (2011), "Macmillan, Verwoerd and the 1960 'Wind of Change' Speech," *The Historical Journal*, vol. 54, no. 4, pp. 1087–1114.

Dudziak, Mary (1988), "Desegregation as a Cold War Imperative," *Stanford Law Review*, vol. 41, pp. 61–120.

Dudziak, Mary (2002), *Cold War Civil Rights. Race and the Image of American Democracy*. Princeton, NJ.

Dunn, D. Elwood (2009), *Liberia and the United States During the Cold War*. London.

Duranti, Marco (2012), "The Holocaust, the Legacy of 1789 and the Birth of International Human Rights Law: Revisiting the Foundation Myth," *Journal of Genocide Research*, vol. 14, no. 2, pp. 159–186.

Eckel, Jan (2010), "Human Rights and Decolonization: New Perspectives and Open Questions," *Humanity: International Journal of Human Rights, Humanitarianism and Development*, vol. 1, Fall, pp. 111–135.

Eckel, Jan (2013), "The International League for the Rights of Man, Amnesty International and the Changing Fate of Human Rights Activism from the 1940s through the 1970s," *Humanity: International Journal of Human Rights, Humanitarianism and Development*, vol. 4, no. 2, pp. 183–214.

Eckel, Jan (2014), *Die Ambivalenz des Guten. Menschenrechte in der Internationalen Politik seit den 1940ern*. Göttingen.

Eckel, Jan and Samuel Moyn (eds.) (2012), *Moral für die Welt? Menschenrechtspolitik in den 1970er Jahren*. Freiburg.

Editor (1967), "Introduction: The Meaning of Human Rights Year," *Journal of the International Commission of Jurists*, vol. 8, no. 2, pp. III–VIII.

Edwards, Mark (2009), "'God Has Chosen Us': Re-Membering Christian Realism, Rescuing Christendom, and the Contest of Responsibilities During the Cold War," *Diplomatic History*, vol. 33, no. 1, pp. 67–94.

Elias, Norbert (2000) (original in 1939), *The Civilizing Process*. London.

Engle, Karen (2001), "From Skepticism to Embrace: Human Rights and the American Anthropological Association From 1947–1999," *Human Rights Quarterly*, vol. 23, no. 3, pp. 536–559.

Ermacora, Felix (1968), "International Enquiry Commissions in the Field of Human Rights," *Human Rights Journal: International and Comparative Law*, vol. 1, no. 2, pp. 180–218.

European Community (1973), *Declaration of European Identity* (Copenhagen, December 14, 1973). Available at: www.cvce.eu/content/publication/1999/1/1/02798dc9-9c69-4b7d-b2c9-f03a8db7da32/publishable_en.pdf (accessed on September 16, 2015).

Ferguson, Niall, Charles S. Maier, Erez Manela and Daniel J. Sargent (eds.) (2010), *The Shock of the Global – The 1970s in Perspective*. Cambridge, MA.

Fischer, Thomas (2009), *Neutral Power in the CSCE. The N+N States and the Making of the Helsinki Accords 1975*. Vienna.

Foot, Hugh (1964), *A Start in Freedom*. London.

Fordham, Jefferson B. (1968), "Introduction: Human Rights – 1968: A Symposium," *University of Pennsylvania Law Review*, vol. 116, no. 6, pp. 967–974.

Fraser, Ronald (ed.) (1988), *1968. A Student Generation in Revolt*. New York.

Friesel, Ofra (2014), "Race versus Religion in the Making of the International Convention Against Racial Discrimination, 1965," *Law and History Review*, vol. 32, no. 2, pp. 351–383.

Gaiduk, Ilya V. (2012), *Divided Together. The United States and the Soviet Union in the United Nations, 1945–1965*. Washington, DC.

Ghanea, Nazila (ed.) (2010), *Religion and Human Rights: Critical Concepts in Religious Studies*, Vols. I–IV. London.

Gilman, Nils (2015), "The NIEO: A Reintroduction," *Humanity: International Journal of Human Rights, Humanitarianism and Development*, vol. 6, no. 1, pp. 1–16.

Glendon, Mary Ann (2001), *A World Made New. Eleanor Roosevelt and the Universal Declaration of Human Rights*. New York.

Glendon, Mary Ann (2003), "The Forgotten Crucible: The Latin American Influence on the Universal Human Rights Idea," *Harvard Human Rights Journal*, vol. 16, pp. 27–39.

Goldberg, Paul (1988), *The Final Act. The Dramatic, Revealing Story of the Moscow Helsinki Watch Group*. New York.

Goldstone, Lawrence (2011), *Inherently Unequal: The Betrayal of Equal Rights by the Supreme Court, 1865–1903*. New York.

Green, Abigail (2014), "Humanitarianism in Nineteenth-Century Context: Religious, Gendered, National," *The Historical Journal*, vol. 57, no. 4, pp. 1157–1175.

Guest, Iain (2000), *Behind the Disappearances: Argentina's Dirty War Against Human Rights and the United Nations*. Philadelphia, PA.

Hajek, Jiri (1970), *Demokratisierung oder Demontage? Ein Prager Handbuch.* Munich.

Hanhimäki, Jussi M. (2003), "'They Can Write It in Swahili': Kissinger, The Soviets, and the Helsinki Accords, 1973–1975," *Journal of Transatlantic Studies,* vol. 1, no. 1, pp. 37–58.

Haring, Bernard (1966), *Road to Renewal. Perspectives on Vatican II.* New York.

Hebel, Kai (2014), "Propaganda Tools and Idealistic Goals: Britain and the Cold War Politics of Human Rights in the CSCE Context, 1972–1973," *Human Rights in Europe During the Cold War.* Edited by Rasmus Mariager, Karl Molin and Kersti Brathagen, London, pp. 113–135.

Herbst, Jeffrey (2004), "Let Them Fail: State Failure in Theory and Practice," *When States Fail: Causes and Consequences.* Edited by Robert Rotberg. Princeton, NJ, pp. 302–318.

Hittinger, F. Russell (2008), "The Declaration on Religious Liberty, Dignitatis Humanae," *Vatican II: Renewal Within Tradition.* Edited by Matthew L. Lamb and Matthew Levering. Oxford, pp. 359–382.

Hoffman, Arne (2007), *The Emergence of Détente in Europe: Brandt, Kennedy and the Formation of Ostpolitik.* Berlin.

Hoffmann, Stefan-Ludwig (ed.) (2011), *Human Rights in the 20th Century.* Cambridge.

Hoffman, Stefan-Ludwig (2011), "Introduction: Genealogies of Human Rights," *Human Rights in the 20th Century,* Edited by Stefan-Ludwig Hoffmann. Cambridge, pp. 1–26.

Hopkins, A. G (2008), "Rethinking Decolonization," *Past and Present,* vol. 200, no. 1, pp. 211–247.

Horne, Gerald (2007), *Cold War in Hot Zone. The United States Confronts Labor and Independence Struggles in the British West Indies.* Philadelphia, PA.

Humphrey, John P. (1984), *Human Rights & the United Nations: A Great Adventure.* New York.

Humphrey, John P. (1994), *On the Edge of Greatness: The Diaries of John Humphrey, First Director of the United Nations Division of Human Rights,* Vol. 1. Edited by A. J. Hobbins. Montreal.

Hunt, Lynn (2008), *Inventing Human Rights. A History.* New York.

Huntington, Samuel (1993), "If Not Civilizations, What? Paradigms of the Post-Cold War World," *Foreign Affairs,* vol. 72, no. 5, pp. 186–194.

Huntington, Samuel (1993), "The Clash of Civilizations," *Foreign Affairs,* vol. 72, no. 3, pp. 22–49.

Inboden, William (2009), *Religion and American Foreign Policy 1945–1960.* Cambridge.

International Commission of Jurists (1961), *African Conference on the Rule of Law, Lagos Nigeria, January 3–7, 1961 – A Report on the Proceedings of the Conference.* Geneva.

International Commission of Jurists (1962), *The Berlin Wall – A Defiance of Human Rights.* Geneva.

International Commission of Jurists (1969), "Reimposition of Censorship in Czechoslovakia," *The Review,* September, no. 3, pp. 5–9.

International Commission of Jurists (1971), "Justice in Guinea," *The Review*, December, no. 7, pp. 4–9.

International Commission of Jurists (1974), *Report on Mission to Chile*, Document E/CN.4/1166/Add. 6. UN Library Geneva.

International Committee of the Red Cross (1987), *Commentary on the Additional Protocols of 8 June 1977 to the Geneva Conventions of 12 August 1949*. Edited by Yves Sandoz, Christophe Swinarski and Bruno Zimmermann. The Hague, p. 1327.

International Consultative Group of Geneva (1940), "Causes of the Peace Failure 1919–1939," *International Conciliation*, October, no. 363, pp. 333–369.

Iriye, Akira, Petra Goedde and William I. Hitchcock (eds.) (2012), *The Human Rights Revolution: An International History*. Oxford.

Irwin, Ryan (2010), "Apartheid on Trial: South West Africa and the International Court of Justice, 1960–66," *International History Review*, vol. 32, no. 4, pp. 619–642.

Irwin, Ryan (2012), *The Gordian Knot. Apartheid and the Unmaking of the Liberal World Order*. Oxford.

Ishay, Micheline (2004), *The History of Human Rights. From Ancient Times to the Globalization Era*. Berkeley, CA.

Jamaica Gleaner (1967), "Jamaica Human Rights Council Inaugurated," *The Jamaica Gleaner*, December 12, p. 27.

Jamaica Gleaner (1968), "Proposal for Human Rights Commission Rejected by House," *The Jamaica Gleaner*, August 2, p. 10.

Jamaican Council for Human Rights (1968), *Government, The Police and Personal Freedom*. May, Kingston.

Jensen, Steven L. B. (2014), "'Universality Should Govern Our Small World of Today': The Cold War and UN Human Rights Diplomacy 1960–1968," *Human Rights in Europe During the Cold War*. Edited by Rasmus Mariager, Karl Molin and Kersti Brathagen. London, pp. 56–72.

Judt, Tony (2006), *Postwar. A History of Europe Since 1945*. London.

Kahn, Paul (1999), *The Cultural Study of Law. Reconstructing Legal Scholarship*. Chicago, IL.

Kang, Susan L. (2009), "The Unsettled Relationship of Economic and Social Rights and the West: A Response to Whelan and Donnelly," *Human Rights Quarterly*, vol. 31, no. 4, pp. 1006–1029.

Katsiaficas, George (1987), *The Imagination of the New Left. A Global Analysis of 1968*. Boston.

Kattan, Victor (2015), "Decolonizing the International Court of Justice: The Experience of Judge Sir Muhammad Zafrulla Khan in the South West Africa Cases," *Asian Journal of International Law*, vol. 5, no. 2, pp. 310–355.

Kelly, Patrick William (2013), "The Chilean Coup and the Origins of Transnational Human Rights Activism," *Journal of Global History*, vol. 8, no. 1, pp. 165–186.

Kennedy, Arthur (2008), "The Declaration on the Relationship of the Church to Non-Christian Religions, Nostra Aetate," *Vatican II: Renewal Within Tradition*. Edited by Matthew L. Lamb and Matthew Levering. Oxford, pp. 397–409.

Keys, Barbara (2010), "Congress, Kissinger and the Origins of Human Rights Diplomacy," *Diplomatic History*, vol. 34, no. 5, pp. 823–851.

Keys, Barbara (2012), "Anti-Torture Politics: Amnesty International, the Greek Junta, and the Origin of the Human Rights 'Boom' in the United States," *The Human Rights Revolution. An International History*. Edited by Akira Iriye, Petra Goedde and William I. Hitchcock. Oxford, pp. 201–221.

Keys, Barbara (2014), *Reclaiming American Virtue. The Human Rights Revolution of the 1970s*. Cambridge, MA.

Khrushchev, Nikita (1959), "On Peaceful Coexistence," *Foreign Affairs*, vol. 38, October, no. 1, pp. 1–18.

King, Jeff and A. J. Hobbins (2003), "Hammarskjöld and Human Rights: the Deflation of the UN Human Rights Programme 1953–1961," *Journal of the History of International Law*, vol. 5, no. 2, pp. 337–386.

Kirkup, Alex and Tony Evans (2009), "The Myth of Western Opposition to Economic, Social and Cultural Rights?: A Reply to Whelan and Donnelly," *Human Rights Quarterly*, vol. 31, no. 1, pp. 221–238.

Kjaersgaard, Kristine (forthcoming), "Human Rights in Europe between Law and Politics. The Scandinavian Complaints Against Greece to the European Commission of Human Rights, 1967–1970," *The Long 1970s. New Perspectives on the Epoch-Making Decade: Human Rights East-West Détente and Transnational Diplomacy*. Edited by Poul Villaume, Helle Porsdam and Rasmus Mariager. Farnham.

Klimke, Martin and Joachim Scharloth (2008), *1968 in Europe: A History of Protest and Activism, 1956–1977*. New York.

Klose, Fabian (2013), *Human Rights in the Shadow of Colonial Violence. The Wars of Independence in Kenya and Algeria*. Philadelphia, PA.

Kotkin, Stephen (2010), "The Kiss of Debt: The East Bloc Goes Borrowing," *The Shock of the Global – The 1970s in Perspective*. Edited by Niall Ferguson et al. Cambridge, MA, pp. 80–96.

Krumbein, Frédéric (2015), "P. C. Chang – The Chinese Father of Human Rights," *Journal of Human Rights*, vol. 14, no. 3, pp. 332–352.

Kurlansky, Mark (2004), *1968 – The Year That Rocked the World*. New York.

Lamb, Matthew L. and Matthew Levering (eds.) (2008), *Vatican II: Renewal Within Tradition*. Oxford.

Lauren, Paul Gordon (1983), "First Principles of Racial Equality: History and the Politics and Diplomacy of Human Rights Provisions in the UN Charter," *Human Rights Quarterly*, vol. 5, no. 1, pp. 1–26.

Lauren, Paul Gordon (1998), *The Evolution of International Human Rights: Visions Seen*. Philadelphia, PA.

Lauterpacht, Hersch (1949), "The Universal Declaration of Human Rights," *The British Yearbook of International Law 1948*. London, pp. 354–377.

Leffler, Melvyn (2007), *For the Soul of Mankind. The United States, The Soviet Union and the Cold War*. New York.

Lerner, Mitchell (2010), "A Big Tree of Peace and Justice: The Vice-Presidential Travels of Lyndon Johnson," *Diplomatic History*, vol. 34, no. 2, pp. 357–393.

Lerner, Natan (1981), "Toward a Draft Declaration Against Religious Intolerance and Discrimination," *Israel Yearbook on Human Rights*, vol. 2, pp. 82–105.

Limon, Mark, Nazila Ghanea and Hilary Power (2014), *Combating Global Religious Intolerance: The Implementation of Human Rights Council Resolution 16/18*. Versoix.

Lindkvist, Linde (2014), *Shrines and Souls. The Reinvention of Religious Liberty and the Genesis of the Universal Declaration of Human Rights*. PhD Dissertation, Lund University.

Lionaes, Aase (1968), Presentation Speech by Chairman of Nobel Committee, December 10, 1968. Available at: www.nobelprize.org/nobel_prizes/peace/laureates/1968/press.html (accessed on September 16, 2015).

Liskofsky, Sidney (1968), "Eliminating Intolerance and Discrimination Based on Religion or Belief: The UN Role," *Reports on the Foreign Scene*, February, no. 8, pp. 1–12.

Lovelace, Jr., H. Timothy (2014), "Making the World in Atlanta's Image: The Student Nonviolent Coordinating Committee, Morris Abram, and the Legislative History of the United Nations Race Convention," *Law and History Review*, vol. 32, no. 2, pp. 385–429.

MacBride, Sean (1968), "New Avenues of Implementation," *Toward an NGO Strategy for the Advancement of Human Rights* [Conference Report], The International NGO Conference on Human Rights, Paris, September 1968, pp. 64–65.

Mackenzie, G. Calvin and Robert Weisbrodt (2008), *The Liberal Hour: Washington and the Politics of Change in the 1960s*. New York.

Manela, Erez (2007), *The Wilsonian Moment: Self-Determination and the International Origins of Anticolonial Nationalism*. Oxford.

Manley, Michael (1968), *The Angry Egalitarian: Roger Mais and Human Rights*. Lecture at the Creative Arts Centre, University of the West Indies, February 29. Kingston.

Manley, Norman (1971), "Human Rights: An Idea in Law," *Norman Manley and the New Jamaica. Selected Speeches and Writings 1938–1968*. Edited by Rex Nettleford, London.

Maresca, John (1987), *To Helsinki: The Conference on Security and Cooperation in Europe 1973–1975*. Durham, NC.

Martin, Andrew (1953), "Human Rights and World Politics," *The Yearbook of World Affairs 1951*. New York, pp. 37–80.

Marwick, Arthur (1998), *The Sixties*. Oxford.

Maul, Daniel (2012), *Human Rights, Development and Decolonization: The International Labour Organization, 1940–1970*. Basingstoke.

Mauss, Marcel (1925), *The Gift: Forms and Functions of Exchange in Archaic Societies*. London.

Mazower, Mark (2004), "The Strange Triumph of Human Rights," *The Historical Journal*, vol. 47, no. 2, pp. 379–398.

Mazower, Mark (2010), *No Enchanted Palace: The End of Empire and the Ideological Origins of the United Nations*. Princeton, NJ.

Mazower, Mark (2012), *Governing the World: The History of an Idea, 1815 to the Present*. New York.

Meier, Benjamin Mason (2010), "Global Health Governance and the Contentious Politics of Human Rights," *Stanford Journal of International Law*, vol. 46, no. 1. Available at: www.unc.edu/~meierb/Meier%202010.pdf (accessed on September 16, 2015).

Miller, Jamie (2012), "Things Fall Apart: South Africa and the Collapse of the Portuguese Empire 1973–74," *Cold War History*, vol. 12, no. 2, pp. 183–204.

Ministerie van Buitenlandse Zaken (1964), *Verslag over de Achttiende Algemene Vergadering van de Verenigde Naties, New York, September 17–December 17, 1963*, 77 edn. The Hague.

Mitoma, Glenn Tatsuya (2008), "Civil Society and International Human Rights: The Commission to Study the Organization of Peace and the Origins of the UN Human Rights Regime," *Human Rights Quarterly*, vol. 30, no. 3, pp. 607–630.

Moeckli, Daniel (2009), *European Foreign Policy During the Cold War: Heath, Brandt, Pompidou and the Dream of Political Unity*. London.

Montreal Statement of the Assembly for Human Rights, March 22–27, 1968.

Morgan, Michael Cotey (2010), "The Seventies and the Rebirth of Human Rights," *The Shock of the Global. The 1970s in Perspective*. Edited by Niall Ferguson *et al.* Cambridge, MA, pp. 237–250.

Morsink, Johannes (1999), *The Universal Declaration of Human Rights: Origins, Drafting and Intent*. Philadelphia, PA.

Moyn, Samuel (2010), "Human Rights in History," *The Nation*, August 11.

Moyn, Samuel (2010), *The Last Utopia. Human Rights in History*. Cambridge, MA.

Moyn, Samuel (2012), "Imperialism, Self-Determination, and the Rise of Human Rights," *The Human Rights Revolution*. Edited by Akira Iriye, Petra Goedde and William I. Hitchcock, Oxford, pp. 158–178.

Müller, Jan-Werner (2010), *Contesting Democracy. Political Ideas in Twentieth-Century Europe*. New Haven, CT.

Naipaul, V. S. (1962), *The Middle Passage. The Caribbean Revisited*. London.

Nathans, Benjamin (2012), "Die Entzauberung des Socialismus: Sowjetische Dissidenten, Menschenrechte und die neue globale Moralität," *Moral für die Welt? Menschenrechtspolitik in den 1970er Jahren*. Edited by Jan Eckel and Samuel Moyn Göttingen, pp. 100–119.

Neier, Aryeh (2012), *The International Human Rights Movement. A History*. Princeton, NJ.

Newitt, Malyn (2007), "Angola in Historical Context," *Angola – The Weight of History*. Edited by Patrick Chabal and Nuno Vidal. London, pp. 72–82.

Niedhart, Gottfried (2008), "Peaceful Change of Frontiers as a Crucial Element in the West German Strategy of Transformation," *Helsinki 1975 and the Transformation of Europe*. Edited by Oliver Bange and Gottfried Niedhart. New York, pp. 39–52.

Normand, Roger and Sarah Zaidi (2008), *Human Rights at the UN: The Political History of Universal Justice*. Bloomington, IN.

Nwaubani, Ebere (2001), *The United States and Decolonization in West Africa, 1950–1960*. Rochester, NY.

Pope John XXIII (1963), *Pacem in Terris: On Establishing Universal Peace in Truth, Justice, Charity and Liberty*. Rome.

Palmer, Colin A. (2014), *Freedom's Children. The 1938 Labor Rebellion and the Birth of Modern Jamaica*. Chapel Hill, NC.

Parker, Jason C. (2006), "Cold War II: The Eisenhower Administration, the Bandung Conference, and the Reperiodization of the Postwar Era," *Diplomatic History*, vol. 30, no. 5, pp. 867–892.

Parker, Jason C. (2008), *Brother's Keeper: The United States, Race, and Empire in the British Caribbean, 1937–1962*. Oxford.

Parkinson, Charles O. H. (2008), *Bills of Rights and Decolonization. The Emergence of Domestic Human Rights Instruments in Britain's Overseas Territories*. Oxford.

Pauley, Garth (2007), *LBJs American Promise. The 1965 Voting Rights Address*. College Station, TX.

Pedersen, Susan (2006), "The Meaning of the Mandates System: An Argument," *Geschichte und Gesellschaft*, vol. 32, no. 4, pp. 560–582.

Pedersen, Susan (2015), *The Guardians. The League of Nations and the Crisis of Empire*. Oxford.

Power, Jonathan (2001), *Like Water on Stone. The Story of Amnesty International*. London.

Prashad, Vijay (2007), *The Darker Nations. A People's History of the Third World*. New York.

Preston, Andrew (2006), "Bridging the Gap between the Sacred and the Secular in the History of American Foreign Relations," *Diplomatic History*, vol. 30, no. 5, pp. 783–812.

Preston, Andrew (2012), *Sword of the Spirit, Shield of Faith: Religion in American War and Diplomacy*. New York.

Putnam, Robert E. and David E. Campbell (2010), *American Grace: How Religion Divides and Unites Us*. New York.

Quaison-Sackey, Alex (1963), *Africa Unbound. Reflections of an African Statesman*. New York.

Quataert, Jean (2009), *Advocating Dignity. Human Rights Mobilizations in Global Politics*. Philadelphia, PA.

Quataert, Jean (2014), "A Review of 'The International Human Rights Movement: A History'," *Journal of Human Rights*, vol. 13, no. 4, pp. 537–540.

Ramphal, S. S. (1962), "Fundamental Rights – The Need for a New Jurisprudence," *Caribbean Quarterly*, vol. 8, no. 3, pp. 139–144.

Ramphal, S. S. (1968), "Toward a Just Multi-Racial Society," *Toward an NGO Strategy for the Advancement of Human Rights* [Conference Report], The International NGO Conference on Human Rights, Paris, September 1968, pp. 72–77.

Ratti, Luca (2008), *Britain, Ost- and Deutschlandpolitik, and the CSCE (1955–1975)*. Bern.

Reddaway, Peter (ed.) (1972), *Uncensored Russia, Protest and Dissent in the Soviet Union*. New York.

Rejali, Darius (2007), *Torture and Democracy*. Princeton, NJ.

Reoch, Richard (1993), "The Silent Shoes of Bosnia," Terra Viva, June 25, 1993, printed in *Human Rights – The New Consensus* (1994). Regency Press and OHCHR.

Reus-Smit, Christian (2013), *Individual Rights and the Making of the International System*. Cambridge.

Roberts, Christopher N. J. (2015), *The Contentious History of the International Bill of Human Rights.* Cambridge.

Romano, Angela (2009), *From Détente in Europe to European Détente. How the West Shaped the Helsinki CSCE.* Bruxelles.

Romano, Angela (2010), "The Main Task of the European Political Cooperation: Fostering Détente in Europe," *Perforating the Iron Curtain: European Détente, Transatlantic Relations, and the Cold War, 1965–1985.* Edited by Poul Villaume and Odd Arne Westad. Copenhagen, pp. 123–142.

Romano, Renee (2000), "No Diplomatic Immunity: African Diplomats, the State Department, and Civil Rights, 1961–1964," *Journal of American History*, vol. 87, no. 2, pp. 546–579.

Richardson, Egerton (1968), "The Perspective of the Tehran Conference," Toward an NGO Strategy for the Advancement of Human Rights [Conference Report], The International NGO Conference on Human Rights, Paris, September 1968, pp. 23–27.

Richardson-Little, Ned (2014), "Dictatorship and Dissent: Human Rights in East Germany in the 1970s," *The Breakthrough. Human Rights in the 1970s.* Edited by Jan Eckel and Samuel Moyn. Philadelphia, PA, pp. 49–67.

Ryan, Yvonne (2014), *Roy Wilkins: The Quiet Revolutionary and the NAACP.* Lexington, KY.

Sarotte, Mary Elise (2009), *1989: The Struggle to Create Post-Cold War Europe.* Princeton, NJ.

Schmidli, William Michael (2012), "Human Rights and the Cold War: The Campaign to Halt the Argentine 'Dirty War'," *Cold War History*, vol. 12, no. 2, pp. 345–365.

Schmidli, William Michael (2013), *The Fate of Freedom Elsewhere: Human Rights and the U.S. Cold War Policy Toward Argentina.* Ithaca, NY.

Schmitz, David F. and Vanessa Walker (2004), "Jimmy Carter and the Foreign Policy of Human Rights: The Development of a Post-Cold War Foreign Policy," *Diplomatic History*, vol. 28, no. 1, pp. 113–143.

Schwelb, Egon (1963), *Human Rights and the International Community.* Chicago, IL.

Sheehan, James (2008), *Where Have All the Soldiers Gone? The Transformation of Modern Europe.* New York.

Simmons, Beth (2009), *Mobilizing for Human Rights: International Law in Domestic Politics.* Cambridge.

Simpson, A. W. Brian (2001), *Human Rights and the End of Empire. Britain and the Genesis of the European Convention.* Oxford.

Simpson, Bradley (2013), "Self-Determination, Human Rights and the End of Empire in the 1970s," *Humanity: International Journal of Human Rights, Humanitarianism and Development*, vol. 4, no. 2, pp. 239–260.

Slate, Nico (2012), *Colored Cosmopolitanism. The Shared Struggle for Freedom in the United States and India.* Cambridge, MA.

Snyder, Sarah (2011), *Human Rights Activism and the End of the Cold War. A Transnational History of the Helsinki Network.* Cambridge.

Snyder, Sarah (2013), "A Call for US Leadership: Congressional Activism on Human Rights," *Diplomatic History*, vol. 37, no. 2, pp. 372–397.

Solzhenitsyn, Alexander (1974), *Solzhenitsyn: A Documentary Record*. Edited by Leopold Labedz. London.

Soutou, Georges Henri (2008), "Paris und der 'Prager Frühling'," *Prager Frühling: Das Internationale Krisenjahr 1968*, vol. 1. Edited by Stefan Karner *et al*. Graz, pp. 355–364.

Steiner, Henry J., Philip Alston and Ryan Goodman (2007), *International Human Rights in Context: Law, Politics and Morals*, 3rd edn. Oxford.

Sullivan, Donna J. (1988), "Advancing the Freedom of Religion or Belief through the UN Declaration on the Elimination of Religious Intolerance and Discrimination," *American Journal of Law*, vol. 82, no. 3, pp. 487–520.

Suri, Jeremi (2003), *Power and Protest. Global Revolutions and the Rise of Détente*. Cambridge.

Szulecki, Kacper (2011), "Hijacked Ideas: Human Rights, Peace and Environmentalism in Czechoslovak and Polish Dissident Discourses," *East European Politics and Societies*, vol. 25, no. 2, pp. 272–295.

Taylor, Charles (2002), "Modern Social Imaginaries," *Public Culture*, vol. 14, no. 1, pp. 91–124.

Taylor, Charles (2007), *Modern Social Imaginaries*. Durham, NC.

Terretta, Meredith (2012), "'We Had Been Fooled into Thinking that the UN Watches Over the Entire World': Human Rights, UN Trust Territories, and Africa's Decolonization," *Human Rights Quarterly*, vol. 34, no. 2, pp. 329–360.

Terretta, Meredith (2013), "From Below and to the Left? Human Rights and Liberation Politics in Africa's Postcolonial Age," *Journal of World of History*, vol. 24, no. 2, pp. 389–416.

Central Committee of the Communist Party in Czechoslovakia (1968), *The Action Programme of the Czechoslovak Communist Party*. Prague, April 5. (English version published by the Bertrand Russell Peace Foundation, Nottingham, 1970).

Thomas, Daniel C. (2001), *The Helsinki Effect. International Norms, Human Rights, and the Demise of Communism*. Princeton, NJ.

Thompson, Andrew S. (2015), "Tehran 1968 and Reform of the UN Human Rights System," *Journal of Human Rights*, vol. 14, no. 1, pp. 84–100.

Thompson, E. P. (1963), *The Making of the English Working Class*. London.

Thompson, W. Scott (1969), *Ghana's Foreign Policy 1957–1966: Diplomacy, Ideology, and the New State*. Princeton, NJ.

Toft, Monica Duffy, Daniel Philpott and Timothy Samuel Shah (2011), *God's Century. Resurgent Religion and Global Politics*. New York.

Tolley, Howard (1983), "Decision-Making at the United Nations Commission on Human Rights, 1979–82," *Human Rights Quarterly*, vol. 5, no. 1, pp. 27–57.

Tolley, Howard (1989), "Popular Sovereignty and International Law: ICJ Strategies for Human Rights Standard Setting," *Human Rights Quarterly*, vol. 11, no. 4, pp. 561–585.

United Nations (1968), *Final Act of the International Conference on Human Rights: Tehran, April 22–May 13*. Geneva.

United Nations (1970), *Declaration on Principles of International Law Concerning Friendly Relations and Co-Operation Among States in Accordance With the Charter of the United Nations.* Document A/8082 available at: www.unmultimedia.org/searchers/yearbook/search.jsp?q=A%2F8082 (accessed on September 16, 2015).

Vik, Hanne Hagtvedt (2012), "Taming the States: The American Law Institute and the 'Statement of Essential Human Rights'," *Journal of Global History*, vol. 7, no. 3, pp. 461–482.

Villaume, Poul (forthcoming), "Anticipating European Détente: Denmark, NATO and the Struggle for an All-European Security Conference in 'The Long 1970s'," *The Long 1970s. New Perspectives on the Epoch-Making Decade: Human Rights East-West Détente and Transnational Diplomacy.* Edited by Poul Villaume, Helle Porsdam and Rasmus Mariager. Farnham.

Villaume, Poul and Odd Arne Westad (eds.) (2010), *Perforating the Iron Curtain: European Détente, Transatlantic Relations and the Cold War, 1965–1985.* Copenhagen.

Villaume, Poul, Helle Porsdam and Rasmus Mariager (eds.) (forthcoming), *The Long 1970s. New Perspectives on the Epoch-Making Decade: Human Rights East-West Détente and Transnational Diplomacy.* Farnham.

Waltz, Susan (2001), "Universalizing Human Rights: The Role of Small States in the Construction of the Universal Declaration of Human Rights," *Human Rights Quarterly*, vol. 23, no. 1, pp. 44–72.

Waltz, Susan (2002), "Reclaiming and Rebuilding the History of the Universal Declaration of Human Rights," *Third World Quarterly*, vol. 23, no. 3, pp. 437–448.

Waltz, Susan (2004), "Universal Human Rights: The Contribution of Muslim States," *Human Rights Quarterly*, vol. 26, no. 4, pp. 799–844.

Waters, Anita (1999), "Half the Story: The Uses of History in Jamaican Political Discourse," *Caribbean Quarterly*, vol. 45, no. 1, pp. 62–77.

Way, Sally-Anne (2014), "The 'Myth' and Mystery of US History on Economic, Social and Cultural Rights: The 1947 'United States Suggestions for Articles to be Incorporated in an International Bill of Rights'," *Human Rights Quarterly*, vol. 36, no. 4, pp. 869–897.

Wenger, Andreas, Vojtech Mastny and Christian Nuenlist (eds.) (2008), *Origins of the European Security System: The Helsinki Process Revisited, 1965–75.* London.

Whelan, Daniel J. (2010), *Indivisible Human Rights. A History.* Philadelphia, PA.

Whelan, Daniel J. and Jack Donnelly (2007), "The West, Economic and Social Rights, and the Global Human Rights Regime: Setting the Record Straight," *Human Rights Quarterly*, vol. 29, no. 4, pp. 908–949.

Whelan, Daniel J. and Jack Donnelly (2009), "The Reality of Western Support for Economic and Social Rights: A Reply to Susan L. Kang," *Human Rights Quarterly*, vol. 31, no. 4, pp. 1030–1054.

Whelan, Daniel J. and Jack Donnelly (2009), "Yes, a Myth: A Reply to Kirkup and Evans," *Human Rights Quarterly*, vol. 31, no. 1, pp. 239–255.

Winter, Jay (2008), *Dreams of Peace and Freedom: Utopian Moments in the 20th Century*. New Haven, CT.

Winter, Jay and Antoine Prost (2013), *René Cassin and Human Rights. From the Great War to the Universal Declaration*. Cambridge.

Zantovsky, Michael (2014), *Havel: A Life*. New York.

Index

Abram, Morris, 155–157, 158, 163–164, 182–183
Achebe, Chinua, 275
Action Programme of the Czechoslovak Communist Party, 188
Ad Hoc Working Group of Experts on Chile, 253
Ad Hoc Working Group of Experts on Southern Africa, 246
Afghanistan, 142
Africa
  and Cold War, 66
  decolonization in, 52, 56–64, 68
Africa Unbound: Reflections of an African Statesman (Quaison-Sackey), 66
African Conference on the Rule of Law, 58
African Human Rights Convention, 58
Afro-Asian states, 45, 54
  anti-Semitism and, 122
  Bizerte incident and, 49
  declaration to end colonialism, 55
  on decolonization, 57
  relationship with Jamaica, 84
  on religious intolerance, 145
  and universality principle, 55
Albania, 111
Alfonsin, Raul, 267
Algeria, 56, 78
Allana, Ghulam, 251, 252, 254
Allende, Hortensia, 248
Allende, Salvador, 246
American Anthropological Association, 31–32, 274

American Bar Association, 31, 180–181
American Civil Liberties Union, 37
American Colonization Society, 218
American Law Institute, 25
Amnesty International, 198–199, 210, 239, 247
  Campaign for the Abolition of Torture, 245
  Chilean case and, 244, 251, 255
  founding of, 42–43
  Kingston Seminar and, 100
  Nobel Peace Prize, 261
  principles of, 198
  and Stockholm meeting on torture, 233
Andersen, K.B., 253
Andropov, Yuri, 179
Angola, 28, 56, 61, 63, 241. *See also* Afro-Asian states
anti-Semitism, 103, 104, 105, 122, 160–162, 169
Anti-Slavery Society, 247
apartheid, 74–75, 97–98, 122
  in human rights conference agenda, 94
  ICJ's ruling on, 165
Arab countries, 122
Argentina, 114, 238–239, 262, 264
  and Convention against Torture, 267–268
  on notion of universal jurisdiction, 266–267
Asian values, 273
Assembly for Human Rights, 189–192
atheism, 155–156

Made in the USA
Middletown, DE
07 September 2020